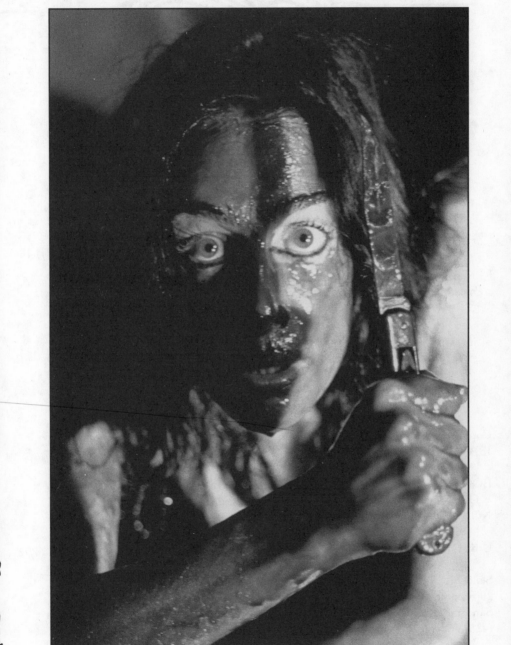

Publishers/Editors:	Andrea Juno & V. Vale
Assistant Editor:	Catherine Reuther
Production Manager:	Elizabeth Borowski
Production & Proofreading:	Anaheed Alani, Curt Gardner, Monique Gerard, Mason Jones, Jennifer Sharpe, Suzanne Stackle, Noah Sternthal, Nick Strauss
Book Design:	Andrea Juno
Flower Borders Drawn By:	Catherine Reuther
Consultant:	Ken Werner
Thanks To:	Mindaugis Bagdon, Randy Koral, Ann LeClerc, Danilo J. Neri

BOOKSTORE DISTRIBUTION: Subco, PO Box 168 or 265 So. 5th St, Monroe
 OR 97456. (503) 847-5274 or 1-800-274-7826. FAX (503) 847-6018
NON-BOOKSTORE DISTRIBUTION: Last Gasp, 2180 Bryant, SF CA 94110
 (415) 824-6636
U.K. DISTRIBUTION: Airlift, 26 Eden Grove, London N7 8EL, U.K. (071) 607-5792

Send SASE for catalog: RE/SEARCH PUBLICATIONS
20 Romolo #B
San Francisco, CA 94133
(415) 362-1465

Printed in Hong Kong by Colorcraft Ltd.
Type service bureau: Pinnacle Type, San Francisco.

10 9 8 7 6 5 4 3 2

Cover Painting: Phoebe Gloeckner
Back Cover Photo: Chris Buck (of Carolee Schneemann)
First Page Photo: Dona Ann McAdams (of Diamanda Galás)

Contents

Introduction

Angry Women is not just about women, but about the future survival of our planet. This project began with the inquiry: "Which artists are most in tune with the times—delving deeply into issues which concern us *now?*" Consistently, women performance artists seemed most perceptive (and poetic) in their criticism of social and political inequities; in their radical public disclosure of personal humiliation, pain and injustice (an act of catharsis which benefits society); and in their calls for a new consciousness which for the first time would integrate political action, cutting-edge theory, linguistic reconstruction, adventurous sexuality, humor, spirituality and art toward the dream of a *society of justice.*

Humanity is clearly on a suicide course—and taking the rest of the planet with it. One has to be in an insane state of denial to not acknowledge that we're in an absolute ecological, economic and moral crisis. Our inherited patriarchal, hierarchical system is breaking apart from within—revealing underlying, foundational flaws. We can no longer do just a "patch-up" job on our problems; we have to *totally reassess* how we as human beings have been tricked into participating in (and perpetuating) systems of domination and oppression whose ultimate destination is self-annihilation. We're in an unprecedented state of emergency—and emergencies can provoke profound reassessments, drastic solutions . . . perhaps even bring about the birth of a new consciousness, a new language, and a new species.

Thousands of years ago, Judeo-Christianity wiped out the pantheon of colorful gods, goddesses and "nature spirits," replacing them with a stern, white-bearded male patriarch known as "God"—a concept which effectively invalidated woman's status as citizen and potential decision-maker in society. Then the patriarchal belief structure implanted the notion of a *mind/body split,* which held that the body was evil—the source of dangerous, lustful impulses and desires which corrupted the mind. Identified with *Woman,* sensuality, pleasure, emotions, the Devil, animals, and Mother Earth—the body was judged inferior and even regarded with horror and self-loathing. Posited as the "superior force" to *subjugate* the body was the mind (reason, logic, the "higher intellect," god-like science) which was identified with *man.* Out of this life-denying, pleasure-denying mindset sprang the archetype of the "logical, rational," scientific male expert—exemplified by the 1950's nuclear physicist who, isolated in an ivory tower of scientific omnipotence, develops nuclear devices—unwilling to acknowledge the disastrous consequences of his research. Our ecological crisis, from ocean pollution to the greenhouse effect, is evidence of a blatant disregard for the body of our planet, just as the second-class status of women reflects the patriarchal system of contempt.

This mind/body split is sibling to a host of other dualisms—binary oppositional pairings which are never equal, which always force a hierarchy: man/woman, white/black, straight/gay, primitive/civilized, self/other, new/old. All dualisms are artificial and must be analyzed as part of a system of *either/or* thinking which imposes restrictive categorizations.

Our society permits in its language abstract generalizations which—unanalyzed, can be repressive, such as the glorification of "nature" which has been used to strait-jacket women. Women have always been considered more attuned to, or akin to "nature"—somehow inherently more "nurturing" or "instinctual." Yet this *essentialism* of nature grafted onto Woman is a subordinating fantasy—"nature" is a hornet's nest of human projections. A "mothering, nurturing" female lioness will also tear apart anything that comes near her cubs—so if that's projected onto women, doesn't that mean they'd also be great warriors?

The gay and lesbian community are pioneers in challenging this concept of "nature" in that they are playing with the fixed biological gender identities of "man" and "woman" which our society has deemed sacred and untouchable. *Identity*—the concept of the Self—has become more flexible and open to multiplicity as people escape the tyranny of unevolved, "instinctual" drives. Today, with the overpopulation crisis, the old "duty" to be fruitful and populate the earth is *suicidal.* Under these circumstances, humans are exercising their option to reinvent their biological destinies. Gays and lesbians are playing with different forms of gender and role switching; they are exploring what it is to love someone in the absence of a *reproductive imperative.* The very act of subverting something so primal and fixed in society as one's gender role, can unleash a creativity that is truly needed by society—like a shamanistic act.

Human inventiveness—the *evolved* human—has produced *technology,* which (following the dualism paradigm) has been constructed as implacably hostile toward nature. Yet the key to self-development is invention and creativity—humans have to freely reinvent themselves and their social relations through play, theatricality, artifice and *technology.* The old ideal of "going back to nature" implied that technology was alien to humanity—*not* a product of humanity's creativity. Yet technology is as "natural" as anything humans create or invent. A silicon chip is just as natural as a flint knife. (A further consequence of equating women with "nature" has been to discourage women from entering the traditionally "male" domains of technology and science—yet when they do, they can bring a fresh, energizing perspective. Theorists such as Avital Ronell or Donna Haraway are rethinking technology's relation to culture, with a radical feminist approach.

There are many philosophic underpinnings to our current crisis, not the least of which is our *hubris*—our thinking that humans are somehow outside (and superior to) the continuum of life. We are still ruled by religious dogmas such as Christianity, which for centuries held that only humans (and ultimately, only white males) had souls—women, "savages" and animals didn't (therefore we could enslave, kill, or experiment on them in laboratories without a qualm). In more ancient, animistic eras, every tree had a "tree spirit," every rock had a "rock spirit"—no distinction was made between the "animate" and the "inanimate"—with the result that there was a conscious sense of "connectedness" to everything in the world.

The Western idea of the autonomous, "individual" self as crystallized by Descartes, and which culminated in the industrial revolution, forced a transition: from a more animistic viewing of the universe as richly imbued with life, meaning, symbols and myths . . . to the present material-istic conception that our world is basically "dead"—there no longer are any "pagan" spirits dwelling in rivers and trees. With this rationale we have been able to exploit and destroy all things with impunity and arrogance. This reflects a hubris and an ego expanded to an ultimate *dead end*—people feel no connectedness or accountability to the earth, other species, or other humans. (Now we are reaching a point where our actions toward the environment have irrevers-ibly destructive consequences.) Yet the irony is: not only are this hubris and ego murderous to the diversity of life on our planet, but to *us* as well—when we believe we exist in a meaningless, mechanistic universe, and are alienated from our own bodies and the earth body (and the pleasure and joy they are capable of bringing), then our own bodies and the earth become incapable of nurturing and sustaining *us*. So when somebody like Annie Sprinkle dares to proclaim an unabashed love of the body and sexuality (which should be taken for granted)—*immediately* this inspires controversy and hatchet-faced censorship. It is a puritanical perversion that this society invests so much of its energy and economic resources in prosecuting drugs and pornography (which only affect the individual) rather than restoring education, health care, and social welfare—or prosecuting the *real* criminals, such as the S&L robber barons (which include the President's son), the Wall Street takeover tycoons, or Oliver North.

We need an electric revitalization of our life force; a reconnection to the world; a heightened conviction that we can *change life*. For the cover of this book, and as a minor antidote to the loss of rich and meaningful feminine mythol-ogy in our lives, we resurrected the image of the Medusa, updated with contemporary power icons. Reflective of the systematic destruction of matriarchal history by the patri-archy, the Medusa expresses *anger*. The complex, powerful pantheon of ancient goddesses such as Medusa, Juno and Artemis were reduced by their conquerors to narrow, negative, fearsome creatures. Medusa's rage, embodied by seething snakes that turned men into stone, seems to be an appropriate response to servitude. Anger is an emotion which must be reclaimed and legitimized as Woman's rightful, healthy expression—anger can be a source of power, strength and clarity as well as a *creative* force.

Recently, when we began approaching people with our title *Angry Women*, a number of women became very defen-sive and reacted negatively, "Oh, *I'm* not angry." (This would not be a customary male response, as males don't ascribe a negative connotation to anger.) In the '60s the expression "Angry Young Man" came into vogue (person-ified by a sexy, desirable James Dean), but there was no corresponding "Angry Young Woman" role model. From the beginning of their lives, women have been conditioned to be [too] polite, compliant, helpful and "nice." Women are very uncomfortable with the idea of being a rebel, and men are *very* uncomfortable with women outsiders. When rebel-liously critiquing society, women have never been cast as sexy or desirable (like a female James Dean)—but rather as a *prime bitch*: grim, humorless and non-sexual.

Women have a different, less destructive relationship to anger than men—especially since it has been a taboo expression for them. Theirs is not the frozen rage of serial killers, which festers internally, but rage that can be chan-neled creatively—as dramatized by performance artists such as Karen Finley. Anger can spark and re-invigorate; it can bring hope and energy back into our lives and mobilize politically against the status quo. Could there have been a Civil Rights movement in the '60s without anger?

We need a renaissance of hope which anger can bring—stuck as we are in the midst of an existential, angst-ridden *culture of cynicism* which has helped implant a widespread attitude of passivity and submissive acceptance. (No longer are people habituated to *create*, but to consume—and desire is escalated to such addictive thresholds that satisfaction remains forever out of reach.) All past subcultural revolts (rap, New Age, punk, the hippies, the beatniks, *et al*) have been appropriated in the service of product marketing strategy. Television commercials present post-punk, leath-er-clad, motorcycle-riding "rebels" whose mean-spirited selfishness is equated with "sexiness."

Yet the romantic Clint Eastwood myth of the nihilistic male loner, unintegrated into society, who inflicts violence in the name of some vague "justice" and then rides off alone into the sunset—in psychoanalytic terms this conjures up a wounded, abused child unconsciously avenging his hurt . . . who is not *conscious* enough to let that hurt and pain emerge so it can be dealt with directly, and healed. That male loner would actually feel *relieved* if he would strip off that character armoring and be vulnerable—actually feel. Peo-ple in our society need that permission to *let go*—it is very strenuous to constantly maintain the mask of being cool, cynical, uncaring and a loner—this is a very difficult act to sustain. (With overpopulation and the loss of our frontiers on earth and in space, cooperation is no longer just an option—it is a *necessity* if we are to survive.) Now there is a definite need in males to be able to relinquish the alienated, self-sufficient macho pose—without, however, lapsing into phoniness or mindlessness.

One of the fundamental contributions of the Women's Movement was the realization that one cannot have a political change without revolutionizing each individual. And that involves each individual's spirituality, personal and family relationships, and emotions—plus the ability to *communicate* those emotions. All personal growth efforts and self-healing are an essential part of the philosophical remapping necessary for political change, so we can fully deploy the imaginations we were born with. We admit that we don't want to see the world blown up; we are *for* the human species.

The feminist project of *liberation for all* is enormous: it involves a total rethinking and remaking of history, culture, law, organized religion (preferably, its total abolishment), psychoanalysis, and philosophy. (And all language which exalts seriousness and fixed identity, which precludes humor and multiplicity of meaning, is ripe for purging. Puns, jokes, and other forms of wordplay that keep alive the spirit of *irony* and *sacrilege*, have always been hated by authority figures, who demand unquestioning reverence.) This is a truly revolutionary time—new linguistics, new theories, new ways of thinking are emerging that must by necessity differ drastically from what is considered "tradi-tional." We look forward to a society which will integrate the female and the male (and all other binary dualisms) toward a new, synthesizing consciousness, with which every indi-vidual can re-ignite the *creativity within*. And there are no shortcuts—every single assumption of our civilization must be challenged. Ultimately, *everything* must be rethought . . . if we are to survive.

—Andrea Juno & V. Vale

Photo: Dona Ann McAdams

Diamanda Galás

The fiery, flamboyant *Diamanda Galás* has carved out her own unique sonic territory as an avant-garde composer, singer, poet, musician and artist. Her pioneering music incorporates influences ranging from gospel to opera to the most atonal electronic imaginings; lyrically, she has deployed poetry from Artaud, Baudelaire and Gerard de Nerval in the service of her uncompromising political/social criticism. As she puts it, "My voice was given to me as an instrument of inspiration for my friends and a tool in the torture and destruction of my enemies." The first artist to compose and perform a "Plague Mass" on the subject of AIDS, she uses her three-and-a-half octave vocal range to spellbinding effect on recordings such as her 3-CD set, *Masque of the Red Death,* and *The Litanies of Satan.*

After a rigorous apprenticeship in classical music (piano, organ, electronic keyboards and voice), in the '70s Diamanda worked in the free jazz and avant-garde music scenes in Europe and America, while launching her career as a solo artist. Nowadays she uses five microphones to spectacularly propel her vocal/electronic musical assaults. Drawing on a power outside herself, she often becomes possessed—turning a concert into a ritualistic, shamanic rally. In 1990 forty Italian newspapers branded her "blasphemous," "cursed," and "sacrilegious" after her performance at the *Festival delle Colline.*

Currently Diamanda lives in New York City, where she manages her own career. She records on Mute Records.

♦ **ANDREA JUNO: This project is about the opening up of definitions/boundaries of women's roles—**

♦ **DIAMANDA GALÁS:** *Strong women,* who don't worry if they *don't* listen to folk music! I picture a life surrounded by the most fantastic women in the world . . . women who are very powerful, very exotic, and even though they don't all have to be beautiful, it would be *nice.* I'd like to be surrounded by soulful, lovely, unusual, strong women, like in that Russ Meyer film—

♦ **AJ:** *Faster, Pussycat! Kill! Kill!* should be shown in every grade school class for girls! That was such a model of inspiration—especially the sexy, fabulous Tura Satana in that one incredible poetic gesture: putting her foot on that guy's back and snapping his neck! Except we'd rewrite the ending so that she triumphs, and rides out of that desert town like Clint Eastwood . . .

♦ **DG:** It's funny—*Forced Exposure* magazine called me, "Tura Satana without cleavage!"

Ten years ago I came up with the concept of "Black Leather Beavers," a group of feminist diesel dykes who went around committing revenge on rapists. We had a veterinarian to perform the castrations, a tattoo artist to engrave "BLB" on the rapists' foreheads, an arsonist to burn their houses down—we'd tie 'em to a tree and castrate 'em. It would be immaculate.

A girlfriend has formed a West Coast chapter in San Francisco, and I would encourage more women to do the same across America. If you can't get professionals for the "meat work," don't worry about it—but the arsonist should be a professional!

♦ **AJ: More artists should be inventing scenarios like that—**

♦ **DG:** Women need to think of themselves as preda-

Performance in 1972 with Bobby Bradford, fluegel horn player, Ornette Coleman and John Carter.

tikon," which was dedicated to Jack Abbott [prisoner who wrote an autobiographical best-seller, *In the Belly of the Beast*]. A lot of my work has been about the concept of a person being caged, treated like an animal, and escaping through insanity. . . One of my texts involves cries to a god invented by Despair—by a person about to be executed. This is not a god in any traditional sense.

In prison, since you don't actually have space, you *invent* it. And you need dialogue—that's why people become schizophrenic: to provide themselves with the dialogue they're not getting in real life. That's also partly why people take drugs—if you're alone and isolated (which is like a whole dope fiend trip) then you lack this dialogue—it's an essential freedom and *need*. If you don't have it, ultimately you *die*.

◆ **AJ: But it's society which has created this isolation—**

◆ DG: That's the caging. However, mental illness isn't just socially created—there are all kinds of realities involved, including biochemical factors. In any case, schizophrenia or multiple personality disorder can provide an essential liberation, a form of freedom from permission—and my work is always preoccupied with *freedom*. I considered "Wild Women with Steak Knives" the homicidal love song of a schizophrenic woman—that was the first work I did with 5 microphones, working with different personalities and using varied vocabularies and languages . . . speaking in tongues (which I'm known for, now) and the training of vocal chords to yield an *übervoice*, a superhuman instrument that's not about being a singer but about being a channel through which the Absolute can manifest (or a bearer of tidings of unsentimental truth, unmatrixed by mere "taste"—a word which speaks of human limitation rather than choice). I wanted to produce an immediate extroversion of sound, to deliver a pointed, focused message—like a *gun*.

tors rather than prey. The other night I threatened a guy who was hassling me, and it felt good. He said afterwards, "I wasn't speaking to you—I was speaking to the woman in back of you." [ha ha] Don't get me wrong; I'm not just coming on *pinchu macha* [a Mexican expression meaning "little macho bitch"].But we need to use *kill* energy on our enemies, not ignore them.

I'm disgusted with the idea of women making themselves invisible as they go down the street—that has to be turned around. The *attitude* is the first thing—whether you back it up with your physical self-defense or a gun is your option, but the attitude needs to be there. Nowadays we're not just talking about being hassled by one or two men at a time, we're talking about *packs* of men.

The Central Park Jogger case comes to mind: a woman who, incidentally, has been insulted more by the liberal press for having been a white woman who was raped by black men, than by the monstrosity of the physical attack itself. It was not "politically correct" of her to have been well-to-do and white. More concern was given to the background of the pigs who raped her. I don't want to know about the constitution of the rapist—I want to kill him! I don't care if he is white or black, if he is middle-class or poor, if his mother hung him from the clothesline by his balls: I only want to *kill* him! Any woman who has been raped will agree.

Speaking of being called an artist—I don't think of myself as an artist at all. I think of myself as "Diamanda": performance is one aspect of life, my personal sex life is another, and I have other sides that may be considered illegal or immoral by cowards—

◆ **AJ: Well, *art has to be war!* You've written eloquent, beautiful lines that are waging war on the status quo—**

◆ DG: Oriana Fallaci [author of *Interview With History* 1976] said, "*Life* is war!" a long time ago. That's been the direction of my work ever since I composed "Panop-

> **I don't care if a rapist is white or black, if he is middle-class or poor—I only want to *kill* him! Any woman who has been raped will agree.**

I used to talk with my singing teacher in San Diego about guns as *necessity* and *metaphor*; we both believe in the idea of "extroversion of energy." For example, the way I sing embodies the concept that diffraction of the personality provides essential liberation from the *self*, thus extroverting the insanity. And when you extrovert the *insanity*, you can live most of the time as a real person, yet be able to change your self and commit actions that your real self would not be capable of.

Training to be a singer is like training in the martial arts. A Japanese martial artist once said that in my performance I use "kill energy," because my singing involves superhuman use of the voice. If you're singing for 4000 people, you're singing for "the Gods." In the Greek or Middle Eastern traditions (Om Kalsoum is an example) singing is not about parlor room nuances of the personality, but a very concentrated energy, an attack energy—the transformation of the body into a weapon. It's about going *beyond* your self. That's how martial artists train: when you hit someone, you're going *through* them . . . beyond that physical dimension. And that's the same way I've trained with voice for many years.

The original nature of woman's voice has always been tied to witches and the shamanistic experience—the witch as transvestite/transsexual having the power of both male and female.

The way I use the voice requires a very athletic discipline—I have the stamina of Wagnerian opera singers (who must sing this work three times a week). My work has an occult, shamanistic, and ritual feeling—that's how it's been described since 1979. Years ago, I decided I wanted to break away from the limited concept of music and speak honestly (perhaps having in mind the ideal of a "divine language"). I called what I did "intravenal song." Others called it "speaking in tongues."

The nature of my work, which involves litanies or liturgical texts, *has* created censorship for me—obviously from churches (with one recent exception), Jesuit-owned radio stations (of which there are many), religious television, and fanatics who take my records to priests for exorcism. In 1982, the New York Public Theater invited me to meet them. In the meantime, someone obtained a copy of the *Litanies of Satan,* and when I showed up, the man said, "We can't present your work in this theater"—like I was the daughter of Charles Manson or something! Yet the *Litanies of Satan* is a beautiful liturgical work by Baudelaire—if anyone actually *read* it, they'd probably be mesmerized. I'm not a fan of Charlie Manson—although I do agree that most record company people in general should receive the treatment he was about to give them!

♦ **AJ: You're taking voice to a powerful extreme, while giving expression to the dispossessed. You pioneered the concept of operatically dazzling performance—**

♦ DG: I started in 1976 or '77. Luke Theodore from the *Living Theater* group who was doing Genet's *The*

Art in the Anchorage, Brooklyn NY, 1983   Photo: Paula Court

Maids saw my work in San Diego. At that point the art world was definitely against what I was doing. Although Eleanor Antin [pioneering performance artist] was very supportive, most people felt the work was emotionally too violent. I would perform dressed in black with my back to the audience; I would wait until *something else* that was *not me anymore* would emerge—until something *greater* kicked out of me. Sometimes people would get irritated—I'm known for making the audience wait 40 minutes—but that's a real diva thing. [laughs]

♦ **AJ: Like a shaman waiting to be possessed by a trance state—**

♦ DG: Right. Not only that—I wasn't finished doing my *eye makeup,* for god's sake. There are priorities—no diva performs without her *full* eye makeup. I perform

Art in the Anchorage, Brooklyn NY, 1983   Photo: Paula Court

sounds, thought into message. And beyond the words (with all due respect to them), the combinations of vocal and verbal energy can be overwhelming. Some French theorists who claim that some of the non-verbal sounds give you more levels of meaning, but I don't necessarily buy that shit.

Oscar Kokoschka, the great Austrian playwright and painter, wrote a play (*Murderer: the Woman's Hope*) which inspired me: a woman is in a cage, and a man is beating her to death. She only says a few words, but those words are explosions or direct lines of expression. When *I* started using non-verbal vocabularies, I designed my lighting to change very radically, in sympathy. I did spatial manipulations of the sound into a quadrophonic sound system; if I have speakers in 4 different locations, the audience is *in my cage*. My sound travels in different vectors; the high frequencies really fuck people up! This isn't intentional—it's just that I need to do this for myself in order to feel a certain *satisfaction*.

My sound monitors would deafen anybody else; over the years their levels have been forced to rise—just like a dope fiend needs more and more! Now I have to *feel* it— I *fry* under that sound. I utilize a specialized high-pass EQ to bypass mid- and low-frequencies, thus accentuating the higher registers—in other words, my sound is very shrill! Ever since I began listening to opera singers on my car stereo, I would never listen at a normal volume—I always cranked it up and distorted it. So I'm doing with voice something like Jimi Hendrix did with the guitar—that's what people in Europe say about my work, and they're right!

♦ **AJ: The power of your voice produces a very visceral, primal, yet almost healing experience—as though poisons are being forced out. This is not abstract, elitist "New Music"; you provide an emotional bedrock which is intense, political and poetic—**

♦ DG: That was always the original nature of woman's voice. From the Greeks onward, this voice has always been a political instrument as well as a vehicle for trans-

with blood, too. Anyway, the *Living Theater* people took me to Gennessee Mental Health Institution, and that's when I started performing at lock-up wards and schizo wards. That's how I started doing the unamplified voice work I do now. I would just sing these words—whatever occurred to me at the time.

♦ **AJ: What was your musical training?**

♦ DG: After many years of basic classical piano lessons, I studied these avant-garde piano works in university graduate school. Then I started playing with free jazz guys like David Murray, Butch Morris . . . post-Albert Ayler, post-Coltrane musicians. At the time it was a very heavy black scene not open to women. But I had played piano for so many years that they couldn't deny I could *do* it.

After playing piano for awhile with all these guys from the post-Ornette Coleman school, I thought, "No, the *voice* is the first instrument." These players have always modeled their mode of expression after the voice. They revered singers like Billie Holiday; often, the way they played was a *reaction* to the voice. The voice is the primary vehicle of expression that transforms thought into

mission of occult knowledge or power. It's always been tied to witches and the shamanistic experience—the witch as transvestite/transsexual having the power of both male and female. People ask me, "How do you feel as a woman onstage?" and I say, "A *what*? Woman, man—I am a fucking nigger, white person, lesbian, homosexual, witch, snake, vampire—whatever!" I don't think in any one of those terms—that's so limited! But on the other hand: how many men can think like that? [laughs] That's the advantage of being a woman or homosexual—

Oh yes, we can sit on men ("Thank you so much for letting me sit on top of you; I really need a urinary tract infection tonight!")

♦ AJ: **You can be more flexible. Whereas a lot of heterosexual males have rigid, ossified gender definitions—**
♦ DG: Of their own volition. I have a lot of straight black friends and I've always terrorized the shit out of them. One of them will come over and say, "Oh, baby, let's get it on—" and I'll say, "Yeah, you know I've been thinking about you *all night*" (and he'll be this big guy, 6'6") and I'll continue, "Man—I thought about fucking you last night with this crowbar, and you were screaming, 'Baby, fuck me!'"—and they have this look of absolute horror on their faces! But they love me, because they want a woman to talk to them like that—it's really liberating.

I want to fuck a man in the ass (so far I haven't had any volunteers; I always ask them and they get nervous and say no) but I want to, because I feel that's a fundamental part of my relationship with them and to myself. I don't want to just be *fucked*—what's *that*? I want to experience this other thing. Someone said long ago that men should be fucked in the ass *first* before they fuck a woman, so they can understand what it feels like to be penetrated in their body. And in this area, I'm all too willing to help! That would be my ideal man, definitely.

Oh yes, we can sit on men ("Thank you so much for letting me sit on top of you; I really need a urinary tract infection tonight!") but after awhile I want to be *paid*—as an ex-hooker, I want that. Really, I wanna fuck men in the ass—I want to *break the flesh*, too—and exorcise my violence on them to show them just how *much* I love them!

We were talking about the concept of the voice as a political force. I also use the voice in the same liturgical way that the Mass has always been used (immediately people say, "Black Mass," because for some reason I'm

identified with "Satan."). All masses are the same; all have the ability to conjure up evil or the devil, because all gods, all powers are connected in the world—nothing else makes sense.

Back to the concept of the Greek voice, which is simultaneously this political/shamanistic/homosexual witches' voice. My father's background is Turkish-Greek-Anatolian, and my mother's is Spartan Greek. The Spartan Greeks were known for their incantations: *moirologi*, which are incantations to the Dead. When mourning, Greek women would scream and pull out their hair. (Om Kalsoum has a certain power relating to this.) The Greeks hate Americans because they want to turn Greece into an U.S. Air Force base; this relates to Medea: "I would rather kill my children than let them be part of your ancestry." (Just like Saddam Hussein's stance: "I would rather my country be destroyed, than be turned into an American army base.")

Medea leaves her homeland for her husband's sake. Then her husband becomes interested in a younger woman and leaves her like some old garbage, and here she is, a transplant in this new country. She sends the future bride a beautiful bridal gown, and when the woman puts it on, her skin starts to melt very slowly; she dies in total agony. (Pasolini made a film about this, *Medea*, starring Maria Callas.) The whole family is destroyed; she kills her children with a knife rather than leave her husband any offspring, so he's left with nothing. And in many versions of the story she kills herself as well—that's very traditionally Greek.

I'm hostile to the act of childbirth—I've always found the concept of childbirth to be a morbid one at best—something *nostalgic*, like a West Coast "return to nature" cult would espouse.

♦ AJ: **Can you explain the *moirologi?***
♦ DG: That refers to the mourning done by the women to incite revenge against the enemy. What the *Maniots* are to Greece, the Sicilians are to Italy; they have the same traditions. When the Turks invaded Greece years ago and came into their houses, the *Maniot* women would decapitate them. They're known for their skill with knives—that's a source of pride. When I went to Greece I heard the same thing all over: "Don't fuck with them!"

Now the women pull out their hair and scream as an incantation to the dead. Because the women would speak directly to the dead, they were seen as a threat to the authority of the patriarchal society and were labeled

(left) Diamanda's brother, Philip-Dimitri Galás, 1979
(above) Diamanda with her brother, 1980

"witches." More importantly, the women would speak *for* the dead, expressing the feelings of the dead. In "Were You a Witness?" I say: "We who have gone before do not rest in peace/We who have died shall never rest in peace/ Remember me, I am unburied/I am screaming in the bloody furnaces of hell . . .There is no rest until the fighting's done."

This is not a bleeding heart, liberal concept: "Pity the poor AIDS victim/Pity the poor homosexual. . ."—none of my friends who are in hospitals want that shit. They'd rather you called them a fuckin' *faggot* than say you feel sorry for them. Patronizing sympathy is revolting; it has nothing to do with a Greek tragedy or Middle Eastern concept of mourning, which not only expresses the mourning of the family, but—more importantly—the *anger* of the dead.

Sometimes people say, "Your work is so angry; it's not sentimental. And your *own brother*—" and I say, "My brother *despised* cheap sentiment. He despised parlor-room sympathy. He was a strong man, a genius, a great writer. He was a fucking homosexual—although he wasn't what is portrayed as 'homosexual' by the media." Here I recall that gospel music was originally military music which was sung by black slaves who were chased through the streets by dogs—music to inspire, to give courage and power in the face of the Enemy—who *always* looms so large.

♦ **AJ: As mourners, the women were speaking not only for the dead but the oppressed—**

♦ DG: It's no mystery that so many of the care-givers in the AIDS epidemic are women, or that so many of my male friends who are sick prefer to be around women. Women and homosexual men have long been friends; there's a spiritual kinship. Sometimes, of course, some drag queen will try to play *diva* around me—then I have to declare, "There's only one queen allowed in this room, dear, and you're out!"

My brother and I had a few fights about gender-blurring—he looked much better in a skirt than I ever will (which I resent him for, even now that he's in the grave!). But speaking of mourning, male journalists will say, "She did this work because her brother died; isn't it wonderful?" and I'll say, "Kiss my ass—it's not wonderful. I'm not a noble person, my brother wouldn't want your fuckin' journalistic sympathy, and not only that— he just called me from Hell the other day and told me he's never been fucked so good in his life! So kiss my ass!" Do you understand?

♦ **AJ: It's so patronizing and simplistic to "explain away" your pro-AIDS involvement because "your brother died." AIDS is a metaphor for all the poisons in our world—everyone has good cause to be involved in this struggle—**

♦ DG: You're either part of the Resistance or you're a collaborator. There's no other option. I was on TV in Finland and some journalists asked, "When do you think there's going to be a cure?" I replied, "If you have to ask this, you're part of the reason we *have* no cure." They were horrified.

In Bavaria I did a performance of *Plague Mass* in its early stages on Repentance Day. If you are discovered to have HIV in Bavaria, you are known to the authorities— they have your name, address, phone number and you get threatened constantly, you lose your job—it's heavy. I appeared on a pop music TV show and immediately started in on the AIDS quarantine topic—they were trying to get me off the air as fast as possible! Because if you have the image of a pop singer in a territory that doesn't know you, they assume you'll talk about some innocuous shit like: you have a big penis—that's what it's usually all about. Whereas I try to subvert all the media accessible to me. And at one "New Music" Seminar, a thousand people wanted me to leave!

◆ **AJ: What did you do?**

◆ DG: I said they were all a bunch of impotent, homophobic, ass-lickers trying to make a buck off the AIDS crisis ("Death as Entertainment"), and this really got people mad. I got in a fight with Lemmy from *Motorhead*—we got to be friends later, though, because he respected my anger. A lot of media wouldn't publicize me because my show had to do with AIDS, which was then very unpopular—especially in England, the Denial Capital of the World. I was exposing and blasting networks that ignored AIDS news and Lemmy said, "If you'd just be less *obnoxious* about this situation"—and this is Lemmy from *Motorhead?!*

◆ **AJ: "If you would just be a nice girl"—**

◆ DG: Right. And I said, "What do *you* know about death, you fucking fake death, post-Sixties motherfucker?" But Lemmy *is* great—and he came to my show in London after that. I really like terrorizing the rock 'n' roll establishment. Recently I was on a panel where Bob Geldof said, "As singers we can only point people in the 'right' direction, and say what we think is the right thing to do." My answer to him was, "Listen—we already have politicians and big movie stars telling us what we should be doing, giving us all this bullshit and false hope—why should we listen to *you?*" Most of the rock'n'roll business is a totally worthless establishment; its music was supposed to be incendiary, it was supposed to be the music of *revolution*—not this fucking wimpy ass shit, "How big is my penis today?" and "I'm a good guy anyway."

I continued, "If we cannot be part of this activism, then rock music is completely worthless; you motherfuckers are worthless, and you're finished!" He was appalled—it was great. He pleaded, "No no, you misunderstand," and I said, "No, I *don't* misunderstand." Also, on this panel he was talking about his wife and kids, and I really have an absolute aversion toward that family unit crap.

I'm hostile to the act of childbirth—I've always found the concept of childbirth to be a morbid one at best—something *nostalgic* that a West Coast "return to nature" cult would espouse. I'm hostile to the idea of being a medium for this capitalist enterprise of childbearing which is about the male ego recognizing itself in the next generation. I exist outside that sort of pedestrian enterprise—so demeaning to women. I prefer the concept of woman as goddess—in a shamanistic society, no shaman has children. So in 1985 I had my tubes tied.

There exists a critic who—I'm told—intends to expose me for being "against nature." The fact that I cut myself apparently is a "rejection of my birth as a wom-

an." (In other words, a woman is defined by the act of reproduction.) To her, my refusal to breed is an intransigence which renders my stage presence "insufficiently feminine!"

◆ **AJ: On this overpopulated planet, the Biblical dictum "Be fruitful and multiply" is suicidal—**

◆ DG: New breeding makes no sense at all—there's already too many kids around; you can *adopt* one. What about protecting the unfortunate children who *already* exist on this planet? I was talking to Rachel Rosenthal [godmother of performance art] about this. I told her I had my tubes tied and she said I should get a fucking *medal* for this!

I try and make my life consistent with my political beliefs; I'm not going to say, "I want a family like everyone else, because *my* children [*of course*] will be 'terribly special.' *Fuck that*—I'll get some goldfish and some cats and *they'll* be 'terribly special'!" Every witch has cats—you never hear of a witch having children!

If you're in the gay community you know there's nothing more sickening than a funeral service in which the minister basically accuses the dead man of being a victim of "divine punishment."

◆ **AJ: On another level, I'm angry that children are not integrated into society. Most mothers exist in a state of cultural non-growth and alienation, and only associate with other alienated mothers. Although it *pretends* to revere the family, America is very anti-family and anti-children.**

◆ DG: If I had a religion, this would be it: since I was very young I knew that having a child would *not* be part of my life. My Greek aunts would ask, "Are you going to have children?" and I'd say, "You can't talk to me like that; I have no place in that reality." The myth I always aspired to was that of Artemis or Diana, the goddess of the hunt. She was a warrior and a fighter who had *nothing* to do with procreation.

I suppose that if a woman insists on having children she can do it [yawns], but I don't want to watch it! I've watched abortions and that was interesting, but I'm not going to watch childbirth—I find it offensive!

In Mani (Greece), years ago, every new son was called the "new gun." Women were accustomed to inciting revenge—the "eye for an eye" idea reflects an *Old Testament* mentality which *is* the reality of things on many levels . . . When the Germans invaded Greece during World War II, the women sang songs of courage to people in prison

who were about to be executed. One song praised the brave dead and the Englishmen who were defending Greece, ending with, "May the German's plane come crashing to the ground and burn him up alive!" and going on to describe the way the flesh would dissolve. This funereal song was an example of "mourning as incitement"—it incited people to be so angry they would fight. It was never mourning in the pacifistic sense—*never*. And in a country like Greece which has very little power—how else do you survive?

♦ **AJ: You're carrying on this tradition of "mourning to incite." It's no use to just *mourn*.**

♦ DG: [spits disdainfully] That's *useless*. If you're in the gay community you know there's nothing more sickening than a funeral service in which the minister basically accuses the dead man of being a victim of "divine punishment." Or, the family of a person with AIDS insisting that the deceased's friends either not attend the funeral, or stay in the background—thus implying that they (or their lifestyle) are responsible for the death of their son. Such funerals don't make sense—they're an *insult* to the *real friends* who've been keeping this person alive to the end. Because often the family shows up *after* the fucking death.

When I do a "Plague Mass," it's done for people in the AIDS community *by* someone in the AIDS community. And with AIDS we're dealing with a "plague mentality"—one almost *has* to have had a firsthand experience with death in order to start taking it *very seriously*. Some

World premiere of *Eyes Without Blood* at NY Philharmonic Horizon Festival, 1984

Photo: Robin Holland

people proclaim that compassion has been erased from our collective unconscious, and that's why so many so-called "Christians" are so coldly contemptuous or condescending toward people with AIDS.

The myth I always aspired to was that of Artemis or Diana, the goddess of the hunt. She was a warrior and a fighter who had *nothing* to do with procreation.

I started working on my AIDS project over two years *before* my brother became ill. Half my friends are HIV-positive; this is my *life*. These journalists who are outside the community look at my work and it scares them because it's the voice of people who are sick themselves. Because it doesn't just offer "entertainment," they can't imagine that people might want to hear it. They look at music as a *placating* medium—it's supposed to be like *Madonna*.

I separated my work from a safe and useless concept of "music" back in 1974. Music that is truly meaningful contains a distillation of reality—and usually that's *tragedy*. At best, most pop music lightly touches on tragedy in ways that people can relate to, shed tears to, maybe even dance to—after which they can then go home, go to sleep, and effectively dismiss it. That's the "We have addressed the issue after all" syndrome. And people like Madonna are only too willing to propagate the idea that, "If you want to feel better about a terrible situation, you can dance!"

Most pop music is descriptive; it's *about* the thing, not the thing *itself*. Whereas my work *is* the thing itself, it *is* the sound of the plague, the sound of the emotions involved. And people object to that—even in the gay community, the Barbra Streisand-type queen looks at my work and asks, "Why are you doing that?" Well, I'm doing music for people who are conscious and who suffer deeply. Fuckin' cocktail drinkers have music that expresses what they supposedly go through; why can't people who experience *deeper* emotions have the same?

This kind of timidity reminds me of a review I got from a *London Times* critic: "There is no point in addressing a perverse situation like AIDS with the perverse music of Galás. I have several acquaintances with AIDS and I admire and almost *envy* their resignation."[!]

♦ **AJ: Your line "Let's not 'chat' about the despair" is apropos . . . You invoked Antonin Artaud when he *became* the plague, when he embodied the disease—**

♦ DG: Artaud was a very strong inspiration on my work. The two people I read over and over again with *interest* are Artaud and Baudelaire. I resent his appropriation by the rock'n'roll establishment who misinterpret him as a dandy or decadent *detached* from society—that's not why he was a great poet. That's just the only thing they can fucking relate to.

I write songs using lyrics by Baudelaire or Gerard de Nerval which are based more on blues or gospel music structures. I also do solo voice and piano performances once in a while—I enjoy that. As a child I was a virtuoso pianist; when I was 14 I was playing Beethoven's "First Piano Concerto" with a symphony. Then when I started playing jazz I was pretty good—I could play almost anything. My father had a gospel choir; he was like a Johnny Otis figure. His

Photo: Emily Andersen

instruments were trombone and bass; he had a New Orleans band and I used to play with him when I was little. But he was also Golden Gloves, and *his* father was a Golden Gloves boxer as well. He taught Greek and English literature. He's done a lot of things and is an interesting man, very strong, sort of like Socrates and Zorba combined—he even looks like Anthony Quinn! (I love Anthony Quinn—why aren't there more men like that?! I feel like Sophia Loren in cowboy country—but all the cowboys are gay.)

♦ **AJ: The whole concept of maleness is shaky nowadays. Misogyny still rules, but now it's mixed with a lot of cowardice, impotence and wimpiness—**

♦ DG: I pity weak men: they should be dragged out into the middle of the street, beaten, humiliated, degraded and sodomized by my friends and me just for sport. I love seeing weak men cry—my heart races.

I feel sorry for men, but if I could fuck 'em in the ass then it wouldn't matter! [laughs] Actually, I think that eventually I won't be exclusively heterosexual by any means. I might go the way of Bessie Smith and Billie Holiday and become a full-on, fuckin' dyke.

♦ **AJ: When heterosexual women get to the point where they possess their independence and soul, and start becoming *truly* discriminating, it makes for a**

more difficult task to find men that are—

♦ DG: I think women should have an "ideal": the only people you treat as equals are other women. And when you want *subordinates*, you can fuck a man in the ass! That basically is probably the future. Some men get angry because they think I view them just as sex objects. But I say, "You don't need to *read* to me—I can read. And conversation—I can get that from my friends. So you should feel lucky that you at least have *this* service you can offer me."

There've been a lot of military men in my life—I like them to be fighters, at least on a physical level. There've been ex-cons—I like violent men; I like the idea that I can terrorize them and they can take it. I don't want 'em to knock me across the room unless I hit them first—and can hit 'em back. In the area of violence and sex, I always warn people. For example, if they want to be bitten, I say, "Either you want to be bitten or you don't, because I might lose control—there will be no halfway measures!" [laughs] And this is a domain that people who worry about being politically correct don't address: the realm of exciting, even violent sex between consenting adults. Most people think that sex should be gentle and peaceful. But if sex is merely gentle and peaceful, I'm not even *interested*. Of course, when I say violence I mean "play

that sexual power relations can be the inverse of "real life." Nowadays women have to take on many roles—especially power roles. What's most threatening to the male status quo? It's a woman like you who is not only extravagant, a terrorist, and an artist but who also proudly proclaims, "Yeah, I've got a *woman's* body."

♦ DG: Right. You don't ask for power; you *take* it! [laughs] That's just the way it is, isn't it?

♦ AJ: **That should be a mantra!**

♦ DG: With regard to relations with men, SM reality has been the only reality that has ever interested me on a psychic level. It *has* presented certain risks, because when you talk to some of these ex-cons the way I talk to them—if you ask for trouble, sometimes you really get it—*unfortunately!* [laughs]

I think it's *marvelous* [upper-class accent] that some women have these nice, gentle husbands who are really kind to them, treat them really well and help them in their work (that kind of thing)—I think that's *really nice* for them. And I'm not saying it shouldn't work for some people—I'm glad it does. *Wonderful!* And I think men should be friends with women in this sense; I think it's good. It just doesn't interest *me*, that's all.

violence" (a topic of discussion in itself)—I'm really not interested in ending up with a broken jaw or collarbone.

I like the man I'm seeing now because he'll say, "You filthy fuckin' white whore, that's all you want, you piece o' shit!" and I'll say, "Listen, you black motherfucker, I'm gonna take you by a chain and lead you through the streets!" This is the way we like to talk to each other— any way we damn well please! Not with this wimpy, politically correct "discourse" [sarcastically].

♦ AJ: **A lot of people in the SM community are exploring this area of role-playing, and discovering**

As for me—I'm my own manager, my own pretty much *everything*. I can't explain why that is, but I like that self-reliance. I don't want to sleep with some fucking guy every night. I don't want him contaminating my bed; I don't want that male energy in my bed every night. I don't want it on the road with me; I want to *choose* when I have it. Usually it's a reward for a job well done—the fact that if I've taken care of my life, then I can have my reward. If you had asked Fassbinder, I'm sure he lived the same way. A lot of these guys, like Pasolini—I'm sure this is the way they lived and worked; *self-reliant.*

♦ **AJ: For a woman, having a relationship often means being "owned." It doesn't even matter whether you aren't, because that's the way society looks at you: as the "girlfriend" or "wife of *so-and-so.*" Yet it's very rare for any man to be referred to as "so-and-so's *husband.*" Also, you rarely ever hear of a woman being referred to as a "genius"; only a man—**

♦ **DG:** I have an *allergy* to "male genius." If I listen to a man talk about his work for more than 2 minutes, I get supremely bored. . . I can certainly understand why lesbian separatist concepts evolved. So "male genius" is something I have to rail against, because I feel it, I understand it—and I'm not interested!

As far as associating with men who do not have ideas, the men that I hang out with, the men that I *fuck,* are not geniuses—they're not even particularly bright. But they don't have any pretensions of cutting-edge theory or cultural analysis—I won't listen to them for that, anyway. And if one woman says to another woman, "I can't understand why you associate with so-and-so"—no one has the right to say that, because in this society the men are so inferior that *we take the best we can get!* We've been forced to—unless we're not heterosexual, that's our choice!

Yet I can't blame a woman for wanting somebody who will challenge her. I had a beautiful breakfast one morning in Germany with William Burroughs—a great man whose genius I respect. We'd done a show on the same bill the night before. He told me that he really liked what I did, and that he had never seen anything that emotional since he was in Morocco many years ago. Then he brought up Martha Graham, who was a great visionary—*that's* what we talked about. A lot of people today wouldn't see her (or her dances) that way, but her ideas have been appropriated by practically every dancer and choreographer today. So he talked about Martha Graham, and I thought, "Oh! He isn't the person he was made out to be—just interested in guns and macho shit—he's a real human being—"

♦ **AJ: He loves cats—**

♦ **DG:** Yes! So that was a revelation . . . Martha Graham, who like Callas with opera, Baudelaire with poetry, and Artaud with the theater—forced her soul to migrate to another place, and stretched her craft with it. The soul and the blood *is* the craft; beauty is revealed through technique after the hard work is done. And just as Callas brought back that primal reality to the opera, and Graham brought it back to dance, so Albert Ayler and Ornette Coleman brought it back to jazz. All these artists start with the scream, with the blood, and then they articulate that. They don't lose sight of *that* being what they're a medium for.

I don't respect the boundaries of any art form; I certainly don't respect music's boundaries. If some journalist tries to describe and circumscribe my work, I say,

"Just use my name—that's sufficient; no one else is doing what I do." The direct statement—I can respect *that.*

On the other hand, technique *is* important. I like the way Japanese martial artists regard technique: if you lack a certain mastery, you can't express or *be* yourself. I aim for something *beyond* what's expected—yet the moment I imagine my suffering as something that's *never* been experienced by someone else, I become boring, effete, self-indulgent—not interesting. Greek tragic theater has a quality of being larger than life, just like great boxing (I like to call myself the "Tyson of the Voice") because it's life or death when you're in the ring. And when you are "singing to the gods" you must have a superlative technique to extrovert the ride—to "ride the outer limits of the soul." Because without technique, Tyson might be known as the baddest fighter in the Bronx, but you and I never would have heard of him!

I think women should have an "ideal": the only people you treat as equals are other women. And when you want *subordinates,* you can fuck a man in the ass!

I can't really relate to most white rock'n'roll singing. I think Aretha Franklin is a great singer, but she grew up in the gospel tradition singing in black churches, where the voice really is a medium for the *soul.* But within the white rock'n'roll establishment, the kind of singing that predominates is *pathetic:* about "your girlfriend left you," or something else that's *weak*—there's never that *shamanistic* sense. Rock singing is something men do to get laid or get their cock sucked after a gig—you can smell it. I don't go to male rock'n'roll shows; I didn't go to that fuckin' Jim Morrison movie. Why do I want to see the motherfucker jerk off in my face, larger than life? What do I have to learn from this motherfucker?

If we're talking Hendrix—well, *there's* a great artist and musician. Oh, he happened to take drugs, but that's not why he was great—that was just the part that people could relate to, because they love the idea of the self-destructive genius, or the "musical suicide." Jim Morrison's *lucky* he died so young, before he became an overweight, drooling drunk. But all this makes me sick—it has nothing to do with anything important. All rock singers are just singing to their dick! Well, *I'm* not singing to my dick!

♦ **AJ: To be a warrior you have to train and be disciplined. Most people have creative impulses, but few nourish and develop them. Every day, whether you're inspired or not, you just have to work.**

♦ **DG:** Actually, I love to answer that question, "Are

you inspired?" I think W.H. Auden once said, "NO—I'm *never* inspired!"

♦ **AJ: You have great technique, which is so vital—**

♦ DG: You have to! Can you imagine someone going to war who didn't know how to fight? [laughs] If you try to reach the emotional levels I try for *without* technique, well—I've seen people in mental institutions hit their head against the wall and say "Mama!" for hours at a time, and I'm sure they *meant* it—but so what? If I see some singer, unless I think he's really *suffered* to be able to do what he does, I don't care to watch him. I mean—I didn't *enjoy* studying voice—it was a lot of hard work. I worked my fuckin' ass off for years and years and didn't see people and didn't go out—I didn't live a "party" life. I lived in fuckin', stinking San Diego for years just to study with this voice coach, but I could have been having fun in New York. . .

♦ **AJ: We were talking about bringing *meaning* back to all the arts—integrating them back into people's lives and the *community.* Music used to actually have some relevance, but now it's just this masturbatory—**

♦ DG: Wank. But we're not talking about music such as Mozart's *Requiem Mass*—I'm sorry, but when I hear that I'm on the floor crying immediately. Now *there* was a master no one can deny.

I did a Mass which I called a "Plague Mass." It was not just for the dead but for the living—people with AIDS who don't necessarily view their disease as a death sentence—although it usually is. I wrote it to encourage action rather than passivity.

I don't want to sleep with some guy every night. I don't want that male energy in my bed night after night. I don't want it on the road with me; I want to *choose* when I have it.

♦ **AJ: Can you tell us about your arrest?**

♦ DG: I got arrested when ACT UP went to St Patrick's Cathedral in December '89 and staged a "Die-In" to protest Cardinal O'Connor's war against people with AIDS. Basically, he was attacking anybody trying to implement condom and preventive measures campaigns. Because he would not meet with any members of the AIDS community, it was necessary for us to go into *his* environment.

It was a peaceful demonstration; there were thousands of people outside the cathedral. I was one of the ones who went *into* the church. When Cardinal O'Connor spoke his cliches about, "We must care for the afflicted and suffering," we exposed the masquerade he was stag-

ing and laid down in the aisles. I shouted, "Cardinal O'Connor, you are responsible for the deaths of . . . you have sinned!" He had the congregation stand up and recite the "Lord's Prayer" (like in the *Exorcist*—that's what you do when there are sinners in your midst and you're trying to exorcise the devil!) And I have to admit I felt sorry for some of the older parishioners, because a lot of them simply aren't informed; they're isolated by society, and for them this is their only "community."

I'm getting a tattoo which says, "We are all HIV Positive." And if I wear the right clothes it will just say "HIV Positive."

So I felt some ambiguity: being raised Greek Orthodox, I didn't like doing that! Nevertheless I felt it was important. The cops asked us to get up without sufficient warning, so they carried us out on stretchers and took us to jail in paddy wagons. A lot of people in ACT UP don't want to go to prison because then they'll be taken out of action for awhile. Going to jail isn't something to romanticize, it's just: you were there for a few hours and it was a drag, but *so what* . . .

♦ **AJ: Do you have any tattoos?**

♦ DG: I'm getting a tattoo which says, "We are all HIV Positive." And if I wear the right clothes it will just say "HIV Positive." A lot of people already assume I've got AIDS because of my work, just as they assume I'm a lesbian—obviously, no *straight* person would be interested in doing what I do! In Sweden I was interviewed: "So, Diamanda, we hear that you are a very famous lesbian." I said, "Oh, am I? I'll have to ask my lesbian friends—I'm certainly not famous among *them!*" I told my friends and they laughed their heads off—could it be I'm the "Colette" of the avant-garde? . . . I'm certainly not the Gertrude Stein.

The questions "Are you homosexual? Are you heterosexual? Are you white? Are you black?"—who cares? I'm a civilized human being and I don't think in those terms. This shouldn't even be a primordial way of thought—people should think of themselves as planetary citizens.

♦ **AJ: In sexuality, we're a continuum; people aren't 100% gay or 100% heterosexual.**

♦ DG: Did you see that cover of *Outweek:* "Marlene Dietrich and Greta Garbo: Bisexual or Cowards?" Give me a break! C. Carr wrote an outstanding piece in the *Village Voice* attacking the practice of outing. *Outweek* wanted to put me on their cover because of my pro-AIDS work, but the editor freaked out, saying, "I *wish* you were a lesbian!" I said, "You exist to 'out' homosexuals, but if somebody is supposedly 'straight', then no matter *what* they do it's not good enough for you, is it?"

♦ **AJ: The enemy has always lived by the tactic of "Divide and Conquer." While we're all fighting each other, the reactionaries of the world are cleaning up! The right wing Christian Fundamentalists, including Meese and his anti-pornography, homophobic campaigns which we're all feeling the effects of, don't fight with each other.**

♦ DG: No one person or faction can speak for the entire gay or AIDS community, yet factions in ACT UP against GMHC (Gay Men's Health Crisis), against CRI (Community Research Initiative) and other groups try to cut off each other's funding or expose "politically incorrect" behavior. That kind of activity is really injurious. I don't claim to be a spokesperson for the AIDS community, I'm one small voice contributing whatever I can. I play the piano for AIDS patients at Veterans Hospital and at Bailey House—the oldest residence house in New York for people with AIDS; I have a lot of friends who work in the community; I try to find out about drugs for my friends and get them in programs . . . but I'm just one fucking person. I always say that even if you spend only one hour a week dealing with the AIDS crisis, at least *do* something! Don't ask me questions like, "When's there going to be a cure?"—be part of it!

♦ **AJ: What does "the Devil" or "Satan" mean to you?**

♦ DG: Baudelaire described "Satan" fairly well. I was in Berlin and some girls came up to me and said, "Oh, you are Diamanda—please do another record for us soon. We have witchcraft rituals and shoot up speed and chant to the Devil and listen to your music." I thought, "Oh *fuck*—you could get a Julie Andrews record and do this kind of stupid shit."

When a witch is about to be burned on a ladder in flames, who can she call upon? I call that person "Satan," although other people may have other names, and it's the same entity that schizophrenics call upon to create an essential freedom they need. It's that subversive voice that can keep you alive in the face of adversity. If you've ever been institutionalized (and I have), then you know what a *descent into hell* is. And if you can come out of it alive, then you are so much the stronger. I have this text: "You call me the shit of God? I am the shit of God! You call me the Antichrist? I am the Antichrist, I am Legba, I am the Holy Fool, I am the Scourge of God" (Legba is the trickster in West African tradition). So you say, "Yes, I am the Antichrist, I *am* Legba, I *am* all these things you are afraid of."

♦ **AJ: It's those "tricksters" (the artists and Outsiders) who reveal society's illnesses—**

♦ DG: But those Outsiders are treated like hunted criminals. There have been warrants out for my arrest, and I think, "Oh—society's going to put me in jail." In court, six ACT UP demonstrators pleaded that they didn't enter the cathedral to disrupt Cardinal O'Connor's

Photo: Dona Ann McAdams

religious ceremony (which is against the law), but to *participate* in it by doing a "Die-In." So it depends on the way you look at it.

I mean: what can they do to you? They can put you in jail—but if you see the ability to survive in any context as a mark of your strength, then that's not going to break your spirit. If I ever go to prison and someone says something nasty to me, we'll have to fight and hopefully I can beat her ass. And if I *can't* beat her ass, then I have to learn how to do it for the next time. *What's the problem?* So I don't get scared, I think: "What are you going to do to me? Are you going to rape me?—I've been raped before. *What* are you going to do? *Next.*"

When I almost got raped for the fifth time in my life, this black guy came up to me while I was opening a door and said (in the dark), "This is a rape!" I said [bored voice], "Oh, really? It's been a long day. Could I ask you a question—do you have a knife?" "No." "Then why don't we just call it off?" And he called it off! It was like: "Darling, I'm terribly bored. I really want to get some sleep and I don't have time for this. You don't have a knife, so let's forget it." And as he walked downstairs with me I said, "Next time you should be careful, because *I* could have had one." It's like: you can get to the point where you're not afraid—then people see that and *what can they do?*

♦ AJ: Earlier we were talking about how society projects onto the Other, the Outcast, the Outsider, the dark side of its psyche which it pretends doesn't exist—

♦ DG: It's a privilege to accept that. If you tell me I wear a cloak of filth, let me tell you: *I wear it real good.* This idea is very dear to me. I grew up in a very isolated situation—my father was very strict: no radio, no TV, no mass media were allowed in the house. And in terms of bringing up kids, being Turkish/Greek is like being Muslim: I was not allowed to wear a 2-piece bathing suit; I was not allowed to have any dates—not until I left the house at the age of 19. I had no friends until I was 18. So my brother and I lived these weird lives: he lived in the attic and I lived downstairs, playing the piano and doing things by myself. And in that isolation you develop peculiarities and inner strengths you can call upon. You discover this early because you're not being constantly distracted.

Later on I got into drugs and had some pretty wild experiences, making that "descent into hell and back." I went through a lot of shit to store up and hone that power that comes from *within*, where you know you can rely on yourself and your judgment—power which doesn't come from *outside*. Some people who have a large support system think they have power and strength, but to me they're like some fucking little ants. Although they might be considered normal or sane, I might consider them very insane, because of the values they live by . . .

I went through a lot of shit to store up and hone that power that comes from *within*, where you know you can rely on yourself and your judgment—power which doesn't come from *outside*.

When I saw Psalm 88 in the *Old Testament*, it was very clear to me that it had to be the first incantation in my work, "Masque of the Red Death." When I started to sing it was in a voice I'd never heard before: it wasn't *my* voice—people have said it sounded like a Southern Baptist on acid. My upstairs neighbors were homosexual priests in the Catholic church working with PWA's (People With AIDS) in hospitals, and I asked them about using these texts: "Did this make *any* sense? Was I just out of my mind?" And they said, "Use them!" That made me feel a little better, because with all due respect to the "artist's" supposed discoveries of realities unbeknownst to anyone else, when one deals with a situation like an epidemic, one hopes that one's vision or intuition is going

to be sufficient—that it's truly reflective of what's going on in the world. Because if you work alone most of the time, you can begin to wonder . . .

I learned a lot about *being a woman* from these black drag queens—the power behind the role, and how you can use it.

Before doing my mental hospital performances, I used to say prayers to the devil—it was like making a connection to some source of power so that I could do what was not socially accepted. It was like: "You know me, you understand me, I can speak for this reality—you can help me do this." I didn't know who I was addressing, really, but that was what I did. The kind of performance I do, the kind of things I have to say, the physical energy I put into it—it's *freeing* but it's very physically demanding. If you're standing in front of 3000 people doing this kind of performance—well, that demands superhuman strength and emotional reserves that are really beyond *me* and my capability as a very fallible human being. Sometimes my performances feel to me like a ripping of the flesh, like a bloodletting. . .

♦ AJ: A kind of voodoo possession?

♦ DG: That's exactly what it is. And in Europe I've had people from Africa ask me if what I do is a witchcraft ceremony. A Ugandan who had brought Miriam Makeba to Cologne, Germany, invited me to Ethiopia and Uganda because what I did in performance (specifically, my Greek junta piece) reminded him of the *samrotsaka* which is practiced in Uganda. He was an old man, and I almost didn't believe him, but he said that if I were performing in Uganda, I would be worshipped as a high fetish priestess. I thought, "Yeah, *right*; what do you want?" but he was very serious about it.

I've heard this over and over again from Africans who've seen my performance—they relate to it in a different way. Because again, it's not about art—it's *not* art. I don't read the fucking *Village Voice* to come up with what I'm going to do. Eight years ago when I worked on my "Plague Mass" it wasn't because I *read* that people were dying of AIDS; I just had this intuition to work on this, but I didn't know *why*. That's why I asked those gay priests: "What am I doing? Is this going to hurt somebody?" That's all I wanted to know—I didn't want to do something to *hurt* someone because my intuition might have inappropriately interfaced with a real life situation.

♦ AJ: Did you study with Linda Montano?

♦ DG: No. Linda and I were at the Center for Musical Experiments; I was working with electronics and she was performing there. That's how I know her.

♦ AJ: She does "performance therapy" which can dredge up hidden emotions and channel them into theatrical artifice. Annie Sprinkle went to her workshop and had to act out her worst experiences, exposing old festering wounds, and this seemed to have the potential to heal—

♦ DG: The act of embarrassing oneself ("em-bare-ass": I like that wordplay) is very painful, especially for dope fiends—they *don't* want to do that. I've lived through some painful experiences because I like to do what I want. My life is my research, you know—I detest mediocrity. On San Pablo Avenue in Oakland, California I worked as a prostitute for awhile under the name "Miss Zina." I was living with some black transvestite hookers: Miss Gina (otherwise known as Butch), Miss Michelle *(transsexual)*, and Duchess, who was another "natural woman" like me. This was way back in 1974. I was in love with a man who was real—he was a major con artist. Previously I had worked in a couple of whorehouses, but that was generally a real bore. One day a Turkish guy came in and—I won't turn a Turkish trick; forget it—not as a Greek . . . so I quit.

Anyway, part of the reason I became a prostitute was because I wanted to be able to walk down the street in the worst fucking part of town and carry a fucking knife and know that it was *my street*—our street, not *their* street. You know that the whole streetwalker "thing" is: stealing money from tricks—that's what you do. So I lived with these drag queens who were basically thieves and sister dope fiends. And how I got started was: one day these drag queens dared me to go out at 6 AM in the fucking rain and raise some rent money, so I decided,

Photo: Dona Ann McAdams

"Okay, I'm not going to turn down a dare."

Basically you'd get into the car and start turning the trick and then steal their wallet and stick 'em up. Some pimps tried to round me up and put me in their cars, but I had my life defended by these great black drag queens. These toothless bitches with knives would say to the pimps, "Mary, I'll cut your fucking dick off—just don't touch this *thing!*" I learned a lot about *being a woman* from these black drag queens—the power behind the role, and how you can use it. Very important—I learned how to walk down the street without fear. Part of the time I worked this drag queen strip with "Miss Gina from

21

Argentina"—we did this fake Spanish-speaking routine together—it was fucking bizarre. This experience was very important to me.

It's like: a lot of men think they have to go to war to be a man. Well, for me as a woman in those days: "You're not going to know anything about sex unless you work the street . . . not until you've done that and lived through the whole violent trip." That is not a suggestion to anyone; it was my trip in '74.

When you rape a whore it's called "stealing"! And a raped whore can't go to the fucking cops, either. One time I was playing in a black band, and one guy waited until everyone else had gone home. He was a black ex-boxer, and the next thing I knew he just knocked me on the ground and did the whole rape thing. Another time— I won't tell you about that time! I put myself in a lot of dangerous situations because I had this *pinchu macha* thing—I felt I had to *prove* something. These days, if there's six punks on the street corner, I'll still walk by them—I'm not going to let them see me cross the street to avoid them! That's ridiculous, I know, but still I won't do it. I prize my freedom. That's why I'm convinced that all women seriously have to get guns. I personally own a .38 Special.

♦ **AJ: The only form of gun control I would support is that women could own guns and men couldn't. Women *should* carry guns. I don't understand how any true feminist could be in favor of gun control—who do they think they're kidding? What masochistic woman could think this? You really *have* to empower yourself. The gun I recommend to friends is also a .38 Special—the Smith & Wesson Model 49 with a lightened trigger pull and Tyler T-Grip adaptor.**

♦ DG: It's like: to some women, fighting is considered a "bad vibe." We're conditioned to the idea that if someone fights back—well, that'll bring you "bad karma." We're conditioned to this idea that if you have a gun, you're inviting trouble. *Newsweek* ran this huge cover story trying to prove how dangerous guns are, talking about "suicides" and people "killed by mistake"—even though all their statistics were lies. But guns don't walk in the middle of the night on 8 legs and blow your head off! So—fuck! A lot of women are conditioned to think that if you get a gun, someone will just take it away from you. Or if you have a knife, then somebody will stab you with it. The same "logic" is cited in the AIDS community: "Bad vibes produce stress, and stress is destructive to a healthy immune system, so *don't* fight back—basically accept your karma. God has chosen you to die, so try to make that happen as slowly as possible—if you fight back, it will just stimulate the virus and you'll die faster." This kind of thinking is really madness!

♦ **AJ: This is another ghettoization of the victim. The status quo wants people to be passive self-victimizers, because then they're just that much more pliable. It's like the Jews going into the gas chamber thinking, "Well, maybe if we're nice, they'll let us go."**

♦ DG: Yes . . . unfortunately, that's it! The guys who

teach people how to fight say: When someone attacks you—just *explode!* You're not yourself anymore, you're this *other* thing. And that's really different from trying to use your supposed "rational center"—which is your fucking *center of sell-out*—and saying [mock sympathy], "Mr Rapist, I know you don't really *mean* to be putting your dick up my ass!"

♦ **AJ: You've got to get into that animal mode and go right for the throat. If you carry a gun, you never wave it around—the moment you take it out you had better kill, instantly! Because otherwise it *will* get taken away from you. [laughs] You keep it totally hidden until the moment you need it, and you carry it in your pocket with your hand on it, not in some purse. And you never shoot to "wound," you shoot to *kill*—two shots in the chest and then one in the head. Because you've got to stop that male attacker.**

♦ DG: My father always told me that with a gun you kill them first, then you put a hole in the ceiling so that when the cops arrive, you say, "Well—I warned him! I *tried!*" [laughs] ♦ ♦ ♦

Recordings

Plague Mass, 1991
Masque of the Red Death, 1988
You Must Be Certain of the Devil, 1988
Saint of the Pit, 1986
The Divine Punishment, 1986
Diamanda Galás, 1984
The Litanies of Satan, 1982

Recording Compilations

The Last of England, 1987
Smack My Crack, 1987
A Diamond in the Mouth of a Corpse, 1986
Double-Barrel Prayer, 1988

Film Soundtrack Work

The Last of England, Derek Jarman, 1987.
Antigone, Amy Greenfield, 1988.
Miscellaneous work for Wes Craven; Golam & Globus.

Video

One-hour documentary of Galás performances from 1980-present now in preparation. Contact Mute Records for information.

Annie Sprinkle

For the past 16 years Annie Sprinkle has worked as a 42nd Street dancer, porno film star (150 feature films, 20 videos, and 50 8mm loops), prostitute in massage parlors, hosted her own cable TV show, starred in the comix series *Miss Timed* by Andy Mangels, and contributed numerous articles and photographs to porn magazines (besides having edited one herself). In 1985 she moved into the world of performance art as a member of the cast of *Deep Inside Porn Stars,* at Franklin Furnace in New York City. Since then Annie has performed all over the world as a "Post-Porn Modernist," breaking taboos and pushing limits—in a number of shows she invited the audience to "demystify the female body" by inspecting her cervix with a speculum and flashlight.

Annie describes her move out of pornography into performance art as a liberation from "junk sex" toward an eclectic exploration of the *outer reaches of sexuality,* combining Eastern philosophy, yoga, meditative breathing, spirituality and healing. She once said, "I was called the Mother Theresa of Porn and the Renaissance Woman of Porn. Before that I was the Queen of Kink. Now I'm the Shirley MacLaine of Porn!" A performance might include a monologue, a one-woman sex show, a play or interaction with the audience invited to participate, and a tantric healing ritual. Promoting her vision of New Age Sexuality, Annie says, "Sex is a path to enlightenment . . . And women producing porn will push things in a positive direction. Women have something really special to offer in terms of helping our society grow sexually."

The *Post Porn Modernist Manifesto* (written by Annie's partner, Veronica Vera) proclaims, "Post Porn Modernists celebrate sex as the nourishing, life-giving force. We embrace our genitals as part, not separate, from our spirits. We utilize sexually explicit words, pictures and performances to communicate our ideas and emotions. We denounce sexual censorship as anti-art and inhuman. We empower ourselves by this attitude of sex-positivism. And with this love of our sexual selves we have fun, heal the world and endure."

Annie Sprinkle's new book, *Post Porn Modernist,* is available for $33 postpaid from The Sexuality Library, 1210 Valencia St, San Francisco CA 94110 (415-550-7399).

◆ ANNIE SPRINKLE: There is nothing in my childhood that would have led anyone to believe that I would end up being "Annie Sprinkle"—nothing. I was not a sexual child—I was very shy and inhibited. It wasn't until I lost my virginity at the age of 17 that I even became *interested* in sex. I think, though, that it was all those years of fear and lack of knowledge that propelled me to learn everything about sex and become a "sex educator" . . .

Annie Sprinkle as 1/2 slut and 1/2 Goddess.

I was never abused, never raped—still have never been raped. Nothing happened that would have led me to believe I would become "Annie Sprinkle" . . . until suddenly I ended up in prostitution—six months after I lost my virginity!

◆ **ANDREA JUNO: How did *that* happen?**

◆ AS: I needed money. I was a hippie—once in a while I'd smuggle some pot in from Mexico but now I was just being a hippie, not making money. This friend of mine was a witch; he cast a spell to help me find a job—and a week later I was working in a massage parlor. For 3 months I worked and didn't even know I was a hooker—I was having such a good time! The men I saw were referred to as "clients" or "massages." But finally, after about 3 months one woman used the word "trick" and I realized, "Ohmigod—they're *tricks!* Oh shit—I'm a *hooker!*"

◆ **AJ: Would you actually engage in intercourse?**

◆ AS: Yes—I would do a little massage and get turned on . . . and then I would fuck 'em! And they'd leave me

Abstinence Can Be Dangerous To Your Health: Abstinence can cause incredible anxiety, frustration, depression, disease, violence and a whole host of other destructive forces. If you like sex, then don't give it up. It's too precious a gift.

Redefine Your Concept Of Sex: Because we are now in the AIDS era, it is essential that we let go of old ideas of how sex is "supposed to be." We have to find new ways to be intimate and express sexual feelings. Learn that sex is about energy, not the way bodies touch. Focus on energy.

Accept The Fact That You Are Living In The AIDS Era: Stop complaining that sex isn't the way it used to be and that you hate condoms. Get over it and accept reality. Learn to love latex. Total acceptance of the reality of being in the AIDS era will get rid of fear and frustration and bring awareness and compassion. Educate yourself on safe sex practices. Use a condom whenever you need to, so we can stop the spread of the AIDS virus and other STD's.

Visualize A Safe And Satisfying Future For Your Sex Life And The Sex Lives Of Future Generations.

Let Your Sexual Energy Flow: If you've been repressing your sexuality because of the fear of AIDS, you don't need to. Realize that AIDS is caused by a virus and not by your sexuality. (That's like saying you will go blind if you masturbate.) Your sexuality will not give you AIDS. There are a trillion, billion, million ways to be sexual without risking any exposure to AIDS, or risking exposing someone else. Enjoy them.

Make Love To The Earth And The Sky: Our earth and sky are painfully polluted. Make love to them, and they'll make love to you. Send them your sexual energy. They love it.

Make Time For Enjoying Sex: If you like sex, give yourself and others the gift of loving sensual/sexual pleasure. THROW AWAY YOUR TV.

Get Rid Of Any Last Vestiges Of Sexual Guilt And Of Any Feelings That You Don't Deserve Pleasure.

Do Not Judge Yourself Or Others: We are all at the right place at the right time in our sexual evolution. Our sex lives, like all the parts of our lives, go through many phases. We learn from all our experiences including our "mistakes." Allow other people their own paths. Allow yourself your own path.

Learn About Your Breath: Sexual and orgasmic energy travel on the breath. Breathing techniques can make sex much more powerful and satisfying. (It's possible to have an orgasm from breathing alone. Is this the safe sex of the future?) Rhythmic breathing is the best thing since the invention of the vibrator.

Know That You Can Choose How You Want To Express Your Sexuality—Self-Lovingly Or Self-Destructively: Many people are shutting down their sexuality because they have come to realize that they had a lot of self-destructive and addictive behavior revolving around sex. But you have a choice, just like you do with what you eat. There is junk sex, health sex and gourmet sex. Try to make self-loving choices, but if you don't, then don't beat yourself up.

Take Care Of Your Body: Eat well, exercise and pamper your body with long baths and obscenely expensive toiletries.

Annie Sprinkle's logo

Ellen Steinberg as a Girl Scout surrounded by her family.

extra money 'cause they'd had such a good time. I figured this was for the massage plus a tip—and the sex was just something I threw in for fun! Because I was really curious—I wanted to try sex with all different kinds of people.

I worked in that massage parlor and ended up coming to New York where I became the mistress of Gerard Damiano (who made *Deep Throat*). I had always wanted to learn filmmaking, so I started apprenticing at a place that made "one day wonders"—really low-budget porno movies. This was when there were porno theaters all over the country, after *Deep Throat* had been released and *porno chic* had arrived.

♦ **AJ: So when you grew up, sex had been—**

♦ AS: —such a scary thing. Menstruation was not talked about; sex wasn't talked about—it was all a big *secret*. All I knew about sex was: *I wasn't having it* (if you did, you were a slut). The suburbs of Los Angeles are very conservative: white, middle-class, conformist—ev-

Ellen Steinberg with Dog.

eryone trying to be the same. There was no juiciness—I wasn't aware of any kind of sexuality anywhere.

♦ **AJ: So what happened at 17?**

♦ AS: I lost my virginity and it was a lovely, wonderful experience. The man was older and had a motorcycle. At the time I was living in Panama (Central America). I had some really nice friends, but high school guys my age didn't interest me. Plus, I was busy exploring Panama, so sex wasn't a big thing. But when I lost my virginity I definitely became interested—because it felt so good!

♦ **AJ: But it seems you bypassed certain liabilities. For a lot of women, sex becomes part of a "neediness" ... a byproduct of getting a *relationship*—whereas you liked sex just in and of itself—**

♦ AS: Yes, sex had nothing to do with a relationship. I actually felt it was a great way to get to *know* people. And I wanted to learn everything about sex—I didn't have to marry the guy or even like him! I wanted to see what sex was like with somebody you couldn't even "stand," so for awhile I had my "Beauty and the Beast" fantasy: being with the "creepiest" kind of guys (that wasn't *my* word, but that's how someone else would have considered them). But at the same time I felt a lot of love for everybody; I was like the "hooker with a heart of gold."

I would do a little massage and then I would fuck 'em! And they'd leave me extra money 'cause they'd had such a good time. I figured this was for the massage plus a tip—and the sex was just something I threw in for fun!

When I was in that massage room having sex, I *loved* that person! I was truly having a *deeper relationship*. And *they* loved me! I think that as a child I didn't get enough attention because there were so many kids in the family—and I needed attention. Our family wasn't very "physical," yet I felt the need to be touched a lot. So in a way prostitution was perfect: I needed to feel sexy; I needed people to tell me I was sexy—because I thought I was ugly. In a way it fit my needs perfectly—that was a big surprise!

♦ **AJ: Then you got into making porno films—**

♦ AS: Right; for 8 months I was an apprentice filmmaker. Weekends I worked in a massage parlor, and during the week worked on these films where I was the set designer, sound woman, script girl—I learned everything about film; I got a full education. Eventually I decided it would be more fun to be in *front* of the camera.

I didn't get into film for the money, because I was making plenty of money as a whore—I just decided to *do it.* When I was growing up I always thought I'd be an art school teacher, and I remember thinking, "Well, there goes *that* career—I won't ever get to teach art school if I do porno movies!" Now, ironically I'm getting all these offers to teach art classes *because* of my porno past! I've always felt I had to follow my muse, go with the flow, and what I was really drawn to was *sexuality*—I wanted to learn everything about it. I really didn't know why, but now I do know why, and it all makes a lot of sense!

♦ **AJ: Why?**

♦ **AS:** I was afraid you were going to ask that! Why? Because *sex is the most interesting subject in the world!* There's a lot of excitement and controversy about sex—both pro and con in terms of people both for and against it—also, politically.

Sex, for me, was always spiritual—not all sexual experiences were spiritual, but there were some that were highly spiritual. For me *sex is my spiritual path, and my spiritual path is sex!* Sex led me into spirituality; I only became interested in spirituality when I found out it could be sexual. And still to this day, the closest I feel to a Oneness and Pure Divine Love . . . to Ecstasy and to Heaven (or whatever you want to call it), is in certain sexual situations. So that's a good reason! Plus: financially, it's a great way to make a living! There are so many great, positive sides to it . . .

♦ **AJ: How did you get your name?**

♦ **AS:** When I was a hooker I began using the name "Annie." Then, when I started doing porno films I needed a name to use on the credits. At first I used "Annie Sands," but then realized I needed something more exciting. I was lying in bed and—it's like it was channeled or the "Goddess" gave it to me—a voice said, "Annie Sprinkle." It was really weird and strange.

I knew I was attracted to the sugar in the sprinkles on ice cream cones (I'm a sugarholic). I was also attracted to the sound of *wetness*—I like waterfalls, piss, vaginal fluid, sweat, cum—anything wet. I love rain, and I practically *grew up* in a swimming pool. So "Annie Sprinkle" seemed perfect!

Look at this photograph that my uncle sent me: the gravestone of an "Annie Sprinkle" who died a hundred years ago at the age of 17. Just a few months ago I visited this gravestone which is in Baltimore. I have a fantasy that she died a virgin, and that maybe she has something to do with *me*—that she gave me her name and guided me on my wild, wanton path . . .

I always had a strong feeling that sex was good for you—that it was really healthy, and that it really made people feel better—and I like making other people feel better (that's the nurse in me). I really resonate with the conviction that *sex makes you feel better.* I have a friend who says it's like getting a chiropractic treatment: you get a whole attitude adjustment and all your molecules change—in fact everything changes—you just plain feel a whole lot better afterwards. So that's another reason.

♦ **AJ: Do you live a healthy lifestyle?**

♦ **AS:** Yes. I don't do drugs (except for special occa-

Ellen Steinberg

sions—I'm not against them, I'm just not a drug lover). Sugar is my biggest problem. I quit smoking 4 years ago. I swim a lot; I try to exercise. When I found out that exercise had a lot to do with sexual energy, that's when I started exercising! And now I actually enjoy it, because I found out that exercise could be sexual.

So it's through sex that I learn about *everything* in life! It's through sex that I see the world. And I can have a sexual experience with someone and realize, "Oh, now I understand why I got into that fight at the bank!" They say that in every grain of sand is an entire universe, and I feel that way about sex—for me it's the most interesting way to learn about life—although I don't recommend it for everyone! [laughs]

♦ **AJ: Did you ever feel exploited in the sex industry?**

♦ **AS:** I think women can feel exploited in every industry! There were times I felt manipulated or exploited— when I'd do something and afterwards felt sorry I'd done it. I guess I always look at the positive side; I look back at what happened as a *learning experience:* learning what I do

and don't want to do, learning how to say No, learning what I like and what I don't like. I made some mistakes. And I think that if I was a victim, in a sense I was just as responsible as the victimizer—that sounds harsh, but whenever that happened I'm sure I created a lot of it. I did have a low self-image and self-worth, which affected how other people treated me. So I take responsibility for any exploitation that occurred.

At the same time we're in a patriarchal society; I was with a lot of men who were far less than "respectful" . . . who were abusive in some ways. But I was also very lucky: like I said, I never got raped. I was never really hurt—I think that *emotionally* there might have been a little psychological damage, but mostly I think I came out a winner!

♦ **AJ: It seems to have been a very positive path for you—**

♦ **AS:** Yes, absolutely.

♦ **AJ: Unfortunately it *is* a patriarchal society and men don't like women to own and *enjoy* sex—but where does exploitation begin . . . and end? Particularly if you enjoy sex and can "own" it—**

♦ **AS:** What I've learned is: there are so many different kinds of sex. And the kind of sex that's exploitative I call

"Look at this photograph that my uncle sent me: the gravestone of an 'Annie Sprinkle' who died a hundred years ago at the age of 17. Just a few months ago I *visited* this gravestone which is in Baltimore. I have a fantasy that she died a virgin, and that maybe she has something to do with *me*—that she gave me her name and guided me on my wild, wanton path . . ."

junk sex (and let's face it: we're a junk sex society, just like we're a junk food society). I think there's a *place* for junk sex—it would be: very fast and quick like MacDonald's food—very genitally focused; not very intimate; selfish—you wouldn't go away feeling really nourished . . .

Whereas *gourmet sex* would take a lot of time, skill and knowledge to prepare—just like a gourmet meal. It would be like Tantric sex—more spiritual, holistic, loving and nourishing. There's also "health sex": just as you would use aspirin or a medicine, you can use sex to heal.

Sex had nothing to do with a *relationship*. I actually felt it was a great way to get to *know* people. And I wanted to learn everything about sex—I didn't have to *marry* the guy or even *like* him!

In fact I once saved Willem de Ridder's [Amsterdam artist, writer, performer] life. All day long we'd been walking around in the dust of Pompeii, so he got the worst asthma attack he'd ever had. Back in the hotel room I tried hot compresses; I tried pounding on his back; I tried full body massages and I swear he was going to die—he couldn't breathe; he was turning blue. I wanted to take him to the hospital but he was a strict macrobiotic and wouldn't set foot in a hospital. So as a last resort I gave him a blow job.

Obviously, neither of us were in the mood for sex whatsoever. But we weren't inhibited, so out of last-ditch desperation I thought, "Maybe this will work!" I started sucking on his cock and was really surprised when he got a hard-on. And what happened was: the surge of sexual energy relaxed him, it took his mind off his breathing and had this *healing effect*—within twenty minutes he was much better, and I knew he wasn't going to die.

When I had gum surgery, the transsexual Les Nichols spent a week in bed with me. I had been given these painkillers, but they really didn't work that well. I had this "tinfoil" on my teeth; I looked like shit; I wasn't in the mood for sex; I didn't feel romantic. So I simply used the sex as a painkiller, and it worked much better—it was a great gift!

We're a junk sex society, and just as sometimes we eat food that's not necessarily good for us, sometimes we have sex that's not necessarily "good" for us. A lot of men go to hookers and it's perhaps not that ideal Tantric loving spiritual situation, but at least it's *something*—not everyone has a partner they can have sex with. There are guys who *like* to pick up a streetwalker and get drugs put in their drinks—get their wallet stolen, or whatever. But perhaps that's exactly what they want! I think we all basically get what we want in terms of sex, and probably in terms of everything else as well!

♦ **AJ: Was there an "evolution" in the kinds of sex you wanted?**

♦ **AS:** I tried everything—well, there's still more to try, but . . . You can have sex for so many different reasons. And I think the problem in society is: everyone's trying to go for that "idealistic" kind of sex—you know: "If it's not love, if it's not marriage then—" They're not willing to perhaps have sex just because it feels good physically. They have to have the whole ideal shebang—everything besides the "ideal" is disappointing to them.

Whereas *I* think, "Today I can have *this* kind of sex; tomorrow, a different kind. Maybe next week I'll fall in love for awhile and have a big loving spiritual experience . . ." So I like to play with the different kinds—there's lots of different kinds, and I think many people who would like to have sex miss out on this variety, because they're always going for that "ideal" that's in their mind.

I was attracted to the sprinkles on ice cream cones and to the sound of *wetness*—I like waterfalls, piss, vaginal fluid, sweat, cum— anything wet. So the name "Annie Sprinkle" seemed perfect!

Some people: if they eat cookies, then they beat themselves up afterwards. Whereas I can eat cookies and then go, "Okay, I wanted to have some cookies and now I feel like shit, but what the heck—there was no stopping me; I had to have some cookies!" The same with junk sex: how much are you going to beat yourself up for it afterward? Because you *can* get in a sexual situation and lose energy or end up feeling not very good . . . but that's part of the learning process. It used to happen a lot, but now I'm really sensitive. When I'm with someone I think, "Am I going to *like* being with this person, or not?" and I get really *clear* so I don't end up in a "mistake"—although *there are no mistakes!* [laughs]

So there definitely has been an evolution. I started out on a very physical level and had a lot of hardcore physical stimulation. Now I've evolved to learning about much more subtle energy levels—more sensual, subtle, and much more cosmic. I hardly feel like I need to fuck anymore—although next month I might be into it, because things change all the time. I'm exploring a whole new avant-garde, experimental sex. It could be sex within ritual, or sex through breathing—learning about breath was a big key, because just by undulating the body (like a

Sex Heals. Photo: Eric Kroll

dolphin) you can go into total ecstasy! It's called "the wave" in Tantra. So now, sometimes I like sex just to please my body, but generally, sex has become more of a "spiritual" act.

There's so much pain and suffering in the world that my purpose in life is to have as much pleasure as possible—to be in perpetual pursuit of pleasure. And I take this very seriously—it's my job! We're a sex-negative society; we call people who suffer "martyrs," and we call people who have pleasure "hedonists." We *respect* suffering but we don't respect people who are always in perpetual pursuit of pleasure. Whereas I do. *Those* are the

Annie Sprinkle and Veronica Vera. "The School of High Heel Journalism."

"Anatomy of a Pinup Photo" by Annie Sprinkle 1991   Photo: Zorro

people I truly admire: the ones who are really having a good time—not the ones who are suffering.

◆ **AJ: You have a philosophy about pleasure—**

◆ AS: Me giving pleasure to others? A Buddhist monk once said, "Not a butterfly flaps its wings in Kyoto that the whole world doesn't feel it." In other words, we're all connected. When the war in the Gulf started, I felt I was really being spurred on to have more pleasure—*that's* how I could help the most. Not by going to Washington, because it was a very long drive and I really didn't know what to do once I got there. So I stayed home, had sex, and enjoyed myself as much as I could—that was my political statement!

◆ **AJ: If everyone did that, we wouldn't have been in that war—**

◆ AS: Yes! Although maybe what some people consider a good sexual experience is *war.*

◆ **AJ: That's the tragedy—they drop a bomb with some sexy woman's name written on the nose. They're taught not to value sex and pleasure *in themselves;* it has to be linked to some commodity or purchasable "experience." When Jesse Helms's censorship campaign began, someone suggested a law be passed that every Congressperson had to spend one day a month fondling and loving their genitals in public—then we** might have far fewer problems.

◆ AS: I think they all do masturbate; that everyone in Congress loves to masturbate.

◆ **AJ: But they don't love and respect their genitals.**

◆ AS: No, they feel guilty about them—well, some do, some don't. As a hooker I got pretty good at being able to judge what men were into, sexually. (I'm not that good at it with women, but I've got men down.) I made a little game out of looking at a person and "reading" them; now I can walk down the street and tell you exactly what a guy likes—I mean, *really close!* And it's so obvious: anyone can pick up on these things—I just do it more consciously.

You can sense someone's sexual energy—who's getting laid and who's not. You can tell who's really letting their sexual energy flow, and who's not. If somebody's very childlike, quite often they're very gentle or masochistic. Guys who are real macho are macho in bed—they want to fuck you in the ass, and they want it to *hurt.* Japanese are very sensual, very gentle, very sweet lovers. Men who live in their "head" a lot (who are in business, and who are very powerful) quite often really want to be dominated. But I hate to generalize too much. . .

We are animals, so we've been given a certain amount of instincts. And one thing: I think sex is repressed a lot, but if we weren't repressing our sexuality, people would think about sex even more!

◆ **AJ: I have the feeling it would be just the opposite. In the '50s, when people were really repressed, they thought about sex *constantly.* When sex is more "natural" and permitted, you don't always think about it. Whereas if you're always all bottled up and tense—**

◆ AS: Maybe that's true for some people, but that wasn't my experience—when I was a teenager my repression came from fear and ignorance. Now I think about sex all the time—it's like a state of being. Actually, it's not like I "think" about it; it's more like: *everything* has become much more sexual in a really nice way. People ask, "Do you mean you're horny all the time?" and I say, "No, I'm just circulating this energy, letting it out—it's not like, 'I've gotta have him!', it's like you're *constantly dancing.*"

◆ **AJ: Our language for sexuality and spirituality is so restricted. Tantric Buddhists who sit and meditate are raising their *kundalini* energy which is actually quite sexual—they talk about this continual orgasmic state. And to refer to this we're forced to use the word "sex," which ends up encompassing fifty million experiences—**

♦ AS: I consider that kind of meditation as having sex—*avant-garde sex*. Of course it's ancient, right? Actually, it would be better to call it New Ancient Sex. It's very ancient, yet there's this new type of sexuality happening where people are playing with energy more, and with breath—with the spiritual aspects of sex. I think that AIDS helped a lot in that sense—at least for me personally. When a dozen of my lovers got really sick and died, that made me a deeper person.

We're a sex-negative society; we call people who suffer "martyrs," and we call people who have pleasure "hedonists."

My lover Marco Vassi and I were living together when he was diagnosed HIV positive—we'd been lovers off-and-on for 10 years. I've tested negative 3 times and have had sex with many people who've died of AIDS—I don't know why I haven't gotten it, but I haven't. So at first we tried *not* having sex, because he had AIDS and I didn't. We couldn't fuck or suck, and using a condom isn't necessarily foolproof, anyway. I visited a condom factory once and found out how many condoms have holes in 'em: a *lot* of them!

So we started to explore sex on other levels; to expand our concept of sex. It became not so much about fucking and sucking, but about energy and intimacy. We started learning about Tantric and Taoist and Native American techniques. We'd do breathing and eye gazing; we'd set the timer for a half-hour and just sit and look into each other's eyes. And we were being *lovers*, we were turned on to each other, and it became so erotic that we didn't even have to fuck—when that timer went off we felt like we'd been fucking for half an hour. We were experimenting, and AIDS helped—because we couldn't always go back to *my clit* and *his cock*. So together we really expanded our concept of sex.

♦ AJ: This is so important: **expanding the concept of all that sex can encompass**—

♦ AS: Many people don't breathe during sex, yet if you get really energetic sex going, it's the breathing heavy that makes you feel good—*that* moves the energy. I've been practicing just breathing myself into orgasm—which I'm getting better at doing, and which performance really helps, because at the end of my performance, I use a vibrator and do a masturbation ritual. If there's 400 people in the audience sending me energy and I'm onstage with a vibrator—we're circulating energy. I have to (in 15 minutes) go into total ecstasy and (hopefully) orgasm. Doing performances put me in a situation where I had to learn fast, so I've gotten really good at "breathing sexual energy." Now I can go into full body orgasms

or breath orgasms onstage in a minute! I can do it walking down the street. Now I say that *ecstasy's just a breath away!*

♦ **AJ: Even without a vibrator?**

♦ AS: Yes, we can *all* do it. And it's not a clitoral orgasm. What happens is: you start breathing it up until you reach a certain point where *it's* breathing *you*—it's doing *you*. And it's similar to when you're having that clitoral orgasm: when you're no longer doing anything; *it's* doing *you*. *Women are capable of having 3-hour-long orgasms; men are capable of hour-long orgasms.* I think it's outrageous that 50% of women have never experienced even one orgasm. According to one study, 80% of the women in Europe between the ages of 14 and 20 have had an orgasm, whereas in the United States it's only 15%—some really low figure.

♦ **AJ: Can you talk about your "Post Porn Manifesto" and performance?**

♦ AS: Veronica Vera wrote the manifesto. I'd been doing performances for years—little ones, and that's what my new book is about. What made me start doing this? The desire *to heal and transform my life.* Before I got into "performance art" I would do fun little shows like the "Bosom Ballet" (in which my breasts literally dance a "ballet") at a birthday party or night club because that would get me excited—it would be fun.

Yin-Yang Breasts Photo: Mare Trunz

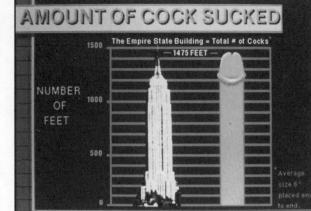

Annie Sprinkle's "Pornstistics."

Then I started working with Linda Montano—that's when I began learning how you can transform issues in your life through a performance. For example, Linda said, "I want you to do a performance about the worst thing that ever happened to you in your life." I'd always done performances about what *fun* life is, so I had to think—I had a week to prepare. Nothing horrible's ever happened to me! I had my tonsils out but I don't remember that; I've never had surgery; I've never been in an accident; I've never really experienced pain; I've never been raped—nothing horrible has ever happened to me. I've never been really scared; I've had this really lucky life.

So I thought, "What can I do this performance about?" Finally I realized, "Okay. I guess the worst thing that ever happened to me was when I was working as a hooker and guys were judgmental or abusive or angry or greedy . . . when I loved and trusted them, and they

---

My lover Marco Vassi and I were living together when he was diagnosed HIV positive. We started to explore sex on other levels. It became not so much about fucking and sucking, but about *energy* and *intimacy*.

---

fucked me over; they *hurt* me."

So I did a performance called "A Hundred Blow Jobs," because out of the two or three thousand blow jobs I'd given, a hundred had been really lousy—really horrible experiences where I'd cry afterwards. I made a tape of all these abusive remarks I'd heard, like, "Suck it, you bitch!" or "Yeah, I bought you dinner—you *should* suck my cock!" or "You're going to hell for this!" or a woman saying, "I hope she gets AIDS!" or "She's such a *slut!*" I filled a cassette with angry, judgmental, or ex-

ploitative remarks like, "Come on, Annie, we'll pay you an extra ten dollars if you do that anal sex scene!"

Then I did a performance where I played the tape, gagged on this huge dildo, and just got in touch with the *pain* of those hundred blow jobs. I really cried and it came from my gut; it was very visceral. All the sexual abuse I'd ever suffered came out of my throat; I gagged—really gagged. After I did that for awhile and the tape stopped, I did a healing ceremony for myself. I'd been having gum problems and my feeling was: it was from those lousy hundred blow jobs. So I put ground-up carrot on my gums and teeth, burned some herbs, and healed myself. And that was my performance—I felt really good afterwards.

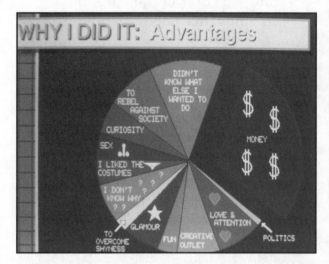

This got worked into more performances, and Emilio Cubeiro (who was my director) came up with a good idea: make a board with lots of dildoes attached, so that I suck all these different dildos of all sizes and colors. I did that; I'd cry and gag and really get in touch with the pain each time, and people in the audience would cry because they could relate to this—especially women; this was a scene primarily for women who'd been in the sex industry. And after a dozen times I would no longer cry or gag—because I'd transformed and exorcised that demon. Now I feel *free*—free from all that abuse I suffered . . .

◆ **AJ: This is good shamanistic therapy: you're exorcising the demons for other people as well as yourself—**

◆ AS: I learn things when I do this.

◆ **AJ: Where did you study with Linda Montano?**

◆ AS: Upstate New York—every summer she invites people up to her home. Each day you work on a different chakra, and each day you do a performance—or two or three or five! And for a week it's the best place to be in the world—anywhere Linda teaches I try to go, because a lot of the seeds of my performances come from association with her—she just totally inspires me to think of good ideas, and *do* them!

◆ **AJ: How did you begin collaborating with Emilio Cubeiro?**

◆ AS: A friend of mine who was a lap-dancer/stripper

saved all her dollar tips and bought a building for a million dollars! It's called the "Harmony Burlesque Theater," next to the Franklin Furnace. She'd seen some of my performances and offered me a show. I'd always wanted to put all my performances together and do a whole evening starring *me!* And I'd seen the piece Emilio had done with Lydia Lunch—it blew my mind, it was so good! I ran into Emilio and he said he'd direct my piece; we set a date, mailed out invitations, and rehearsed for about a month. He taught me a lot about theater. That was a year and a half ago; the piece has evolved a lot since then.

Basically, it's a story of my sexual evolution. It starts out with how Ellen Steinberg became Annie Sprinkle. I used slides, and wrote a little piece about it:

"I was born 'Ellen Steinberg' but I didn't like being Ellen very much so I invented 'Annie Sprinkle.' Ellen was excruciatingly shy; Annie was an exhibitionist. Ellen was fat and ugly and unattractive and no one seemed to want her, but Annie was voluptuous and sexy and everyone seemed to want her. Ellen desperately needed attention; Annie Sprinkle got it. Ellen had to wear ugly orthopedic shoes and flannel nightgowns, but Annie got to wear six-inch spiked high heels and fetish lingerie. Ellen was scared of boys and absolutely terrified of sex, but Annie was fearless. Ellen was dull; Annie was exciting. Ellen was a nobody from the suburbs of Los Angeles; Annie Sprinkle got a little bit famous and people even stopped her and asked her for autographs. Ellen Steinberg sometimes still wants to get married and have

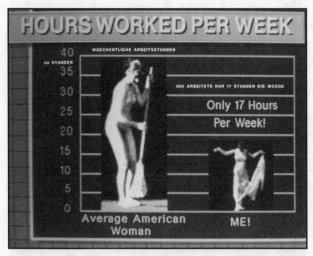

children, but Annie Sprinkle wants fame and fortune and a career. After all these years I've finally come to realize that Ellen Steinberg really must be Annie Sprinkle, and the truth is, Annie Sprinkle really is Ellen Steinberg."

Now, the show (and my life) has evolved to the point where I've invented a new personality. After 19 years of being "Annie Sprinkle," now there's "*Anya*":

"Annie Sprinkle loves everybody; Anya loves herself. Annie Sprinkle seeks attention; Anya seeks awareness. Annie Sprinkle is a feminist; Anya is a goddess. Annie Sprinkle wants a career, fame and fortune; Anya wants

peace, love and freedom. Annie Sprinkle likes an animal attraction; Anya likes a spiritual connection. Annie Sprinkle loves men; Anya loves men but absolutely adores women. Annie Sprinkle is a modern woman; Anya is ancient. Annie Sprinkle likes sex with transsexuals, midgets and amputees; Anya makes love to the sky, mud and trees. Annie Sprinkle masturbates; Anya meditates while she masturbates. Of course, Anya *is* today only because Annie Sprinkle *was* yesterday."

The reason I got out of porn and moved into art is because there's more room for experimentation in art—I can be *myself*.

So the show tells the story of my evolution through slides and performances. I've grown to know and love and accept Ellen Steinberg now. Because previously, I totally denied her and became everything that she wasn't—I became her total *opposite*.

◆ **AJ: And Anya is the integration of both?**

◆ AS: Anya is neither Ellen nor Annie Sprinkle; a whole new person evolved. But Annie still pops up every so often, and even Ellen Steinberg pops up—they're all still around, but Anya's more where I want to be. Anya's really exciting—a goddess . . . older and wiser, more intelligent.

◆ **AJ: This is a journey into the self—**

◆ AS: That's what the performances are about: my*self*. All I do is talk about myself. I'm political in that sex is political, but it's all about *my* sexuality.

◆ **AJ: "The personal is political": if your personal life isn't together, how can you change the world?**

◆ AS: I guess that's true . . . Maybe there's a little porn star in some of you (or maybe not), but there's a lot of "you" in every porn star. In other words, I found out that being in prostitution was nothing like it's portrayed in the movies—the reality was so different. I just loved

the women I met. As a result of that I did a "Sluts and Goddesses" workshop that's about exploring the different sexual personalities inside yourself, and accepting them.

♦ **AJ: What else is in your show?**

♦ **AS:** I also did a piece illustrated with statistical graphs called "Amount of Cock Sucked." I figured that all the cocks I'd sucked, if laid end to end, would equal the height of the Empire State Building! Plus, I show my cervix to the audience. And that's really a fun piece—it sounds sleazy and shocking, but it's very sweet and innocent. People are shocked that they aren't shocked! If you hear about it, you might go, "Oh—that's gross, that's disgusting; how can she do that?" I show a chart of the female reproductive system (now I can say "cervix" and "fallopian tube" in four languages) and I show what to look for: the cervix.

In a way I wanna say, *"Fuck you guys*—you wanna see pussy? *I'll* show you pussy! "

Why do I show my cervix? I tell the audience that the reason I show my cervix is: 1) because it's fun—and I think fun is really important, and 2) because the cervix is so beautiful that I really want to share that with people. There are other reasons: I think it's important to demystify women's bodies. It wasn't until recently that anyone was allowed to *look* at pussy—really get down and look at them. A lot of women have never even seen their own! And the other little thing is: in a way I wanna say, "Fuck you guys—you wanna see pussy, *I'll* show you pussy!"

So, I put a speculum in and have an usher help police the line, because usually about a third of the audience gets up and wants to take a look! Hundreds—they *all* want to see it! And I don't act embarrassed; I don't act like it's anything abnormal, shocking or strange—and suddenly, neither do they!

Usually a few people are shocked. But I think that if I took the time, *everyone* would get up and look. They look inside, and I have the microphone by their mouth, and they say, "Wow! That's beautiful! Thank you so much!" They speak their reactions into the microphone; it's like playing doctor—it's very playful and funny and fun. I like the fact that this creates a bizarre reality—like, "Isn't this a world?" Because here people are invited into *my* world where sex is okay, and the body's not dirty or shameful, and where you can play. A few people walk out—I guess they can't take it, it's not for everybody—but mostly they're sitting there laughing, surprised that they aren't shocked.

Then I do a masturbation ritual with the vibrator and the breathing and usually I have an orgasm. I'm just now getting to where I can have clitoral orgasms on top of the

other kinds: energy orgasms, breath orgasms, kundalini orgasms, heart orgasms, Third Eye orgasms . . . it's like: things really kick off! Plus, the energy of being onstage is so incredible; it's like my favorite sexual experience. To tell the truth, I do the whole show just so I can do the masturbation ritual at the end—that's like my payoff! That's what *I* get off on—it's such a turn-on. But also, I feel it's important that people *hear* the sound of an orgasm—it's like hearing a baby cry; it's a very pure, healing sound.

I think it's important that people see the power of a woman's sexuality. And I'm used to showing my sexuality openly, so I make a lot of noise, I do a lot of breathing, I become an animal, I become a goddess, I get pretty wild, and I think that a lot of people have never seen that. And I've had some of the best orgasms of my life at the end of the show, literally! I just totally go *out,* because of the energy of being onstage: everyone there is supporting me. Plus, whenever I enter a new theater I call upon tortured spirits and Taoist spirits and old sexy spirits for help . . .

It feels like ecstasy—it's not like doing a live sex show. It's not like being in a porno movie; to me it's a whole other reality: the sexuality of Anya, the sexuality of a more mature woman. I'm not being anyone else's fantasy; I'm being myself. I try to be totally honest in my expressions and my feelings . . .

♦ **AJ: How did that evolution come about—from being other people's fantasies to becoming Anya?**

♦ **AS:** I think I personally paid my debt; I can't be other people's fantasies anymore—well, occasionally I can! But certainly not that mainstream middle-class average American fantasy—I just can't do that anymore. Take go-go girls—they dance that way because they're being paid to do this—you can make good money being someone else's fantasy; that's what your job is. You can also learn for yourself along the way; you can get turned on gyrating your hips and use those feelings to nurture

"I tell the audience that the reason I show my cervix is: 1) because it's fun—and I think fun is really important, and 2) because the cervix is so *beautiful* that I really want to share that with people. There are other reasons: I think it's *important* to demystify women's bodies."

Photo: Leslie Barony

Photos: Leslie Barany

"I did a performance called 'A Hundred Blow Jobs' where I played a tape of all the abusive remarks I'd heard, like, 'Suck it, you bitch!' and I sucked on all these different dildoes. I'd cry and gag and really get in touch with the pain each time. After a dozen times I would no longer cry or gag—because I had *transformed* and *exorcised* that demon."

yourself, but mainly your job is: you're working for *them*. And the reason I got out of porn and moved into art is because in art there's more room for experimentation—in art I can be *myself*. I can be as weird as I want to be, and I don't have to please anybody but myself! [laughs] And that's really good.

> I know my show has inspired a lot of people. It's inspired *women* much more than men, and it's really nice to communicate *for* women or to work with women—not men.

Anyway, at the end I go into this totally other world—as far as I can go sexually (and it gets better and better—it's like forced learning—well, some days the energy's low). And I've learned not to have sex beforehand; I save up all my sexual feelings for that scene—otherwise I wouldn't have that same power. So when I'm traveling, all the sex I have is onstage. Of course I feel that just walking down the street or communing with a tree or being by a fountain (I really get turned on by fountains) is having sex. But "actual physical partner sex?"—never when I'm performing. Actually, I should *Never Say Never!*

♦ **AJ: Do you feel it was necessary to be all those male fantasies in order to finally become yourself?**

♦ AS: For me it was. Some people know what they want and who they are right away, but I didn't. I wanted to understand Sex and Society; I wanted to understand men's sexuality, because that's what I was most afraid of as a teenager. Once I learned about that, I felt safe that it was time to move on. Now, ironically, I'm much more

into women—I still like some men occasionally . . . but very few.

♦ **AJ: I think that as women get more in control of themselves and understand themselves better, they find it very difficult to get just basic human considerations from men—**

♦ AS: Well, I don't know if it's that! I just think that I've sort of fallen more in love with *myself*. And being with women is like loving yourself a little more . . . than being with men, which is like loving *differences* in the world. Lately, I really like women's bodies because they're a whole new challenge, a whole new area to learn about—unexplored territory! Even though I've had sex with a couple hundred women over the years, my heart wasn't into it—it was a physical kind of thing or it was in movies or I was being paid to do it. I experimented a little bit, but it never meant much. Now it's like I'm in love with women! And I probably have some emotional wounds from years of being with men—which I'm not ready to face.

But there's a few men I like! My last lover, Les Nichols, was a transsexual: a woman who became a man, and that was quite nice. He's wild—very wild. He looked like a man (on the street, you'd never know that he wasn't a man) but he had a cock and a pussy—*both*. He had a cock that was surgically constructed, but kept his female organs intact. And he was very into S&M . . . very sensual—he abused his hormones and took way too many, so he was always horny. And what a performance artist—this person was so off the wall!

We made a video in which he talked mainly about transsexualism (leaving out his more "outrageous" side), but he's the kinkiest person I've ever met—and also one of the sexiest. He's with another woman now; he's not in my life at the moment—I gave him to this other woman because I wasn't getting anything done. We were having too much sex all the time—I'm not kidding. He didn't work, he just hung out, and all he wanted to do was have sex, and I always agreed—

Anya, a Goddess. "After 19 years of being 'Annie Sprinkle', now there's 'Anya'. Anya is neither Ellen nor Annie; *a whole new person* evolved. Anya's really exciting—a goddess . . . older and wiser, more intelligent."

Photo: Rick Silvarnes

♦ **AJ: Did you know him before the operation?**

♦ AS: No, but after the surgery I was the first woman he tried his new penis out with. He's a total masochist, but with his own style and his own ideas—for example he likes to be "installed" in the furniture for days at a time. I've found it's unusual to find a woman that kinky or fetishistic. And he's a total foot fetishist. Sometimes I'd want him to sleep next to me and I'd command, "Come up here!" yet 5 minutes later he'd be back down by my feet—he slept at my feet or *under* the bed, kind of like a cat. Then he'd want to be shut up in the closet—I just had to give him a little water once in a while. He liked to be walked on, too. And here I was, a New Age girl (I thought I'd become more "spiritual," more "Tantric," more about the "heart" and "love")—and I end up falling in love with this kinky masochist! He didn't want to hear, "I love you!" he wanted me to say, "I hate you! Fuck you—you piece of shit!" That meant "I love you!" to him.

This was a whole *other* learning experience, because I wanted to please this person—he really turned me on. That's when I learned that the "Slut" or the "Whore" side is just as valid and wonderful and perfect as the "Goddess" or the "Spiritual" side . . . one is not better than the other, they're just different—it's your *intention* that matters. Because when I said, "Fuck you—I hate you!" he knew that meant, "I love you!" And having learned about "affirmation" and "positive thinking," this went totally against my grain. But here again I had to go with my muse, go with my feelings, and my feelings were saying, "Step on him! Kick him! Because that's what he likes!" And *I* liked it too when I did it!

I'd never want to hurt him *for real*, but we played with a lot of violent fantasies, and a lot of pain and piercing and every kinky thing you could think of—but I was getting this new awareness. Because in reality, putting him in the closet is no different from a Vision Quest out in the woods overnight! And walking on him in high heels isn't all that different from a shiatsu massage! So it's our judgments of these things that get in the way—the problem is not our "Slut" side but our *judgments* of our "Slut" side. Because we all have different sexual sides or personalities: sometimes we want to be real animalistic and down-and-dirty and raunchy, and other times we want a more "spiritual" experience. (Well, some people are happy with one thing all their lives—or two or three things . . . and there's others of us who change week-to-week or month-to-month or even several times in a night!)

So at last I learned how to really accept my extremes. I had already done a lot of kink; I'd worked as a dominatrix. And I was judgmental of that when I became a New Age girl. So it took Les Nichols to get me back into *not judging*—just going with the feeling . . . replacing judgments with acceptance and compassion.

I think that in terms of society in general, Jesse Helms wants everyone to be like *him*; and we want Jesse Helms to be like *us* . . . which is ridiculous because everyone's different. The Gays think that everyone's kind of Gay, you know (or that everyone has that side); the Bisexuals

Photo: Eric Kroll

think that everyone's really Bisexual; kinky people think that *they're* the liberated ones and that everybody else really wants to be kinky, and monogamous ones think, "People can't be happy if they're not monogamous—you *have* to have monogamy." So everyone's trying to make each other just like them. Whereas my feeling is, "It's much nicer just to accept our differences . . . to enjoy our differences." I *like* Jesse Helms.

♦ **AJ: Yes, but Jesse Helms would like to *shut you up*. He'd like you to stop what you're doing—**

♦ AS: Right, and I think that makes it more interesting. I taught a class recently on the history of "Sex and Performance Art," and no one was "against" it, there was no controversy—it was a boring class! Usually someone will ask, "Well, what about child pornography?" or "I don't like that garter belt you're wearing because it symbolizes the subjugation of women"—but not this time! I'm glad there are Jesse Helmses in the world, and I'm glad there's Women Against Pornography, and I'm glad there are people that aren't like me, otherwise I think it'd be pretty boring.

♦ **AJ: Yes, but nothing's happened to you: you're not in *jail*, you're not like Lenny Bruce who was fighting "obscenity" charges—**

♦ AS: Well, I don't *look* for that kind of thing; I stay out of trouble. I was arrested once—for sodomy, conspiracy to commit sodomy, and for amputee sex (for a magazine I was editing). But the charges were dropped. I've never been arrested for prostitution—I've been very lucky. But I kind of feel like the world is perfect, just the way it is . . . *in a way*. And I still do what I do.

Annie says of her last lover, Les Nichols, "He is a transsexual: a woman who became a man. He's wild—very wild. He has a cock and a pussy—*both*. He's the kinkiest lover I've ever met—and also one of the sexiest."

Photo: Vivien Maracevic

♦ **AJ: So far we've been "indulged"; we haven't gone through Fascism as in Nazi Germany; we haven't gone through McCarthyism at this point, and just because they've stopped a few NEA grants—well, nobody's gone to jail *yet*. But there is a momentum in this country pushing in that direction and it's getting scary.** *2 Live Crew* **were arrested—even though fortunately they were released. The photographer Jock Sturges could be going to jail—it's estimated that the FBI has spent over $2 million of taxpayers' money trying to "frame" him. If Helms had his druthers . . .**

♦ AS: Well, that's my way of coping with the problem: "Thanks for the publicity, Jesse!" And another side of me is thinking, "Jesus—I know they're going to burn me at the stake!" But my way of coping is to say that it's *really fun!* Even though I do get scared at times, I try not to. It is scary. I did have my freedom taken away once for a couple days in jail, and I was quite blown away. But I don't want to put energy into the idea that this might happen to me—I'll move to another freakin' country; I'll just *move*. I'm going to continue having a good time.

♦ **AJ: It is crazy to live in fear of something that hasn't happened yet—**

♦ AS: Nothing's happened, but I think that's partly because I was never afraid. I know women working in the same places I did who have been arrested 5 or 6 times—they were so afraid of being arrested, that they *were* arrested!

♦ **AJ: There's something about "positive energy" that definitely helps grease you through life!**

♦ AS: I've been very lucky. Look at Larry Flynt—you can get shot and even killed! There are people out there who don't want women masturbating on stage and calling on spirits and going out of their bodies and having orgasms that last longer than theirs do! And I enjoy the controversy and excitement—at least I want to, otherwise I can't do it. I can't get up there on stage if I'm really scared of that repression. And if it gets too hot in the kitchen I'm going to get out! I'm not into being a martyr, or being arrested—I'll change what I do. If I go too far

Les Nichols has a surgically constructed penis as well as his original female organs.

I'll drop back a little bit—for a *while*.

♦ **AJ: But what you're doing is so healing for others. People all over the United States need to see your show. And you have a big heart, too; you enjoy giving sex to—**

♦ **AS:** The needy—a lot of mercy fucks! I've gotten a lot of positive response; I know my show has inspired a lot of people. It's inspired women much more than men, and it's really nice to communicate *for* women or to work *with* women—not men, for a while. And my show has especially helped women who've been in the sex industry.

♦ **AJ: How many performance artists have been in the sex industry?**

♦ **AS:** Almost all the top women performance artists have told me (because I've met all my favorites) that they were in the sex industry as streetwalkers, go-go dancers, etc. I think that the sex industry is a much bigger funder of the arts than the NEA—I'm sure of it!

♦ **AJ: If you're a creative and independent woman— well, in the "olden days" you really had only two choices: to be a wife/mother or a whore—there wasn't really much of a middle ground . . .**

♦ **AS:** The book *Sex Work* cites this statistic: globally, one out of ten women has been in the sex industry. And that's a lot! I'm so open about this that people come out of the woodwork all the time and confess what they did 10 years ago—people you wouldn't expect: your sisters, your brothers, your mothers, your fathers—people all over.

Photo: Dona Ann McAdams

I like to go where I'm *wanted*; I don't like to rub things in people's faces—*if they don't want me to put my tits on people's heads, I won't!*

♦ **AJ: Didn't you do a show in Cleveland?**

♦ **AS:** Yes, there were police in the audience and I would have been arrested if I had showed my cervix, or posed for polaroids with my tits on people's heads at intermission. I didn't want to be arrested so I decided not to do it, because I was on my way to Europe. I like to go where I'm *wanted*; I don't like to rub things in people's faces—*if they don't want me to put my tits on people's heads, I won't!* [laughs] But the show became about censorship: I talked about how I couldn't do my full, planned performance. Everyone in the audience *wanted* to see my cervix—too bad. Now a lot of places are afraid to book me; I don't have any shows scheduled right now in the U.S., just in Europe—it's really easy in Europe!

I think people hear about what I do and are horrified and shocked: "Oh, she masturbates on stage; she sucks on dildoes; she shows her cervix—it sounds disgusting; it sounds really sleazy!" Yet those descriptions take everything out of context. For example, before I show my cervix I take a douche—a very nice little douche—be-

cause people are going to be looking inside me. *I* like all the flavors and smells and tastes inside my pussy, but not everyone likes them, so I take a little douche.

If I have to pee I just say, "Oh excuse me; I have to take a little pee," and it's like being in my home: if you have to pee at my house, you don't have to close the door. And nobody in the audience is shocked—they might be kind of amazed that I'm peeing—they're trying to remember, "Aren't you not supposed to do that?" but I do it very innocently, it's not like [bellows], "I'M GOING TO PEE ONSTAGE!" It's meant to be a natural part of life—we have the toilet on stage, and I use toilet paper; I wipe—it's all very nice! I do it to defuse the issue; to show that it's not shocking—we've all seen people pee. But then of course, if you *hear* about it, you're either going to be horrified . . . or run out and buy a ticket! [laughs]

♦ **AJ: You were talking about pursuing more sex research—**

♦ **AS:** If you asked me, "What do you do?" I'd say that I'm a sex researcher. That's what I've devoted my life to, and it looks like that's what I'm going to continue doing: researching sex . . . my own sexuality, other people's, sex in ancient society, sex all over the world. People I meet just tend to tell me everything about themselves sexually, because—that's all I talk about, so they talk about it too! I'm still learning, exploring, thinking about, talking about, and researching through video and photography . . . *all about sex!* ♦ ♦ ♦

Films

Deep Inside Annie Sprinkle. Full length 35mm film, written, directed by & starring Annie Sprinkle.

Consenting Adults. Full length 35mm docudrama conceived, casted by & co-directed by Annie Sprinkle. Producer: Gerard Damiano.

Annie. Ten minute 16mm film by Monika Treut, about how Ellen Steinberg becomes Annie Sprinkle.

Success. 16mm feature film by Monika Treut; Annie has a leading role.

Videos

Rites of Passion. Written, directed & edited by Annie, produced by Candida Royalle.

Linda/Les & Annie—the First Female to Male Transsexual Love Story. Docudrama written, co-directed & co-edited by Annie, featuring Les Nichols & Annie.

The Sprinkle Salon. NY Cable TV show, aired weekly for 6 months, w/Annie, Veronica Vera & Willem de Ridder.

Portrait of a Porno Star, Inmost, Inside, Annie Sprinkle. 68 minutes, directed by Michelle Auder.

Deep Deconstruction. One hour documentary by Steven Kolpan.

Current Flow. Safe lesbian sex demonstration.

Magazines & Booklets

Sprinkle Report. Newsletter devoted to Piss Art, w/Willem de Ridder.

Annie Sprinkle Hot Shit Book. 80 page magazine, published by LOVE magazine.

Annie Sprinkle's ABC Study of Sexual Lust & Deviations, published by R. Mutt Press.

Annie Sprinkle's Bazoombas. 48 page magazine from Red Lion.

The Kinky World of Annie Sprinkle. 48 page magazine from Hudson Communications.

Love 83; Post Art Art in America. 86 page magazine about Annie & Veronica Vera, designed by Willem de Ridder, published by LOVE magazine.

Some Live Performances

"Strip Speak," burlesque performances at various theaters across the USA.

"The Prometheus Project." Directed by Richard Schechner, at Performing Garage in NYC.

"Deep Inside Porn Stars." With 6 other women at Franklin Furnace, NYC.

"Sex Three." By Linda Montano, performed in Cleveland, Ohio.

"Annie Sprinkle—Post Porn Modernist." One woman play/performance written and performed by Annie, first directed by Emilio Cubeiro, later by Willem De Ridder. Performed at the Kitchen, LaMaMa, Joseph Papp Theater (NYC); LeKliene Comedie Theater (Amsterdam); Schmidt Theater (Hamburg); COCA (Seattle).

Other

Has written over 300 articles on sex for *Penthouse, Hustler, Cheri, Adam, Stag, Velvet,* etc. Has produced 11 audiotapes for the Radio Art Foundation, Amsterdam. Has lectured at Tyler University, Museum of Modern Art (NYC), Columbia University, etc. B.F.A., School of Visual Arts, NY. Attended 3 sessions at Linda Montano's Summer Saint Camp, Kingston, NY. Chairperson of P.O.N.Y. (Prostitutes of New York).

Has appeared in *Cheri, High Society, Club, Playboy, Penthouse Forum, National Lampoon,* and posed for painter Alice Neel and photographer Joel-Peter Witkin.

---

101 Uses For Sex or Why Sex is so Important by Annie Sprinkle

1. Sex as a sedative. It helps you go to sleep.
2. Sex to fight addictions. It helped me quit smoking.
3. Sex as a laxative. Regular sex helps have regular shits.
4. Sex to get to know somebody. You can tell a lot about a person by fucking them.
5. Sex as a meditation.
6. Sex to relieve boredom.
7. Sex to improve concentration.
8. Sex to make money.
9. Sex to create magic. Some witches believe that the most powerful time to cast a spell is during orgasm.
10. Sex for manipulation. It can get you what you want.
11. Sex as a reward. Either to yourself or to someone else.
12. Sex for relaxation.
13. Sex for rejuvenation. It keeps you looking and feeling younger.
14. Sex to increase energy. A great pick-me-up.
15. Sex to cure an asthma attack. I saved a man's life once.
16. Sex to make you laugh. It can be hilarious.
17. Sex as a gift. A present for birthdays, anniversaries, Bar Mitzvas...
18. Sex to get high.
19. Sex to achieve an altered state.
20. Sex to create life.
21. Sex for waking up. Helps get rid of that groggy feeling.
22. Sex to cure back pain.
23. Sex to keep warm in the winter.
24. Sex as a pain killer. It's far more potent that aspirin, and most prescription pain killers.
25. Sex as an anti-depressant. It will cheer you up.
26. Sex for stress reduction.
27. Sex as a spiritual experience.
28. Sex for exercise. It's aerobic and burns calories.
29. Sex for thrills and adventure.
30. Sex to relieve headaches. Even migraines.
31. Sex as a cure for writer's block.
32. Sex as a good deed. Give the needy an occasional mercy fuck.
33. Sex as an art form. It can be very creative and a great way to express oneself.
34. Sex to control appetite. It can be so filling.
35. Sex for cardiovascular health.
36. Sex to create intimacy.
37. Sex as an expression of love.
38. Sex for itching mosquito bites. Apply sperm to afflicted areas.
39. Sex for barter. Trade it for all kinds of things.
40. Sex to get in touch with emotions, like sadness.
41. Sex to avoid working. I can always finish this some other time.

Karen Finley

When the National Endowment for the Arts (NEA) censored performance artist Karen Finley, she became a cause célèbre. Attacked by Jesse Helms for her live performances which involve partial nudity, political satire, social criticism and the exploration of sexual taboos, she replied, "I use certain language that is a symptom of the violence of the culture. If I talk about a woman being raped, I have to use the language of the perpetrators." The content of her performances (dealing with child abuse, wife-beating, sexism, suicide, abortion, homophobia, racism, dysfunctional families and addiction in general) was generally overlooked, as was the seriousness of her commitment to exposing moral, cultural and social decay—always, however, with irony and black humor.

Karen's performances are moving and powerful. With passion and anger she gives voice to the alienated and dispossessed: "A lot of people feel the same way I do, but they *keep it in* because it's socially unacceptable to mourn in public or to show feelings. If you did, you'd be vulnerable or abandoned— maybe no one would love you. But I have the ability to reveal my feelings— so in a sense, I'm getting even. Revenge can be art."

In addition to hundreds of performances over the past decade, Karen has released videos, disco/spoken word albums, and created paintings, drawings, sculptures and installations. Her book of monologues and short stories, *Shock Treatment,* was recently published by City Lights Books. Currently she lives in upstate New York.

♦ ANDREA JUNO: How did your childhood shape you?

♦ KAREN FINLEY: Fortunately, I grew up in a university town where education was the Number One priority. Like many children, I remember always feeling "different"—like a loner. As soon as I started school I began "taking a stance"—perhaps because my parents were so outspoken in their social convictions. In my family, if you saw someone hurting, you would go help that person—you would put yourself *out.*

At home, if there was a racist comment, that person was thrown out of the house—physically. That's just how it was: *you would put yourself on the line.* My mother was very involved in environmental issues like banning DDT;

I grew up hearing Martin Luther King and Jesse Jackson. I started working for Operation PUSH on the weekends—we'd do neighborhood breakfast programs and collect food for them. Later on I was in "Punks for Peace" and other groups . . .

Now I'm creating work that has "social consciousness"—that deals with the *true history of aesthetics.* Because these are not *my* aesthetics—they have been given to us by men for thousands of years. You go into museums or read "histories of art" and women just aren't included—you only see women as the "Nude" or as the Object of Desire, really. And I can't create work that would contribute to or encourage that "aesthetic"—with all its underlying hatred and misogyny.

Photo: Dona Ann McAdams

When I was growing up, I thought that a lot of artists were women—for example, I thought *Jean Dubuffet* was a woman! I remember doing drawings in the first grade and because I "showed promise," the nuns encouraged me in the arts. I think they were struggling with "liberation" themselves; they told me, "This is the first time in history that women have had so many opportunities . . . however, you really are going to have to *work.*" I was only 7 years old, but this had quite an impact on me.

Something else that really had a big impact on me was seeing the Chicago 1968 Democratic Convention riots and demonstrations on TV while I was having a slumber party—immediately everything changed for me. I remember seeing the "Chicago Seven" talk at town meetings, and they became my heroes. For the first time I felt the excitement of the possibility for *political change.*

When I started attending art school, I didn't have the money to fully work on my craft the way other people did. And I thought this was wrong: just because I came from a working class background, I couldn't afford to be an artist?!

♦ **AJ: You have a sensitivity toward "lower-class" women that's very powerful in your work. In America the class system is never spoken about, yet it blatantly exists. In a lot of feminist discussions this is neglected—**

♦ KF: I think so. And I was determined to make a mark for my gender—to have someone listen. I didn't want to channel my "art" into a painting that some rich person would buy and hang in his study and then close the door.

So I made a conscious decision to do something that couldn't be bought or sold that easily.

The trouble with museums and the history of "aesthetics" (in terms of writing, music, dance, theater, film, television, and popular culture) is: women really are restricted to certain identities. For example Madonna, as much as she is her own woman in certain situations, has basically just exploited what was expected of her as a female. And in some ways that's sad. I feel she's very talented and a good businesswoman and has style and is very generous, but she still exploits "what's expected of a woman." And that's something I'm out to *destroy*: looking at the woman as an object first—which encourages that whole sexual violence that women live with.

I was really upset when the NEA tried to censure my work as "obscene," because I think my work is extremely moral. I'm trying to speak out about sexual violence and how hateful that is, and make it *understandable.* Yet many times I'm just viewed as "hysterical"—as a sexual deviant who's "out of her mind." But people still use stereotypes of women—if a woman doesn't fit one pattern, they'll fit her into another. And in the process they'll use some really ugly names . . .

♦ **AJ: That's how women are marginalized. There are very few places for women—unless you're a "quiet good girl" you're going to fall off into the periphery. When you are onstage, you almost *become* the abuse so that we're able to critically examine it. How do your performances evolve?**

♦ KF: I do a lot of psychic work. Many times when people just walk by I can pick up energies or see or feel other things, like a *medium*. I like to look at my work as a ritual or ceremony that's more pagan—before the idea of the "One Male God" emerged. In Brazil there's an African/Indian religion where women dress in white, take on "evil spirits" and "shake it out." I feel *I* sort of do that. In my performance I wish I could relieve the audience of its suffering, but for women, that's really what relationships are about: somehow *feeling* the suffering and being the nurturer; somehow letting those feelings come through so they can be dealt with. I want to expose that private, secret process *in public*.

In theater, I could never have anyone see me being raped. That would be degrading, futile, and would only contribute to a perpetuation of oppression—it would be more like co-opting someone else's pain. There's no reason to see the act; it's more important to deal with what you're left with *after* the act. So I want to show what that is: a day-to-day feeling of *despair* which I think many oppressed people live with in this culture . . . the reality that: women (or gays or people of color) don't have the same freedom as men to just walk down a dark street—because that fear is such a daily part of life.

Fear has really repressed us; for thousands of years we've just been trying to "maintain"—keep plodding along. But we've got to get rid of this—we must have that equality and acknowledgment. So I'm trying to *break through*, and I hope the next generation can contribute even more.

Photo: Dona Ann McAdams

That's the "male" way of dealing with suffering: "thinking" about it instead of *feeling* it. And my way is to *feel* it, *acknowledge* it. As a culture we kind of have the thinking part down pat, but not the feeling—

Real art is supposed to embrace current political and social issues, but capitalism wants to prevent that process from happening in the culture, because if society embraced it, that might bring about the possibility of getting *rid* of capitalism! And that's just too threatening. Since art is based on a capitalist commodity structure, I try to think of ways to use that for my ends—that's why I'm trying to do more public sculpture and installations.

♦ AJ: Describe your public sculpture—

♦ KF: I took my poem, "The Black Sheep," had it cast in bronze and now it's set in a concrete monolith near a place where a lot of homeless people live. In a way this was a memorial for the homeless, the outcasts and the

artists living on the Lower East Side. I think the only reason I got to do it is because no one wanted to do a public sculpture there—they want to do things in Central Park or some place that's "cool and hip." I wasn't sure what the response would be, but it's been really positive. The people who live there put flowers on it; when Nelson Mandela visited, people added ribbons in African colors—people leave things there. Also, a cottage industry started where people do rubbings and then sell them for a buck—I love that, too.

I want to do public sculpture that really acknowledges social conditions rather than just presents "form." A huge red cube or big blue circle in some public square—I can't relate to something like that; it doesn't make me feel good. I'm never going to get $500,000 for work like that, anyway. I mean—just a few years ago I was working 3 jobs and getting free food from a food pantry for the poor.

I was getting thrown out of apartments and living in places that didn't have a bathroom—I had to pee in jars. So when I see a huge red cube or some abstract-shaped public sculpture—well, that just doesn't give me anything. Maybe for a man who's gotten everything he wants, and now has an opportunity to "experiment with shapes," this represents his big sense of freedom. But for me, something like that is as *least* threatening as it can possibly be.

I want to *give* something—do work which helps people connect emotionally in a sense of *sharing and*

clarifying emotional pain. Because that's more important to our culture.

◆ **AJ: Well, your "Black Sheep" poem is so powerful in that it binds all people who are displaced and marginalized. You're a voice for a lot of the Black Sheep in this dysfunctional society—**

◆ KF: I don't like art that covers up; I like to do work that deals with *hurt*—where there's pain I want to point a finger. I'm not a fatalist or an existentialist—I really do believe in the human spirit. I don't by any means believe suicide is the answer, and I don't believe in giving up. I think people feel a lot better when they examine pain, and know that they don't necessarily have to forgive.

A lot of Judeo-Christian ethics are about "forgiving and forgetting." But I don't necessarily believe in forgiving at all! I feel that forgiving is: *never letting go.* I think that forgiving is a *myth* by which you in actuality think you can still maintain control over someone—and that's a falsehood.

I think this is why sometimes people feel better after seeing my work: because a lot of people are spending their adult lives trying to "forgive and forget" things that happened to them in their childhood. Whereas in my work, it's more like: "These people are bad, they're assholes. They had a fucked-up life, and it's fucked up!" Then you go on, having *accepted* it being fucked up, rather than giving excuses for people.

◆ **AJ: Only total *acceptance* of what happened—no matter how horrible it was—can sever the emotional enslavement to the past. You have a great line about "people who intellectually 'rationalize' suffering"—**

Photo: Dona Ann McAdams

◆ KF: That's the "male" way of dealing with suffering: "thinking" about it instead of *feeling* it. And my way is to feel it, acknowledge it. As a culture we kind of have the thinking part down pat, but not the feeling—

◆ **AJ: —because it's so scary to acknowledge that there are things you can't *think* your way out of, like death and suffering. This is a whole "society of denial"—denial of even the suicidal path it's going on. Society doesn't want to acknowledge there are things in human life like death and sex that you can't just "rationalize" away—**

◆ KF: I think everyone's confused about these topics . . . but I feel that death—well, *killing*—is wrong. I feel we are *more* than our physical bodies . . . and that everything's related—all people's "bad" actions affect other people, and jail isn't necessarily the "cure."

◆ **AJ: We don't even have a "community" anymore; society's so fractured. People are so alienated that they don't feel any connection with others, so it's getting easier and easier to fuck other people over—**

◆ KF: I think we don't feel. To me, what's important is a connection and a centering: really listening to our selves, because we're always listening to things *outside* of ourselves. Of the male and female, the female is more apt to *listen*, be instinctual, use the "sixth sense," nurture and heal—and I want to show that. Many times when a woman is trying to express what she truly feels, a man will say, "That's hysterical, perverted, domineering"—all these words that reveal the existence of a double standard. For example, it's interesting that there's no male word for "nymphomaniac." If a man has sex with a lot of different women, that's looked upon as *good*, but if a woman does—! There's a lot of negativity and jealousy toward women's sexual abilities: they don't have to refuel!

All this relates to the War in the Gulf, which typified very negative masculine behavior without negotiation—almost fearful of the "feminine." And this behavior is grounded in philosophies and religious systems that rule the world. Our religious principles are anti-women; our philosophy even toward "saving the planet" is anti-women; America's whole social structure is anti-women and anti-family—there are no childcare programs. Yet what are our taxes going for?

In terms of the family, the responsibility is put on the woman: most mothers still have to work, because the father can't earn enough to support the kids, or has left home. Society makes it as hard as possible for a woman, who should have the *right* to pursue and develop her talents and her job. It's almost as if society *wants* to destroy the family structure, as it disregards the health and welfare (never mind the "happiness") of an entire generation of people who are growing up. American society sticks the whole burden of raising kids on the woman.

We're the only industrialized country outside of South Africa that doesn't consciously do more for children. Anywhere else, you can look at children and see that they're happy. Here, when a woman takes pregnancy

Photo: Dona Ann McAdams

leave, it's as if she were getting away with something. Other employees whisper, "She's being given more than we are." What no one ever remembers is: everyone had a mother, and what did she do for you?

♦ **AJ: There's no support for a single woman—**

♦ KF: —or even a woman with a man. There's *nothing*. And besides the absence of health care, one thing I feel strongly about is RU-486. It's not just a "morning after abortion pill"—it's considered a "miracle drug" because it can do a lot more. For example, a study done in France

Photo: Dona Ann McAdams

showed that 9 out of 12 women with breast cancer went into remission after taking it. Also, it seems to diminish certain brain cancers, treat hormonal diseases that affect mostly women, and it could be very important in AIDS prevention and cure. Yet this drug is prohibited—probably because it mostly deals with women's diseases. If it concerned prostate cancer, you bet it would be available *now!* And it wouldn't be illegal.

There is so much hatred of the woman's body. If you watch Sunday morning TV which has a lot of religious programs or political shows, when the topic is "women's problems," it's mostly older white men talking (with a token woman). And very curiously, you'll see a lot of commercials for mammography dealing with breast cancer, and that's very strange and sick. In fact, this truly shows the sickness of our culture—which intersperses commercials of diseased women between David Brinkley's political comments. Is this the only voice a woman has in the political arena? And in these breast cancer commercials, the woman is portrayed as dirty and diseased—more diseased than a man . . . Yet you don't see prostate cancer commercials—can you imagine a rubber-gloved hand with fingers pointed, ready to give a rectal exam? I've been studying this for a couple of years—someday I'd like to do a video installation.

♦ **AJ: And those breasts are the property of men—**

♦ KF: Right: if they can cure it, they can control it. Also, having too many mammographies (X-rays) can *cause* cancer! And these commercials present and display women in all kinds of ways that upset me. Also implied is the idea that the woman's body isn't the woman's—particularly in the anti-abortion groups.

♦ **AJ: The taking away of the right to abortion is the biggest travesty. On Earth Day 1970, Abortion Rights and Zero Population Growth were the biggest issues, but on Earth Day 1990 there was no mention of these— yet overpopulation is *still* one of the heaviest issues we face. We can't even *have* an effective ecological movement with this many people on the planet! And it all comes back to the issue of the "Woman's Body": who owns that body, and who owns the body of the earth?**

♦ KF: In the same way that we bomb the earth, we rape women. Mother Earth is universally regarded as "feminine," and the way we treat it is very similar to the way we treat women. I think it's no coincidence that the day Bush started the War (January 15) is the same day he declared "Pro-Life Day."

♦ **AJ: And now there are 300,000 Iraqis dead—"collateral damage," right?**

♦ KF: We slaughtered this long caravan of people for no justifiable reason—they weren't attacking, they were *fleeing*. We bombed them and melted them into their machines—there was no reason to do that, it was highway massacre. I look at all the men behind this as *murderers*. Because these same men, with their corresponding "politics," will stop a pregnant woman from getting healthcare at a Woman's Clinic.

I've been talking with WHAM, which is sort of an ACT

U.P. version of women's healthcare, and they've inspired me to think about doing a new study on women's healthcare—an updated *Our Bodies, Our Selves.* Something that tells what's really going on. Because a lot of people don't know that in certain parts of America you can't *get* an abortion even if you want to—that's how bad it is! In many places, even if you're not going for an abortion, you'll be denied entrance to a clinic, or be subject to extreme harassment. Planned Parenthood is really suffering—

We treat Mother Earth in much the same way we treat women. I think it's no coincidence that the day Bush started the War (January 15) is the same day he declared "Pro-Life Day."

♦ **AJ:** *Planned Parenthood* often provides the only healthcare in general for poorer women. And these Fundamentalist blockades prevent low-income women from getting something as basic as a pap smear. I think the next generation will view the Pro-Life people of today as *murderers,* because so many adults are going to die from the consequences of overpopulation. For Pro-Lifers, life ends *after* birth—they're only concerned with that little fetus (which is really just a metaphor for the possession/control of Woman's body and sexuality). There are almost no resources directed toward life after birth—

♦ **KF:** Or even before birth—there are no resources anywhere. Society basically wants to tell a woman what to do—to prevent her from making decisions. As a woman, I do not have the same prospects as a male. When I grew up, I didn't have the *capability* to dream about becoming President. I couldn't dream about being an astronaut, a baseball player, or even an artist—just a *mother;* a woman in this society is only valued if she's a mother. And after you've reached a certain age, society's view is: "If you're not a mother by now, something's *wrong* with you."

And when a woman is over childbearing age, she's basically considered useless—she's just waiting her time out. That's the reason all these women (from Cher to Raquel Welch to whoever) are desperately trying to maintain the look of a woman of child-bearing age. Many women over 50 are still very sexual and appealing. It's pathetic that to most of society, they've lost their worth.

If you examine TV newscasters, none of the women are as old as the men—they don't even have a chance past a certain age. Of course, in all highly visible professions there's the Token Exception syndrome they give to shut us up: Barbara Walters, Sandra Day O'Connor, Margaret

Thatcher. They like to give us these little exceptions—

I have a problem, too, with monarchy (besides the fact that it even exists). In Britain, the only way you can become Queen of the country is if all the men die . . . only as a last resort! And I look at all the media professions: why are there no female game show hosts and no male assistants? Because they could never allow a *man* to turn the letters on "Wheel of Fortune"! Can you imagine a man dressed like Vanna White in a skimpy little outfit doing that every day? That would be considered *degrading.*

♦ **AJ: One topic I wanted to talk about is this need to marginalize artists in society. There's the myth that artists are unstable, unhealthy, and hysterical—therefore they can be dismissed. Yet *you* have one of the most healthy, stable, holistic lives I've ever seen. That in itself is a powerful, radical statement helping to keep you from being trivialized, even though you're very much disturbing the status quo—**

♦ **KF:** A lot of male artists "bought into" the myth that "Men are more unstable; they don't take responsibility as much as a woman does." Meaning that: women don't *kill* as much as men; women don't abandon their children and then not support them, like men do. For generations, women have learned many skills: how to live with less . . . how to take on different challenges and manage. So there really isn't anything so exceptional in how I live. I look at my mother and what she did in terms of handling her life, and *her* mother, as well as other women around me—they had to do a *lot* . . .

In terms of the "artistic personality," the male artist seemed to always be on the verge of going out of control—even though men are always putting down women for the same thing! And women trying to be artists had to become more like men in order to be accepted—Janis Joplin is a good example: she tried to be just as irresponsible as men, and live "on the edge." But I don't buy this idea that for thousands of years, women couldn't (by their nature and biology) possibly be artists, because to be an artist you had to have a certain misfit, irresponsible, drunken, lifestyle. Really, that was all created to keep women *out!*

Installation at The Franklin Furnace: "A Woman's Life Isn't Worth Much." Granite sculpture.

Photo: Dona Ann McAdams

After a funeral someone said to me
you know I only see you at funerals
it's been three since June —
been five since June for me.
He said I've made a vow —
I only go to death parties if I know
    someone before they were sick.
Why?
'cause — 'cause — 'cause I feel I feel so
sad 'cause I never knew their lives
and now I only know their deaths
And because we are members of the
Black Sheep family.

We are sheep with no shepherd
We are sheep with no straight and narrow
We are sheep with no meadow
We are sheep who take the dangerous
    pathway through the mountain range
    to get to the other side of our soul.
We are the black sheep of the family
called Black Sheep folk.
We always speak our mind
        appreciate differences in culture
        believe in sexual preferences
        believe in no racism
        no sexism
        no religionism
and we'll fight for what we believe
but usually we're pagans.
There's always one in every family.
Even when we're surrounded by bodies
we're always alone
and you die alone.
You were born alone
and you die alone —
written by a black sheep.
You can't take it with you —
written by a former black sheep.

Black Sheep folk look different
        from their families —
It's the way we look at the world.
We're a quirk of nature —
We're a quirk of fate.
Usually our family, our city,
our country never understands us —
We knew this from when we were
        very young
that we weren't meant to be understood.
That's right, that's our job.
Usually we're not appreciated until
        the next generation.
that's our life, that's our story.
Usually we're outcasts, outsiders
        in our own family.
Don't worry — get used to it.
My sister says — I don't understand you!
But I have many sisters with me tonight.

My brother says — I don't want you!
But I have many brothers with me
        here tonight!
My mother says — I don't know how
        to love someone like you!
You're so different from the rest!
But I have many mamas with me here tonight!
My father says — I don't know how to hold you!
But I have many many daddies with me
        here tonight!

We're related to people we love who can't say
        I love you Black Sheep daughter
        I love you Black Sheep son
        I love you outcast, I love you outsider.
But tonight we love each other
That's why we're here —
to be around others like ourselves —
So it doesn't hurt quite so much.
In our world, our temple of difference
I am at my loneliest when I have something
        to celebrate and try to share it with those
        I love but who don't love me back.

Photo: Dona Ann McAdams

There's always silence at the end of the
    phone.
There's always silence at the end of the
    phone.

Sister — congratulate me!
NO I CAN'T YOU'RE TOO LOUD.
Grandma — love me!
I DON'T KNOW HOW TO LOVE
SOMEONE LIKE YOU.
Sometimes the Black Sheep is a
    soothsayer, a psychic, a magician of
    sorts.

"The Black Sheep" was taken from
Karen Finley's book, *Shock Treatment*,
published by City Lights Books, 1990.

Black Sheep see the invisible —
We know each others thoughts —
We feel fear and hatred.

Sometimes some sheep are chosen to be
    sick to finally have average, flat
    boring people say I love you.
Sometimes Black Sheep are chosen to be
    sick so families can finally come
    together and say I love you.
Sometimes some Black Sheep are
    chosen to die so loved ones and family
    can finally say —
        your life was worth living
        your life meant something to me!
Black Sheeps' destinies are not
    necessarily in having families, having
    prescribed existences —
        like the American Dream.
Black Sheeps' destinies are to give
    meaning in life
        to be angels
        to be conscience
        to be nightmares
        to be actors in dreams.

Black Sheep can be family to strangers
We can love each other like MOTHER
FATHER SISTER BROTHER
    CHILD
We understand universal love
We understand unconditional love
We feel a unique responsibility, a human
    responsibility for feeling for others.
We can be all things to all people
We are there at 3:30 AM when you call
We are here tonight 'cause I just can't go
    to sleep.
I have nowhere to go.
I'm a creature of the night —
I travel in your dreams —
I feel your nightmares —

We are holding your hand
We are your pillow, your receiver
your cuddly toy.
I feel your pain.
I wish I could relieve you of your
    suffering.
I wish I could relieve you of your pain.
I wish I could relieve you of your
    destiny.
I wish I could relieve you of your fate.
I wish I could relieve you of your illness.
I wish I could relieve you of your life.
I wish I could relieve you of your death.
But it's always
Silence at the end of the phone.
Silence at the end of the phone.
Silence at the end of the phone.

Karen Finley's painting, "God is a Woman."

♦ **AJ: And to keep the artist from being taken seriously. Because then they could be dismissed—**

♦ KF: —as a freak. I still feel that a person can live any way they want; it's their business. But I really can't stand the way the life of the artist is identified with *suffering*. I don't have to "suffer" with my art—I've suffered in my own personal life just being sensitive to things that seemed "wrong," and just from the fact of being "born a woman." So I don't need to be suffering in my leisure time by drinking 2 gallons of bourbon while hanging out in some cafe—I don't buy that. Behind a lot of very famous artists are really exceptional women whose *own* work is important: Pollock's wife, De Kooning's wife, Courbet's wife and Picasso's wife. And you can see how a lot of the wives' work—and *thought*—influenced the men. Frida Kahlo and Diego Rivera are another good example—

> **Then I stick little candy hearts (symbolizing "love") all over my body —because after we've been treated like *shit*, then we're *loved*. And many times that's the only way people *get* love.**

♦ **AJ: She was so much more responsible than he was. Most women really can't carry off that completely irresponsible, over-the-edge lifestyle (Janis Joplin's an exception) because even when they try, they're still holding down the fort—**

♦ KF: —you gotta get that tampon in once a month.

♦ **AJ: That really is a very male myth of how "art and life" can be conducted, because men are not connected to that *menstrual center* in terms of responsibility—**

♦ KF: I don't need to destroy myself to find pain! And I think the male privilege is: many times they're so fearful of "femininity" that they just won't feel their real pain—

♦ **AJ: —and that's part of why we're on this suicide course: because men don't want to *feel*.**

♦ KF: I think that "male myth" has destroyed a lot of male artists. I heard Oliver Stone talking about Jim Morrison and I thought he was completely wrong in saying that part of Morrison's "edge" derived from the fact that he had to go out and get himself completely fucked up—even put himself in dangerous situations—to do his art. I just don't buy that. Maybe it's because I'm a woman, but I have a certain fear: when I tried hitchhiking after reading Kerouac's *On The Road*, I got picked up and at gunpoint had to give someone a hand job—

♦ **AJ: Females have to face the fact we can't even play *that* game.**

♦ KF: There's no *On The Road* for *us!* I looked at Kerouac's work, and from a feminist viewpoint felt it was a lie. Yet I feel that as women we're naturally *Dharma Bums*—we just get paid less! I mean, we don't have to "slum it"—we're slumming already. Actually, I liked Kerouac's work and thought it was important in some ways, but I also felt it was uneven . . . it was a *lie*. In the same way that I felt Picasso appropriating African imagery was a lie . . .

♦ **AJ: Right now we can ask: "What is contemporary? What is really needed? What art really speaks for the society right now?" These are the issues. And women are doing a lot of the most cutting-edge, positive work because the male experience is no longer providing enough . . . One thing I love: in your performances you take off your clothes and are so at home with your body. It's refreshing to see you walk around as if you truly own your body, and are not walking or moving for the male gaze—**

♦ KF: I think I purposely do that because I felt resentful of what was going on in the '60s and '70s with the cutting edge male "Body Artists" (Chris Burden, Vito Acconci, the Kipper Kids and Bruce Naumann) who did use their bodies—well, as soon as *I* (a woman) tried to do that, the situation changed, because the female body is *objectified*. The men using their bodies are seen as "artists," but for women a new element is introduced . . . and putting on a flesh-colored leotard just doesn't cancel out that layer of "embarrassment" or "hiding" associated with female nudity. Women basically have to protect themselves against the male gaze which is *always there*. Like, you won't wear a short skirt if you're walking by yourself down the street—you "dress down."

When I first started out, there were times when male artists would relate to me *not* on a professional level but on a sexual level—and that confused me a lot. I thought about this and realized how much I wanted to do away with this. Usually, we only see the nude female body in a sexualized way, like when a man is going to fuck her. Rarely do we see the woman's body in situations other than that—just look at movies or commercials!

Yet I only disrobe when it's necessary for what I'm

Photo: Dona Ann McAdams

shit, then we're loved. And many times that's the only way people *get* love. Then I add the alfalfa sprouts (symbolizing sperm) because in a way it's all a big jack-off—we're all being jerked off . . . we're just something to jerk off onto, after the "love." Finally, I put tinsel on my body, because after going through all that, a woman still gets dressed up for dinner.

A woman knows that if she wears that skirt, dresses herself up and feels good about herself—that at the same time she's potentially risking sexual violence. And the fact that this is accepted as "normal" makes me almost want to cry. In a way women are like Christmas trees: normally they're not part of life (or a "man's world") . . . but adorned and decorated, they're an accepted accessory. The man has his life, then he comes home to "the wife"—and that's what it's all (supposedly) about.

At the end of the performance, when I wash myself off, it's like knowing you're washing your own shit off . . . you purify yourself. You know that you have your own gods, your own goddesses—that you are alone . . . alone with your pain.

The final scene involves the deathbed: a *female* Jesus Christ in the tomb, after the body has been wrapped in a sheet. The chocolate bleeds through the sheets like dried blood seeping through. I look at women as being this sort of martyr, in a way. I think this piece is about AIDS, but it's also about dying, of being there at death, and holding *in* pain . . . and finally, all of us coming together again.

♦ **AJ: In a culture of alienation, only in the entertainment world can you have anything approaching a "shamanistic ritual." You function as a shaman empowering people to better understand themselves—and that's threatening—**

♦ KF: I think society is still fearful of the Woman having power, meaning: if we had more of a feminine culture, we wouldn't be needing the army, we wouldn't be needing to kill 300,000 Iraqis; we wouldn't need to be doing a lot of things—

♦ **AJ: We practically destroyed their entire ecosystem; their entire sea is polluted.**

♦ KF: Did you see Kuwait City on TV? They don't have any sunlight; it's dark every day. If you live there you're supposed to wear a gas mask.

♦ **AJ: . . . Regarding "anger": women aren't allowed to be angry, whereas a man can be angry—*no problem.* Anger is even "sexy" for a man, but for a woman it's always going to have a tainted, "bitchy" connotation, like: *"What's Your Problem?"***

♦ KF: What's weird is: often when a woman gets angry at a man, he'll say this cliche: "You turn me on when you get mad!" as if to tame her. And there's something about "taming" (or controlling) a woman struggling to assert herself, that's really hideous. I'm angry, but I feel like I'm doing something about it—so it feels good. And that's what a lot of my work is about: trying to get people angry so that they'll *do* something about it. I look at my performance as a pep rally—really I think of myself as a *motivational speaker!* ♦ ♦ ♦

doing . . . to express a certain sense of freedom or abandonment, where I'm not going to be violated. So onstage I create an energy of *freedom and safety*. And I help people feel more comfortable with their selves: "Here I am, this is it." Thus, in a sense, I wipe all the surface crap off myself—get rid of all the decoration.

When I come onstage I don't wear any makeup. I do that purposely—when a male performer comes onstage *he* isn't wearing makeup; same thing! And I don't fix up my hair—I try to keep that sort of thought away. See, I'm just doing my job, my task. And when all that artifice is done away with you're just supposed to be seeing the soul now . . . there's the body up there, but you're going to see the *soul*.

Then I cover myself up in ways that I feel society covers up a woman—as in the ritual where I put chocolate all over myself. I could use *real* shit, but we know that happens already—just read the news: Tawana Brawley was found covered with shit in a Hefty bag. I use chocolate because it's a visual symbol that involves eating as well as basically being treated like shit . . . so it works on different levels. There are so many occasions where you go into a job or situation and you just have to *eat the shit*—there's no other way out.

Then I stick little candy hearts (symbolizing "love") all over my body—because after we've been treated like

Linda Montano

In performances over the past 25 years, Linda Montano has steadily sought to erase the barriers between "art" and "life." Her demonstrations of the theory that *attitude, intent,* and *awareness* are what transform "life" into "art" can be viewed as a terminal assault on the art-as-commodity establishment, redefining art as a vigilant *state-of-mind.*

The history of Linda Montano's performances reads almost as a scientific investigation (or transgression) of the limits of previous conceptions of "art." Themes have been "endurance, transformation, attention states, hypnosis, eating disorders, death, as well as obliterating distinctions between art/life." Some highlights include the 1969 "Chicken Show": "Once I decided that I could show chickens in the gallery, all kinds of creative ideas began to flow. The chicken show taught me how to laugh—plus I became the Chicken Woman." In 1973 she did "Handcuff," during which she was handcuffed to conceptual artist Tom Marioni for 3 days and nights. In 1975 she lived blindfolded for 3 days in a gallery and never spoke. Probably her most famous performance was the *year* she spent tied at the waist with an 8-foot rope to artist Tehching Hsieh; they never touched. On December 8, 1984 she began "7 Years of Living Art," which she described as "a multi-layered personal experiment in attention which will last for 7 years. I will wear only one-color clothes, each a year a different color; listen to one note 7 hours a day; stay in a colored space 3 hours a day, and speak in a different accent each year."

Linda Montano has written 5 books (including *Art in Everyday Life* and *Before and After Art/Life Counseling),* produced 20 videotapes, and created over 50 major performances. For years she has been an art instructor; currently she teaches at the University of Texas in Austin. Her book *Art in Everyday Life* can be purchased for $12 ppd from Astro Artz, 1641 18th St. Santa Monica CA 90404 (213) 315-9383.

Linda will do a tarot reading by mail on any subject (sex/money/death, etc). Send $7/per question and a self-addressed stamped envelope (SASE) to Linda Montano, c/o The Art/Life Institute, 185 Abeel St, Kingston NY 12401. For a Saint/Performance Artist certificate send a donation and an SASE to the same address.

♦ **ANDREA JUNO: Tell us about your early life—**
♦ LINDA MONTANO: I grew up in a small upstate New York village where there wasn't much access to psychological or "New Age" ways of dealing with life issues. I had quite a strict Catholic upbringing; I believed *all* the doctrines. Catholicism to me was pre-television theater; living MTV; it's where I got my imagery and my fear . . . I took it really seriously. I think kids now have the advantage of knowing that it's *just* TV . . . having a distance, a savvy and sophistication. But I took what was

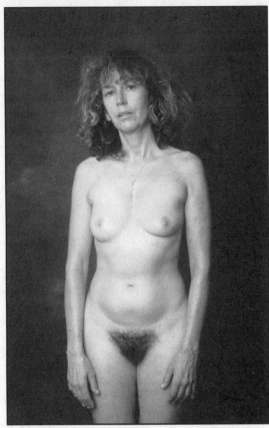

Linda Montano as "Herself"

Linda Montano as "Guru Leendah"

Linda Montano as "Biker Mama"

Linda Montano as "Lenny"

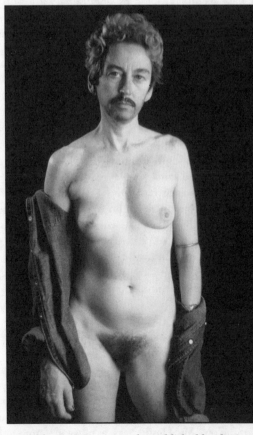

The many faces of Linda Montano, as photographed by Annie Sprinkle. From a soon-to-be published book, *Sacred Sex. . . 1 + 1 = 1.*

happening in Catholicism *verbatim,* and everything came out *verboten.*

Everything was a sin—not to be done. A positive aspect was: at least Catholic ritual is really high drama and theater. At an early age I was aware of the power differential in the church between men and women: that the women were the "nuns" whose job was to "shepherd" the children, keep them quiet and keep them going to confession. And the men were the "priests" officiating up on the podium, with altar boys serving them while they performed the "magic" (not that taking care of the kids *wasn't* magic, but . . .). *I* certainly wanted to be a priest!

I appropriated some of Catholicism's mythology—I created my own religion in which *I* could be what I used to adore; *I* could start receiving the attention I used to give to the saints.

So you could say that my work really stems from jealousy over the fact that I couldn't be a priest! Plus . . . in my background is a lot of psychodrama; I grew up in a small town without access to therapy, and I had to heal a lot of things. Yet I had a strong will to live and to live *my own way,* in my own style. . . As a result of training in Catholic imagery and rituals, in my life the recipe of *rituals* and *neuroses* produced performances which were not "schooled" . . . but personally *necessary* to express insanity and therefore maintain sanity.

◆ **AJ: There's the idea that this world is an *illusion;* it's a backdrop for a play in which our goal is to evolve and really get to know ourselves. You've taken that a step further and consciously made life into a play called "performance". . . You were a nun, too?**

◆ LM: I didn't want to go on to college. As a young child I had read *Maryknoll* magazines, about a particularly adventuresome order of nuns who go to Africa to cure leprosy or go to China and learn to eat noodles . . . peddling Jesus around the world, the implications of which I didn't really think about—I just thought, "Well, I'll be able to travel and Do Good." And so for many years I wanted to be a Maryknoll nun.

Then I had some major disappointments in sex when I was 16-19, so I went into a nunnery by default; my decision didn't spring from pure motives of either service or spirituality. I was running away from my confusion over sex, plus what I felt to be a betrayal. And I didn't have a way to analyze my situation or to communicate my confusion. My family was a musical family; they listened well, but they didn't really stimulate conversa-

tion or dialogue or monologing. My father was quite fervently religious, but he was also dogmatic—therefore genuine creativity in thought wasn't exactly encouraged.

So I made the dramatic gesture of entering a convent. I was so enthralled that I stayed in that spiritual world for 2 years, not knowing that as an artist I would create similar rituals which would become my own "thing." I enjoyed the freedom from all kinds of external responsibilities; there I found structure with a built-in ritual.

I also made the dramatic gesture of gaining a lot of weight, then losing it—when I left I weighed 82 pounds. I went from 145 to 82; that was probably my first *body alteration.* I didn't have the skills to deal with my psychological issues, and had acquired an eating disorder—I was anorexic.

◆ **AJ: That's typical of a lot of saints—**

◆ **LM: Did you see the book, *Holy Anorexia?***

◆ **AJ: Yes, and *Holy Feast & Holy Fast*—there are two of them out.**

◆ LM: So that was quite exhilarating, it was like performing, because I became very alert, very conscious, very in control, very empowered—but I was doing it with food and denial of food. There was no other place I could do *my will,* because I had given my life over to the convent—to "Mother."

◆ **AJ: You felt empowered?**

◆ LM: I was focusing; I was creating all the rules; I was creating the scenario and being very "one-pointed"—but all this was specifically about food. I know some people who are into macrobiotics and that's all they do: think about food. They go on retreats, they spend hours eating, cooking, and discussing food theory. My preoccupation eventually became non-healthy, obviously, because it turned into fasting which *did* increase my alertness—but to distract me from *myself.*

I would do a performance on a street corner for a day, or for 3 days I would handcuff myself to an artist, or for a week live at home and *every minute would be art.* I was just being in this "state of art" which was really a state of meditation.

Then I went to college, majoring in art. I felt that the only way to communicate was with art. I started out being extremely non-verbal and confused, but gradually began doing things and began to shine, becoming a leader and organizing public pieces that everyone else could be in. I became the energy of the art department, getting applause for expressing my feelings in a way that was socially acceptable—in a way that was *possible* for me. I could modify my body and my psyche by creating "living sculpture" (as it were) or "performances."

Of course, with all that I had to do *more*, so I went to Italy for a year and studied sculpture. I was still very Catholic-oriented, so my sculptures were often crucifixes involving Jesus. But by the end of my stay I was doing what I called "happenings" on the roof of the art school. I had painted all these found objects and numbered them. People would come in, take a number, find the object corresponding to that number and add it to the existing "non-frame" that eventually became the sculpture. I was getting hot and excited—this was really wonderful—it wasn't addressing my psychology then (as much as my later performances would) but I felt I was *really living*.

♦ **AJ: That "happening" took Duchamp's idea that the spectator completes the work of art to its literal realization, and also challenged the notion of "sole artistic responsibility" for a work of art.**

♦ LM: Then in 1965 I went to a graduate school dominated by all these serious minimal artists, students and teachers. That's when I hid out in the agriculture department. I took on the persona of a chicken, worked with chickens and did an entire "happening" with chickens presented in 3 large cages, 3 to a cage. A chicken video was continually playing; I exhibited 9 hand-tinted photos of chickens; I rented a car loudspeaker and drove around the city playing chicken sounds, etc. In a humorous way I felt I was dealing with these Minimalist questions of size and structure and concept—breaking the definitions of what is sculpture or what is art.

♦ **AJ: What did chickens represent to you?**

♦ LM: Just recently I was talking to someone who had taken an acid trip where she followed chickens around for 8 hours! She was talking about the size of their brain in relation to this body that doesn't fly, that has this day-

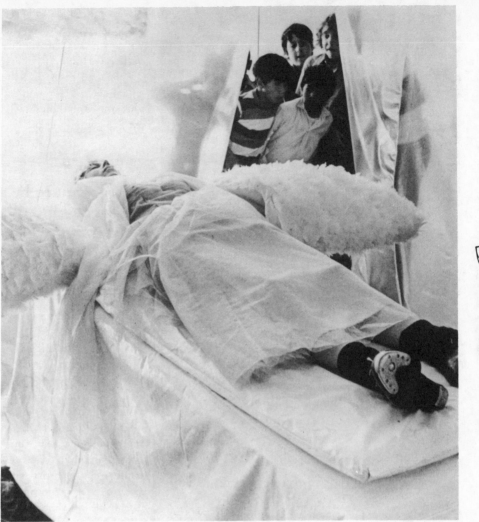

Photo: Mitchell Payne

LYING: DEAD CHICKEN, LIVE ANGEL
Berkeley Museum, Berkeley, California 1972

Art

For three days, from twelve noon to three, I laid in a chicken bed which had a twelve-foot wing span. I wore a blue prom dress, tap shoes and a feather head band. Polyethylene curtains surrounded the bed. Fig leaves covered the floor. A bird tape played during the event.

Life

This is the San Francisco version of the lying down piece... except I had moved from the east to the west coast and as a result, everything was more fairy tale like...more whimsical. I was curious about female imagery and tried making art that looked as if it were made by a woman but felt that feather-covered female, donut-shaped sculptures didn't satisfy me. Wings did. I provided sound this time and yet was still talked to/with and even kissed on the lips by a self-designated prince. It was the time of silence.

long function of gathering enough food to keep the body alive. It's a very large body and a very small brain, whose *one-pointed* task is to keep pecking at food on the ground

fly up in her face and escape! I think this was some kind of empowering action, in that even if you're not able to talk, you can communicate to get what you want. My father was a first-generation Italian who didn't speak English, so perhaps I thought of this as some kind of comment on communication. I may have remembered this story and thought, "Oh—chickens in art galleries! A way to communicate!"

"I want to be an artist with the same kind of alertness a *brain surgeon* would have performing microsurgery . . ."

♦ **AJ: Well, it's a creative act: to produce an egg out of this one-pointed, frenzied activity—**
♦ LM: —which they then sit on. They really live a life of bipolar, opposite actions. When I took these chickens into the gallery, it marked the beginning of a realization that I had a *function:* to do things that would stretch my mind and the minds of others. In Zen training they talk about "waking up!" and "paying attention" and "playing with the mind"—various ways to do that yet remain "one-pointed." When I teach or talk I want to be alert. I want to be an artist with the same kind of alertness a *brain surgeon* would have performing microsurgery on a 3-year-old neighbor's brain. I want that critical edge of awareness and surgical precision, and I want to get it in *this* lifetime.
♦ **AJ: Isn't that also part of being priestly or doing what a shaman does for the community: being a kind of "communicating vessel" for the gods?**
♦ LM: I've shied away from that title, but recently I've been disguised as a man in a setting where people come up and want their Sex Chakra to open up, and I help them. So finally I'm really a priest handing out communion! I guess I'm finally getting less shy. In a sense it's only right that I've waited until my fifties to feel comfortable with that title.
♦ **AJ: There's a transparency in your life; an openness to explore what people consider private. Your personal process of evolution is also for the society? Can you talk more about your chicken performance?**
♦ LM: After working with chickens, I started presenting myself as a "chicken woman" who was also a nun and a saint as well as a statue. I appropriated some of Catholicism's mythology and tied it to my own life and needs— I created my own religion in which I could *be* what I used to adore; *I* could start receiving the attention I used to give to the saints. So I would put on wings, mummy wrappings and whiteface makeup (and later on, a dance dress). This really was my chance to be looked at, to be seen, and to be witnessed here on the earth—balancing

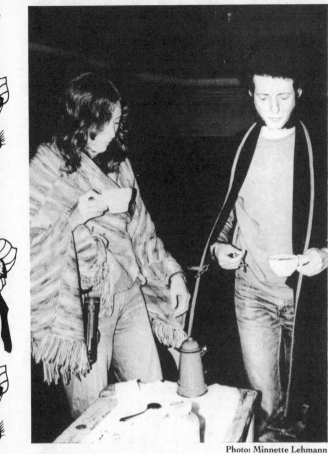

Photo: Minnette Lehmann

HANDCUFF: LINDA MONTANO AND TOM MARIONI
Museum of Conceptual Art, San Francisco 1973

Art

For three days Tom Marioni and I were handcuffed together. For ten minutes each day we made a video document of the event. The time together became a study in movement and mutual signaling.

Life

Somehow this event, more than any other one, raised questions about public/private, and I felt a tension between my ability to be permissive in my work and yet not in my life. I needed to redefine marriage and tried to do so with art. Despite the conflict, it was a magical piece and I discovered that Tom and I had probably been related long ago.

(sitting on eggs is the other task). This involves a peculiar energy of concentration—they are constantly busy. Also they have a strange non-functionality in that they have wings but can't fly—it's all very strange, like a Zen parable.

My father told me that when his mother wouldn't let him go to the movies, he would put chickens in the kitchen so when she opened the door, the chickens would

out my tendency to live in the mind and to *leave*, so to speak. Intuitively I knew that if I got other people to look at me, then I would really be *here*. Once I found that out, it was as if I had discovered this secret. I did everything and anything to keep that going, because it was pretty satisfying. And I could do this on my terms with my costumes and my time frame; people would (not at the beginning, but eventually) *pay me to be ME* . . . to be alive. It wasn't quite that easy—I could only be *me* if I was performing, but . . .

I got addicted to the performing process—that's where I was creative, truthful, abandoning ego and doing all these wonderful things. I was *curing myself* through exhibiting my existence publicly. (Although . . . once I came off stage, it was almost like the comedian who isn't funny off-camera.) But I got to cure my feeling that "others are better than I am."

◆ **AJ: Which others?**

◆ **LM:** Like saints and martyrs and priests. I wanted so badly to have "the best" that I found ways to creatively give it to myself—the audience became surrogate parent, friend and teacher . . . the audience started teaching *me* how to pay attention to myself so I could drink in this attention. And when I did get the audience's attention, I felt this was because I had succeeded in universalizing my "message"—although I did this instinctively, not consciously.

Now I can be more *conscious* about how to achieve this. People have other ways of getting "conscious": they go to therapy, they have friends they open up to, they have relationships, they have family, they have a diary, they have music (or whatever) in their private worlds. And now, after years and years of accruing much attention from audience and voyeurs, I've gotten to the place where things are more manageable—although I still to this day like the energy of a performance; I make sure I do more than one a year. After finding out that I was good at making a living by the "art of public suffering," I wanted to pull back a little.

◆ **AJ: When did you start making your life a constant performance, so you never went "offstage"?**

◆ **LM:** I began doing that piecemeal. I would do a performance on a street corner for a day, or for 3 days I would handcuff myself to an artist, or for a week live at home and *every minute would be art*. I would endure things by taking things into my body, listening to my body, being blindfolded. And this became very satisfying—I wasn't running around *looking* for art; I wasn't running around *doing* anything; I was just being (for a week, or whatever period of time) in this "state of art" which was really a state of meditation.

◆ **AJ: What made it "art"?**

◆ **LM:** Just the *statement*, the *intention*. I sent out an announcement to people that I'd be home for a week, and document all food, all clothing, all dreams, all conversations, all phone calls, etc.

◆ **AJ: And instead of relabeling inanimate objects like Duchamp did, you're making "living" the art piece—**

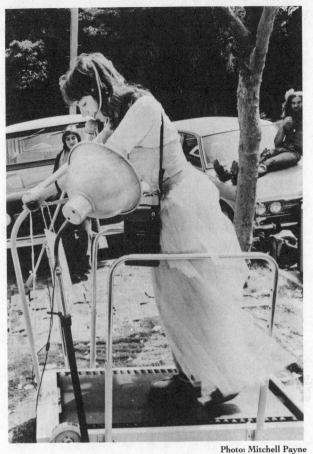

Photo: Mitchell Payne

THE STORY OF MY LIFE
San Francisco Art Institute, May 1973

Art

For three hours, noon to three, on a Wednesday, I walked uphill on a treadmill while telling the story of my life into an amplification system which slightly echoed the sound. I wore a blue prom dress over my clothes, had dye on my teeth and wore a permanent smiling device on my mouth. A tape recorder hung at my waist and played bird sounds. A green carpet covered the ground. A light was on my face... A family photo album was on a chair.

Life

I wanted to get into myself so deeply that I would be able to get out of myself and knew that it was just a matter of time before that would happen. Actually the piece produced physical euphoria and as a result I couldn't stop walking once the piece was over because my legs had been programmed to move in one way and couldn't stop. My body had a mind of its own. Preceding the event a dentist had embarrassed me by proving (with dye) that I had dirty teeth. I asked him for some dye and exposed my condition publicly therefore ameliorating the dentist's probes into my hygiene.

◆ **LM:** And it dovetails nicely with Zen. In something like Hinduism or Karma Yoga you're doing things for "god," so to speak. But in Zen there isn't necessarily a separation between sitting in meditation and doing the

dishes—*all* actions (in fact, everything!) are opportunities for consciousness. And I was *on* to that; I knew that was the direction I wanted to go in. I think Duchamp said that *breathing* could be the highest art. That's really my goal—I'm begging Duchamp's ghost to teach me that!

We had a contract with witnesses that said we would be tied at the waist with an 8-foot rope, never touch, and be in the same room the entire time. And we lived that way for a year.

I had a lot to learn about consciousness—about "Why Create?" Or, "Why do I like to create?" Then, when I met Pauline Oliveros, I started something called "Living Art." I was still doing things like living for days at a time in art galleries and talking about the fact that living was the highest art. Then I started to think, "Living art, hmmm" . . . if anybody wanted to live with me for a period of time, we would call it art, we would "intend" that. We would draw up a contract, have lawyers sign it, and choose what activities we would do. The whole thing would be art, but we might just want to "live," or just want to work. Because I liked being in creativity at all times, I didn't like the division that "this was art" or "this wasn't." Then I met and started working with Tehching Hsieh, who really is the *master* of Living Art. I feel he's Duchamp's son—philosophically and aesthetically, he's a direct descendant.

♦ **AJ: Where did you meet?**

♦ LM: I worked with him in upstate New York in a Zen monastery and had seen his ads on the streets of New York—he was very good at PR. He was advertising the street piece where he just lived on the streets of New York for a year. And I had just broken up with a lover and was mourning a bit too long. I realized that I could stay in the monastery and be a nun, or I could get out, do something harder and be an artist. So I called him; we had an interview, and then in '83-'84 we were tied together. For 6 months we worked, saw each other, became lovers; then we got tied at the waist.

♦ **AJ: How did that happen? You had a contract signed, too?**

♦ LM: We had a contract (with witnesses) that said we would be tied at the waist with an 8-foot rope, never touch, and be in the same room the entire time. And we lived that way for a year.

♦ **AJ: Why the "never touching" clause?**

♦ LM: It was an attempt to *universalize;* to *not* be lovers, so that more people could relate to the piece—so that it wasn't just male-female, but was 2 people. We talked for probably 3 months straight; either we talked or fought. We became very used to each other's needs. By the end of the year it was like a ten-year marriage—we were so totally bonded we were *non-verbal* [laughs] . . . I was considering that he would be my mate for the rest of my life! It was probably the most powerful art experience I've ever had.

♦ **AJ: Wasn't a lot of the performance about interpersonal development? What kind of relationship problems did you solve? What did you learn?**

♦ LM: Well, it took 2 very special people to do this. We both shared enough of the same philosophy to endure this; we both knew *consciously* that we had chosen to do it. I knew I was training myself for other kinds of life issues—for example, that it was possible to live creatively in a jail, or if you were terribly handicapped or an AIDS victim. So while I was tied to him I escaped by creating a future. What I did was daydream; I created a structure that would keep me in a "job" and alive and learning and active and plugged into a creative mindset or consciousness.

♦ **AJ: But was anything wrong?**

♦ LM: What was wrong was: I got out of a lot of the pain of being tied by making a new piece. I thought about that new piece a lot—instead of feeling how awful it was every time I had to get up and go to the bathroom.

♦ **AJ: So in a sense you were escaping the pain of the moment—**

♦ LM: I escaped to creativity instead of just sitting it out. And it's a great piece, I did a great job, I escaped beautifully. But I have some regrets about that experience because I feel I wasted a lot of good "grounding" time by not fully dealing with the pain of the moment. Because thinking about or daydreaming about the future can be a terrible opiate, a terrible drug . . .

I spent many years devouring a *smorgasbord* of spiritual disciplines. Each had a different message, a different methodology, a different way of meditating. I thought, "Migod, what do I do?"

♦ **AJ: It's so tempting to want to escape the pain of life—**

♦ LM: Really now, in retrospect, what bothers me is: I didn't *know* I was escaping. And now I know more about this. If I'm going to escape, I want to be *conscious* before I go. I want to say, "Okay, you're *going* now—for the next 3 hours you're going to think about [fill in the blanks] . . .

◆ **AJ: But since life is for learning, in a sense you didn't waste any time—**

◆ LM: And there is no time to waste, anyway!

◆ **AJ: It's an illusion. The ultimate goal is to be able to say: Everything is perfect.**

◆ LM: Right! Well, I feel I *did* do something perfect, then. Besides, time heals all wounds . . .

◆ **AJ: But if you were doing it now you'd do it differently— [laughs]**

◆ LM: Anyway, I guess I'm still trying to *teach myself* . . . I give myself incredible permission when it comes to art. I'm really ballsy, I'm really gutsy, I love what I do, I'm really good, I have great respect for myself. And what I'm trying to teach myself is, "Listen, this is *life*; there's no difference between art and life. So start seeping some of that life over to the other side." It's almost like I've created this schizophrenic persona of an *artist*, but then there's also this *life* . . .

◆ **AJ: So now you want to integrate them both. In sum—what did you learn about yourself?**

◆ LM: The fact that I'm extremely stubborn and one-pointed, and the fact that I love challenges—I love doing difficult, strange things. Tehching Hsieh helped me touch the "Good Girl" paradigm in me—I had always been the Nuns' or the Teachers' pet. I'd been the bad girl in my *art*, but the good girl in *life*. That piece aroused rage and anger and got me into therapy again, where I realized that *art was not enough*—I needed more help than what I was giving myself. Then I had to find a way to make everything "art," so that the fact that I was going into therapy would be just as valuable as making an art work. Then I came up with the idea of the *7-year piece, 7 Years of Living Art*: Dec 8, 1984-Dec 8,1991.

---

7 YEARS OF LIVING ART 12/8/84 — 12/8/91
An experience based on the 7 energy centers of the body.

PART A: INNER: The Art/Life Institute
Daily, for 7 years, I will:

1. Stay in a colored space (minimum 3 hours).
2. Listen to one pitch (minimum 7 hours).
3. Speak in an accent (except with immediate family).
4. Wear one color clothes.

PART B: OUTER: The New Museum

1. Once a month, for 7 years, I will sit in a window installation at the New Museum and talk about art/life with individuals who join me.

PART C: OTHERS: International

1. Once a year, for 16 days, a collaborator will live with me.
2. Others can collaborate in their own way wherever they are.

Photo: Mitchell Payne

BECOMING A BELL RINGER FOR THE SALVATION ARMY
San Francisco, December 1974

Art

I became a Salvation Army bell ringer during the Christmas season. I sent out announcements to friends who visited me.

Life

I began discovering that in reality I was different characters/people and photographed myself as these for a few years. Somehow I found all the Salvation Army clothes in my closet, except for the hat, pin and bell. I also needed work. As a result the Salvation Army character emerged.

◆ **AJ: You're at the end of the piece, right? And it's related to the 7 chakras and the 7 primary colors?**

◆ LM: It's based on the 7 energy centers or chakras in the body which are psycho-physical-spiritual-physiologic-glandular sites of nerve endings or ganglia or glands or spiritual vibratory black holes—moving black holes that Hindu or Tibetan Buddhist or other religious and metaphysical systems have cited. I spent many years devour-

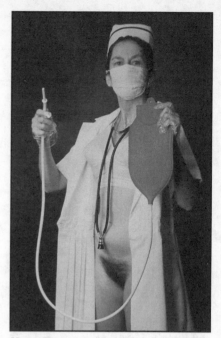

Linda *Hell*—"Professional Dominatrix"   *Lindy*—"Girl Scout"   *Nurse Montano*—"Stern Enema Nurse"

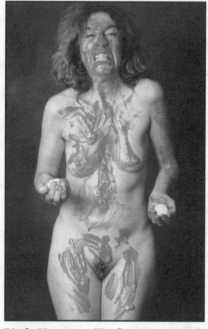

Juicy Lucy—"Stripper"   Linda Montano—"Performance Artist"   *Mõntañïëra*—"Ethnic Girl"

ing a *smorgasbord* of spiritual disciplines—I went in and out of many different spiritual worlds. And each had a different message, a different methodology, a different way of meditating, a different place *in* or *on* the body. The focus might shift from the top of the head to the nose, to between the eyes, to the heart, to the nipples, to the abdomen, to the sex center, to the toes, to the bottoms of the feet—I thought, "Migod, what do I do?" I didn't know where to be.

So that was one reason to create the piece—take one center to each year and just *do* it. And I needed a way to do more art and to do public art, because that year-long piece had been so rich and delicious that I wanted *more.* And I love structure; I've always worked with structure, design, number, and time or duration. So I designed a wonderful job for myself: for the next 7 years to live each year in a different energy center or chakra, very disciplined. The first year was Red, the sex center, and for this

Linda *Monroe*—"Hollywood Sex Queen"

Miss Montano—"Victorian Lady"

Lola—"Naturalist"

Linda *Page*—"Bondage Babe"

Prissy—"Prom Queen"

◆

The Many Faces of Linda Montano

◆

All photos by Annie Sprinkle

◆

I chose a French accent. I selected a pitch which I listened to on an oscillator every day for 7 hours. Every day I spent 3 hours in a red room; every day I wore only red, and it was just totally wild.

◆ **AJ: What kind of experiences did you have in that year?**

◆ LM: I had 5 lovers at the same time—probably one of the greatest loves of my life came into my life (I can't name the person). And I had people knocking on my

door thinking it was a whorehouse because it was painted a vibrating red. I had the excitement of having chosen a wonderful piece and a great job; the confidence that I was really on the right track—that I had done something really good. It felt *revolutionary*.

◆ **AJ: Dec. 8, '84 — Dec. 8, '85 was your Red year?**

◆ LM: Yes. But in 1977 (described in my book, *Art in Everyday Life*) I had done this piece, "Learning To Talk," which featured these 7 characters, each identified with a different chakra and theme. So seven years later in '84 I resurrected this work, adding a different color, accent, and musical note. And each year I "channeled" a different guide or mentor—for example in '84-'85 when I brought in the French accent, I asked Joan of Arc to be my guide. So this year I'm "channeling" a doctor I met at Ananda Ashram who's from India and has delivered 2000 babies and has 8 children. She's my model for the year.

The 1977 list of characters was:

1. Lamar Breto	1st Chakra	Sexuality
2. Sister Rose Augustine	2nd Chakra	Security
3. Kay Pryo	3rd Chakra	Courage
4. Linda Lee	4th Chakra	Love
5. Dr Jane Gooding	5th Chakra	Communication
6. Nadia Grozmolov	6th Chakra	Bliss
7. Hilda Mahler	7th Chakra	Union

I had to modify this for the "7 Years of Living Art" project.

♦ **AJ: What color are you in now?**

♦ **LM:** I'm in white, the crown. And as the years went on the accents dropped, the sounds dropped—I had to break my own rules, although I kept the basic structure together for 3 years—I never once broke the *dress code*. People would say, "Well, you didn't sit in your room today!" I noticed that I was fighting too much, that I was *forcing* it to happen, that I was messing around with my Will, and that life was starting to mess around with me. I was trying to stick to my original plan, but Life told me, "Okay, *try* doing it under these circumstances—go ahead and see if I care!" I could not keep going—life won.

♦ **AJ: In the Red Year, did you find that you resolved issues of sexuality?**

♦ **LM:** No, but in the yellow year I met Annie Sprinkle and it's like I opened the door to unconscious sexual imagery and sexual issues. I've been dealing with that ever since, and it's still not resolved, although it's getting better and better. I'm much more comfortable with where I am sexually, but there's still more to be said and done. When I opened the "door," I found the reluctance to leave was so great that I decided I needed 7 years for *each* chakra—that I had made a mistake—the piece was wrongly developed. It needed to be a *49-year* piece.

♦ **AJ: Do you still think that?**

♦ **LM:** I really don't know . . . The second year was *orange* for *security,* and one of the issues of being a nun or being in any institution is security, because there that's a given. The horizontal plane is taken care of by them, so you can go up and live in the "spiritual"—and I wanted to get a handle on that, because some people hide out in institutions so they don't have to deal with the nitty-gritty of everyday life, and that's an issue for me. I want to be able to handle the everyday life, because *that's* where the real saintliness is. People who maintain their clothes, their tastes, their cars, their relationships, their mothers, their fathers, their shoes, their things, their relationship to money, their relationship to food—with-

out possessing and territorializing and having greed . . . who do all this and just *share* and just *laugh* . . . well, it's not easy for me to do all that.

The third year was *yellow* for *courage;* the accent was Spanish and the guide was Theresa of Avila. My life in those first three years was quite spectacular: I would get up and meditate and do karate and listen to the sound and live in those clothes (which people brought to me, or they came from thrift stores) and speak in that accent. That was the year I met Annie Sprinkle and Veronica Vera . . . when I allowed myself to look at all aspects of sexuality and sensuality—and this was pretty courageous for me. I also allowed Annie and Veronica as collaborators into my life. I had done that with Tehching Hsieh and the rope, but I saw that I could continue doing that—and with a woman. I had lived with Pauline Oliveros who had influenced both my life and my work—her work with listening and using long tones certainly inspired my use of a drone in a piece I did for my ex-husband who was killed. Pauline's the real mother of all women composers—a totally avant-garde, wild, pioneering electronic musician. She plays accordion and composes meditation music. And we were partners (and lovers) for years. Pauline and Maryanne Amacher are the most devastatingly wonderful female composers in the world.

The next year's color was *green* for the heart chakra. I moved into Maryanne Amacher's home which Pauline was renting, and I sublet it from Pauline. I said, "Okay heart—open!" because in that year my mother died, my brother-in-law died, my dog died and I had no place to live. All that was quite a test of the heart, like: "Okay, you asked for something—*here it is!*" It was like dynamite, a volcano erupting and an earthquake all combined. That was the hardest year.

That year I "manifested" a house for myself in mourning for my mother's death. I worked like a zombie creating the "Art/Life Institute" in a building that had been empty for 20 years and was totally trashed (I filled two 25x25-foot dumpsters with refuse). I brought this "victim" back to life—recycled this building, recycled myself, and cleaned out all the confusion (not *all!*) and the pain of loss.

When I was living in San Francisco I had the "Living Art Museum" because I get uncomfortable if I have to live in a "home"—a home means nurturing, food, security, and raises issues about family and communication. So no matter where I'm living, I call it a museum or an institute and that makes me happy, because then I am *art living in art.* Doing this also gives me permission to make a place a "work of art" instead of a "home." The "Art/Life Institute" is divided into two equal spaces, one of which is completely empty and painted the color of the year I'm "in." The other space is for living, with a kitchen and bathroom; upstairs is for sleeping and storage. And it's wonderful—very minimal and nun-like. It's a work of art—a monument to mourning and a monument to a woman doing a really big sculpture. It's a great feat, and

I'm proud of it.

People can come study with me. That was part of the structure I'd envisioned, because I was living alone in Kingston, without a live-in relationship; without *stimulation*. When I first moved here it was like a North Dakota outpost on a winter day—intensely isolated. Now it's becoming very Soho. During the past 7-year piece I've gone once a month into New York City to do Art-Life Counseling at the New Museum, as an extension and testing of my "inner work." Also, once a year I have someone live with me for a couple weeks and work and collaborate, or I give workshops to them.

♦ **AJ: Annie Sprinkle described attending your workshop with Veronica Vera, doing performances about her life and discovering things about herself. She said she learned to appreciate toilet paper—only using one square. . .**

♦ LM: Yes, the workshop is like living in a convent for 2 weeks—everything's regulated, it's very strict. I don't let them rustle through the icebox, you know.

SAMPLE SCHEDULE

1. All lights off when not in use.
2. Silence most of the time.
3. Use very little water, dish soap, toilet paper.
4. A performance every evening based on a chakra.
5. All is subject to change.

Wed. *I Ching*, Tarot, Pendulum. Orientation.
Thur. 1st Chakra: Sex, Earth.
8:30-9:30 Exercise
9:30-10:00 Tea
10:00-12:00 Meditation, chant, visualization.
12:00-2:00 Do interview
2:00-3:00 Lunch
3:00-5:00 Meditation
5:00-7:00 Free
7:00-8:00 Snack
8:00-10:00 Meditation and performance.
Fri. 2nd Chakra: Security, water.
Sat. 3rd Chakra: Power, fire.
Sun. 4th Chakra: Heart, air. We will do a 6-hour Vision Quest.
Mon. 5th Chakra: Throat, ether.
Tue. 6th Chakra: 3rd Eye, ether.
Wed. 7th Chakra: Top of the head.

♦ **AJ: In your workshop, your intention is to get people to make performances out of very deep and personal past experiences . . . to get us to externalize our deepest personal shames and fears—in order to get control over them, instead of *them* controlling *us.***

♦ LM: If inside you is a little girl who's snickering at something you do, then you bring that little girl *out* and

LIVING ART
The Annual San Francisco Christmas 1975

 Art

For four days, Pauline Oliveros, Nina Wise and I lived together and called that time art. Each of us had a separate environment and we laid motionless for long periods of time in the environment.

Life

Instead of feeling creative, human and spontaneous, I felt like a harried hostess during this event, probably because the complexities and paradoxes of relating were too problematical—I decided to go back to life.

give her the attention she needs—you reveal her "sins" in public so that she can get on with her life—i.e., *disappear!* So that the next time you make love to your favorite lover in the world, there's not that little snickering 7-year-old there to create static amidst your ecstasy—you know what I mean?

So . . . it's really to our advantage to houseclean our interior soul, and bring what we found *out* into visible, witness-able form, and have other people say, "That's not so bad!" or "That's great!—you really did well with that sludge!" Someone might say, "Oh wow—now let me

ART / LIFE ONE YEAR PERFORMANCE

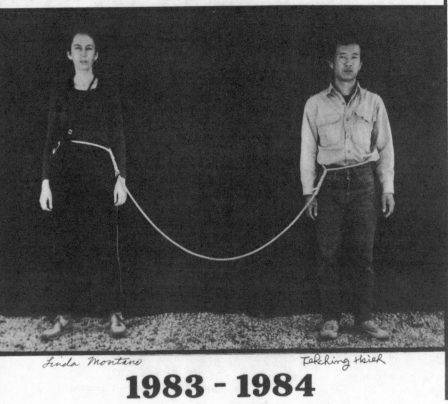

Linda Montano   Tehching Hsieh

1983 - 1984

Linda Montano and Tehching Hsieh together day in and day out for a solid year.

Each year I had an ailment that corresponded to the chakra of the year—whether it was head or my eyes or heart trouble. By then I knew that it wasn't just *me.* I thought, "Okay life, let's play together—if you want me to do something, go for it. I'm going to see what you want."

Last year was really a whirlwind for me; it involved screening out *everything;* obtaining clarity of vision—*clear sight.* This year has been extremely angelic, pure, scary. I'm all in white and living at an ashram where all is light. Then when I go to Kingston, I'm like in the movie *Wall Street*—I get on the phone and buy a car and make arrangements to go to my next teaching job.

Now my life is about *integration.* I'm trying not to judge anyone as good or bad or white or black; I'm not trying to be the good girl or the bad girl, or to judge something as better or worse . . .

I'm planning another 7-year project. I'll be going four times a year to the United Nations, giving myself as a *living art object,* because the United Nations is filled with gifts of art from other countries. So I'll be an "unofficial" American donation. I'm also going to Texas to teach—that's how I've survived for the past 20 years: teaching freelance—6 weeks here, 6 months there . . . whatever.

In the yellow year I met Annie Sprinkle and it's like—I opened the door to unconscious sexual imagery and sexual issues. I've been dealing with that ever since . . .

♦ **AJ: You're in direct contact with students; do you see any evolution in how people are dealing with things?**
♦ LM: I think that role models for women are gaining momentum; I think we're fired up now. We can go for whatever we uniquely need to do, and we also have

show you *mine!*" Everybody should do this some time in their life: look at your sexual history, and if you have no public place to do this, then definitely at least do a performance privately for yourself.
♦ **AJ: Annie Sprinkle had such praise for your workshop—**
♦ **LM:** I feel Annie is extremely and importantly bound to my process and my "good" sexual self. Our finding each other was a boon! And we constantly trade information. Annie told me, "Look, Linda—you're really sexy . . . have fun with it!" Sex is her *gift.*
♦ **AJ: Tell us about your "Blue Year"—**
♦ **LM:** During the "Blue Year," I lived like a total bum. I had no water, no gas heat—only electricity. Given what I was thinking about, I think I needed to suffer—I was in such heavy mourning that I didn't want to "nurture" myself, I had to do it this way—this was the best "nurturing" I could give myself. Tehching had showed me how to pee in a jar and [shit] in a bag—he'd had to do that when he lived on the streets of New York for a year. So life was reduced down to the "nitty-gritty." Yet it was a really satisfying experience; I was Katherine Hepburn that year, and the chakra was the *throat* or *communication.* My persona was Meridel LeSeur, 90-year-old poetess and incredible ex-stuntwoman.

permission to fall back . . . permission to be pre-women's movement and pre-consciousness raising. I'm finding that we can have it *all;* that we have permission to *fail* and to be floundering humans. Maybe that's more important than "making it." I think what I'm trying to say is: there are days when I feel trapped, and I still need support. There are times when I need nurturing and I have to ask for help for my next step—which might be no step at all.

In the '90s we artists are doing *death*—it's the great preparation for letting go completely.

The goal is to relax into my *true nature.* Menopause has come and gone, and as the political arena gets messier and the world gets more desperate by the moment, I try to tap into my own clarity and spiral away from my own confusion. Actually, I think *interviews* give me a chance to learn more and appreciate myself—maybe the moral of the story is: we all need to interview ourselves once a week . . .

♦ **AJ: With all the pain that's going on in the world— well, how do you *deal* with pain?**

♦ LM: I don't have a TV and I don't open a newspaper—I'm a *wimp!* I won't look. And now I run to a therapist and live in an ashram because I just can't take it—I'm not strong enough; it's *too much.* And I don't know if that's correct, but right now I need all my resources just to get through the next day. It's a weak time and I'm coming out of it—I'm being kicked out of it because soon I'll have to teach publicly for a period of time. But one of my survival modes has been: as much isolation as possible. The revolution is not just in the world; it's taking place inside yourself.

Something strange is going on—people are acting very odd, and things are happening that you would *never* think would ever happen. It's the breakdown of the nuclear family and the political world and the world itself—so I'm just clinging to the side of the ship in the only way I know how. But I think everybody's trying to find their way of *making sense* before everything sinks . . .

♦ **AJ: I'd like to think we're on the brink of an incredible new consciousness and human evolution— but it's like a birth, it's most painful. And it's personal, too—you can't even have a "revolution" without personal healing. Actually, how can there be a revolution when two people can't even have a personal relationship without lying to each other almost every day? Without total personal transformation, you'll just be perpetuating the same authoritarian bullshit . . . where the revolutionaries become just like the oppressors**

they overcame. And for thousands of years women's rights and their more personal mode of living have been negated—yet without their integration, there can never be a lasting revolution. Anyway . . . your personal life and art have become transparent models for us: watching *your* growth is like watching *our* own growth . . . you're making personal evolutionary changes *public*—

♦ LM: As artists, in the Bohemian years we did *food*—it was bread, wine and cheese, and that was all because of lack of money. In the '60s and '70s, artists did *sex,* with all these live models and alternate role playing. In the '80s we did *money*—rich artists; much money being made (Andy Warhol started that). And now in the '90s we artists are doing *death*—it's the great preparation for letting go completely and going to the next cycle. We're going into a *technological convent* (or something) because of AIDS and the gay world who helped us with sex . . . who liberated sex so that now we can have a *liberation of death* . . . now that death has become like the common cold and it can't be hidden anymore—now it has to be acknowledged; it can't be lied about. So I have a piece where I ask everyone to say the word "death" 4000 times a day; to talk to it, to start making friends with death, because that's the *new word.* We've taught each other everything else; we still have to teach each other about death. It's been romanticized, it's been disguised, it's been camouflaged, it's been watered down—everything but *dealt with* . . . and it can't be denied anymore.

Death has to be acknowledged; it can't be lied about . . . we have to start making friends with death, because that's the *new word.* It's been romanticized, it's been disguised, it's been camouflaged, it's been watered down—everything but *dealt with* . . . and it can't be denied anymore.

Karen Finley's doing the Death of the Good Girl; Annie Sprinkle's doing the Death of Taboo. I also hope to be contributing; I have my own need to understand the aging process. I want to be a *scientist* uncovering all I can about death and the fears surrounding death—that's my next 7-year scheme. I've done the martyr work; the next 7 years will be about the appreciation of the chakras in the body— not opening, not pushing, not fucking, but *appreciating* them. And in that desire for the fullest possible appreciation, I'm inviting a dialogue . . . with *Death.* ♦ ♦ ♦

Brief Biography: "Life Is Art"

Jan 18, 1942, 7:35 AM: Born Capricorn with Aquarius rising. 3 days old, a minor operation for an inverted nipple. Congenital heart murmur. Got shoe and foot caught in toilet bowl.

1942-48 Played with brother & sister; insist on being Virgin Mary

1949 Had worms. All 3 of us have 2 enemas a night until worms are gone.

1952 Played doctor under the house.

1953 Took tap dancing lessons. Took piano lessons.

1954 Won a drawing award for picture copied from magazine.

1955-59 High school. Devised a smell patrol—friends who would tell me if I smelled or not. Wore ten different deodorants at one time.

1957 Work at father's shoe store, bus girl at resort, sandwich counter at Thruway Hot Shoppe, child care at resort.

Late 50s. Grandmother dies. Introduced to Italian opera. See movies: *Joan of Arc, Bernadette, Seven Brides for Seven Brothers, Annie Get Your Gun*.

1959-60 College of New Rochelle, Art Major. Spike heels.

1960-62 Maryknoll Sisters. "I wanted to be the female Albert Schweitzer and cure leprosy." Leave weighing 82 pounds.

1963-65 Back to college. "Did short, impromptu plays about college life, shaving legs, dating, etc. Like Catholic rituals, the skits also seemed to be the prototypes for performances I would do years later."

1965-66 Villa Schifanoia, Florence, M.A. degree in sculpture. "I had a 'happening' at my opening which seemed more provocative and spontaneous than my sculpture. It was then that I began questioning the need for *permanent object making*."

1966-69 Univ of Wisconsin, MFA degree. Agriculture school with chickens.

1970 Car accident, car turns over. I "die" and leave body but experience coming back in.

1970-71 Do first performance in Rochester with dead chickens: "everybody who saw it was shocked. People wondered if it was about Yoga or Vietnam or Vegetarianism or whatever." "The Chicken Woman was born— she was a nun, saint, martyr, plaster statue, angel, absurd snow white dreamlike character and the chicken became my totem and twin. I began a series of experiments with myself that allowed me to explore physical, spiritual, psychic spaces which had been previously taboo, frightening, or obscure. To intensify these events I would alter my consciousness with hypnosis, duration, sound or repetition. My work was now giving me the freedom to practice the things that

I needed in my life: confidence, courage, stillness, endurance, concentration." Begin Yoga. Marry Mitchell Payne. Honeymoon in Niagara Falls. Move to San Francisco, car accident on way. Belongings all over the highway.

1971-75 Study Yoga with Doctor Mishra; study acupuncture. Yoga Therapist at St Mary's Hospital. Buy nurse's dress and wear it on the street. "In 1972 I performed a chicken dance in 9 different outdoor places in San Francisco. The suicide prevention squad picked me up for dancing on the Golden Gate Bridge and said that I was holding up traffic for 5 miles on each side and if any accidents occurred while I had been dancing, that I would have been liable. I quickly realized that art had a 'public ethic.'"

1973: Do "Handcuff" piece with Tom Marioni: "The piece with Tom was wonderful. We moved together immediately. As soon as the handcuffs were on, we started moving together. That continued for 3 days: going places, getting up, eating, changing, going to the bathroom. Whatever we did was absolutely synchronized at all times. It just seemed so easy—he was so easy and I was so easy—and the kinds of closeness that happened and the Siamese twin feeling of the piece was amazing; the kinds of things we didn't have to say because we had become so bonded just by doing everything together. So for 3 solid days, everything we did was with awareness."

1974 Begin going to therapy. Fix up house at Shotwell Street. Dog "Chicken" dies Nov 2, All Souls Day, during performance of me lying in a crib listening to my mother talk about me as an infant.

1975 Scream uncontrollably after Motion performance. Kindness of friends makes me want to come back. Separated from Mitchell Payne.

1976 Move to San Diego & live with Pauline Oliveros.

1977 Took refuge with Buddhist Lama Kalu Rimpoche. He lived in a cave for 13 or 16 years. I experienced being a Catholic, Yogi, Buddhist and have done EST, Gestalt, TM, Mind Dynamics, Zen, Rolfing, Polarity and Acupuncture. Become saint in Universal Life Church. Mitchell Payne is shot Aug 19 and dies instantly in Kansas City. Mourning. Begin Karate classes with Lester Ingber, founder of Institute for the Study of Attention. First real taste of discipline.

1978 Teach art.

1979 Teach performance at San Francisco State & SF Art Institute. Cut my hair so I'll appear punk. Hike 45 miles in the Sierras. Collaborate with Pauline Oliveros.

1980 Begin small business, Art-Life Counseling.

1983 Begin one-year performance with Tehching Hsieh

tied to 8-ft rope by waist.

1984 Begin 7-Year Performance, *7 Years of Living Art.*

1980's *The Sister Rosita Summer Saint Camp.* Come to Sister Rosita's Summer Saint Camp and learn discipline,* how to look for miracles, talk in accents, wear a habit (all yellow clothes), get up early, exercise into oneness, take pilgrimages to sacred places (tour Woodstock and swim in the Hudson); take cold showers and prepare for next winter, eat sparingly (rice and beans); fast one day a week, research stories about the saints (performance artists). Here, structure gets substituted for worldly success, dreaming for TV, walking for cars, and awareness for entertainment. In 7 days we visualize and experience the 7 chakras, one a day, and then "perform" from that chakra each night, after having spent the day coming from that particular energy.

At the successful completion of these hardships you will receive saint papers and a performance certificate from the St. Rosita Art/Life Institute.

Living Art: Time Spent Artfully Alone or Not Alone

Section 1: *Purpose & Intent:*

Friends often intend to collaborate but rarely find the opportunity. The purpose of LIVING ART is to allow artists/nonartists to designate specific times; hours, days, weeks or months to work and live, together or alone. This time then becomes ART. The intention of LIVING ART is to redefine relationships by living together in a marathon fashion after having drawn up a mutually workable contract. The contract lasts as long as the ART.

Section 2: *Living Art Defined:*

Living Art is any work/play which artists/nonartists are willing to perform together or alone. The rules can be determined by the needs of the participants. For example, they may explore silence, fasting, psychic discoveries, eating, basketball, etc in the search for new styles of relating. LIVING ART becomes LIVING ART when the times and activities which the artists perform are *intended* to be art. The announcement may be public or private.

Section 3: *Time Defined:*

LIVING ART divides time into actual time and ART. Actual time is divided in terms of seconds, minutes, hours, days, months, years. The artists may choose as much of this time as they think they need to *transform* and *change* themselves. When it is intended that a specific time together will be designated as time for LIVING ART, then that time will become ART and not time.

Section 4: *The Contract:*

The contract is an agreement made by the artists before the event. It states that the time together and activity performed will be ART.

Section 5: *The Activities:*

The activities are *anything* that the artist/nonartists would like to perform together. These activities, when documented and performed together as ART, can change the *values* and *personal vision* of the artist.

Section 6: *Directions For Performing Living Art:*

1. Choose a person/persons with whom you wish to perform LIVING ART.

2. Select an activity that you would both like to perform.

3. Draw up a *contract* stating what the activities are, time it will be, and place/places.

4. Decide on a mode of documentation for the LIVING ART event.

5. Spend the designated time together and perform the events.

6. Present the result of your experiment to one or more friends, either with documentation, talking or live performance.

Section 7: *Documentation*

The document of the time can be in any mode comfortable for the artists. Record making should be done *without stress* so that the process of the art itself can be fully *experienced.*

Personal Living Art History

1973 Home Endurance. Home for a week.

1973 Handcuff to Tom Marioni. Three days.

1974 Garage Talk. Available to others for 3 days.

1974 Husband-Wife Fashion Show. Modeled resort clothes.

1975 Listen To Your Heart. Three days living in a gallery wearing a stethoscope.

1975 Living Art. Anza-Borrego Desert with Pauline Oliveros.

1976 When I was Young I Thought that I was Going to Die when I was 34. Living on Leucadia beach for three days.

1983-84 Living tied to 8-foot rope without touching for a year with Tehching Hsieh.

---

* Thrift; how to walk and smile like a nun; how to live without hot water, art, or sex; how to remember to turn the lights off when leaving a room; how to make a hair shirt and enjoy wearing one; how to live on air when hungry; how to live without the use of your refrigerator over the Christmas holidays; how to spot a martyr.

Photo: Chris Buck

Carolee Schneemann

Since the early '60s Carolee Schneemann has been a pioneering, taboo-breaking performance artist, filmmaker and writer on the subjects of feminism, sexuality, and the *ecstatic, erotic* body as a source of knowledge. Investigating denied aspects of the unconscious, she has created hundreds of solo improvisations and multi-media "happenings" which incorporate dance, film projections, poetry, painting and sculpture.

In 1962 she transformed her New York loft into a kinetic environment in which she did a series of "actions," thus anticipating the "Body Art" movement of the '60s and '70s. She choreographed the Judson Dance Theater (whose members included Meredith Monk and Yvonne Rainer) exploring the use of anti-gravitational devices and emphasizing intensive physical contact and *risk*. By 1964 she had established her Kinetic Theatre, a racially mixed group whose performance *Meat Joy* mingled blood, fish, chicken parts and raw sausages with the naked bodies of the celebrants. Her infamous film, *Fuses* (1965) revealed transgressive images such as a penis transforming itself into a vagina, and a penis stained with menstrual blood. During the Vietnam war, public screenings of her anti-war films *Snows* and *Viet-Flakes* were harassed by police. Since then Carolee has done more performances, including *Up To and Including Her Limits* (in which she was suspended from a rope harness); *Fresh Blood—A Dream Morphology* (exploring taboos of female sexuality); and a major installation, *Cycladic Imprints,* at the San Francisco Museum of Modern Art.

As Carolee put it, "I've always been amazed when I create a scandal. I don't do it on purpose, but you do get an instinct for *where the repression is* and you go for it. I always thought that my culture would be gratified that I was putting it out, but instead they want to punish you." Her latest works have not stopped critiquing bodily taboos. She currently resides in New Paltz, NY.

♦ ANDREA JUNO: **Where did you grow up?**

♦ CAROLEE SCHNEEMANN: In rural Pennsylvania. My earliest inspiration was my godmother who always arrived wearing furs and smelling of perfume—she was an actress who'd run away to New York City. She gave me the most exquisite attention when I was four years old, and was the first adult who encouraged me in a visionary way. I was drawing before I knew how to talk—drawing was like breathing for me. All kids draw, but I drew in sequences like stills from a

film. I also started keeping notebooks—not only of dream notes, but of dream *drawings*.

Early in life I recognized that there was a certain ecstasy (akin to the sacred and holy—*orgasm*, even) involved in creating images within a frame. I discovered this was a place where I could go for a "higher" integration of where I was and what I could feel. So for me, drawing and the erotic had this early bond—whenever the adult world would try to inhibit or discourage or confuse me, I would recognize that they were trying

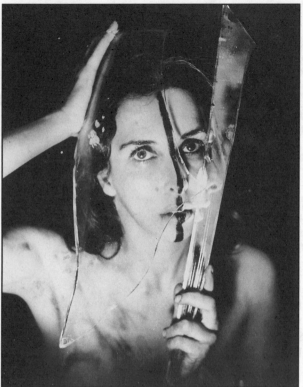

"Eye Body," 1963   Photo: Erró

to separate these two realms.

♦ AJ: In the '60s, you made a statement that "Painting Was Dead"—

♦ CS: Yes, that was a real crisis for me. What I was trying to find was a way to—in effect—paint with words, with video, with film, with the body, with extended structures in space. So I'll probably die saying I'm a painter, even though there's no brush or paint around. As a young artist I had to overcome all those Western culture standards of "how to see, how to draw, how to hold the chalk . . ." And back then the term or the idea of "Performance Art" did not exist.

What truly inspired me was what I called "double knowledge": the existence of a secret, separate history to research and investigate.

♦ AJ: Who else influenced you?

♦ CS: Virginia Woolf—when I was 14 I found a book by her in a bookmobile van. You'd go meet the book van and rent books for two weeks, then the van would return and you could get new ones. I remember reading *The Waves* in a barn, with a huge spider web next to me, crying because I knew I wanted to do things with this kind of density and fragmentation, this slipperiness and

tenacity where an image could be both imprinted and released, like a film image in motion. That book gave me something which is still a key to my method . . .

Actually, my main influences were *secret*—I had lived in and absorbed and survived and even done well within male culture, but what truly inspired me was what I called "double knowledge": the existence of a secret, separate history to research and investigate (for example, Maria Bashkirtseff's diaries from the turn of the century). She was an impassioned young Russian who went to Paris and studied with the best teachers before dying of tuberculosis. Her journal chronicles this incredible struggle and turmoil about what she's painting, what she's sculpting, what she's etching, how she's struggling to keep her strength, and how much blood she's coughing up . . . And she died at the age of 22!

. . . at the end the performers (who were mostly nude—if they'd been totally nude they would have been arrested) were smearing each other with dead fish, chicken parts and raw sausages in an absolute *frenzy!*

The more I research, the more this terrible pattern emerges—all my favorite female predecessors seem to meet a terrible end! Margaret Fuller drowns; Paula Modersohn-Becker dies after giving birth; Virginia Woolf drowns—others are simply ignored by history, or worse—absorbed into a body of work done by their male lovers (or fathers or associates). For example: Judith van Leyster, who painted an enormous number of the works attributed to Franz Hals. Marie-Joseph Charpentier's most significant works were re-attributed to David, because then they'd be worth a lot more. There's a whole litany of histories like this. I was an amateur digging this stuff up in the early '60s; now, thank goodness, there's "feminist research . . ."

When I started really developing my own work such as "Eye Body" (1963) and "Meat Joy" (1964), the impetus came from a combination of the writings of Wilhelm Reich, Antonin Artaud, and Simone de Beauvoir's *Second Sex*. "Eye Body" was a performance in my New York loft which I had transformed into an "environment"—with 4x9-foot panels, broken mirrors and glass, lights, photographs and motorized umbrellas. Then in a kind of shamanic ritual I incorporated my own naked body into the constructions—putting paint, grease and chalk on myself. At one point I had live snakes crawling over my body! Only later did I realize the affinity of this to the famous statue of a Cretan goddess whose body is decorated with serpents.

♦ **AJ: Your performances show your own life—**

♦ CS: But I mistrust intensely whatever you might call your "own life" because whatever it is, it might already be colonized by principles and aesthetic ideals that society offers you. So my work has to do with cutting through the idealized (mostly male) mythology of the "abstracted self" or the "invented self"—i.e., work involving another kind of glorification/falsification where you direct *someone else* to do an act you wouldn't do yourself . . . so you retain power and distancing over the situation. In my work in performance and film, nothing happens that I haven't first tried myself—usually with a lot of fear and uncertainty, because I *need* risk—I need to push my own boundaries.

♦ **AJ: Your book, *More Than Meat Joy* (1977) seems so contemporary, although it includes writings from the 1960's—**

♦ CS: We live in a *culture of oblivion* that perpetrates a kind of *self-induced denial* in which the meaning of the recent past is continually lost or distorted . . . much like feminist history was always lost or distorted. The cultural history each generation creates is immediately turned into waste: "That's *old shit!*" Whereas my work is addressing issues involving 3000 years of Western patriarchal imposition. So if I'm fighting with some younger artist about the past 15 years—I'm already suspicious: those are not the right stakes!

My performance "Meat Joy" came from a dream. It was a celebration of the flesh as well as an assault on repressive culture. The performers were untrained, so we

"Meat Joy," 1964   Photo: John Haynes

had to have a lot of rehearsals. It was performed for Jean-Jacques Lebel's "Festival for Free Expression" in Paris and caused a scandal—at the end the performers (who were mostly nude—if they'd been totally nude they would

"Meat Joy," 1964

"Meat Joy," 1964

have been arrested) were smearing each other with dead fish, chicken parts and raw sausages in an absolute frenzy! One man came out of the audience and tried to strangle me, but three older women realized this was not part of the performance and came up and saved me!

◆ **AJ: In *Fuses* you were filming your lovemaking with your partner. What themes were you exploring?**

◆ CS: That's a silent film. One issue was: *the permission to see.* As the daughter of a rural doctor, I grew up seeing first-hand blood and guts and limbs that were chopped off—there was *no editing*—when there's an accident, body parts "you're not supposed to see" are sticking out! Then I worked in animal husbandry where if you're artificially inseminating a cow, you don't put a drape over it or close your eyes and hope that the syringe finds the right spot . . .

As a painter you have to *see.* I always felt there was something in a fruit that was as taboo as genitals were— where the stem comes out. You were never forbidden to look in a concavity or convexity of anything that was animal or mineral or vegetable . . . only *human fractures* were explicit and therefore taboo. So when I made the film of my longtime lover [composer James Tenney] and I lovemaking, basically I wanted to see if the experience

of what I *saw* would have any correspondence to what I *felt*—the intimacy of the lovemaking. It was almost a Heisenbergian dilemma: will the *camera* distort everything? (There was no camera person present.)

In my experience men would rather tear a relationship apart than adjust, adapt and change what needs to be changed in their psyche. They prefer the "heroics" of *evasion*.

The camera brings back very strange hallucinatory imagery, and it's *not real*—its representations are imprinted on this material and then projected. And to imagine that it's "real," and therefore can be censored, seems to me almost a depraved attitude, because it's not real, it's

"Infinity Kisses," 1981-87. Ongoing performance with Carolee's kissing cat.

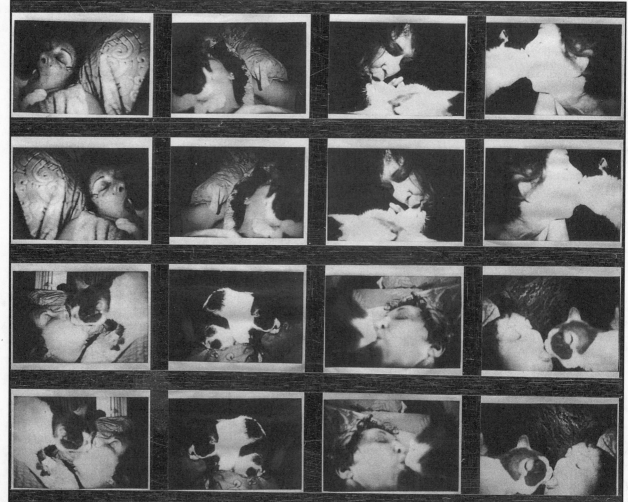

"Axis in Parallel"

Photo: Shelley Farkas

film, and mine in particular is baked, stamped, stained, painted, chopped and reassembled. And I wanted to put into that *materiality* of film the energies of the body, so that the film itself dissolves and recombines and is transparent and dense—like how one feels during lovemaking. Even though the film doesn't fulfill a pornographic expectation in terms of its editing or rhythms or organization, everything *normal*—which is to say everything in heterosexual lovemaking—is there. It is *different* from any pornographic work that you've ever seen—that's why people are still looking at it! And there's no objectification or fetishization of the woman.

◆ **AJ: How did people react?**

◆ CS: Women would come up after a showing and say, "Thank you for restoring me to my whole body; I have always been in some alienation from my own genital self—thank you!" Some people said, "This makes me sick—I want to throw up!" Or, "I don't get a hard-on—this isn't really about sex!" The Jungians discerned the Aphroditean aspects of the "return to water" and "the light streaming from the window" in the house I still live in. And there's also the presence of the cat, Kitch, who in some sense was the medium through which the film evolved—or was it the director?—because it was this cat's pure pleasure, her shameless attention watching us make love, that made me want to see what *she* saw!

I love cats; I had one kissing cat, Cluny (they're very rare). He died, but just recently came back into another carnate form; his name is Vesper. And he's an obsessive kisser. In front of the house there are acres of fields and squirrels and mice, and he'll poke his face out the door, then suddenly think, "*Wait*—I think she's upstairs at the

desk!" and come tearing up the stairs. Then he'll sneak up and perch on my shoulder while I'm typing and suddenly there's this cat tongue in my mouth and I say, "Oh—where did *you* come from? *Vesper!*" and he's purring and his little ears are down and his paws are on my cheek. I have a lot of cat-directed, cat-inspired work. . .

◆ **AJ: How did you develop your performances?**

◆ CS: Performance, for me, developed from the place where I had to extend the principles of painting and construction into *real time*, out of a pressure of imagery

"Up To And Including Her Limits," 1973-76

Photo: Henrik Gaard

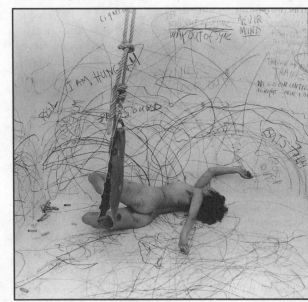

71

"Body Collage," 1968   Photo: Michael Benedikt

built up an incredible momentum and started to turn me, like a pendulum. Suddenly I was in motion—but I hadn't shifted my body or done *anything!* And sometimes it was wickedly fast.

Basically, my work deals with the "sacred erotic" or the "ecstatic." And the body is not injured or terribly stressed—even in its most energetic, intense physicality it's not concerned with deformation or violence or denial of pleasure—the body is enacting something *ecstatic* for me. *That's* where I want to go!

♦ **AJ: Your work involves eroticism, the embracing of the body, whereas Stellarc calls his hanging the "Obsolete Body," the denial of the body—**

♦ CS: Well, *that* has to do with endurance, punishment and fragmentation. Nevertheless, *all* of these approaches are valuable in a society which has denied the intelligence and the primacy of the body. Some artists want to explore guilt, shame, repression or revulsion with the body; I don't choose that role. And this is used against me; critics complain, "Oh, you make it too easy!" or "This is fluffy" or "sensualist" or "regressive" or . . .

♦ **AJ: To dismiss that as "fluffy" indicates sickness in this society—**

♦ CS: Yes, it's still working within the patriarchal constructs but taking them to another degree of suppressiveness, because to the degree it refuses to address the ecstasy of the body, and to the degree to which it denies the particularity of female sexuality and insists that it's a *construct*—well, there's no way that female orgasm is a "construct" for me!

In one performance, "Interior Scroll," [1975] I stood naked in front of the audience, extracted a paper scroll from my vagina and read a text on "Vulvic Space"—about the abstraction of the female body and its loss of meanings. I saw the vagina as a "translucent chamber of which the serpent was an outward model." I related the

and didactic information that could only be vitalized *in that way.* Because the body, taking that energy into immediacy, has a value that static depiction won't carry, representation won't carry—it has to actually be in real time.

When you're submerged in your material you have to have intense concentration; here *entrancement* involves *repetition.* In one trance piece, "Up To and Including Her Limits," I suspended myself in a harness from a rope for 8 hours. I got on the rope when the space opened and when it closed I stopped, so it was like a day's labor frame. And the ecstatic anti-gravitational sensation of being suspended—like floating free in space—required a lot of muscular balance so I didn't tip over or fall down. The concentration was totally on the rope—the harness was very light, very free, but it also required a lot of strength. And this piece had to do with getting rid of intentionality or repetition—trying to change my own *habits.* Because I was a point of weight on this rope which

womb and the vagina to "primary knowledge" by which our woman ancestors measured their menstrual cycles, pregnancies, and lunar observations.

♦ **AJ: That whole mindset which would dismiss your work as "fluffy" would also dismiss environmental concerns: the earth body—**

♦ **CS:** Let's call it "trivial" instead of "fluffy," because even to use the word "fluffy" confuses the issue . . . The dominance of the sex-negative imagination fuels itself on the denial of the body, its denigration, its split from spirit, its split from nature—the whole construct as really a *techno-metaphysics* where the godhead is so strangely devitalized, his form itself is a crucified body that no longer speaks or acts or moves but is filled with genital suppression. You worship this dead genital figuration with its exclusionary propriety of being "male" . . . so that the authenticating source of vitality is a distanced male god, a Holy Ghost, a crucified phallus. And all the female attributes are completely distorted so you get this demented mythology where the god is born from a Virgin [!] or from a god's forehead or from an underarm . . . *anything* that can *usurp* the female primacy!

Not only do we have to live out this male schizophrenia culturally, but we have to live it out in our personal lives. First the truth is sacrificed, then *you're* next. It's a mess—it's sad and wasteful. And the patterns of male self-aggrandizement, low self-esteem and castration fantasies fulfill themselves in endless adventures and penetrations—then *denial* of what they have built up with a partner that might become "coherent." In my experience men would rather tear a relationship apart than adjust, adapt and change what needs to be changed in

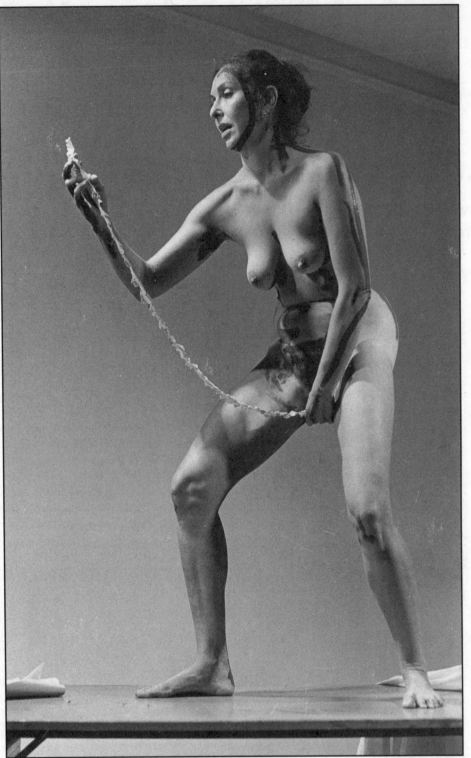

"Interior Scroll," 1975-77

Photo: Anthony McCall

their psyche. They prefer the "heroics" of *evasion*.

♦ **AJ: How do you maintain your relationships with men?**

♦ **CS:** Well, my primary bedrock relationship with the composer/musician James Tenney confirmed and inspired me to take risks, because I had this one loving, comprehending partner who knew what the conceptual and erotic truth was behind the work; we did a lot of parallel intellectual research. And I realized recently that when

"Thames Crawling," London, 1972

I've lost a primary relationship, I usually stop performing. But that's a pattern—I see that now.

♦ **AJ: Is it because the sexuality and eroticism are—**

♦ **CS:** —yes, *energizing.* Also, it means that I can release this energy into the universe without feeling I'm going to be *alone* with the reactions—whether depraved, unpredictable or positive. But now I've been learning that I *have* to do it all alone, because I lost a very loving partnership—he left. And I had a magical inspiring cat—I felt that as long as I had "Cluny" with me I'd be okay—but he died from a rat bite. Then my best friend died; I slit my thumb in half—the list of misfortunes just went on and

"Dirty Pictures," a performance with slide projections

Photo by: Lisa Kahane

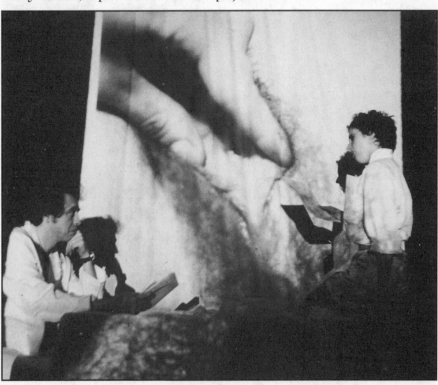

on. But I crawled out of that . . . we're *all* doing it!

It's difficult to find a really intelligent man who shares a commitment to feminist issues and practice, who reads the same material I read . . . someone who knows what's happening with this reinvestigation of "inherited culture."

♦ **AJ: A lot of men just feel guilty and offended by the information—**

♦ **CS:** —as if personally they're responsible . . . or will lose some "self-definition" by dismantling 3000 years of crap. Give us our daily bullshit!

♦ **AJ: This is the first time I know of in history where a large group of women are defining their own roles, their own genitality, their own eroticism, and their own rules—**

♦ **CS:** —and their own language and their own repositioning of lost history. However, some very remarkable, essential feminist research has been done by male scholars. Bram Dijkstra's *Idols of Perversity* is an extraordinary examination of misogynist genitalphobia in the history of the past 100 years of Western painting. There's another book all about the penis, *The Durable Fig Leaf* by Mark Strage, which contains a cultural analysis of the male regard, and depictions and distortions of the penis. And, of course, behind all this is Bachhoven and those early Victorian pioneers who readdressed the aspect of the mythic feminine, and the pioneering examination of misogyny, *The Dangerous Sex* by H.R. Hayes.

♦ **AJ: Do you read theorists such as Derrida?**

♦ **CS:** I find him femalephobic also, with a very elaborate "re-construction" which involves repossession . . . a way to dominate and reincorporate the female principle. Baudrillard is equally creepy! Lacan, Freud, Jung, Engels— they all have to be subjected to a more thorough analysis. Derrida's language is exclusively male: he only has one pronoun!

♦ **AJ: You've tried to truly remake your language—**

♦ **CS:** I've fought about language from the beginning—what I called the "Missing Pronoun" and the "Missing Genital." In college back in the '60s I wanted to study Simone de Beauvoir in philosophy class. And my teacher was a very gracious, charming Southern gentleman who said, "Why Carolee, you don't want to study the writings of the *mistress;* you want to study the writings of the *Master.* You can read Sartre." And it was the same with wanting to study Woolf—no, you could read Proust, Joyce, Mann, or Kafka! For me, unearthing the female mind has really inspired the use and meaning of "the body." I research non-Western cultures to establish connection to other forms of depiction of the body.

♦ **AJ: Art is not divorced and alienated from life; when exteriorized in performance it can become a healing for the audience or the society—**

♦ CS: A healing or a shock; an imposition; a slicing. The healing may be slower but sometimes there's a glimpse of feelings and conceptual connections that take off . . .

♦ **AJ: Who else was influential in your life?**

♦ CS: When I was four years old, my Scottish nanny would wake me up at 4 AM and take me to a window where we would look at the moon. She taught me to study it and to pray to it, so that my grandfather, who had recently died, would appear and speak to me. She taught

me things I never forgot, such as: I was only half a soul, and that there was a little boy who was my other half wandering somewhere in the world, and we would find each other. And she told me about herding sheep in Scotland with her brothers—they would sleep out in the open huddled next to the bodies of the sheep when it was cold, and eat dried meat and cheese—that freedom and connection with the "animal self" seemed so clear and

"Is this what you're so scared of: this moist pussy? Is *this* the Terrifying Other—the clitoris that has to be excised or chopped off or rendered mute?"

appropriate to me. And she taught me my first Zen joke: "Do you know what's inside your knuckles? Little nuggets of gold!" So if you're ever all alone in the world and feel helpless, you can get a hammer, crack open your knuckles and retrieve that gold. What a dilemma!

Carolee directing the film *Water Light / Water Needle*, 1966

Photo: Chris Buck

told about this Gulf War were psychotic.

♦ **AJ: To have any awareness, man or woman, you can't help but be, to some degree, angry.**

♦ CS: That courage derived from righteous energized anger; it was part of the energy to change things—to challenge the closed suffocating forms . . . Now the goddesses are back and no one knows what to do with them! And we ask, "Is this what you're so scared of: this moist pussy? Is *this* the Terrifying Other — the clitoris that has to be excised or chopped off or rendered mute?"

♦ **AJ: Back in the '60s, you had a whole generation of women that needed—**

♦ CS: —to masculinize and neutralize . . . but now in San Francisco women are *adorning*—I've never seen so many amazing earrings.

♦ **AJ: You did an incredible performance recently—**

♦ CS: —based on the "vaginal orgasm": that suffusing, intense energy. I've read a lot of descriptions of orgasms, and some women will say, "The vagina was sensitive enough." Different women have different physicalities; if you don't have vaginal orgasms you might think it's an invention or a lie or another masculinized deformation. The clitoris really *isn't* a correlative to the male, because the male orgasm is so propulsive, intensive, with tremendous acceleration. Whereas the clitoris is really a very subtle, delicate organ. The idea that it's like a penis is wrong; male and female genitals are *not* homologous.

♦ **AJ: You did a political performance, "Snows," which was based on the Vietnam War—**

♦ CS: I've done another work on the destruction of Palestinian culture in Lebanon, which displays a series of paintings and a sculpture with a video, "War Mop." It's

♦ **AJ: That's a devilish one . . . You made the observation that women probably made most of the early artifacts that have been discovered—**

♦ CS: I assume those ancient "goddess" figurines were made by women.

♦ **AJ: You also wrote that women need a base of strength, self-confidence and validated achievement to have a directed anger—**

♦ CS: Well, *rage* and *humor* are two of the reins—I don't want to let go of either one! They fuel your ability to take the next step; they advance you. We have a tremendous base of outrage: all the lies and destruction

76

an ordinary mop moved by elegant plastic gears; it slaps a video monitor every 10 seconds. On the monitor is a very seductive pan through this village that looks vaguely like Santa Barbara, with a shimmering sea off to the left . . . then there's all these *smithereens:* fragments of colored glass, wrought iron and ancient stone . . . and then it pans down a totally desolate road with some burnt-out automobiles into the house of a Palestinian woman who's screaming at the camera—her living room is behind her, and it almost looks normal until you see birds fly through it, and you realize it's been bombed apart—half of it's intact, and the rest is gone! There's a lamp and a bookshelf and a sofa there, but no walls.

I studied the history of Lebanon, the history of the Palestinians, and charted day-by-day the systematic destruction by the Israelis. I went to the Lebanese tourist bureau the day before it closed and they gave me all their touristic slides of people weaving nets, making pottery, fishing, skiing, swimming . . . I had all this "before-and-after" material in my hands, and then did this slide lecture which was the most despised piece I ever did—people just did not want to acknowledge this information. Because Lebanon really had no equal armaments, no sophisticated defense systems, no air force!

The Gulf War was so carefully calculated and the news such a video masquerade that—I can't deal with it. And it's no accident that the most technological, milita-ristic Western "culture" was destroying all these ancient goddess sites with no overt consciousness that *this* was being obliterated. We don't know if the Hanging Gardens of Babylon or the Gate of Ishtar, the largest ceramic arch in civilization, still exist. Key archeological sites are in areas that our tanks moved through.

♦ **AJ: You said this war is too much for you—**

♦ **CS:** It's a phallocentric mania, it's psychotic, and the language of this war has all been about "creaming them, surrounding and killing them, pounding them relentlessly" . . . it's the jerk-off language of men who can never cum. It's like a gang-bang, an endless rape with the heaviest battering ram, the battering cock.

♦ **AJ: Someone sent me a newspaper clipping claiming that Air Force pilots were being shown porno films prior to the bombings—**

♦ **CS:** —A displacement whereby orgasmic energy becomes pure destructive energy.

♦ **AJ: It's thought there may be as many as 300,000 Iraqis dead, yet this has been referred to as a "bloodless" war using "surgical" air strikes.**

♦ **CS:** Well, now they're saying they overestimated the damage . . . it's all just one confabulation after another. The few bizarre reports that come through are so horrific: blasting away at thousands of camels because they saw "something" moving and didn't know what it was, so they *obliterated* it . . . There's just that increasing degree of *technological abstraction,* so you have no vision of what you're affecting—no concept, no vision, no contact.♦ ♦ ♦

Photo: Chris Buck

Books

Early & Recent Work. NY: McPherson/Documentext, 1983.

More Than Meat Joy: Complete Performance Works & Selected Writings, NY: McPherson/Documentext, 1979. 280pp, illus.

Cézanne, She Was a Great Painter. NY, Trespass Press, 1976.

200 Mattresses. Catalog, Wash, DC, 1975.

Parts of a Body House Book. Devon, UK: Beau Geste Press, 1972.

Numerous interviews & articles have appeared in periodicals such as *Interview; Act: Journal of Performance Art; Performance; Red Bass; Heresies 23; Theater in Sight; Enclitic* (USC); *Exquisite Corpse; Guardian (London); Millenium Film Journal; Afterimage 7; Performing Arts Journal; Ear Magazine;* and in books such as *Notations* by John Cage; *Fantastic Architecture* (eds. D. Higgins & W. Vostell); *Theater of the Female Body* (ed. Dianne Hunter); *Esthetics Contemporary* (edited by Richard Kostelanetz); *A Critical Cinema* (intv by Scott MacDonald); *Down and In: Life in the Underground* by Ronald Sukenick; *P.S.1 Catalog, 1983,* etc.

bell hooks

bell hooks has pushed feminist theory to new limits in her writing—integrating postmodern speculations, cultural criticism, neglected literature and autobiographical disclosure. Slashing the superficial platitudes which typify these *ahistorical* times, she calmly and dispassionately revises "politically correct" views on issues such as racism, male supremacy, and female separatism. Seeking the broadest possible philosophical base for reforming our nihilistic, terrorized world, she has written, "There is such a perfect union between the spiritual quest for awareness, enlightenment, self-realization—and the struggle of oppressed, colonized people to *change* our circumstances, to *resist.* . . We must focus on the importance of domination and oppression in *all its forms* in our lives if we are to *recover ourselves.* Resisting oppression means more than just reacting against one's oppressors—it means envisioning new habits of being, different ways to live in the world. And I believe *true resistance begins with people confronting pain*—whether it's theirs or somebody else's—*and wanting to do something to change it.*"

A professor at Oberlin College as well as a writer, *bell hooks* has published *Ain't I a Woman: Black Women and Feminism; Feminist Theory: From Margin to Center; Talking Back: Thinking Feminist, Thinking Black;* and *Yearning: Race, Gender and Cultural Politics* (available from South End Press, PO Box 741, Monroe ME 04951. 1-800-533-8478). She has written numerous essays, plays, novels, short stories, poems, and regularly contributes a bi-monthly column, "Sisters of the Yam" to "Z" magazine.

Part I

◆ ANDREA JUNO: How did your childhood lead you to your present position: fighting political, racist and sexist oppression?

◆ bell hooks: Well, it's funny—I've been trying to assemble a collection of essays that are both autobiographical and critical about *death*. Because when I think about my childhood—the kind of early experiences (or what I think of as imprints) that have led me to be who I am today, they really revolve around the death of my father, mother, sister. . . In our work we use autobiographical experience from our childhood. I wrote this detective novel entitled *Sister Ray* (my grandmother's name is Rachel, and that's the name of the detective) and a childhood

event I really remember was: my grandmother dying in the bedroom next to mine. My mother put all of us children to bed (allegedly "to take a nap") because she did not want us to *know.* So there was this incredible air of mystery about this, and I for one was *not* going to go to sleep. . .

I got to witness the men from the funeral home coming in with the stretcher, and—it's funny, but one of the things I deeply remember is the way they *smelled*—and to this day I have trouble with men who wear sweet colognes. But the most amazing thing was watching my mother closing my grandmother's eyes. Because I saw this and thought, "Wow—if this is death and it can be looked at and faced, then I can do *anything* I want to in life! Nothing is going to be more profound than this moment!" And I see this as *a moment in time that shaped who I became* . . . that allowed me to be the rebellious child I was—daring and risk-taking in the midst of my parents' attempts to control me.

♦ **AJ: They thought they could control death by keeping it hidden—**

♦ bh: Absolutely. It's interesting to me that this intercession of death and the death of a *foremother* (the women who go before us) is tied to my development as an independent, autonomous woman. My father's mother lived alone; she was a powerful figure. And I talk a lot with other women about our experiences as women working to be artists—and in my own case, working not only as an artist but as a cultural critic/intellectual in a world that still isn't ready for us . . . that still hasn't adapted to who we *are*.

♦ **AJ: We're all struggling to make these parts fit together into a whole. Your writing is not only philosophical and theoretical but also informed by your personal life. One of the barriers we're trying to break down is that artificial separation between the so-called "objective" and the "subjective," the personal and the political—**

♦ bh: People have written to me about my new book (*Yearning: Race, Gender and Cultural Politics*) saying, "It's such a heartbreaking book . . . it's so sad." I think that a lot of what's going on in my work is a kind of *theorizing through autobiography* or through storytelling. My work is almost a psychoanalytical project that also takes place in the realm of what one might call "performance"—a lot of my life has *been* a performance, in a way.

In an essay I wrote about Jennie Livingston's film *Paris Is Burning*, which is about black drag balls in Harlem, I reminisced about myself cross-dressing years ago. I was thinking about this as a kind of re-enactment of a

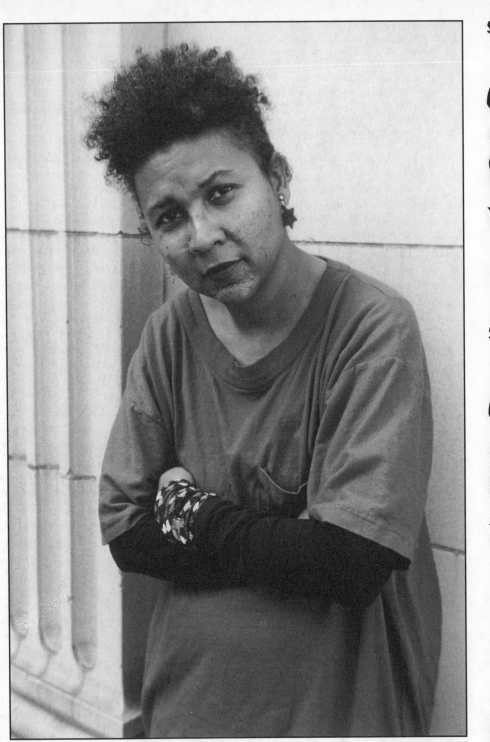

Photo: Jane Handel

past performance, but it's also a moment of autobiographical sharing that is a kind of *stepping out:*

"There was a time in my life when I liked to dress up as a man and go out into the world. It was a form of ritual, of play. It was also about power. To cross-dress as a woman in patriarchy meant, more so than now, to symbolically cross from the world of powerlessness to a world of privilege. It was the ultimate intimate voyeuristic gesture.

"Searching old journals for passages documenting that time I found this paragraph: 'She pleaded with him: "Just once—well every now and then—I just want us to be boys together. I want to dress like

79

you and go out and make the world look at us differently and make them wonder about us, make them stare and ask those silly questions like, 'Is he a woman dressed up like a man? Is he an older black gay man with his effeminate boy/girl/lover flaunting same-sex out in the open?' Don't worry, I'll take it all very seriously. I won't let them laugh at you. I'll make it real 'Keep them guessing' . . . do it in such a way that they will never know *for sure*. Don't worry; when we come home I'll be a girl for you again. But for now, I want us to be boys together."

Then I wrote that "Cross-dressing, appearing in drag, transsexualism, are all choices that emerge in a context where the notion of subjectivity is challenged . . . where identity is always perceived as capable of construction, invention, change."

I was thinking about this a lot, because today, even before we can have a contemporary feminist movement or a discourse on postmodernism, we have to consider "positionalities" that are shaking up the idea that any of us are inherently *anything*—that we *become* who we are. So a lot of my work views the confessional moment as a transformative moment—a moment of *performance* where you might step out of the fixed identity in which you were seen, and reveal other aspects of the self . . . as part of an overall project of *more fully becoming who you* are.

There was a time when I liked to dress up as a man and go out into the world . . . to symbolically cross from the world of *powerlessness* to the world of *privilege*.

♦ **AJ: This is very important. You write about how separatism or exclusionism really reinforces the older patriarchical hierarchy—therefore we need to analyze all the processes of separation operating within the black community, the women's community, etc. You're talking about reintegration with a whole new set of rules—**

♦ bh: —as well as a different vision of *expansionism* (and not that *imperialist* expansionism that was about, "Let's go out and annex more land and conquer some more people!") but about allowing the self to grow. I think of Sam Keen's popular book, *The Passionate Life: Stages of Loving*, which declares that one wants to grow into a passionate human being, and that to some extent having fixed boundaries does not allow that kind of growth.

I really shudder when people tell me, "I only want to associate with [this little crowd]," because I think, "Well, what if what you really need in life is over there in another group? Or in another location?" It's interesting: the way in which one has to balance life: because you

have to know when to let go and when to pull back—the answer is never just to completely "let go" or "transgress," but neither is it to always "contain yourself" or "repress." There's always some *liminal* [as opposed to subliminal] space *in between* which is harder to inhabit—because it never feels as safe as moving from one extreme to another.

♦ **AJ: There are lots of paradoxes to deal with; where are our *lack* of differences?! In a "*Z*" magazine article [reprinted after interview] you wrote about seeing your father beat up your mother—can you talk about that, and your feelings of murderous rage and terror mingled together?**

♦ bh: It's funny—when you reminded me of that I felt really "exposed." I know that my mother and father don't read "*Z*" and would probably never read it unless someone sent it to them, but they would be very devastated and hurt that I was exposing something about their private life to the public. At the same time I deeply needed to express something, I was also frightened by the kind of "construction of difference" that makes it appear that there is some space of rage and anger that *men* inhabit, that is alien to us *women*. Even though we know that men's rage may take the form of murder (we certainly know that men murder women more than women murder men; that men commit most of the domestic violence in our lives), it's easy to slip into imagining that those are "male" spaces, rather than ask the question, "What do we *as women* do with our rage?"

I've found that most children who have witnessed parental fighting (where a man has hurt or hit a woman) identify with the woman/victim when they retell the event(s). And I was struck that what *I* didn't want to retell was the fact that I didn't just identify with my mother as the person being hurt, but I identified with my *father* as the hurting person, and wanted to be able to really hurt *him!* My play daughter (who's an incest survivor) and I were talking about this recently—

♦ **AJ: What do you mean by "play daughter"?**

♦ bh: When I was growing up, that was a term used in Southern black life for informal adoptions. Let's say you didn't have any children and your neighbor had 8 kids. You might negotiate with her to adopt a child, who would then come live with you, but there would never be any kind of *formal* adoption—yet everybody would recognize her as your "play daughter." My community was unusual in that gay black men also were able to informally adopt children. And in this case there was a kinship structure in the community where people would go home and visit their folks if they wanted to, stay with them (or what have you), but they would also be able to stay with the person who was loving and parenting them.

In my case I met this young woman, Tanya, years ago when I was giving a talk, and I felt that she really needed a mother. At the time I was really grappling with the question, "Do I want to have a child or not?" And I said, "Come on into my life; I need a child and you seem to need a mother!" And we've had a wonderful relationship; I've watched her become more fully who she's meant to *be* in this world. From her talking about the experience of incest, a theory emerged: if you were in some traumatic moment where you felt a particular emotion, and then you repressed that emotion (let's say, for 10 years), and didn't allow yourself to feel anything . . . then, when you open the door to those emotions you've closed off, you *still* have to work through that last emotion you were feeling. In other words, this is not like some other kind of emotional *coming out*—it's like: you've made that emotion incubate by locking it away, so when you reopen those doors, the emotion that first emerges is *monstrous*—

◆ **AJ: Like facing "the belly of the beast"; facing incredible rage—**

◆ bh: Absolutely. I still think men have not fully named and grappled with the *sorrows of boyhood* in the way feminism gave us as women ways to name some of the tragedies of *our* "growhood" in sexist society. I think males are just beginning to develop a language to name some of the tragedies for *them*—to express what was denied them. If I imagine myself as a boy witnessing the grown father hitting the mother—well, what "positionality" does the boy feel himself to be in? Clearly he doesn't think, "I'm going to grow up to be a woman who will be hit." So does he then have to fear: "I will grow up to be this person who hits—therefore I'd better live my life in such a way that *I never grow up*"? Like a lot of women, I feel that I've loved men who made that decision to never grow up "because then I'll become that monstrous *Other*." I think that's why so many men in our culture don't allow those doors to ever be opened: because there's *something* in the experience of boyhood they witnessed—

◆ **AJ: —which is just too traumatic . . . Beyond merely polarizing the men as "victimizers" and leaving it at that, we have to recognize that men are just as crippled as women. What's very liberating here is the whole notion of not identifying with victimization— that there could be an empowerment if you would just *feel* that rage, instead of merely shutting down and being victimized—**

◆ bh: In Toni Morrison's *The Bluest Eye* (one of my favorite novels), there's a moment when the little girl, a victim of rape/incest, says to another little girl whom she wants to be angry, "Anger is *better*—there is a *presence* in anger." I was always moved by that contrasting of victimization vs. being victimized; it's important to maintain the kind of rage that allows you to *resist*.

◆ **AJ: Yes. When I was a young girl I was petrified of horror films, particularly the psycho/slasher ones, and I'd even have dreams that they were "coming to get me." So I'd force myself to watch *Halloween*-type films where usually a male figure kills hundreds of women (or men, whatever). And I decided to try to identify with that male . . . and it gave me such a sense of power. Of course this is in the "safe" area of creative expression (film)—so it isn't like I'm going to go around killing people! But there was this incredible**

sense of empowerment when I realized I didn't *have* to identify with the victim—

◆ bh: Certain feminist writings by lesbian women on SM discuss what role playing is in terms of power. A woman can take on ritualized role playing in terms of *confronting a dragon*, and realize that in the *confrontation* of that dragon (through the role playing), it no longer has power over you. I think it's been really hard for some feminists to "hear" that the ritualized role playing in eroticism and sexuality can be *empowering* . . . because there's such a moralistic tendency to only see it as a *disempowering* reenactment of the patriarchy's sexual politics. Whereas: in all forms of ritual and role playing, if it is empowering and if one is truly only engaged in play acting, so to speak, there's the possibility of re-enacting the drama of something that terrifies you . . . of working symbolically through it in a way that touches back on your *real* life, so that ultimately you *are* more empowered.

> I still think men have not fully named and grappled with the *sorrows of boyhood* in the way feminism gave us as women ways to name some of the tragedies of *our* "growhood" in sexist society.

◆ **AJ: I think that so many women really need to do this: confront those fears.**

◆ bh: In an essay on the construction of "whiteness" in the black imagination, I wrote about black people really being fearful of white people, and how it's really become a cliche or a "no-no" to talk about having that fear. I gave this paper recently at a university, and a young black man who was my host said that my paper really disturbed him—finally he had realized that he really *did* feel a certain fear of white people, without ever having thought about (or faced) that fact.

In our culture, black men are constructed as such a *threat*: they can pose on the street corner or on the street as people who are in power, in control. And the culture doesn't ever give black men a space where they can say, "Yes—*actually* I feel *scared* when I see white people coming toward me." When we think of an incident like Howard Beach [where a mob of whites killed a young black man who had "invaded" their neighborhood], we recognize that here were these black men who were not positioned in people's minds as being potentially afraid— that it might be *scary* for 3 black men to be in the space of dominating whiteness. Instead, all the fear was projected onto *them* as objects of threat, rather than as people who might inhabit a space of fear. . .

There was a whole controversy around the fact that

these men said that they wanted to use a telephone, and that they passed by a number of phones (which is what the opposition cited to prove that they weren't really being "honest"), and yet there's no suggestion that maybe they bypassed a number of phones because they were looking for a location in which they would feel greater safety. We have so little understanding about how black people fear white people in daily life. . .

Recently I was staying in New York. Sometimes I would get in the elevator and then see a white person approaching—so I'd try to hold the elevator . . . and most times they would brush me away! I would just be amazed at the idea that possibly they were afraid to go up in the elevator with me because I was black. And I thought about how afraid I am to go up in elevators with white people.

A woman can take on ritualized role playing in terms of *confronting a dragon,* and realize that in the *confrontation,* it no longer has power over you. It's been really hard for some feminists to "hear" that the ritualized role playing in eroticism and sexuality can be *empowering* . . .

◆ AJ: **Well, in a way blacks and other people of color become the disembodied shadows of the power structure; they symbolize the guilt the power structure can't acknowledge that is then projected on to them as fear.**

◆ bh: And I think it's really dangerous for us if we internalize those projections, because it means (and I think this has particularly been the case for black men) that we then shut off those areas of vulnerability in ourselves. It's a kind of defense to imitate those who have wounded you, because: to the degree that you become them, you imagine you are *safe.* (Or rather: to the degree that you become the way they *say* you should be, you imagine you are safe.) So I try to talk about the process of "assimilation" as a kind of mask, as an amulet almost, whereby you feel, "I can ward off the evil of this by becoming it, or by appearing to be it." It's a kind of *camouflage.*

◆ AJ: **Can you give an example?**

◆ bh: When I enter a room where other black people are present, I might want to speak to another black person and acknowledge them—and that person might look away as if to say, "Don't think that just because we're black we have something in common." To some extent that person has decided to imitate the behavior of

the larger white culture that says, "Color is not important . . . don't use *that* as a basis for bonding." And the fact is: the person may imagine that by adopting that behavior they're safer, they're more *part of the group* . . . when in fact we know that they're not necessarily safer, and that their safety might actually come from bonding with the other person of color.

I think the same can be said of women who enter spheres of power, and who feel, "It's important for me never to show bonding or allegiance to another woman, because that will show I'm weak." Whereas the irony is: we're more strengthened when we can show the self-love expressed through bonding with those who are like ourselves.

◆ AJ: **It's always threatening to the male power structure when women get together and are friends.**

◆ bh: And I think right now we're at a historical moment when we all have to talk about, "How can I be bonded with other black people in a way that is not constructed to be oppressive or exclusionary to other people?" I think that this can be viewed as a *magical moment:* "What does it mean to try to affirm someone, without excluding somebody else?"

I just gave a talk at Barnard College in front of a large audience, and a black woman came in late who seemed somewhat distressed. I wanted to reach out to her and say, "Hey, you're really welcome here, I'm glad to see you!" (and I always think about: "How do you do that in such a way that you don't make other people feel that somehow her presence is more important than anybody else's?" because it isn't—all the presences are important. So I always try to give off a real aura of warmth and welcome to everyone.) When she came in, I walked over and stuck out my hand to her and . . . I got this sweet letter from her saying that this action meant so much to her: "I was stunned by the spontaneous lovingness of the gesture you made toward me. It will take some time before I fully internalize the lessons of relatedness and sisterhood it showed me."

Part of what I try to express in my work is that racism, sexism, homophobia and all these things really wound us in a profound way. Practically everybody acknowledges that incest is wounding to the victim, but people don't want to acknowledge that racism and sexism are wounding in ways that make it equally hard to function as a Self in everyday life. And . . . something like having a person reach out to you with warmth can just be healing. . .

◆ AJ: **I think a lot of people need integrating philosophies now. Things are so alienated, fascistic and polarized—it's very sad that we're all sort of "Displaced Others". . . . Everyone who really wants to change the world needs so much to be bonded together with our differences, instead of separated.**

◆ bh: That was one of the ideas I tried to express when I chose *Yearning* as a book title. At dinner last night when I looked around me across differences, I wondered, "What is uniting us?" All of us across our different experiences were expressing this longing, this deep and profound yearning, to just have this domination *end*. And what I feel unites you and me is: we can locate in one another a similar yearning to be in a more *just* world. So I tried to evoke the idea that if we could come together in that site of desire and longing, it might be a potential place for community-building. Rather than thinking we would come together as "women" in an identity-based bonding, we might be drawn together rather by a *commonality of feeling*. I think that's a real challenge for us now: to think about constructing community on different *bases*.

Eunice Lipton, a woman art historian, said, "What would it mean for us to look at biography not from the standpoint of people's accomplishments, but from what people *desired*." I thought, "Wow—what a different way to conceptualize life and the *value* of life." Again, this goes away from the imperialist model where you're thinking of life in terms of "who or what you have conquered," toward: "what you have actualized *within* yourself?" So her question concerned: "What if biography were to tell about *desire*, not achievement—then how would we tell a woman's life?" I think that's really powerful.

◆ **AJ: Our identities are so constructed that you hit a brick wall if you attempt to say what women "are," because one can always think of exceptions. All constructed identities such as "Black" or "Chicano" are sort of negative identities against the world of white Wasp "ideals." For many women, what bonds us is: what is *against* us.**

◆ bh: Right, and that's not enough to build community upon—one has to build community on much deeper bases than "in reaction to." You heard about the Korean woman shopkeeper and the young black woman she murdered? In Los Angeles, this woman came into the store, took some juice and put it in her backpack, then held out the money to pay for it and was shot to death by the shopkeeper (who claimed she was being attacked). But when the video was replayed, people could see clearly that she was *not* being attacked. And this can become the way relations between Korean/Asian women and black women are projected. Those of us who have had very different kinds of relations (where we've learned about one another's cultures) haven't been vocal enough to propagate a representation that counters this—so that we see it for the individual moment of madness it is, rather than a representation of Black/Asian relations.

When Trinh T. Minh-ha [Vietnamese author/theorist] and I come together in love and solidarity, it's usually in private spaces—in our houses, where we talk about what we share, the cultures we come from and ways they intersect. And one challenge I put forth is: it's no longer enough for us to do that—we need to also come out of those houses and name our solidarities *publicly* with one another.

I became fascinated by how a lot of the stereotypes for Asian women ("passive," "non-assertive," "quiet") are just the opposite of the stereotypes that plague black women ("aggressive," "loud," "mean"). It's like we exist in 2 radically different poles in the economy of racism.

And it's those positionings that make it hard for Asian women and black women to come together . . . but I think we have to be more *public* in naming the ways that we dare to cross those boundaries and come together.

Black men are constructed as such a *threat:* they can pose on the street as people who are in power, in control. Yet the culture doesn't ever give black men a space where they can say, "Yes—*actually* I feel *scared* when I see white people coming toward me."

◆ **AJ: Right. Wanda Coleman said that when she goes to a party and is the only black woman there, suddenly she has the burden of being the "representative of black culture," particularly with well-meaning "liberal" types, and that this was exhausting—she just wanted to have a *good time!***

◆ bh: Right—you may think of race as just one facet of "who they are," but that facet doesn't mean they inherently know the "collectivity"! I went to a dinner party where a young white woman who seemed to be an admirer of my work wanted to sit next to me . . . but immediately she said, "I'm having problems with my black woman roommate, and I just wanted to know if you could tell me why she's behaving this way?" I replied, "You know—if you wanted to know about Buddhism, would you grab the first Buddhist priest you met and say, 'Really tell me all about it in the space of a half hour'?"

I think that often, when it comes to race or meaning *across* difference, people just lose their rational capacity to know how to approach something—I think a lot of white people give up their *power of knowing*. As soon as I said that to this young woman, she knew she should learn more about black culture and black history herself—not think she should go to some other black person to solve this problem. I asked her, "Why would I understand this situation better than you, when you're in it?" But on her part there was this whole sense of: "As a white woman, I couldn't possibly understand what a black woman is going through," when in fact (as Thich Nhat Hanh says) understanding comes through our capacity to empty out the self and identify with that person whom we normally make the Other. In other words, the moment we are willing to give up our own ego and draw in the being and presence of someone else, we're no longer "Other-ing" them, because we are saying there's no space they inhabit that cannot be a space we can connect with.

◆ **AJ: These days relationships are so superficial, cliched, and stereotyped . . . but if anyone really talks**

to somebody, after 10 minutes one forgets or loses one's self in that other person's emotions—

♦ bh: When people ask, "How do we deal with difference?" I always refer them back to what it means to fall in love, because most of us have had an experience of desire and loving. I often say to people, "What do you do when you meet somebody and are attracted to them? How do you go about making that communication? Why do you think that wanting to know someone who's 'racially' different doesn't have a similar procedure?" It's like: if I saw you on the street and thought you were cute, and I happened to know someone who knew you, I might say to that person, "Oh wow, I think so-and-so's *cute*. What do you know about them?" I think that often the empowering strategies we use in the arena of love and friendship are immediately dropped when we come into the arena of *politicized difference*—when in fact some of those strategies are useful and *necessary*.

I mean—how many of us run up to somebody we are attracted to and say [breathlessly], "Tell me all about yourself right away." We usually try to *feel out* the situation. We don't want to alienate that person; we want to approach them in a manner that allows them to be open to us . . . giving to us. I think it's interesting that often when *difference* is there (like a racial difference or something), people *panic* and do crazy, bizarre things . . . or say crazy, stupid things.

♦ AJ: Within any politicized group that is formulating a platform for social change (claiming "gayness" or "political correctness")—well, what does that really mean? For example, if you're in ACT UP, you can have less in common with a Republican gay than with a "straight" political anarchist—

♦ bh: Absolutely. I said something similar about the film *Paris Is Burning:* even though the subject matter *appears* "radical," it doesn't necessarily *mean* it's radical. Just to portray marginalized black gay subculture is not necessarily to be giving a portrait of subversion and oppositional life. One has to question more deeply what authentic terms of opposition might mean for any of us in our lives.

♦ AJ: Particularly in this society which has appropriated all the forms of rebellion . . . where you have Lee Atwater playing the blues—

♦ bh: Absolutely. My friend Carol Gregory made a video of Lee Atwater [now-deceased campaign manager for George Bush, responsible for the blatantly racist Willie Horton commercial], which contrasts him talking about how *much* he loved black music, with examples of the political racism he generated. The separation was so intense. . .

♦ AJ: He fomented the most flagrant racism—

♦ bh: Yes. She said, "This is what's so tragic . . . that he was not able to allow his fascination with black music to alter his perceptions of race." This also reminds us how easily we can appropriate and commodify an aspect of a people's culture without allowing any personal transformation to take place—I mean, he was *not* transformed

by his involvement in black music! A lot of what's happening now with Madonna and black culture is also raising those kinds of questions.

♦ AJ: When I saw Lee Atwater with Chuck Berry, there was such an implied colonialism—a certain "slumming" quality as he was "playing the blues" with these black musicians. You felt that the power structure had not been breached whatsoever.

♦ bh: And yet, when I read recently of his death from a brain tumor, I kept wondering as to what extent his inhabiting that *schizophrenic positionality* had affected his physiological well-being—

♦ AJ: When he found out he had brain cancer, apparently he had a genuine realization that he was going to die, and tried to apologize to all the people he had hurt.

♦ bh: One of the myths of racism in this society and patriarchy is: "Those who oppress, do not suffer in any way." Yet if we just look closely, we see that this—the most materially luxurious country on the planet—is beset by all forms of disease and ill health. This in itself is such an *interrogation* of the price people have had to pay for what has been taken in conquest.

Racism, sexism, and homophobia wound us in a profound way. Everybody acknowledges that incest is wounding, but people don't acknowledge that racism and sexism are wounding in ways that make it equally hard to function as a Self in everyday life.

♦ AJ: And people are so profoundly lonely. I saw this commercial that struck me like a brick—about a hospital outreach program for alcoholism, drug abuse or addiction in general. It cited this statistic: "One out of four people will have a mental breakdown." I thought: "What a claim for this society!"

♦ bh: And of course we never know about black people or people of color who are breaking down (in some way or another) every day, because the political forces we contend with in everyday life are so grave that they render us helpless. There's no way to even chart those breaking-downs, those dysfunctionalities, those moments when people just feel like—as black woman law professor Patricia Williams wrote in an essay, "There are days where I *just don't know* . . . I look at myself in a shop window and I think, 'Is this crazed human being *me?*' I don't know who I am." And she talks about how all the effort it takes—the forces involved in just *dealing* with sexism and racism and all those things—can just destroy our sense of grounding.

◆ **AJ: You were talking about black women professors and hair loss?**

◆ bh: It's interesting that while a lot of professional black women in this society have achieved a great deal, a major factor undermining that achievement is stress. One of the things about stress as a response to racism, homophobia, sexism . . . is that it's not something you can chart. I think about a black woman in a high-powered job who may be losing her hair—she may start wearing scarves or hats and nobody sees that—nobody registers the crisis she may be in. But it may be made visible by all kinds of physiological breakdowns that are happening to her.

◆ **AJ: In the nuclear family structure, dysfunction is intrinsic. Women in the '40s and '50s were always having "nervous breakdowns"—that was part of the "culture"—**

◆ bh: In her film, *Privilege*, Yvonne Rainer shows how the white medical establishment dealt with menopause and how women were constructed as hysterical, sick, breaking-down human beings. She also ties that to: how we look at race and difference.

◆ **AJ: As a response to this society which is so unhealthy, anyone with any sensitivity at all has to embody *some* form of madness—**

◆ bh: Absolutely, and I've written a lot about the necessity for black people to *decolonize our minds*. One of the things that happens when you decolonize your mind is that it becomes hard to function in the society, because you're no longer behaving in ways people feel comfortable with. For example, white people are often much more comfortable with a black person who doesn't ask any direct questions, who acts like they don't know anything—who appears *dumb*, in the same way that men are often more comfortable with a woman who doesn't appear to have knowledge, strength, power, or what have you—who assumes a positionality of [timidly], "Oh I don't know what I'm doing." And when that person becomes empowered, it can totally freak out the people that they're with, and around, and work for.

On the other hand, when you begin to move out of the dysfunctionality (as we know from our movements of recovery) . . . when you begin to change toward health in a dysfunctional setting, it becomes almost impossible to remain in that setting . . . yet here we are in a whole dysfunctional society with *nowhere to go!* [laughs] So I feel that we have to create what Thich Nhat Hanh calls "communities of resistance"—so that there are places where we can recover, and return to ourselves more fully.

◆ **AJ: Can you explain this more?**

◆ bh: Well, he's created this village in France called Plum Village. It's a place where different people go and grow things, and live a "mindful" life together. Sometimes I get really distressed by the extent to which we, in the United States, have moved away from the idea of *communities*—of people trying to have *different* world views and value systems. In the '60s there was a lot of focus on such communities, but that sort of died out, and a refocus on the nuclear family emerged.

In fact, the whole focus on "yuppiedom" was really like a public announcement: "If you want to be cool, you'll return to the patriarchal nuclear family!" And we know that small alternative communities of people still exist, but they don't get a lot of attention. If I think about the communities that have gotten a lot of attention from the mass media (such as the Rajneesh town in Oregon), it was always *negative* . . . never attention on shared worship, shared eating of vegetables (and not being meat-eaters), or being peace-loving—*that's* not the attention it got. But whenever something goes wrong—

> **A lot of people took the failures of the '60s as a sign that, "See—you cannot really *make* an alternative space." Whereas I'm convinced that you *can*.**

◆ **AJ: —The media are right there to report it. However, many "alternative" societies in the '60s brought their same dualistic oppressional thinking to their would-be "paradise"—they just inverted it a little, but it became just as oppressive—**

◆ bh: Even then though, the question becomes: "Do you give up on making the beloved community . . . or do you realize that you must make it a different way?" Because I feel what happened was: a lot of people took the failures of the '60s as a sign that, "See—you cannot really *make* an alternative space." Whereas I'm convinced that you *can* . . . if, as you say, you have changed your consciousness and your actions *prior* to trying to create that space.

I think that when we enter those new spaces with the same old negative baggage, then of course we don't produce something new and different in those spaces! It's like—I remember going to this town and working with a number of other black women. I said to them, "We should buy a building together. Why should we all be paying rent to some nasty white landlord?" And they all looked at me and said weird shit like, "Why would we *want* to live in the same space? What about *privacy?*" They raised all these negative issues and I realized, "These people would rather be victimized than think about taking some agency or control over their lives." And all the values that were being raised (such as "privacy" or "individualism") were really myths—I mean, what privacy do we really have? I didn't feel I had any privacy in my little building where my landlady watched my comings and goings like a hawk. I didn't feel I had any autonomous existence there. Because this wasn't a *helpful* watching—it wasn't like someone who cared about me was watching me, wanting my life to be richer and fuller, you know?

◆ AJ: Right—"privacy" in this country is usually just a euphemism for extreme loneliness, alienation and fragmentation—

◆ bh: And privacy becomes a way of saying, "I don't want to have to attend to something outside of myself." So it really becomes a screen for a profound *narcissism*. And people "privilege" this narcissism as though it represents the "good life." A lot of people will say to me, "How can you live in this small town of 8,000? It would just drive me nuts for people to *know* me, and to run into people." And I say, "Well, you know, if you live your life in the open. . ."

I love that pulp book by M. Scott Peck, *The Road Less Traveled*. He has an incredibly fun section on *lying*, where he says that if you are dedicated to truth and you live your life without shame, then you don't really have to care whether your neighbors can see what you're doing . . . I feel I don't really care if people can see how I live, because I *believe* in how I live. I believe that there is beauty, and joy, and much that is worthy of being *witnessed* in how I live. And I consider it a sign of trouble and confusion when I start needing "privacy," or to hide.

I think about how privacy is so connected to a politics of *domination*. I think that's why there's such an emphasis in my work on the *confessional*, because I know that in a way we're never going to end the forms of domination if we're not willing to challenge the notion of *public* and *private* . . . if we're not willing to break down the walls that say, "There should always be this separation between domestic space/intimate space and the world outside." Because, in fact, why shouldn't we have intimacy in the world outside as well?

◆ AJ: I really believe in the idea that people break down the power structure through the confessional . . . that just telling the truth in a society that's based on lies, is a radical act—

◆ bh: Yes—a culture of lies.

◆ AJ: And truth is always liberatory. The very thing one lies about is usually something one is *ashamed* about. And this shame basically enslaves people to the status quo. For example, in the '50s blacks were trying to be white; they were actually ashamed of their blackness—whereas *racism* should have been the thing to be ashamed of. Or, take a woman who is ashamed of being sexually active and feels "used"—

◆ bh: Also, I think that only in a truly supportive environment can we know the real meaning of privacy or "aloneness." Because the real meaning is not about secrets or clandestine activity; I think that "real" (I'm struggling with the word "real") or "authentic" privacy has to do with being capable of being alone with one's self. And one of the sadnesses of a culture of lies and domination is: *so many people cannot be alone with themselves.* They always need the TV, the phone, the stereo—*something* . . . because to be alone with the self is to possibly have to see all the stuff we spend so much of our time trying *not* to face.

◆ AJ: Right—it's the things we don't want to face that enslave us. So it's very liberatory to say, "Well, this

is who I am." There's something very cathartic and transformative in accepting all the victimizations we've gone through—somebody described their incest as a "wall of shame." It's incredibly liberatory to "come out" of the closet of shame—

◆ bh: That's why I like that book *Shame: The Power of Caring* [by Gershen Kaufman] because one of the things the author says is: There's no experience that we cannot heal . . . there is no space where we cannot be reconciled . . . but we can never be reconciled as long as we exist in the realm of denial, because denial is always about *insanity*. And sanity is so tied to our capacity to face reality.

If you are dedicated to truth and you live your life without shame, then you don't really *have* to care whether your neighbors can see what you're doing.

I remember when I was really struggling around my own issues with men and with my father. One day I called up my mother (I think I was 22) and was crying, "Daddy didn't love me!" Usually my mother would say, "Of course he loved you; he did this and that . . ." But this time, after an hour of torturous conversation, she suddenly said, "You're *right*—he *didn't* love you, and I never understood why." And that moment of her acknowledging the truth of what I had experienced was such a moment of relief! The moment she affirmed the reality of what had taken place, I was *released*, because somehow what we all know in our wounded childhood experiences (what the Swiss psychoanalyst Alice Miller tried to teach us) is: it's the act of *living the fiction* that produces the torturous angst and the anguish . . . the feeling that you're mind-fucked. I was watching Hitchcock's *Spellbound* again and I love it when that moment of truth—breaking through denial and re-entering one's true reality—becomes the hopeful moment, the promise: when we can know ourselves and not live this life of running in flight from reality.

◆ AJ: When you were talking about being raised in the black community, I was reminded of Philip Aries' *Centuries of Childhood*—

◆ bh: One of my favorite books in the world—

◆ AJ: In the Middle Ages, children weren't raised in a nuclear family, but in a healthier extended family—

◆ bh: Something I think a lot about is the question of *destiny*. It seems that this technological society tries to wipe out cultures who believe in forces of destiny . . . who believe there are forces moving in our lives beyond ourselves. Because such beliefs suggest that one could never be confined to the realm of one's skin, or one's nuclear family, or one's biological sexuality (or what have you), because one has so much awareness that there are forces *beyond* at work upon us in the universe. And I think that part of what man's technological society tries to do, is to deny and crush our *knowing* of that, so that we lose ourselves so easily.

I think that ironically, despite all its flaws, religion was one of those places that expanded our existence. The very fact that in Christian religion Jesus made miracles—well, kids growing up in the Christian church may learn all this other reactionary dogma, but they'll also learn something of an appreciation for mystery and magic. I was talking to an Indian Hindu woman friend whose son is fascinated with Christianity, and I said, "Yeah, those stories fascinated me too!" He's into David and Goliath; Moses parting the Red Sea... Not only are those stories fascinating, but they also keep you in touch with the idea that there are forces at work on our lives beyond our world of "reason" and the intellect. So this turning away from religion (in black culture: from traditional black religion) has also meant a turning away from a realm of the sacred—a realm of mystery—that has been deeply helpful to us as a people.

This is not to say that one only finds a sense of the sacred in traditional Christian faiths, because I find this in the realm of spirituality and in the realm of occult thinking as well. It just seems to be a very tragic loss: when we assimilate the values of a technocratic culture that does not acknowledge those high forms of mystery—nor even tries to make sense of them.

Part of what people like Fritjof Capra (author of *The Tao of Physics*) are doing is reminding us that a true technological world has *respect* for mystery. I think they're trying to reclaim the aspect of physics and science that in a sense was suppressed by the forces—the mentality—that would only *dominate* and *conquer*.

♦ **AJ: "New science" seems to almost be confirming older occult postulations. The newest physics, astronomy or "super string" theories sound so much like cabalistic notions—**

♦ bh: Absolutely! Historically, when we study the lives of someone like Madame Curie, we discover that in fact it isn't just "logical" scientific methodology that allows her to make her "grand discovery," but the work of the *imagination*. And with Einstein we can see the role of *mystery* in the discovery of things—as opposed to this notion that everything can be worked out in a logical paradigm.

♦ **AJ: Some of the writers like Evelyn Fox Keller (*Reflections on Gender and Science*) and Donna Haraway discuss how the philosophy of science has been informed by a patriarchal colonialist mentality, and how that's being reformulated by different perspectives like feminism . . . I wanted to talk more about black community—**

♦ bh: One of the more important things I want to say is: it wasn't just that I grew up in a black community, but

that I grew up in a *caring* black community—again, we don't want to get stuck in false essentialisms . . . I don't want to suggest that something magical took place there *because* everyone was black—it took place because of *what we did together* as black people.

One of the sadnesses of a culture of lies and domination is: *people cannot be alone with themselves.* They need the TV, the phone, the stereo—*something . . .* because to be alone is to see all the stuff we spend so much of our time trying *not* to face.

I was in Claremont, California, with a black cultural critic from England. Every day we would take walks, and be the only people on the street. I felt like we were in the *Twilight Zone*, because there were all these grand houses with lovely porches, but we never saw any people. And I was reminded of growing up in a small town of black people (Hopkinsville, Kentucky) on the black side of town where if you went walking you would always be able to greet people on their porches and talk with them and spread messages. Some elderly person might say, "When you get to so-and-so's house, tell them I need a cup of sugar!" There was this whole sense of being connected through that experience of journeying, of taking a walk.

But where I live now, when I walk to my friend's house I won't see people out. Even though this is a small town and everyone has these grand porches, people will not be outside—the whole bourgeois notion of "privacy" means they don't want to be seen—and they particularly don't want to have to talk to strangers. Yet at least we have more communication around issues of "race" and "difference" than in most Midwestern towns, because of the Underground Railroad [Civil War] having gone through here, and the old black community that still exists in Oberlin, Ohio. Nevertheless, a lot of people who come here to college from New York City or other cities just think it's horrifying to be seen daily by the same people.

♦ **AJ: Yet if you walk through a lot of ethnic Jewish, Hispanic or black neighborhoods in New York, usually the older people still take their chairs and sit out on the street with their coolers—that's their living room. They talk to people, and it's really quite wonderful and relaxed.**

♦ bh: I struggle a great deal with the phone, because I think the telephone is *very dangerous* to our lives in that it gives us such an illusory sense that we are *connecting*. I

always think about those telephone commercials: "Reach out and touch someone!" and that becomes such a false reality—even in my own life I have to remind myself that talking to someone on the phone is *not* the same as having a conversation where you see them and smell them.

> **I think the telephone is *very dangerous* to our lives in that it gives us such an illusory sense that we are *connecting*.**

I think that the phone has really helped people become more privatized in that it gives them an illusion of connection which denies looking at someone. Telephone commercials can be "great" because they actually let us see that person on the other end—see how they respond and give off this warmth that is never really conveyed just through the phone, so that we're not just having a diminished experience of the non-person you don't really see on the other end. And it's hard to always remember this—because we're seduced. I love Baudrillard's book, *Seduction*, because he talks a lot about the way we're seduced by *technologies of alienation*. We know that all technologies are not alienating, so I think it's good to have a phrase like "technologies of alienation" so that we can distinguish between those ways of transmitting knowledge, information, etc, and other ways of knowing that are more fully meaningful to us.

♦ AJ: **Don't you think that in our addictive culture, these seductions set up addictions which can never be satisfied? The telephone gives this impossible promise of connection; its "900" numbers promise a simulation of friendship and community (like a long-distance nightclub) which can never be fulfilled. An incredible sense of longing and desire is evoked—**

♦ bh: Absolutely. When I spoke at a conference on the "War on Drugs," I tried to talk about how a culture of *domination* is necessarily a culture of *addiction*, because you in fact take away from people their sense of *agency*. And what restores to people that sense of power and capacity—well, working in an auto factory in America right now gives few workers a sense of empowerment. So how do you give them an illusory sense of empowerment? We could go to any major plant in America and look at what people do. And a lot of what people do when they get off work is: drink. Many of the forms of "community" (set up to counteract the forces of alienation on the job) are tied to *addiction*—because the fact is: it's simply *not* gratifying to work fuckin' hard 10 hours a day for low wages and not really be able to get the things you need materially in life.

In fact: if people weren't seduced by certain forms of addiction, they might rebel! They might be depressed,

they might start saying, "Why should any of us work 10 hours a day? Why shouldn't we share jobs and work 4 hours a day and be able to spend more quality time for ourselves and our families? Why shouldn't workers who don't know how to read be able to go to a job where you spend 4 hours working and another 4 hours looking at movies and having critical discussions?" I don't know of any industry that has tried to implement those kinds of self-actualization moments in the experience of workers engaged in industrial work in this society.

♦ AJ: **What do you think are the underlying mechanisms of the "Drug War"?**

♦ bh: I think the mechanisms of the Drug War have so much to do with the mechanisms of capitalism and money-making. Also, many people have shown the ways in which our state and our government are linked to the bringing in of masses of drugs to pacify people—starting with drugs like aspirin which make people feel like "you shouldn't have any pain in your life" and that "pain means you're not living a successful life." And I think this is particularly hard to take. Black people and the black community have really been hurt by buying into the notion that "If I'm in pain, I must be a *miserable* person," rather than, "*Pain can be a fruitful place of transformation.*"

> **In this society it's easier for us to build our sense of "community" around sameness, so we can't imagine a gay rights movement where 80% of the people might be non-gay!**

I think that early on, in the black communities I grew up in, there was a sense of redemptive suffering. And it's really problematic for us to lose that sense. James Baldwin wrote in *The Fire Next Time* that "If you can't suffer, you can never really grow up—because there's no real change you go through." Back to M. Scott Peck who tells us that "All change is a moment of loss." And usually at a moment of loss we feel some degree of sorrow, grief—pain, even. And if people don't have the apparatus by which they can bear that pain, there can only be this attempt to avoid it—and that's where the place of so much addiction and substance abuse is in our life. It's in the place of "let me not feel it" or "let me take this drug so that I can go through it without having to really feel what I might have had to feel here." Or, "I can feel it . . . but I'll have no memory of it."

♦ AJ: **And ultimately we go back to the whole issue of anger: to "not feel it so I won't erupt with the kind of anger that pain has caused."**

♦ bh: I think that's it, precisely. What I see as the

promise is: those of us who are willing to break down or *go through* the walls of denial . . . to build a bridge between illusion and reality so that we can come back to our selves and live more fully in the world. . .

Part II

♦ **AJ: What do you write?**
♦ bh: I started out writing plays and poetry, but then felt I'd received this "message from the spirits": that I really needed to do feminist work which would challenge the universalized category of "Woman." Years ago certain ideas were prevalent in the feminist movement, such as, "Women would be liberated if they worked." And I was thinking, "Gee, every black woman I've ever known *has* worked (outside the home), but this hasn't necessarily meant *liberation.*" Obviously, this started me posing questions: "*What* women are we talking about when we talk about 'women'?"

So I began doing feminist theory challenging the prevailing construction of womanhood in the feminist movement. I wrote *Ain't I a Woman: Black Women and Feminism,* which initially met with tremendous resistance and hostility because it was going against the whole feminist idea that "Women share a common plight." I was saying that in fact, women don't share a common plight solely because we're women—that our experiences are very, very different. Of course, *now* that's become such an accepted notion, but 12 years ago people were really pissed.

I remember people being enraged because the book challenged the whole construction of white woman as victim, or white woman as the symbol of the most oppressed . . or *woman* as the symbol of the most oppressed. Because I was saying, "Wait a minute. What about *class* differences between women? What about racial differences that in fact make some women more powerful than others?" So that's how I started out. I continued to do my plays and my poetry, but my feminist theory and writings became better known.

♦ **AJ: And you're also a professor?**
♦ bh: Yeah, although I'm on a leave of absence. It's funny—lately I've been thinking a lot, because I'm having this life crisis right now and I'm just trying to pause for a moment—I call this a "pause-itive life crisis" [laughs] . . . I'm taking this time to focus more on creative work and on questions of performance. I have a desire to write little mini-plays and performances—dramas that can be acted out in people's living rooms.

I'm really into the *de-institutionalization* of learning and of experience. The more I've been in the Academy, the more I think about Foucault's *Discipline and Punish: The Birth of the Prison* and the whole idea of how institutions work. People have this fantasy (as I did when I was young) of colleges being liberatory institutions, when in fact they're so much like every other institution in our culture in terms of *repression* and *containment*—so that now I feel like I'm trying to break out. And I've noticed the similarity between the language I've been using, and the language of people who are imprisoned—especially with regard to that sense of what one has to recover after a period of confinement. . .

♦ **AJ: I like your idea that theory *can* be liberating, but that so often it's encased in a language *so* elitist as to be inaccessible. In the lecture I saw, the ideas you presented seemed so understandable—plus, it seemed you brought your heart and soul to the "lecture" format—**
♦ bh: That's where I think *performance* is useful. In traditional black culture: if you get up in front of an audience, you should be performing, you should be capable of moving people, something should take place—there should be some total *experience*. If you got up in front of an audience and were just passively reading something—well, what's the point?

♦ **AJ: Right—why not listen to a tape recording?**
♦ bh: There has to be this total engagement—an engagement that also suggests dialogue and reciprocity between the performer and the audience that is hopefully responding. I think about theory; I use words like "deconstruction." Once someone asked me, "Don't you think that these words are alienating and cold?" and I said, "You know, I expect to see these words in rap in the next few years!"

The less we engage in denial, the more we are able to recover our *selves*. *Hope* lies in the possibility of a resistance that's based on being able to face our reality *as it is*.

In my new book, *Yearning: Race, Gender and Cultural Politics,* I talk about going home to the South and telling my family that I'm a *Minimalist* . . . explaining to them what the significance of Minimalism is to me (in terms of space, objects, needs and what have you). Because meanings can be shared—people can take different language and jargon *across* class and across experiences—but there has to be an intermediary *process* whereby you take the time to give them a sense of what the meaning of a term is. You've got to be able to express that complicated meaning in language that is plainer or translatable. This doesn't mean that people can't grasp more complex jargon and utilize it—I think that's what books like *Marx for Beginners* had in mind: if you give people a basic outline or sense, then you are giving them a tool with which they can go back to the primary text (which is more "difficult") and feel more at home with that.

♦ **AJ: Do you feel that you as a black woman are changing things in the Academy?**
♦ bh: Black women change the process only to the degree that we are in revolt against the prevailing pro-

cess. However, the vast majority of black women in *Academe* are *not* in revolt—they seem to be as conservative as the other conservatizing forces there! Why? Because marginalized groups in institutions feel so vulnerable. I've been rereading Simon Watney's *Policing Desire*, and thinking a lot about how I often feel more policed by other black women who say to me: "How can you be out there on the edge? How can you *do* certain things—like be wild, be inappropriate? You're making it harder for the rest of us (who are trying to show that we *can* be 'up to snuff') to be 'in' with the mainstream."

♦ **AJ: So it's like an assault from both sides. You were talking about the "internalization of the oppressor" in the minds of the colonized—**

♦ bh: Simon Watney was talking about marginalized communities who will protest certain forms of domination (like a notion of "exclusion/inclusion" whereby they are excluded) but then invent their *own* little group wherein the same practices determine who is allowed into their "community." We see that happening now with the recent return to a black cultural nationalism where a new, well-educated, cool, chic, avant-garde group of black people (who perhaps five years ago had lots of white friends or mixed friends) now say, "I really want to associate *only* with black people" or, ". . . black people and people of color."

I'm very much into the work of the Vietnamese Buddhist monk Thich Nhat Hanh; I consider him to be one of my primary teachers and have been reading him for years. He talks a lot about the idea of resistance to the construction of false frontiers—the idea that *you* make or construct someone as an enemy who you have to oppose, but who in fact may have more in common with you than you realize. However, in this society it's easier for us to build our sense of "community" around sameness, so we can't imagine a gay rights movement where 80% of the people might be non-gay!

I was working from Martin Luther King's idea of the "beloved community" and asking, "Under what terms do we establish 'community'? How do we conceptualize a 'beloved community'?" King's idea was of a group of people who have overcome their racism, whereas *I* think more of communities of people who are not just interested in racism, but in the whole question of *domination*.

I think it's more important to ask, "What does it mean to inhabit a space without a *culture of domination* defining how you live your life?" In Thich Nhat Hanh's book *The Raft Is Not the Shore* (1975) he says that "Resistance at heart must mean more than resistance against war. It must mean resistance against all things that are *like* war." And then he talks about living in modern society . . . how the way we live threatens our integrity of being, and how people who feel threatened then construct false frontiers: "I can only care about you if you're like me. I can only show compassion toward you if something in your experience relates to something I've experienced."

We see an expression of this in Richard Rorty's book, *Contingency, Irony, & Solidarity*, where he argues that white

people in America can be in solidarity with young black youth if they stop seeing them as "young black youth" and look at them as Americans, and declare, "No American should have to live this way." So it's a whole notion of: "If you can find yourself in the Other in such a way as to wipe out the Otherness, then you can be in harmony." But a "grander" idea is: "Why do we have to wipe out the Otherness in order to experience a notion of *Oneness*?" I'm sort of a freak on the left in that I'm really dedicated to a spiritual practice in my everyday life, yet I'm also interested in transgressive expressions of desire—

♦ **AJ: Like what?**

♦ bh: *"Like what?"* she says! Well, for example, I just had this fling with a 22-year-old black male. A lot of people felt, "This is politically incorrect. This person isn't political; he's even got a white girlfriend. How can you be non-monogamous in the Age of AIDS?" Likewise, if you say you have a spiritual practice, people immediately think you're plugged into a total good/bad way of reading reality—

♦ **VALE: Or that you can't have a wild sex life . . . You're 38 and he's 22, so you're breaking an "age" taboo?**

♦ bh: Actually, less the taboo of age than the taboo of being involved with somebody who isn't involved with my work, who doesn't talk, and who's not politically correct—

I'm really into the de-institutionalization of learning and experience. People have this fantasy (as I did when I was young) of colleges being *liberatory* institutions, when in fact they're just like many other institutions in our culture in terms of *repression* and *containment*.

♦ **AJ: Almost as if *you* could be the exploiter?**

♦ bh: No!—rather, "You're letting us down—how could you be involved with a sexist terrorist?!" Because from *jump* I wasn't trying to pretend that this guy was a wonderful person—I said he was a "terrorist"—referring to people who are into "gaslighting," that great old term we should never have abandoned: men who seduce a woman, and just when you think you're in heaven, they suddenly abandon you. The syndrome of: seduce and abandon; seduce and betray. This theme really was popular in Hitchcock movies.

I like that term "gaslighting"; I want to recover it. It makes me think of emotional minefields, of someone you might actually have this ecstatic experience with, someone who inspires in you feelings of belonging and homecoming—you're walking along and suddenly you get blown up! Some part of you falls away, and you realize that all along this has been part of the other person's agenda: to give you a sense of belonging and closeness—then disrupt it in some powerful way. Which is what I think sexual terrorism does . . .

In a more general sense: in this country I always relate terrorism to the idea of *sugar-coated fascism:* where people really think they are free, but all of a sudden discover that if you cross certain boundaries (for example, decide you don't want to go fight in that Gulf War), suddenly you find you can be blown up—some part of you can be cut off, shot down, taken away. . .

I think about the soldiers that people were spitting on—the ones who *don't* want to happily get on the planes and go kill some Iraqis . . . just how quickly their whole experience of "America" was altered in the space of, say, even a day. If you juxtapose the notion of "Choice"/ "Freedom of Will" (that mythic projection) against the reality of what it means to say, "Well, I really would like to exercise my freedom in this *democracy* and say that I don't really support this war, and I don't want to go to it!" then WHAM! You find out there really was no such freedom, that you really *had* signed up to be an agent of White Supremacy and White Western Imperialism globally—and that you get punished quickly if you choose against that!

♦ **AJ: This really was a White Supremacist war, yet the way it was presented on TV sidestepped that reality.**

♦ bh: It's funny, because I was just talking with a friend about *Dances With Wolves.* We were disturbed because so many "progressive" people had been seeing this film, crying, and saying what a wonderful film it is. And while it is one of the best Hollywood representations of Native Americans, the fact remains that the overall package is completely pro-war, completely conservative.

I was interested in this because I've written a new book, *Black Looks: Race and Representation,* with an essay that examines the whole history of Africans coming to the so-called "New World," and the kind of bonds that developed between Africans and different nations. All of a sudden we began to think of Native American Indians as light-skinned people with straight hair, whose cultures have nothing to do with African-American (or any African) culture . . . when in fact, in the 1800s and early 1900s, there was still lots of communication—a lot of black people joined Native American nations legally. You could declare yourself a citizen of a particular nation.

♦ **AJ: Do you have any thoughts regarding the presentation of people of color in mass media?**

♦ bh: I think one of the dilemmas in film or performance for people of color is: it's not enough for us just to create cultural products in reaction to prevailing archetypes—we must try to create the *absences* in Hollywood cinema. For example, we think a Spike Lee film is "good" because it has different images from what we've seen before. But we need more than merely "positive" images—we need *challenging* images. When people say to me, "Well, don't you think that at least Spike Lee's telling it like it is?" I say, "You know, the function of art is to do more than tell it like it is—it's to imagine what is *possible.*"

Martin Luther King said that the black revolution is not just for black people, but also to expose systemic flaws in society: *racism, militarism,* **and** *materialism.*

♦ **V:** —to tell what *could be.*

♦ bh: Yes. And I think that for all people of color in this culture (because our minds have been so colonized) it's very hard for us to move out of that location of *reacting.* Even if I say, "I'm going to create a drama where Asian women's sexuality is portrayed differently than the racist norm," I'm still working within that sense of, "We only respond to the existing representation." Whereas actually, we need some wholesale re-envisioning that's outside the realm of the merely reactionary!

I'm fascinated by the appearance of transgression in an art form that in fact is no transgression at all. A lot of films *appear* to be creating a change, but the narrative is always "sewn up" by an ending which returns us to the status quo—so there's been no change at all. The underlying message ends up being completely conservative.

♦ **AJ: Can you think of any examples in mass media that work in a positive way?**

♦ bh: We haven't seen enough. Black heterosexuality in cinema and television is always: basic, funky and sexist, like in *Mo' Better Blues* by Spike Lee where nothing different takes place—even though we know that people's real lives can have far more complex constructions. For example, nobody says, "Let's have different arrangements—I don't think I want to be monogamous. Let's reorganize this." A location where one *can* imagine possible different constructions is performance art: we think of Whoopi Goldberg's early performances when she took on many different identities, such as the "bag lady" she gave voice to.

There was a point in my life when I needed a therapist. I was involved in this horrible, bittersweet life with a black male artist/intellectual. There was no one I could go to and say, "This is what's happening to me, and I have no apparatus for understanding it." So I *invented* this figure: this therapist, this healer, and I could get up and do an improvisational performance on this persona. I realized you could invent something you need.

I was just reading a quotation from Monique Wittig's *Les Guérillères:* "There was a time when you were not a slave," which evokes the idea of *remembering who you were.* I was thinking about being in that emotionally abusive, bittersweet relationship, and was trying to remember when I was *not* in a matrix like that. But coming from a family where I had been routinely tortured and emotionally persecuted, it was hard for me to even imagine a space where I wasn't involved with people who seduce and betray—who make you feel loved one minute, and then pull the rug out from under you the next—so you're always spinning, uncertain how to respond. The point is: performance art, in the ritual of inventing a character who could not only speak through me but also for me, was an important *location of recovery* for me.

It's like having a sickness that gets more fierce as it passes on to *wellness*. We don't have to view that period as an invitation to despair, but as a sign of potential *transformation* in the very depths of whatever pain we are experiencing. . .

◆ **AJ: As far as the position of women or people of color goes, it seems that the deception levels are getting far worse. The illusions are so much tighter, and the grip of control—**
◆ bh: There's an incredible quote by Martin Luther King in his last essay, "A Testament of Hope." He says that the black revolution is not just a revolution for black people, but in fact is exposing certain systemic flaws in society: *racism, militarism,* and *materialism.* And while there are a lot of progressive people on the Left who oppose militarism, many do not oppose *materialism.*

One thing we can learn from Thich Nhat Hanh, who lived through the Vietnam War, is how much this culture is so profoundly materialistic . . . people think they need *so* much. When I teach a course on Third World Literature, I spend the first few weeks trying to get people to unlearn thinking with a First World mindset, which means: when you watch a show like "Dynasty" and see all this material opulence, you measure your own life by that. You might say, "Oh God, I don't have anything—I only have an old car and an old stereo, but just *look* at this opulence!" Whereas if we think about the rest of the world . . . I remember myself as a naive teenager going to Germany and finding out that everyone *didn't* have a stereo!

When we think *globally,* we're able not only to see how much we have (compared to others), but also to think about what goes into the production of what we have. I tell my students, "In the first two weeks, in order to not think with a First World context—if you eat a steak, you have to take out your pen and paper and write down what goes into producing that steak." Thus you have a sense of being part of a world community, and not just part of a First World context that in fact would have you deny your positionality as an individual in a *world community.* It's not enough to just think of yourself in terms of the United States.

Even friends on the "Left" would rather not discuss the Gulf War in terms of *challenging materialism;* using so much of the world's resources—exploiting so much of the world's resources. Because then we might begin discussing what it would mean to change our way of life . . . to realize that being against war also means changing our way of life. In his Nobel Prize speech the Dalai Lama said: "How can we expect people who are hungry to be concerned about the absence of war?" He also said that peace has to mean more than just the absence of war—it has to be about reconstructing society so that people can learn how to be fully self-actualized human beings—fully alive.

◆ **AJ: Possessions become substitutes, covering up for a loss of meaning and connection (you *are* what you own). The things I love most don't cost that much—yet have special meaning for *me,* such as gifts that link me to certain people or objects that remind me of a certain time period. Whereas Western Industrial society promotes items whose original function has been forgotten: a car isn't just a box on wheels that gets you around—it's this expensive commodity you buy to "communicate" status.**
◆ bh: I think our materialism is often totally disconnected from the idea that aesthetics are *crucial* to our ability to live humanely in the world. To be able to recognize and know beauty, to be able to be lifted up by it, to be able to *choose* the objects in your surroundings . . . I've always been interested in Buddhist room arrangement: how do we place something in our house so that we can be made more fully human by glancing at it, or by interacting with it? And there's *so little* of that in our culture.

For example, for some time I'd wanted this expensive coffee-table book on Amish quilts. And I was really sad when I got it and discovered it was just about the *Esprit* collection! On the one hand, we're made to feel "grateful" that these wealthy people who are buying these quilts are making them "available" to the public. But no one talks about how yuppie consumers have turned quilts into something that totally abandon the homes of the people who had them as historical or family legacies—all in the interest of *money.* There's nothing that tells us, "Well, this is how we acquired this quilt." There's nothing about the process of acquisition in the context of capitalism—nothing about that whole *process of collecting*

(and what it implies) —

♦ **AJ:** —which takes it out of the community. In certain American Indian tribes, spirituality and a profound community sense would be deeply integrated into the making of objects whose function was also necessary for the survival of the tribe . . . I grew up in New England where old ladies used to have sewing bees which gathered women together and provided a valuable sense of community. And then suddenly for this community craft to get shunted off into a *collector* status — you've just alienated and *consumed* that spiritual, cultural reservoir . . .

♦ **bh:** I know that when I have the money to buy a thing, I struggle a lot with the question the meaning of that thing in my life. Do I want to possess something *just* because I have the money to buy it? What would be the way that I or *Esprit* (or any group of people) could own a collection of something, and not be participating in this process of cultural alienation? *Esprit* seems to think that hanging the quilts in their offices is a way of *sharing*.

I was trying to analyze why I felt violated when I got this book titled *The Amish Quilt* — thinking I'm going to learn something about Amish quilts, only to realize that what I'm really learning about is this *Esprit* collection of Amish quilts. This brings in the question of *repackaging*, as well as the question of this fantasization of Amish life that's taking place in the United States. I think it's not untied to White Supremacy, because if we think about the Shakers or Mennonites or other groups who have welcomed people who are non-white into their midst, we find that one of the groups which has stayed more solidly *white* has been the Amish. And when white people are looking at them with a kind of nostalgia and evoking this ideal of "the Amish way of life" — whether we see them being grossly exploited (as in the movie *Witness*) or in the many books that have been published recently . . .

This culture is so profoundly materialistic . . . people think they need *so* much.

There's a new book by a white woman who went to live among the Amish; it describes the peace and serenity she found. I think we *all* have something to learn from the Amish way of life, their habits of being and thought . . . but it's interesting that this particular group which is most *white* is the one that gets fetishized.

♦ **V:** How can exploitation in general be prevented?

♦ **bh:** I always think that whenever there's the possibil-

ity for exploitation, what intervenes is *recognition of the Other*. Recognition allows a certain kind of negotiation that seems to disrupt the possibility of domination. If a person makes a unilateral decision that does not account for *me*, then I feel exploited by that decision because my needs haven't been considered. But if that person is willing to pause, then at that moment of pause there is an opportunity for *mutual recognition* (what I call the "subject-to-subject" encounter, as opposed to "subject-to-object"). This doesn't necessarily mean the person will change what they intended to do, but it means that (at least temporarily) I am not rendered an *object* by their carrying forth with their objective.

To have a non-dominating context, one has to have a lived practice of interaction. And this practice has to be *conscious*, rather than some sentimental notion that "you and I were born into the world with the 'will to do good towards one another.'" In reality, this non-exploitative way to be with one another has to be *practiced*; resistance to the possibility of domination has to be *learned*.

This also means that one has to cultivate the capacity to *wait*. I think about a Culture of Domination as being very tied to notions of efficiency — everything running smoothly. I mean, it's so much easier if you tell me, "I'm leaving!" rather than "I desire to leave and not come back — how does that desire impact on you?" and I reply, "Is there a space within which I can have a response?" All this takes more time than the kind of fascism that says, "This is what *I'm* doing — fuck you!"

I often think: What does "resistance" *mean* (our resistance against war, sexism, homophobia, etc) if we're not fully committed to changing our way of life? Because so much of how we *are* is informed by a Culture of Domination. So how do we become liberated within the Culture of Domination if our lived practice, every moment of the day, is not saying "No!" to it in some way or another? And that means we have to: *pause, reflect, reconsider*, create a whole *movement* . . . and that is not what the machinery of capitalism in daily life is about. It's about "Let's do it all swiftly — quickly!"

I hope that what's happening now for many people is: a lot of the *denial* is being cut away, because denial is always about *insanity*. So we know that the less we engage in denial, the more we are able to recover our *selves*. *Hope* lies in the possibility of a resistance that's based on being able to face our reality *as it is*.

♦ **AJ:** And yet I see the denial getting more and more fierce, building up —

♦ **bh:** There's one way you can look at this: it's like having a sickness in your body that gets more and more fierce as it is passing on to *wellness*. We don't have to view that period of intense sickness as an invitation to despair, but as a sign of potential *transformation* in the very depths of whatever pain it is we are experiencing. . .♦♦♦

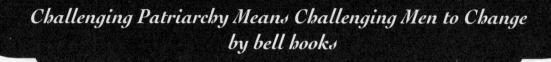

Challenging Patriarchy Means Challenging Men to Change
by bell hooks

Almost forty, when I chart the journey that moved me—a southern black girl who had been raised to be a "lady" at all costs, to be a victim—into that space where I could embrace revolutionary feminism as a liberatory politic, I always return home. I return to that hot summer night when I first heard my father's angry voice threatening to kill mama, to that moment when I saw the blood trickling down her mouth where he had struck her, to the strength of his words as he repeatedly yelled, "I'll kill you. I'll kill you." I do not forget the sense of helplessness that I felt standing there, making my presence bear witness (my siblings were all willing to retreat from the scene) and I do not forget the fear. Yet what stays with me most is the memory of the intense violence that surged in me. I wanted to kill this man, my father whom violence had turned into a stranger. If someone had to die, I did not want to see mama sacrificed to this male rage. There was no question in my mind that if there had to be a choice, I would choose her over him. Intimately, I shared with him at that moment the overwhelming killing rage that can lead to the taking of another life, that makes blood sacrifice possible. The memory of my rage has stayed with me, a constant reminder of the violence I am capable of, a violence just as strong, just as intense as that of any man.

What stays with me most is the memory of the intense violence that surged in me. I wanted to kill this man, my father whom violence had turned into a stranger.

My rebellion against patriarchy, like that of many Sister and Brother comrades, began in the home of my childhood. I can still remember the stunned look on mama's face when I turned to her one day walking up the stairs to my bedroom and looking down yelled: "I will never marry, I will never be any man's prisoner."

Perhaps I would have thought believing in revolutionary feminism was all about a struggle against men, if I had not spent my childhood struggling with mama, with her violence against her children, with her sense of woman's place, with her sexism that was at times deeper and more entrenched than dad's. With insight honed by experience, I left home knowing that the "real" feminist deal was not just about the struggle to stop men from hurting women but about ending sexism and sexist oppression and being able to confront head-on the "enemy," no matter what form the enemy might take—man, woman, child, state, church, school, friend, lover, and most frightening, "the enemy within."

Within me there will always be a young girl who fears men and male power indiscriminately, a hurt and frightened girl who has no ability to be selective, to choose among men as though she had the power to intuit, "These men are the enemy, and these comrades." That young girl holds the memory of pain and rage so intense it can burn flesh, like the heat of that summer night, when she should have stood bearing witness, watching her father dominate, humiliate, and brutalize her mother, watching a man dominate and hurt a woman. That young girl who still lives inside me was "traumatized" by all that she witnessed. She spent years of her life reliving that night. In her dreams she heard again and again the voice of her father saying, "I'll kill you. I'll kill you." She grew up to be a women who would lie next to a man and wake up screaming with a fear so naked and raw that the dream became reality. Ultimately, it changed. It was no longer the mother who was being attacked. It was her life the man was taking, her death she witnessed. The nightmare of patriarchy, the ritualistic drama of male domination over woman, reenacted in her sleep, served as a constant reminder of the horror that sexism and sexist oppression make possible.

My mother and father reconciled after that night, living an uneasy peace. It was within me that the terrorizing fear lingered. Working for self-recovery, coming to grips with this past, I have had to face and claim both the terror and the rage of that night, to see them as intimately linked—that moment of separation when I felt I had to choose the mother over the father, the female over the male, and that moment of connection when the rage I shared with the father linked me to him, denying our difference, making us one. That terrorized young girl who lives inside me no longer dominates my life. I no longer watch everything through the lens of her fear, looking at the world through her terror. I do not see men through her eyes, even though I understand the forces that shape and determine the nature of her gaze.

Intimately knowing both the terror and the rage, the fear of abusive male domination and the will to meet it in kind, has been the lived experience that has not allowed me to naively imagine that men hold all the power to act in ways that dominate and hurt. That recognition has been redemptive for me. It has enabled me to be ever mindful of the need to construct feminist theory and practice so that it addresses females and males, so that it will be a revolutionary political movement that is fundamentally committed to ending sexism and sexist oppression in all its forms.

In most of my work I have been critical of a lifestyle based on a radical feminism that sees feminist movement as primarily being for and about women. Thinking about feminism in this way, women cling to notions of hierarchy, privileging the experience of women as being more important and more worthy of attention than the experience of men. Such logic is not essentially a radical critique of domination but more a rebellion against a politic of domination that makes women its victims. Embedded in its standpoint is the assumption that if men were the sole victims of patriarchy and male domination, there would be no need for women to challenge and resist this abuse of power. Concurrently, by evoking a gendered rhetoric that holds to notions of good and bad, innocent and guilty, one that places women always on the winning side, radical feminists avoid the call to accountability and responsibility that would signal a fundamental break with the logic of Western metaphysical dualism that undergirds the politics of domination.

Remembering my own past, and linking it to the many autobiographical narrations of women who have been the objects of male violence that has known no limits or boundaries, I understand fully and know intimately the impulse, usually rooted in essentialist rage, that can lead feminist thinkers to see all men as the "enemy" and all women solely as victims, or potential victims. Yet when women accept such a simplistic account of female experience, what are we called to suppress and deny in ourselves? Raising this issue in *The Oppositional Imagination*, Joan Cocks urges a critique of an instrumentalist approach that denies woman's capacity to be self-determining: "Radical feminism's romanticization of women as essentially innocent or good may be more benign than the dominant culture's degradation of women, and it may be more well-meaning than the culture's idealization of women in a backhanded way that suggests they are really the weaker and less dramatic sex. Still, it is absolutely infantilizing and embalming. It implies that women are not complex enough in desire, sophisticated enough in imagination, and dynamic enough in will to act in vicious as well as virtuous ways, out of passions, predilections, and motive forces that are not men's but their own."

Accepting a version of female experience that sees us solely as victims, as the dupes of men, enables us to ignore both the violence we do to other women and children and to less powerful men. Most importantly, it acts to obscure the extent to which females can assert autonomous agency and therefore have the power to choose whether to support sexism, patriarchy, and male domination. The danger of this simplistic account of female experience should be obvious. By denying female agency it implicitly disallows our capacity to rebel, to resist, to act in a revolutionary way. A despairing vision, it acts to reinforce patriarchal power; it does not subvert

or undermine it.

Radical feminist demands that women choose the representation of innocence over recognition of experience and agency posits a world view that ultimately makes separation from men a necessary component of female liberation. By inverting the logic of misogyny and phallocentrism that has socialized males for centuries to believe their safety can be maintained only by staying away from or dominating females, we in no way advance our understanding of gender. It is fundamentally rooted in a denial of reality. Most women cannot choose lives where they have little or no contact with men. Vast numbers of heterosexual women continue to seek and desire such contact. It belittles women for any radical feminist to assume that all these women are mere dupes, victims of their internalized sexism. Since so many women are in daily contact with men whether that contact is chosen or not, it is dangerous for privileged groups of women — who need not have contact with men because of class, race, or sexual preferences that position them where they have options — to promote the notion that the "real" feminist is a woman who has no need or desire to be in contact with men.

Refusal to think in either/or terms empowers feminist activists to search for and invent strategies that address the complexity of feminist movement.

Many radical feminists assume that any feminist woman concerned about male domination who desires a feminist agenda that includes a focus on men (note the emphasis on *include* rather than *centralize*) is somehow failing to fulfill her true feminist mission, and worse, betraying the cause. This brand of "guilt tripping" has pushed many women away from feminist politics because it has demanded that they devalue or deny their ties with men. Years ago in a women's studies class filled with women of all ages and races, many of whom were lesbians, sex radicals, or consciously choosing celibacy, we hotly debated whether one could be woman-identified and remain involved with men. Rather then deny female agency, we chose collectively to acknowledge that it was indeed possible, and that the degree to which women understood that contact with men need not correspond with solidarity or allegiance to patriarchy would stand as testimony to the power of transformative feminist thinking. We made this choice with full awareness that the vast majority of women would need to unlearn internalized sexist thinking before this could be a concrete possibility in daily life. We also acknowledged that

separatist space often facilitates coming to feminist critical consciousness, even though it is not a precondition of sustained feminist commitment.

Given the politics of patriarchy, feminist agendas that include a focus on men must be formed with full understanding that most people have been socialized to assume that the experiences and concerns of women are not as important as those of men. This reality makes it necessary for us to vigilantly centralize women's experience in ways that critically intervene and disrupt conventional ways of thinking about gender. When considering questions about the place of men in feminist movement, or to what extent feminist agendas should include a focus on males, feminist activists must creatively develop strategies that do not reinscribe a focus on women as secondary. Those radical feminist agendas that dismiss a focus on men avoid addressing these issues. While woman-only space makes it easier to generate a sense of solidarity among women, if in such settings all focus on men is deemed reactionary and anti-feminist, then they become sites where feminist revolution that acts to eradicate sexism and sexist oppression, that empowers women to challenge and confront patriarchy and men, that offers a transformative vision, is undermined.

My father was dying. That the only time I would feel free to touch him without feeling threatened by his power over me was when he lay dead—it's unbearable to me.

In keeping with conventional patriarchal notions of allegiance, it is often sexual preference that shapes and informs individual feminist response to issues concerning men. The assumption that choosing lesbianism automatically means that one is no longer male-identified remains popular within feminist circles. And not surprisingly, it is often individual separatist lesbians who most outspokenly oppose making space for men on feminist agendas. Audre Lorde addresses this issue in her essay "Man Child" and grapples with what it would signify if she attended a lesbian/feminist conference that would not allow boys over ten to participate. With her partner, she wrote the conference this insightful message: "Ten years as an interracial lesbian couple has taught us both the dangers of an oversimplified approach to the nature and solutions of any oppression, as well as the dangers inherent in an incomplete vision. Our thirteen-year-old son represents as much hope for our future world as does our fifteen-year-old daughter, and we are not willing to abandon him to the killing streets of New York City

while we journey west to help form a Lesbian/Feminist vision of the future world in which we can all survive and flourish. I hope we can continue this dialogue in the near future, as I feel it is important to our vision and our survival."

Stating clearly in her essay that both as a black person and as a women she has, at times, the need for noninclusive space (a need many of us share), Lorde does not privilege this longing over the desire for collective space where difference does not prelude the possibility of solidarity. Refusal to think in either/or terms empowers feminist activists to search for and invent strategies that address the complexity of feminist movement. There has not been enough fruitful dialogue between women who would exclude focus on men from all feminist agendas and those of us who believe such focus is necessary if we are to end sexism and sexist oppression.

Black women/women of color feminist activists have brought to feminist theory and practice some of the most insightful ways to think about questions of inclusion and exclusion. By sharing with white women the meaningful solidarity we have forged with men of color in struggles to end racism and class oppression, we have demonstrated by our lived experience that it is possible to maintain a woman-identified commitment to feminism even as we work with, alongside, and for the liberation of our brothers. Recognizing that race and class domination challenges any monolithic construction of a universal category we can call "woman," we have maintained ties with white women, growing and learning in struggle, even as we are ever vigilant in contesting and challenging racism. Concurrently, knowing the ways black men/men of color perpetuate and maintain male domination, we maintain ties even as we continually resist and challenge sexism. We advocate coalition because domination affects us all and we know that it can only be effectively addressed by collective struggle.

Often white women active in feminist movement, particularly individuals with class privilege, feel no such bonds with white men. Indeed, white female struggle to break complicity with white male abusive power may fuel an anti-male standpoint. Separating from men, and most specifically from white men, may be the easiest way for these women to project the image that their political allegiances have been radicalized, are different, even if that is not truly the case. Often these women are most fierce in their condemnation of any group of women who want to make a feminist agenda that includes a focus on men. They are the women who can be heard stating that they "refuse to give their energies to men."

Revolutionary feminist activism must avoid at all costs investing in simplistic forms of gender separatism that offer women the luxury of not having to engage in ongoing confrontation and struggle with men. Most women do not have the option to choose. Black women, whether we are revolutionary feminists or simply beginning the process of examining sexism and its impact on our lives, collectively share the awareness that there must be feminist education for critical consciousness for black men if sexism and sexist oppression is to cease in black communities.

Recently, I was invited to speak at a benefit for the opening of a day-care center by an Afrocentric group with black male leaders. An atypical event, the audience was extraordinarily racially and ethnically diverse, many more black men were present than is normally the case, and there was a definite presence of individuals with diverse sexual preferences. Indeed, the audience appeared to be the lived embodiment of the feminist vision of a diverse movement.

> ## It is possible to maintain a woman-identified commitment to feminism even as we work with, alongside, and for the liberation of our brothers.

As I began speaking there were problems with the sound system. Men of color and white men tried to remedy the problem. The audience laughed when the problems did not disappear. Yet when black women rose to help, segments of the audience cheered. During the question period, the first speaker was a South African black man, who said he was troubled by seeing white people in the audience laugh at men of color while expressing through cheers their solidarity with black women. He wanted to know whether this display could not be seen as affirming the notion that feminism is not only anti-male but is a movement that seeks to divide women and men of color. As he spoke he was mocked by segments of the audience. This experience highlighted for me the way in which continued investment in sexual hierarchy informs feminist movement, undermining the possibility that there will be a mass conversion to feminist thinking. Until women committed to feminist movement fully accept men as comrades in struggle who have every right to participate in the movement (and no right to dominate) and recognize that they (men) would then be called by political accountability to assume a major role in feminist struggle to end sexism and sexist oppression, the transformative vision of revolutionary feminism will not be concretely actualized in our lives.

Women cannot accept men as full participants in feminist movement if we cannot address the depths of our anger and fear of them. One of the most moving confessions of such fear is expressed by Barbara Deming in Mab Segrest's book *My Mama's Dead Squirrel* as they talk about women's responsibility for radicalizing men. Speaking of her father's death, Deming confesses: "It was on a weekend in the country and he'd been working outside with a pick and shovel, making a new garden plot. He'd had a heart attack and fallen there in the loose dirt. We'd called a rescue squad, and they were trying to bring him back to life, but couldn't. I was half-lying on the ground next to him, with my arms around his body. I realized that this was the first time in my life that I had felt able to really touch my father's body. I was holding hard to it— with my love—and with my grief. And my grief was partly that my father, whom I loved, was dying. But it was also that I knew already that his death would allow me to feel freer. I was mourning that this had to be so. It's a grief that is hard for me to speak of. That the only time I would feel free to touch him without feeling threatened by his power over me was when he lay dead—it's unbearable to me. And I think there can hardly be a woman who hasn't felt a comparable grief. So it's an oversimplification to speak the truth that we sometimes wish men dead—unless we also speak the truth which is perhaps even harder to face (as we try to find our own powers, to be our own women): the truth that this wish is unbearable to us. It rends us."

That wish to see men dead, felt by me so long ago, on that hot summer night, surfaces every time I hear about any horrific act of male violence against women, of male domination. When this visceral response passes, my zeal to make my feminist life and work critically intervene in the lives of men in such a way that it serves as a catalyst affirming and promoting male feminist transformation is renewed. Unlike some women, I do not feel the luxury of choice. Not only does patriarchal power continue to affirm the use of violence as a means to subordinate and subjugate women, the resurgence of antifeminist backlash also exposes the extent to which antifeminism is pushed as an appropriate response to feminist movement that is perceived as anti-male. As a black woman, I know that we continue to be the objects of sexist violence that knows no boundaries. Black communities are in crisis. Revolutionary feminist theory and practice indicates that the inclusion of a focus on men within feminist agendas is necessary if we are to fully challenge and confront sexism and sexist oppression. I willingly give my energies to work with men who are committed to feminist change, who want to make a world where women no longer suffer patriarchy's heavy hand, where transformative feminist visions are daily realized in the way women and men live with and among one another.

Reprinted from "Z" Magazine February 1991. For subscription rates contact "Z," 150 W. Canton St, Boston MA 02118 (617) 236-5878.

Holly Hughes

Performance artist/playwright Holly Hughes gained nationwide attention when her grant was revoked by the NEA in election year 1990 (along with grants to Karen Finley, John Fleck and Tim Miller). She said, "I think the reason my work was overturned is because it is chock full of good old feminist satire, and secondly, I am openly lesbian."

Since 1983 Holly Hughes has written and performed plays and monologues. She grew up in Saginaw, Michigan in a very Republican, upper-middle-class family before moving to New York and *agitating* in the underground performance art/theatre scene. Prior to becoming a playwright/ "lesbian scientist exploring the polymorphous perverse," she was a feminist painter and sculptor. To date her performances have included *Well of Horniness, Lady Dick, Dress Suits to Hire, World Without End,* and *No Trace of the Blond* (in collaboration with Ellen Sebastian) . . .

◆ ANDREA JUNO: You were in the eye of the hurricane when your NEA grant was revoked and you got massive nationwide publicity—

◆ HOLLY HUGHES: I keep wondering, "Who will be the new scapegoat?" There's a part of me that *wants* to be the enemy of the White Patriarchal Class Structure. On the other hand, when the machinery is turned against you, it's *scary.* This reminded me of '50s McCarthyism.

All this builds on a certain hysteria in the culture about sexually explicit materials—if you're *accused* of being a pornographer, then you *are* one. This was the only time I agreed with Richard Nixon: he said how difficult it is to turn something around once it's been publicized.

◆ AJ: Why were you targeted by the NEA?

◆ HH: The mere *whiff* (if you will)—the *je ne sais quoi* of lesbianism wafting out from my work—was enough. In the summer of 1989 Congress equated homoeroticism with obscenity. To the heterosexist imagination, all gay and lesbian experience is assumed *a priori* to be oversexualized. If only that were the case! [laughs]

There are not that many openly gay or lesbian artists making work about their experience who receive funding. I think lesbians tend to be legitimately terrified of what might happen to them outside their own communi-

ty, and how they're going to be represented. A lot of lesbians have told me, "This is *exactly* what we thought would happen: that you would be humiliated because you were cheeky enough to be openly queer."

◆ AJ: —meaning that you're not supposed to be "out"?

◆ HH: Right, and I've always made the decision to go *outside.* I feel that the coffee table art books of the future should not be exclusively about white male upper-middle-class artists. Yet I think it's very difficult to work outside the lesbian community on your own terms—it's a *minefield* out there. Everywhere I go people tell me I'm the first openly lesbian performance artist they've seen— yet I can't represent the whole smorgasbord of lesbian experience. I'm just a white girl from the Midwest and that's what I talk about . . . let's have some diversity of experience here!

I often am told, "You're not like those ugly angry dykes!" And then I show them that they're wrong—that I *am* very ugly and very angry! [laughs] One of the current issues is: whether you're inside your ghetto or outside it. Outsider artists face pressure from the dominant culture to make their specific experience universal and risk watering their work down. There's always that seduction to make work that's not about your own experience—pull a Tennessee Williams, as it were. Yet artists like Truman Capote and Edward Albee successfully used their experiences as gay men to illuminate the oppression of others.

There's a "pyramid" scene that often happens in the art world. If you look at a performance place, you'll see they produce mostly white men (generally straight or closeted), one or two African-Americans, one or two lesbians (or one lesbian and one gay man), one Latino, and you're encouraged to think that's *diversity*. Any person who gets produced is encouraged to think—*another trap*—that the cream always rises to the top, and the reason there are no other women around you (or it's so white) is because *you're the best!* Who *can't* fall for that: "You're the best, babe!"

◆ **AJ: That's tokenism in action—**

◆ HH: Right. And on the other hand, if you *do* achieve some visibility, does that mean you've sold out? *No*—I think you can use your visibility in beneficial ways. And society wants all Outsider Artists to be each other's enemies. They want heterosexual feminists and dykes to be enemies; they

Photo: Dona Ann McAdams

want white people and people of color to be enemies; and it's very easy to fall into those traps. Just within the queer community, people of color are asserting themselves and wanting power, dominance, and visibility. I think this mirrors some larger cultural change: America is no longer primarily white. The white male heterosexist middle class privilege is being eroded, so now there's a huge amount of anger and backlash.

One woman said to me: "You know, I'm a white lesbian, but I don't *feel* privileged—even though people describe me as such." Yet her white skin *does* buy her a certain privilege in this culture, and that's important to acknowledge.

◆ **AJ: This complicated web of awards and privileges, ranking and hierarchy, ultimately falls apart because we're all really victims. Society tries to prevent you from getting a larger picture of what victimization means. Even the most macho white dude is to some extent a victim, but since he has a more privileged position, he can't see that. For example, if he's in the army he may not realize that he's just "cannon fodder." What is your art about?**

◆ HH: Well, all of my pieces deal very specifically and exclusively with *lesbian desire*, with trying to uncover or *recover* women's sexual power in a fucked-up context. My performance ranges from the slapstick to the Theatre of the Absurd—hopefully it's not overly pretentious!

The mere *whiff* (if you will)—the *je ne sais quoi* of lesbianism wafting out from my work—was enough for the NEA to target me.

Do you know the work of Joanne Llewellyn, a lesbian therapist who's written a number of books on lesbian sexuality? She talks about how *de-eroticized* the women's movement was. Perhaps this was the only way we could get some distance on sexuality, in order to be able to *re-invent* what it meant to us. I know that when I was "coming out," the lesbian movement meant something very painful to me. With butch-femme identity polarization, the lesbians sort of fell for a heterosexist view that was an aping of male-female desire, rather than a very specifically lesbian experience. Then came a whole de-sexualization toward androgyny. Now *that's* completely changed: women are really getting into pussy in a big way, and it's great.

◆ AJ: And embracing the notion that makeup is not just for seducing men, it's for themselves. Also, it's not even for another woman; it's for the tribal act of adornment—

◆ HH: It's true. I really do feel that I can wear makeup (whether I'm lesbian or straight) and determine what I think it's *about* for myself, more than any previous generation could. My piece "World Without End" deals a lot with my relationship to my mother. She was an incredibly fucked-up person, and I think much of that just had to do with the choices available (not to absolve her of responsibility)—but what choices did a woman born in Michigan in 1917 and growing up in an upper-middle-class WASP family have at that time?

I clearly felt the conflict in her. She *wanted* to be sexual, she *wanted* to be creative, but none of that dovetailed with her notion of what it meant to be a "good woman." She feared she would not be loved; to her the love of a man was something that redeemed the life of a woman—it almost made up for this huge waste of her potential creative life.

◆ AJ: The reality is: she probably *wasn't* loved, and this man's "love" was equated with her economic survival.

◆ HH: Right. While I feel my work involves a critique of certain branches of feminism or where the movement is going, nevertheless I wouldn't be here without 1970's-style feminism. I would never have believed in *separatism* because it seemed too white and too bourgeois for even *me* to participate in—originating as it does in privilege. On the other hand, I wouldn't *be* here without years of lesbian separatism. Now *nobody* has to apologize for being a lesbian or for being a person of color or whatever.

◆ AJ: There's a big problem with the linguistic process of labeling. You're this "lesbian" or "feminist"—yet what do these terms mean? Everyone has a different interpretation.

◆ HH: Well, lots of lesbians will tell you I'm not a lesbian! I guess I'm not hardcore enough for them.

◆ AJ: There's the idea that those linguistic definitions take away from the wholeness of your being. Oversimplification (for example: you being labeled as a "spokeswoman for the lesbian community") is a frequent form of abuse. But at your last reading you were talking about really universal experiences—such as being a waitress at the "Red Lobster." Within a dispossessed community somehow the totality of life gets defined in a really artificial way—

◆ HH: That's another one of those traps you get stuck in. In performance, I rarely feel I have the luxury to be a human being—I have to always present content explicitly linked to sexual identity. Only straight white men have had an extended period of experience where they aren't continually hit in the face with how their sexual identity sets them apart—because their identity is seen as *normative*. The "good cop/bad cop" of any kind of liberation movement is "assimilation vs autonomy."

They want heterosexual feminists and dykes to be enemies; they want white people and people of color to be enemies; and it's very easy to fall into those traps.

◆ AJ: On that level there's a power in the reclaiming process . . . proclaiming, "I'm a lesbian!" or, "I'm a whore!"—taking those once-negative labels and turning them around. Our culture's language structure alienates us. Part of our legacy from the Industrial Age is: widespread fragmentation and compartmentalization of our psychic and bodily life—

◆ HH: Right. For example, even though I'm a self-identified *femme*, when I'm fucking my girlfriend a lot of my fantasies are about *being a guy fucking a woman*. I've finally gotten to a certain point in my life where I don't *judge* that anymore; I've accepted that because it *works* for me—*I have a dick and I know what to do with it*. But there remains that critique in the lesbian-feminist community: that there's *no language for female desire* . . . And perhaps

I'm so saturated by heterosexual images that I can't conceive of something that's uniquely my own *and* lesbian. That might be true, but my feeling would still be, "*So? So can I still have my dick?*"

I continually feel the poverty of the words and language that supposedly express women's sexuality. There are a lot of descriptions of what happens to a man's dick from the moment it's flaccid to the moment he shoots his wad—minute descriptions that are part of our collective unconscious. But what happens to woman's genitalia? There's no language—and I think about that.

One of the things I like about being a lesbian is: I do feel freer in my sexuality. If I wanna penetrate someone, I can do that. And I can fuck in any orifice. I can take my imaginary dick off, and there are less values attached to it, because if I'm a lesbian "top" or "bottom," those roles don't translate to the rest of the world, whereas male/female ones *do*. And what happens in bed gets mirrored in the world, and values—positive and negative—get attached.

♦ **AJ: You're forced to *reinvent* language, because women's sexuality has largely been delineated by male writers—**

♦ **HH:** I know. The other day I was sitting around with my girlfriend and we were talking: "You always say I have a big clit, but I have a *tiny* clit, it's so hidden!" Then we realized the male referent: about *clit size?!* This was like a humorous remembrance of times I had been with guys who had anxiety about their penis size. It didn't seem like the same thing, yet—! I realized that since 15 years ago when I first fell in love with a woman, I spent far too little time really *thinking* about female sexuality: sizes of clits, characteristics of vaginas . . . what it was I *liked*. I spent far too little time really *inventing* or being inventive. So much of my own shame and lack of imagination kept me from really exploring and defining . . .

Women's sexuality in this culture, in any of its specific permutations (gay, straight, ambidextrous, of various classes and races) has really been invisible or has been lied about. It's interesting to think about coming up with a new language for lesbians . . . so women can express the reality of their own experience—

♦ **AJ: —without referencing to men . . . What are your thoughts on the Gulf War?**

♦ **HH:** I feel angry that we could effortlessly come up with a billion dollars a day to spend on the War, yet nothing, ever, for education. And that a $5000 NEA grant to a lesbian performance artist is a threat to National Security. Congress passed the AIDS-Care bill, but there are no funds to implement it. The homeless and the environment are completely neglected. Obviously we have the money to *kill* people, but we don't have the money to do anything else!

I feel so far outside of this culture, yet I know this is an illusion—I *am* part of it. There's that whole temptation to just drop out. I keep wondering what the strategies are so I can remain sane, have an impact—but not burn myself out. One thing I've done is join a group of about

"World Without End"   Photo: Dona Ann McAdams

10 people called GANG in New York. It's mostly lesbian and gay visual or performance artists including people who've spent time in direct action groups like ACT UP. We've been doing guerrilla postering and some guerrilla performance, and it's been really exciting. First of all, as someone who has mostly done personal or autobiographical work, it's such a relief to work on something else . . . to sit around over coffee and collaborate and fight (in a really good and productive way) about projects with people you respect, and come up with something and then *do* it.

In Sheridan Square in the West Village, right across from a big Marlboro billboard, we put up a billboard of a cowboy with Bush's face superimposed on it, and in the

"World Without End"   Photo: Dona Ann McAdams

same typeface as "Marlboro" it said, "AIDS CRISIS!" and in the "Surgeon-General's Warning" box it read, "WARNING: WHILE BUSH PLAYS COWBOY THERE'S ONE DEATH FROM AIDS EVERY EIGHT MINUTES IN THE UNITED STATES, AND 37 MILLION AMERICANS CAN'T AFFORD HEALTHCARE."

Even though I'm a *femme*, a lot of my fantasies are about being a guy fucking a woman —*I have a dick and I know what to do with it.*

We also did a piece at the BESSIES (the GRAMMYs of Performance Art), which is just as bloated and pretentious as the GRAMMYs. So much of the NEA controversy focused on the individuals, whereas in my case I felt it could have been about *any* lesbian performance artist. The reasons why I was the one who was chosen are complicated, but it was so transparent that the issue was completely about *my sexual identity*. Why was this so difficult to grasp? After all, the art world's riddled with queers—it's a fruit bowl! Ask any woman in the art world who tries to get a date on Saturday night! But why is there so little art that speaks about that experience?

So we did this whole piece: everyone thought I was supposed to come out on stage, but the curtains opened and I didn't come out and I didn't come out—finally they got the joke. Then a gay man and a lesbian came out and talked about why I'm not speaking . . . and that this is what the right wing would *like* to have happen: they'd like artists of color, lesbians, and gay men to simply disappear! Then we asked all the queers in the audience to stand up—a huge number rose to their feet. Then we asked anybody who'd *ever* slept with a person of the same sex to stand up, and there was a whole other wave . . . and then, anybody who'd done work that contained lesbian or gay content to stand up, and there was another wave.

We talked about the issues of community: why some people were sitting or standing, and what did it mean? . . . about putting your body on the line in terms of what you care about. Then we tried to address this trickier issue of: people who say that their identity, race, class or sexual preference has nothing to do with their *reception* of the work (because we'd like to tell the right wing that it has *everything* to do with that). And it ended by us saying to the people who were still sitting down, "If you're uncomfortable with being identified as 'lesbian' or 'gay', let's remind ourselves that we can talk all we want about homophobia, but unless you're willing to put your body on the line, it's not going to end. So if you're uncomfortable, and have a need to relentlessly assert your heterosexuality, there's a word for that discomfort: *homophobia.*"

We had various "plants" in the audience come onstage to pick up these bags of pink triangle badges while this Jewish faggot told this story: *In 1940 when Denmark was annexed to Germany, Hitler told the King of Denmark to order all the Jews to wear yellow stars. The Danish King's response was to put on a yellow star! Thousands of Danish citizens also put on yellow stars; as a result Denmark was the only country who didn't have mass exportation of Jews.* Then we said, "Would everybody who's a gay or lesbian please stand up," and we passed out pink triangles.

Now the amazing thing is: we already had about 98% compliance. But there were still a lot of people in the audience who were just furious; they wouldn't get into it. They knew what was being asked of them but weren't willing to stand up, and were angry. At intermission I heard all these people complaining, "What are these pink triangles about?" and somebody saying, "I think it's some sort of ACT UP thing." And this is the arts community in *New York City!*

I constantly wonder, "What can I do to really become an ally with people of color?" It's the responsibility of white people to cash in their *privilege chips* and really put their foot down. There's a way the lesbian/gay movement could really be important—because it's so inherently *mixed.* It's multicultural—male and female queers are everywhere and in all economic classes, ages, races and countries.

On the other hand, we're all infected with a sensibility which is so uncomfortable with "the Other" and with "difference"—this is baked into our religion. In our Judeo-Christian tradition, you take what you can't understand or incorporate about yourself and project it onto a *scapegoat,* so that then you're "free" (i.e., no longer responsible). It used to be an animal or a young human sacrifice (as in the story of Abraham & Isaac). We've built a whole culture on the psychological foundation of the *scapegoat;* we evade responsibility by relying on this mechanism that is *projecting* rather than *integrating*—

◆ **AJ:** —like projecting onto the "devil" all our repressed desires.

◆ **HH:** Also, we can talk about patriarchy and power in terms of being *too* successful predators who are proceeding to *do ourselves in.* We can talk about how human beings can be better in the future, but perhaps these impulses of aggression, territorialism and all that aren't necessarily *male*—perhaps they're not *inhuman.* They may really be in our blood and in our flesh; it may be horrifying and yet very normal for us to kill other humans over territory and resources. Maybe through admitting how normal this is, and how this is something we're *driven* to do . . . maybe through acknowledging that under the grip of this "animal nature to control a turf" we're *powerless,* we might reclaim some power. . .

With butch-femme identity polarization, the lesbians fell for a heterosexist view that was an aping of male-female desire, rather than a very specifically lesbian experience. Now *that's* completely changed: women are really getting into pussy in a big way, and it's great.

◆ **AJ:** A premise of our Judeo-Christian society is that humans are gods not beholden to "animal" creatures. Men think they are *superior* to animals. And this refusal to accept the animal (or devil) nature in man has created the psychotic serial killer—a creature who hasn't accepted his own animal blood, predatory nature and territoriality—in a sense, the devil inside him. Yet only through acceptance can one become integrated, whole, and creative again—

◆ **HH:** Rather than say that Saddam Hussein could be the next Hitler, I'd rather say, "We *all* could have been

Hitler! We're all Hitler! We all could *be* Hitler!" Let's start from that point, because we all have that capacity for fascism—that egomaniacal potentiality, that desire to extrapolate from personal pain into a horrific external manifestation, and label that "politics"—whereas really what it is is an *armor* against *personal pain.*

I've always resisted in feminism the notion that women are *innately* "better" or more "nurturing" or "closer to Nature," because this shows signs of the *Bambi* mentality. First of all: Is Nature *good?*

Something that I've always resisted in feminism is the notion that women are *innately* "better" or more "nurturing" or "closer to Nature," because this shows signs of the *Bambi* mentality. First of all: Is Nature *good?* No—nature is *without value.* If you look closely there's a lot that's horrifying, offensive and *not pretty* in "Nature". . .

◆ **AJ:** The Civilization vs. Nature duality is a projection of the Judeo-Christian idea that "Man" (that is, "White Men"—blacks and Indians weren't considered human) alone possesses a living soul which could return to God; everything else is condemned to hell. Now certain scientists are claiming there's not only a continuum between Man and Animal (chimpanzees can learn language) but between man and the machine. For instance, no longer can we in good conscience feel separated from the other "animals."

◆ **HH:** Feminism, in associating women with "nature," has sparked some very complicated considerations. A feminist friend of mine who's in her '50s says, "I used to be more of a conventional feminist, but now I'm a sociobiologist by avocation. I feel that we're a primate society, and if you look at primate societies they're all male-dominant. . ."

◆ **AJ:** But there are female-dominant "animal" societies, like bees—

◆ **HH:** Right. But I worry about any liberation movement putting on blinders—that maybe we're *not* going to "save the world" because we refused to face some unpleasant idea or fact. As a queer, I don't want to be imbued with any "divine" qualities. I think there are great deeds or events or people in queer culture that have been hidden or erased, and that it's important to reclaim them. And I think that all Outsider cultures have something that the dominant culture really needs. But we're not going to save the world by pretending that we're more "divine" or more "natural" or more "archetypal" or more truly *this* or *that*—

Photo: Dona Ann McAdams

◆ AJ: It's a trap for women to think they're that separate. If you start defining what you "are," you start getting so many exceptions that any argument can be whittled down. Actually, there's nothing you can say that women are, that men aren't (and vice versa).

◆ HH: In the '70s, feminist art criticism got lured down a *cul-de-sac* attempting to define qualities that "women's art" had. Absurd generalizations were aired: "that it resembled their mother's tuna-noodle casserole," etc—

The prevailing view in this country is that the role of art in this culture is not to *disturb* anyone.

◆ AJ: Or showed more "gentleness"—

◆ HH: It's more useful to go into the *actual work*, than to make theories about how you can separate women's art from men's art. There's a certain *scapegoating* mentality that happens in all liberation movements. I was in consciousness-raising groups in the '70s, and any time I was a pain in the ass I was told I was "acting like a man." When I was competitive and assertive (let's say *aggressive;*

let's go beyond the sanitized *YMCA/Learning Annex* term "assertive") then I wasn't being "nurturing."

As a woman I really like children, although I don't want to *have* them; I have a lot of problems with all those soft spots, plus their floppy necks. I suppose it's good for the species that there seems to be an *overabundance* of people who think that babies are the cutest things in the world. I'm sure my negative attitude derives from ways I was neglected as a baby, etc. As a "woman," as a mark of my "humanness," I'm supposed to be *overwhelmed* by babies. But I'm much more overwhelmed and moved by *pre-pubescence*—young people caught in puzzling intersections of childhood and adulthood. Yet as a woman I'm supposed to be able to bake bread, love babies, and—

◆ **AJ: Isn't that the dominant culture's definition of how a woman's supposed to be?**

◆ HH: But the feminist movement, in a lot of ways, certainly emphasized nurturing, cooperation, ways of relating to people other than war and abuse—and all these were important values to assert in the world. But— I just don't want to assign a *gender* to them. I can't assume that just because someone is a woman, they're going to be more nurturing or more understanding or more humane in their administration of power than if they're a male. We do ourselves a disservice if we make such generalizations—

◆ **AJ: A word like "nurturing" is quite meaningless until you get into specifics. We have to beware of a tendency toward a *fascism of labeling*. For example, I really love certain horror films that are filled with gore and blood. As much as I think the Gulf War was totally evil, I have certain "male" likes: I loved watching those planes swooping down on the CNN news broadcasts. I feel insulted if anybody's going to tell me what I as a female am supposed to enjoy or not enjoy—**

◆ HH: I think everyone's afraid, because all those values that were successful for such a long time are now being threatened. In this horrifying spiral that the world is in, what are some values worth holding onto? I think the word "values" is just a buzzword, a euphemism for very white, very Christian agendas. During the whole NEA controversy I was told over and over again (by people who should know better), "This is a *Christian* country." But the First Amendment guarantees us freedom *from religion* and establishes our government as a democracy, as a republic *without* a state religion. This clear-cut separation of church and state is really *news* to people. And this separation is really being eroded by the current Supreme Court, as is the part of the First Amendment that guarantees free speech and the right of assembly.

Really, the prevailing view in this country is that the role of art in this culture is not to *disturb* anyone. And another serious problem is *collective amnesia:* Nobody remembers anything. George Bush can make a statement . . . deny he said it six months later, and nobody *ever* confronts him on that. But we all know: it's not just what you say, it's who you are . . . and what you can get away with . . . ◆◆◆

Lydia Lunch

A thorn in the side of the performing arts establishment for over 15 years, Lydia Lunch is a "confrontationalist" whose musical onslaughts and spoken word invectives ravage middle-class, male-oriented morals and dogmas. Starting at age 16 as primal screamer/guitarist for the seminal New York punk band, *Teenage Jesus and the Jerks*, Lydia has continued her assault on complacency via music, film, video, theater, spoken word, and writing. Besides doing hundreds of performances, she has appeared on over 30 records, starred in a dozen films or videos, written 4 books, and produced/written a play (*South of Your Border*, with director Emilio Cubeiro in New York City). Over the years she has collaborated with numerous musicians including Nick Cave, Rowland S. Howard, *Foetus, Sonic Youth, Einsturzende Neubauten,* Henry Rollins, and Michael Gira. Her own bands have included *Eight Eyed Spy, 13.13, Beirut Slump,* and *Harry Crews.*

Legendary underground filmmaker Richard Kern worked with Lydia to realize her personal vision of the roadmap of sexual violence and desire in the classic shockers *The Right Side of My Brain* and *Fingered.* She starred in Beth and Scott B's films *Vortex* and *Black Box* and also appeared in Penn & Teller's *The Invisible Thread* and *BBQ Death Squad.* Recently Lydia completed *Kiss Napoleon Goodbye,* a film for Dutch TV co-authored by herself and also starring Henry Rollins and Don Bajema.

In 1984 Lydia founded Widowspeak Productions to release her work and the work of other cultural instigators with whom she tours—such as Wanda Coleman and Hubert Selby Jr. Many of her early rare recordings are now back in print. For a catalog offering *incendiary inspiration,* send $2 to Lydia Lunch, Widowspeak Productions, PO Box 1085, Canal St Station, NY NY 10013-1085.

Part I

♦ **VALE: Do you think it ever will be possible to have a society without exploitation?**

♦ LYDIA LUNCH: No. Absolutely not. Because I think it's man's nature to exploit power, position, authority, money, and it stems basically from greed. Exploitation and greed are tied together.

♦ **ANDREA JUNO: You mean "man's" nature—literally. So far the history of our planet has been—**

♦ LL: —Male-dominated! *Completely* male-dominated. And the general disrespect that human beings have come

to accept—to take for granted—astounds me. It doesn't seem like there's going to be any reversal of that . . . so exploitation, ownership and greed prevail.

♦ **AJ: But isn't that disrespect exclusive to a male-dominated society? Would that be transferred to a woman-dominated society?**

♦ LL: At this point still (which is astounding to me), I don't see the improvement of the position of women in the social, political, or economic echelons. I don't see the "equality" at all. I still see chronic domination by white middle-aged men in positions of power who will remain there forever, because *they decide who gets to decide.* Nothing short of *total war between the sexes* is going to eliminate that!

Photo: Jane Handel

as standards: we have this woman in a position of power, so we don't need another. I don't soon foresee equality of the minorities, of the races, of the sexes—and that's all in a certain order! I don't see any closing of that gap. I see a widening all the time.

Where I grew up, Rochester, New York, I saw black-and-white race riots outside my door in the '60s. But now, instead of people in a community banding together to protest their position in society, people are going, "Fuck you, man, I know I can't get ahead—I'm gonna get *mine.*" Not, "Let's bind together and show them we can't take this shit!"

♦ **AJ: How can the position of women improve***?*

♦ LL: I like the concept of the *Conspiracy of Women;* of a political party run *by* women *for* women. I'd like to encourage other women to become more political, to bond together, and to spread communication outside of their small circles. I'd like to see *more organization—*

women encouraging others: putting out books, newspapers, magazines, TV shows, radio programs, videos, and branching out in all media networks. Women have to find their own realm of politic, which doesn't necessarily play any of those male games, or go by those male rules or use those male formats, but which can somehow unite and cause change and enlightenment! And that's what the hope for *my* future is—I know that!

♦ **AJ: We don't have the luxury of being thoughtless about the earth anymore.**

♦ LL: We're at the breaking point.

♦ **AJ: We used to have a lot to kill: you could kill many people, animals and plants, but the earth wouldn't die.**

♦ LL: But now it's the opposite: they're killing too much of the earth and not enough of the people! *Another reversal of intelligence.*

♦ **AJ: So how do you view yourself regarding all this?**

Equality hasn't happened—not in the past ten years; and just examine the "progress" that's been made in the past twenty or forty! I don't know when that generation will finally die out: of the men who think like dinosaurs, and behave like their ancestors.

♦ **V: A woman like Margaret Thatcher behaves just like a man—**

♦ LL: —but using a single example like Margaret Thatcher is irrelevant. It's like, how many Ronald Reagans and George Bushes and Khadafys and Saddam Husseins and Fidel Castros, Manuel Noriegas, Charles Mansons, Ted Bundys—how many of these can we name to *one* woman in a position of power who acts like everyone else? That example means nothing!

♦ **AJ: Also, it's the male power structure that *allows* someone like Thatcher in—a women they know and trust will play by their rules.**

♦ LL: Yes; she is useful as a token. Tokens are often set

◆ LL: Merely as the *instigator*. Merely as the cattle prod. Instigation can be a fine art in itself! I never claimed to have any answers or solutions to the world situation; I merely report on it as I see it. But a common complaint about me is: "offers no solutions." Just because I call what's going on "disintegration" or "apocalypse now," *I'm* supposed to provide the salvation?!

You answer the fuckin' question . . . and answer it for yourself. Politicians offer solutions—they never work. My job is just to question the roots of the madness.

◆ **AJ: We all live in a brutal world, yet some people see this more clearly than others. I think everyone on some level is brutalized by existence—**

◆ LL: Absolutely. And that's why when people ask me, "How can you tell those *really personal* stories to everyone?" I reply, "These are *universal* stories. Merely because I use myself as an example . . ."

First of all, you shouldn't feel shame about the abuse you've incurred because—first rule, to all the victims—*it is not your fault*. Too many people take that guilt and shame upon themselves. Secondly, I'm only using my own example for the benefit of all who suffer the same multiple frustrations: fear, horror, anger, hatred . . . I speak for those who can't articulate it, that's all. And the stories aren't just personal—often they're very political, too. But the sexuality, the politics, the abuse—it's all interrelated, it's so historical. It goes beyond and before my lifetime—it goes back to the fucking *cave*.

◆ **AJ: Your childhood was pretty wretched, right? You were sexually molested by your father—**

◆ LL: It's quite brutal to realize at the age of six that one is no longer a *child*. You feel that something has snapped that will never return to you. And you can rationalize this, without the intelligence to truly understand it. That's the biggest obstacle to overcome: the point when you realize everything has suddenly changed, and will never go back . . . *until* . . . you return the power to yourself that has been stolen by that other person—and that's very difficult, and takes a long time to master.

I *like* the idea of a community sense. I like the concept of the *Conspiracy of Women;* of a *political party run by women for women.* I like the idea of this threat . . .

Because no matter how petty or how intense the abuse that a child has to go through—physical or psychological or self-induced environmentally, financially—everyone feels as if something has been *stolen* from them, or that they have been battered beyond repair. People are so insecure; they hate themselves or they hate their parents (or both), because they don't know what love is, and don't want the love they never knew. And that lack or void (which they've never dealt with) has twisted and demented their entire reality. So much of the problem is: *fear of intimacy* . . . not knowing how to love or be loved or nurture or encourage *without* controlling, manipulating, hurting, perverting. I think this stems both from just the repetitive cycle of abuse we had to withstand, and also a reaction against the '60s Love/Hippie shit. Two forces that converge on the same generation to really make people cruel, mean, and unconcerned . . . not only about themselves and others, but about the situation. Hence: apathy, lethargy, destruction, mayhem, boredom, drug abuse and death.

◆ **AJ: Yet you've used your art as a catharsis to not only speak for other people, but to heal yourself.**

◆ LL: From the time I was about 10, I was writing poetry and stories. So I had started to channel that painful energy while quite young. But also . . . I think the way most victims perpetuate the cycle is by *experimenting* on others and turning *them* into victims to relieve the pressure of their own pain. And I think I began doing that very early as an outlet—at 11 or 12. I became the "Bad Seed," like so many of us were. I kept notebooks or journals of these "experiments." I considered every relationship from the time I was 11 as a *psychological test* of strength, will, power, control, and pain.

◆ **AJ: For a woman, that isn't exactly a conventional outlook; it's an inversion—**

◆ LL: But it's just the other side of the victimization; the mirror image. Instead of *turning it around,* this merely perpetuated the cycle of abuse. But I think you can divorce yourself from that repetitive cycle of pain and victimization and channel the negative energy into creative outlets so that you *don't* have to continue to experiment on people. That's the growth process: to understand your psychoses and neuroses by spending enough time *by yourself* . . . to know yourself, and *love* yourself (not needing anyone else, of course, to love you). Yet also: not being in a position where you *reject* love because—god forbid, it's the four letter word!

Victimization steals the capacity to love or be loved, and that's a waste—in fact, many *generations'* worth of waste. Defensiveness, insecurity, ego and inadequacy plague the people of our country, because that's what they're taught: they're not good enough, they're not rich enough, they're not white enough, they're not smart enough. And that's inbred, generation after generation. The thing is: with patterns and cycles of abuse, the rhythm of the psychology and the drama behind these occurrences is what pumps the adrenalin through most people, because otherwise their lives would be unbearably numb and deadened from the pain they've witnessed before.

To be free of these negative, self-defeating, painful, alienating, lonely feelings, is to really accomplish a *great achievement*. Because "they" don't want you to feel anything but what they've drilled into you; they want to steal your pleasure—your pleasure zones; they know that when you're miserable you're not as effective or strong as when you're happy. And when you as a woman can *make yourself* happy, empowered, strong, loving, concerned, nurturing and encouraging (especially toward other women) . . . when that empowerment can be restored or regenerated in a loving fashion without threat, abuse, violence, cruelty or ego . . . *that's* when you start developing.

They're killing too much of the earth and not enough of the people! *Another reversal of intelligence.*

Instead of being a flaky blonde who works for somebody else, I'd rather be a shrewd businesswoman *any day,* thank you very much. *I know how to get what I want done—* that's my job.

♦ **V: Actually, how did you *become* a shrewd businesswoman? By demanding that every detail of every contractual arrangement be brought to light?**

♦ LL: Exactly—instead of just *agreeing* with whatever was proposed. By *organizing. Conceive, execute, document, desist, go on.* That's being a shrewd businesswoman. Make sure that everything you do is documented to your satisfaction. You don't take No for an answer—whatever it takes, you get it done!

♦ **AJ: What was it like back in the beginning of punk rock? You were a pioneer—**

♦ LL: "Annie Oakley of the Wild East."

♦ **AJ: How old were you when you moved to New York?**

♦ LL: Just turning 17, I think.

♦ **AJ: Did you run away from home?**

♦ LL: Of course. I just left. The End, Chapter One. I had been going to New York since I was 14; I'd run away from home a few times to check out the CBGB's scene—that was *happening*. The sense of community was very strong; people were having a good time and feeling good—it was before the big self-destructive binge when punk declined into death, destruction, and drugs. It was more positive.

When I first started going to New York, people went to these wild discotheques—5 stories, with incredible "happenings": just people performing—gays, lesbians, blacks, drag queens, glam rockers, whatever. All different types—all the sexual minorities—were blending together in these huge discotheques which were left over from the late '60s.

♦ **V: The punk scene started with poetry as a focus, somewhat like the Beatniks started.**

♦ **LL:** I think Emilio Cubeiro started doing the first performance art/poetry at CBGB's in '72; he lived right around the corner from there—he still does. When I first arrived in New York I stayed with some hippies including Lenny Bruce's daughter, Kitty Bruce. She was moving out of this loft and I took her room. Then I met James Chance . . . and then my band started. But his *stage antics*—he was *far* too expressive to be in *Teenage Jesus and The Jerks*. Because I wanted a very rigid regiment of almost military precision—this band was not to be a spontaneous combustion, it was about uncompromising, percussive stabs of pain. And his was a much more free-floating, lugubrious expressiveness. Finally we had to decide, "James, you have to do your own thing, *please*. You shouldn't be held back. I'm not going to tell you not to do that—just don't do it here!" Other bands like *Mars* and *DNA* were already rehearsing at my house—since everybody knew each other, the whole scene quickly bonded together . . .

♦ **V: It must have been like punk rock in San Francisco, 1977—it wasn't just about music—people were remaking and rethinking *everything*. It was a complete cultural rebellion.**

♦ LL: Yes! It was a very good time. It was the upswing. It was still riding the crest of the '60s "liberation."

♦ **AJ: What ideas from those days do you still hold?**

♦ LL: First and foremost: *no compromise*. As soon as I started writing, doing a band, recording records, going to Europe, touring . . . all that just made me realize (as I had always known): *"You want to do something, YOU DO IT. Listen to no one but yourself. DO IT."* I think that's the most important lesson. Being able to do something at such an early age intensified in me the idea: "Don't take No for an answer. If you want to do it, you get it done. You've got to do it yourself. Don't listen to *them;* don't listen to anyone else. Do it the way *you* want it done."

The manifestations of these themes have changed . . . have gone from one pain, one heartache, one broken bone, one mood swing, one emotional dystopia, one stab in the dark . . . to another. Well, that's just part of the developmental procedure of examining yourself and trying to get over your personal story . . . then looking at the greater picture. Because until you're over your personal problems, you are so self-obsessed, so wounded-animal-in-the-cave, that when you finally salve the wounds: *admit, eliminate denial, go to confession, get over it* . . . when you can see the bigger picture—you realize that not only are you *not* alone, but there's even less hope for the whole picture than there was with you just crying in your bedroom with the gun in your hand! Now you need *two* guns—one in each hand!

♦ **AJ: —and they're no longer aimed at yourself. You wrote two of Richard Kern's films, *Right Side of My Brain* and *Fingered*—two very powerful films. How do you feel about the impact they've had?**

♦ LL: Well, I'm very happy with the way the first film, *Right Side of My Brain* turned out. It was made for only $500, I believe. It's very black-and-white *noir,* with a soft poetic explanation about the cycle of feminine abuse and violent relationships and why possibly that carries on . . . how the energy connected to that, and the adrenalin that goes along with that, is what abates all the pain. I look at it in the same way I think Polanski's *Repulsion* is a *romantic* film: it's tragic in a way, but it's not sappy—it's very sad.

Fingered is an uglier rendition of a similar theme. It shows again how the cycle of abuse turns the victim into the victimizer—sometimes completely accidentally through being a "victim of circumstance"—through being willing to "go along with" the situation to see what the end result of the experiment will be. *The thrill of the kill.*

◆ **AJ: The intensity in *Fingered* is an achievement in itself. It's like looking at the world through the eyes of a psychotic.**

◆ LL: It's not meant to be erotic, or pornographic—it's just *reality*—and that means *pornography!* Most people don't want to take that chance . . . to test or learn. And that film was a *learning process:* to try to show that sometimes ugliness and pain, when they're in your face, are very attractive from a close distance. We were trying to show how the *rules of attraction* may be *quite different* from the way they seem—well, there are no rules. *First rule: no rules!*

So much of the problem of the generation I speak for is: *fear of intimacy* . . . not knowing how to love or be loved or nurture or encourage *without* controlling, manipulating, hurting, perverting.

◆ **V: Do you think it's possible to have a personal relationship without exploitation?**

◆ LL: I don't know. I have to admit that exploitation (in my own personal experience) was part of the learning process—there was no choice. Because I'm not writing fiction; I'm not dealing with *dis*-reality. So in order to stop the exploitation that goes on in my personal relationships . . . every character that goes through my life ends up in a story. They're interesting characters that need to be documented, because they won't do it *themselves* and their stories need to be told. Exploitation always has a bad and negative connotation given to it. But it just depends on how it's done: willingly, secretively, against one's will, or with full approval for therapeutic or educational purposes.

◆ **V: One antidote to exploitation is communication or honest confession—**

◆ LL: And here a lot of men shut down; the walls come

crashing down whenever a heavy emotional confrontation might threaten to force some deeper communication. Yet that's when they become *men* and no longer act like boys, because boys are the frightened ones that don't want intimacy because they fear it . . . because they might get hurt—as if anything is going to hurt . . . and so what if it does?—you'll *live.*

◆ **AJ: Exactly. To shatter your ego—*so what?* What are you losing? Just your previous sense of your Self. Hopefully you can learn and get wiser. You can't learn about yourself in a vacuum—only by taking risks can you gain valuable lessons that increase maturity.**

◆ LL: What amazes me is that people feel it's better to shut down and *not* experience something, than to experience possible pain. Women deal with chronic and constant pain throughout life: physical, emotional, psychological—living in our society as the second-class citizens they still are.

Fear of rejection and possessiveness often go hand-in-hand, and that's where things really get dangerous and unattractive. People fear rejection because they really need to possess (or be possessed by) someone else. Because basically *they don't want to be alone.* They don't want to be with themselves. They're frightened to be alone. They don't know how to live with themselves; therefore, they always have to be living with someone else . . . *through* someone else. I really don't think people should live together; I think they should live separately—completely. Because that freedom is so important. Even if you're working on separate creative projects, you still need time to be alone in order to *center.* I think that "codependency" is the first bullshit that has got to go. Society chronically reinforces the notion that you need a mate, you need a partner, you need a husband, you need a lover, you need a mother, you need a father, you need a fuck—or fuck you!

◆ **AJ: Let's get on to another subject. You did the screenplay, "Psycho-Menstrum," based on your study of female diseases. You learned how there's really very little research being done on them—**

◆ LL: I'll talk about my diseases if you talk about yours! *Let's play doctor.* PID interests me incredibly, because pelvic inflammatory disease first publicly reared its head in the early '70s, mostly because of the Dalkon Shield lawsuits. This was an IUD which a lot of women could have been suing for *if* they read the *one* article printed in the paper last year, because Dalkon was handing out $6 billion dollars to women who had been injured by their IUD. And any woman who has had an IUD has no doubt suffered in one way or another. I don't know *one man* who would allow a copper rod to be inserted into the tip of his penis and left there to rust for years . . . and continue to function as a sexual human being.

◆ **AJ: PID is an intense "set" of diseases that they know nothing about. The AMA would never tolerate knowing so little about a male disease that affected the male penis—**

◆ LL: —and that affected so much of the population.

At least 25-30% of the female population have suffered from PID, because it *is* sexually transmitted. And once you have it, you tend to get it again—under stress, bad diet, no sleep, or different sexual partners. Every time a new unprotected partner is introduced into your feminine body (we forget how raw and exposed the feminine genitals on the inside *are;* how close they are to the inner organs; they're the gateway to the whole body) pollutants run rampant—whether they're something that you notice and smell or not. *Very unhygienic!* All sorts of feminine cancers (which they don't want to call feminine cancers, like PID) are transmitted sexually through unprotected contact that *women* pay the cost of. *Ladies,* invest $1.99—get yourself some condoms, please! (Or: if men are too fuckin' cheap to afford 'em, they're outta luck! You don't need "it"!)

That's the growth process: to *understand* your psychoses and neuroses by spending enough time *by yourself* . . . to know yourself, and *love* yourself.

To me AIDS is not as frightening as all the other things that lead up to it. People have a *focus* on AIDS, but no one is talking about the twenty other *common* sexually transmitted diseases which plague mostly women (which men *do* transmit, but have no symptoms of) like chlamydia, which many people have, and which can also go into the bloodstream and cause what is commonly known as "Yuppie Disease"—chronic fatigue.

◆ **AJ: In a performance you cited a litany of these diseases that sounded so poetic—**

◆ LL: —just like a Greek chorus: Chlamydia, Candida Albicans, Condyloma Acuminata (genital warts), Trichomonas, Vaginitis, Endometriosis, Pelvic Inflammatory Disease, Herpes, Syphilis, Gonorrhea—to name a few. Let us not forget non-specific urinary tract infections (NSU) . . .

◆ **AJ: In your screenplay you're also talking about PMS: another underreported—**

◆ LL: —problem we all suffer from. [laughs] It's about a biology student who's dissatisfied with the lack of research about many ills, but especially the *monthly monster:* premenstrual tension. Unable to comprehend how half the population could possibly suffer from this *every single month* (the cramping, the bloating, the weight gain, the irritability, the insatiability, the mood swings) she sets out to experiment on herself with steroids and hormones in order to discover a solution hopefully beneficial for the entire female population.

Her experiments come to unfortunate ends, because she tries injecting steroids, hormones, estrogen and pro-

gesterone, causing an imbalance which causes her to start acting like a man—*not* the desired effect! She becomes extremely sexually aroused and *bloodthirsty,* acting out fantasies [which have been illustrated by cartoonists Robert Williams and Charles Burns]. Each fantasy is experienced not only as a hallucination but as an actual chemical imbalance which causes indescribable mood swings—just like premenstrual tension—only *exaggerated* under the influence of the drugs.

I'm hoping that with a caricatured, slightly comedic portrayal leaning toward futuristic sci-fi *sex horror,* some controversy may be instigated (if at first as a joke). At least the film will pose the question, "Why isn't there research being done about this?" What if women *did* begin taking hormones and steroids and acting like men—what would the consequences be? Women should start pioneering . . . experimenting with different drugs and hormones, to find a remedy that is not harmful and that possibly could be administered holistically.

◆ **AJ: It's amazing that PMS and PID are still tittered about. If you talk about prostate cancer, nobody's tittering about *that*. But somehow PMS is "funny": "She's on the rag," and it's not taken seriously. The whole field of women's gynecology—**

◆ LL: —is 50 years behind the times. And the lack of holistic research—well, holistic medicine is not an abusively profitable business, so that's why there are no holistic cures. It's practiced by individuals who are not necessarily linked to medical associations—therefore they usually can't charge too much for a given herb.

◆ **V: There are over 9,000 "medicines" in pill form. Think of all the profits—**

◆ LL: At $15 to $35 a bottle, or more!

◆ **V: They're an ideal capitalist commodity: cheap to manufacture, invested with a mystical aura—plus you can charge whatever the market will bear.**

◆ **AJ: Also, most drugs don't really heal, they just relieve symptoms, so you have to constantly come back for more—**

◆ LL: Absolutely. Drugs often relieve one problem and replace it with another. Antibiotics often eliminate one form of infection just to make the body vulnerable to another—which they can treat you for again. Thus they perpetuate your cycle of sickness and discomfort and weakness and suffering. But I'm not a doctor; I can only *complain* about this. I'm not inventing any new cures; I can only ask, "Why aren't *you* doing something about this?"

It's unbelievable, but before 1970 the American medical society would not admit that women actually had cramping every month—it was a figment of your imagination! During the Victorian era it was, "Don't get out of bed!" God forbid—she might get crazy, she might do something horrible, she might become violent—so *stay in bed.* But during the Depression women were out in the fields working, because female manpower was needed. Cramps?—you worked *through* them—"it's all in your head!" So society has treated the menses differently throughout history: hiding women in huts when they're menstruating (Rastafarians did that).

♦ **AJ: The menses is a very powerful time, when you're connected to your deepest sense of self . . . but we're not in an inner-directed world, we have to be external; we have to answer the phone—basically we're thrust into this frenzied capitalist world—**

♦ LL: All the stress, the caffeine, the work, and the pressure make the menses all the more uncomfortable. The fact that you have no time to go *into* yourself and actually rejuvenate makes it worse. And of course cramping and frustration are just going to feed off each other. Everything is compounded; there's no time to just allow the menses ritual to take its time for regeneration, like animals do who are more in tune with themselves—who are not blinded by the 9-to-5 paycheck chase.

♦ **AJ: . . . Why did you choose "Widowspeak" as a name for your record company?**

♦ **V: —like the Black Widow Spider?**

♦ LL : More like the woman without a husband who doesn't *need* the man . . . or who's *outlived* the man. I think it sums up a philosophy: *the sisters are doing it for themselves.*

Part II

♦ **V: Do you always get up at 6 AM?**

♦ LL: I like to, because the first four hours of the day are the most peaceful. No one's calling you on the phone, I can assure you of that. No one's knocking at the door, and even the mailman doesn't come 'til noon. So I like to get an advantage on everyone else; have some *peace* time. Also that's just my natural rhythm—that's when I wake up. I'm not really a night person like *so many artists* [sneers]—fuckin' clowns. (Yeah, the circus happens at night, too!) I prefer to rise with the sun. That doesn't mean I go down when it goes down—if *only* I were so lucky. So many of the nights of my childhood were based around fear and apprehension of night which has to do with the fact that my night life was *stolen* from me as a child at a very early age.

♦ **AJ: What do you mean: that your nights were stolen from you?**

♦ LL: Well, by an intruder in the form of the father figure.

♦ **AJ: And this started when you were really young?**

♦ LL: Yeah; I think that's when my whole "night sickness" came in. And that's why I'm probably much more active in the day. Because at night I would have to—as a preservation or a survivalist tactic—*shut down.* When I lived in L.A., I was in a constant state of night panic, because it's such a violent place. It seemed like people committed the most random violence just for pleasure, and I really felt I could be the next target . . .

So it might seem that I would be so panicked at night that I wouldn't be able to fall sleep until 6 AM. But it's the *opposite*—if I can get to bed before midnight, I'll be okay. But if I don't get to bed until 3 in the morning,

then I won't be able to go to sleep.

♦ **AJ: I read that statistically at *least* one out of three women have been victims of incest as children—**

♦ LL: And what about men?

♦ **AJ: Well, they don't collect statistics like that because they want to protect male sexuality, right? But I wouldn't be surprised if it's high for males, too. Little girls *and* little boys are basically—**

♦ LL: Fodder for abuse.

♦ **AJ: Yeah. Passive, powerless receptacles. But I think there's a lot of self-empowerment coming out of that now. People are really starting to deal with that issue—deal with that rage.**

♦ **V: You mentioned an idea for a seminar?**

♦ LL: To do a seminar for women only, that would bring together a lot of concepts about reparation, self-empowerment—getting over addictions, co-dependency, self-destruction, and loneliness.

That's why I moved to New Orleans: to do a lot of research, reading, writing, and pull together different sources of information to try to arrive at some kind of "non-school-of-philosophy" basic *how-to* guidelines to help yourself *not* continue doing the same things you've always done . . . holding yourself back in the same ways.

I'd also like to set up a women's art coalition—an art therapy house where women artists and writers from all around the country (or the *world*) can come to just relax or work. So that they can have *input* from other women who are also doing progressive and creative endeavors, and also try to get over their own personal disabilities.

♦ **AJ: What are some of the philosophies you'd initiate?**

♦ LL: Well, to get over all bullshit *now,* and to quit harboring pain from the past. Now is the time to take your stand and to empower yourself. We all have been beaten down repeatedly in every relationship that involves another person—to one extent or another. The seminar would be just for women to be able to look to themselves, empower themselves, and *need* only themselves. Instead of looking for another person to make your life happy, have the potential in *yourself* to make other people happy—not to satisfy them or cater to them, but to be secure in your own desires and intentions so that you can inspire other people to get their act together. I think that's the priority.

♦ **AJ: How did *you* achieve this for yourself?**

♦ LL: Thirty-one years of crawling through the shit . . . slowly and surely eliminating all the destructive patterns, habits and rituals, one by one. Trying to analyze where they came from, and where certain attractions, addictions and patterns originated.

I asked myself, "Who am I? Where the hell am I, and at this point why aren't I further along the road than *this?*" I think people have got to give up the fear of being alone, *especially* women—and especially when after twenty-five they start feeling that already they're too old. They don't realize that they're reaching their *peak* at *thirty-five* or even older—not twenty-one, not fifteen. If

Photo: Birrer

women could just be strong enough, secure enough, and happy enough to live by themselves—*satisfying* themselves—ultimately they'd be satisfying other people as well. This is a very important lesson. Most people are more lonely with someone else than they are when they're by themselves.

◆ **AJ: That's for sure. A live-in relationship leads to a daily dose of dulling ritual—**

◆ **LL:** It's a pattern—and patterns are not good. What I originally started dealing with was my own personal internalization of the abuse of the world, because you have to externalize your frustration and anger in order to see it and get over it. You can't just keep it bottled up inside, because eventually that will drive you *insane*.

◆ **V: What if you're not a painter, writer, or sculptor?**

◆ **LL:** There are other forms of expression. Even the ability to just confide in other people, and get things off your chest—that's in the oldest tradition of storytelling.

◆ **V: Would you work with meditation?**

◆ **LL:** I think meditation is a good thing. Meditation gives you that twenty or thirty minutes where you don't think about anything else . . . except for energy and healing. I think that has a very positive effect—because you *need* that free time, that free space.

People don't give themselves that time; they don't allow themselves to just give it up. They have to chronically *obsess* on what they're going to do next, or what just happened. As opposed to just sitting back, shutting down, shutting up, and letting it out. This is such a basic concept, you know?

I mean—physical exercise is good for that. Bike riding is good, taking a walk—anything that puts you out of contact with everyone else and into contact with your *self*. I think even just breathing and physical exercise helps you concentrate more. Improving your physical condition can have a powerful effect on your mental health—just through the oxygen intake you can improve your outlook. Look at someone who's neurotic, hyperventilating, panicking—meditation could be a necessary *must!*

◆ **V: You were talking about "letting go"—I think that's easier said than done: to let go of past pain, guilt and unresolved trauma from childhood—**

◆ **LL:** The key is to resolve them and let them go. To distance yourself also—

◆ **V: You mean forgive yourself?**

◆ **LL:** Yes—to not take the burden. Most victims take on the responsibility as if *they* caused the problem. That's the whole syndrome with child abuse: they always feel that *they're* the ones that brought it on, *they're* the guilty party. They take on the guilt because usually the violator does not. And the guilt has got to go somewhere.

I think the first step in self-recovery is to be able to say, "I am not the guilty one. It was not a personal thing against *me*. I was just the convenient battering ram. I was just used as the receptacle; I am *not* the receptacle." I think that's a big key to getting over personal pain overload—to distance yourself from personal responsibility about the act that was committed against you without your desire—when you were either too young or too weak to defend yourself. The first key is to forgive yourself and to take *back* yourself, reclaim yourself, and to heal the self-hate that these situations have forced you into. Because that's the biggest plague of our generation anyway: *self-hate*.

Also, people propagate their own abuse. They get stuck in that pattern, it's all they know, it's what they can respond to, it's what they know how to deal with. A great quote from Bataille's *Guilty:* "The greatest desire is a wounded person's need for another wound"—very true. Because that's what you know, that's what you can deal with, that's what you understand, and that's what you respond to—because through pain you have blocked out just about everything else.

I think that feeling of dislocation, limbo, and disorientation is the first thing that's got to be healed or clarified in a victim's life: "You are here now! That shit *happened*, but now it's over!" Easier said than done, but—you first have to realize that *the past is the past*. And in order to prevent the future from mirroring and mimicking that, you have to take control immediately and focus on your emotional conditions which are not intrinsic to your true self, but that were ground into you.

So many responses that you have are not real responses—they're *conditioned* responses. And that's the first thing that's got to be given up: "I'm acting this way because *they* did that, and this is the conclusion." Also I find in the communication between people (especially two pained, frustrated, unwhole people) that between intention and interpretation there is so much *perversion*. Because people take a communication or response and then start twisting or perverting it to mesh with their own cycles and abuses and patterns. And that's very dangerous. That's also what locks people into cycles that propagate themselves in a relationship: so many things just keep getting misinterpreted, become cyclical and destructive: "Well, you said that, and you did that, but you must have meant *this*. So I'll act like *that*." PAIN ATTRACTS PAIN. The more capacity you have for pain—well, when your pain threshold is your greatest accomplishment, that's not much of an achievement! And being the *Queen of Pain*, I can tell you: There are other things that are more important!

♦ **V: Aren't we always striving toward the goal of being nonexploitative in our relationships with our friends?**

♦ LL: Absolutely. However, I do think most people are more interested in conflict, because it's more interesting and it's what they're familiar with. It's more exciting (it gets the adrenalin going) than a "peaceful, happy, loving" relationship—which to most of us sounds pretty fuckin' boring (although it doesn't have to be).

I think the basic key to a long-lasting relationship is to realize that that person is not there to satisfy your desires and goals, but to satisfy their *own*. And if you at the same time are clear on *your* goals and desires and satisfactions, then you can coexist (and I don't say cohabitate). And then, if two people share so much in common that they can continue in a relationship for an extended period of time . . . freedom and respect for the other person have got to be the priorities: "You want to do that? Do it!"

Women are denied masturbation even more severely than men . . . that's another method of control— they're not taught to please *themselves*. It takes most women a while to warm up to the "situation," but once they get into it, they're hooked— well everyone I know is!

I think that's where most relationships begin their downfall: when one person tries to please the other—one person tries to live for the other, satisfy the other— be the ideal of the other. Why not be the ideal of yourself? Why not make yourself as satisfied and happy and full as possible? And if the other person can enjoy that ride, there's a sidecar—"Strap yourself in! Put your helmet on—it might be rough!" But I think people are too dependent on other people for their happiness, their satisfaction, or to alleviate their loneliness.

I also think women are denied masturbation even more severely than men, and that's another method of control—they're not taught to please themselves. Whereas men jack off from the time they're nine years old! Most women—it takes them a while to warm up to the "situation," but once they get into it, I'm sure they're going to get just as hooked as—well, everyone I know is! I think if women were taught to love themselves from masturbation on upward, that would make the whole sexual conflict a little easier to deal with. If women could really take themselves as their own lover, and enjoy their bodies and their sexuality, with and to and by themselves—that's 50% of the battle. My favorite line is: "Masturbation satisfies what reality cannot withstand."

♦ **AJ: [laughs] That's a good one. Most women don't even *know* their own genitals!**

♦ LL: It's not like they don't have mirrors in the house, honey. They're all *over* the place. Get down there and

Photo: Beth B.

been pounded into them, and have taken their own stance—it's beautiful. Women should find encouragement in the fact that there *are* men out there that are capable of rising above the bullshit. I wouldn't shoot 'em for the world!

I'd also wipe half the *female* population off the face of the fuckin' earth if I could—because they're not doing their job; they're buying the game; they're swallowing it whole—they're fuckin' choking on it! What makes *them* better? Just because they're not *running* the fucking game—why should they get more credit? They're allowing it to continue in the same fashion too. So it's not as if this side is good just because they're *women*—that's bullshit. You can't just cut the population in half. It's not that easy.

◆ **AJ: One of the dangers in a separatist community is that through hatred and conflict toward men, they internalize the very attributes they are against, thus perpetuating the same old game—**

◆ LL: Absolutely.

◆ **AJ: What do you think about pornography in general?**

◆ LL: I think the problem is not getting rid of what's there—just expanding the boundaries of what exists. Mine is not to dictate—it's to *encourage*.

Men have these concepts of female submission in the first place, and pornography caters to that. Pornography is a symptom of the problem which is sexual inequality. Eliminating one of the symptoms doesn't solve the problem. You've got to go to the root cause and redress the imbalance.

◆ **AJ: It's very important to distinguish what is fantasy and what is reality.**

◆ LL: Absolutely, because denying women pleasure and making them feel guilty about it, is to deny them power—that's the bottom line.

◆ **AJ: Right. If people really gave pleasure a top**

start doing a little investigative research—unlock those mysteries. Because 98% of the men out there aren't going to able to.

◆ **AJ: So what do you think of the lesbian separatist view that men are incorrigible—that this world has gone *too* far, and men really cannot be coped with?**

◆ LL: I don't think we have to disregard half the population just because 75% of them are chronic assholes. We've got to think about the ones that are willing to change, and the ones that are capable of change, and the ones that are really fighting (in their own way) for the right side, anyway. I don't think all men are bad, or that all men are evil and stupid. I'm not a lesbian and have no desires of becoming one in the near future. I don't think it's that simple—to just wipe out half the population. It would be nice, but I'd miss a few of the buggers myself. I think they're *useful*. When men have gotten over what's

114

priority, who in their right mind would go into an alienated office and sit and type all day—40 hours a week (plus commute time)—for some corporation that doesn't give a damn about them? How do you keep an *insane* system like that going—in which people willingly consent to the taking away of their own lives?

♦ **LL:** If the American white male-dominated society is based on violence and war, then if women really want to get ahead, that's the only route they can take. They can't try to reason. We've been trying to reason with men for thousands of years, and it *doesn't work*. Men are not reasonable people, for the most part—they're too territorial. So now it's time to say, "Well, this is *our* fucking planet. We gave birth to it, and it is in *our* likeness that it is created. You are fucking with us—so fuck you." Because that's the only language they can understand. They're not going to understand reasoning. Not at this late a date.

♦ **AJ: How do you see women evolving—getting together and organizing?**

♦ **LL:** I think there's no choice—*someone's* going to have to start organizing coalitions. What would I like to predict as the ultimate outcome? A complete overthrow. And real revolution, and for women to just *shut the whole fucking country down.* Just say No. Don't pay the rent. Don't pay the gas bills. Don't pay any insurance. Just say, "No, I'm not working anymore!" But it has to be done totally—I mean, people have *all* got to be ready to take that stance. It can't be ten isolated people or you'll get squashed. It can't be just a few women here and there sneaking into positions of power. It has to be done in the only way they understand, which is to dominate them and to completely overthrow them. Because otherwise it's not going to happen.

♦ **AJ: So what would you like to see right now?**

♦ **LL:** I'd like to see a women's army storm into the White House with Uzis and shotguns and eliminate at least half the population who work in politics. They're killing you slowly—what's the alternative? Kill them quickly, kill them now—before they kill everything else, okay? That's the only choice. Sorry—I didn't make it up, you know? Revolution is not a new concept—it just hasn't been practiced for a long time in this country . . . not in the way other countries are willing to practice it. And there *is* no time left.

♦ **AJ: So what are *you* doing?**

♦ **LL:** I'm rallying the troops. That's my job. Everyone should assume a position in the ranks of this army, because it *is* war, and that's it. As I've said before: if 1% of the population controls 80% of the money, *that shit has got to change.*

♦ **V: . . . Would you advise women to keep journals and diaries?**

♦ **LL:** I think diaries and journals serve a function, at least to be able to have something (if not someone or somewhere) to put thoughts that totally plague you. But you've got to be willing to *learn* from the repetition that will be written in those pages. I always used to *burn* all my notebooks when they were finished!

♦ **V: Really?**

♦ **LL:** Yes, like: "Well, I know that now—time to torch!" I don't think that you need a specific *artifact* to express what you know, or what you're going through, or what you're doing, or what you're creating. I think you just have to be able to open the floodgates—to be able to let that out in a way that's going to *heal* . . . whether it's into a book, into someone else's face, into a tape recorder, into a typewriter, onto a canvas—I don't think the *format* is so important as the fact that you just have to be ready to let it out . . . give it up. And also, if need be, open that wound to scrutiny by other people (as opposed to the "male thing" of just closing down, shutting up, and keeping it inside). Women "naturally" tell other women what's going on—they don't seem to have that inhibition. They're more open to expounding upon the *disease of the day*.

♦ **AJ: Shame is what the control system's all about. The power system wants you to feel ashamed and secretive. For decades women's sexuality has been a source of *shame and denial*—and that has just perpetuated the status quo. Secrecy and keeping things inside are all part of a mechanism to keep you down and powerless.**

♦ **LL:** Absolutely.

♦ **AJ: Where do you think you derive your strength from?**

♦ **LL:** I always gathered my strength from knowing that it was *the rest of the world* versus *me*. I took *comfort* in that fact—as opposed to other people who feel so alone, and get buried by it. I know that every problem I speak about (no matter how personalized it is or how unique the details are) is *universal*.

We forget how raw and exposed the feminine genitals are on the inside; how close they are to the inner organs. Every time a new unprotected partner is introduced into your feminine body —pollutants run rampant!

No matter how well I knew anyone else or how well anyone understood me, or how well I got along with anyone, still: *you stand by yourself,* at the end of the day and at the end of your life. So why not get used to that fact? Why not grow to become your best friend, your biggest *confidante,* and your staunchest supporter?

Maybe that started because within my family structure, I felt as though I didn't *belong* to them. I didn't *look* like them, had nothing in *common* with them—I felt I had been exchanged in the nursery—which my parents had told me and I always *believed*! So feeling separate within the family was a good introduction for me to the rest of the world. I felt isolated from the time I could walk, think, and talk—and with the abuse and all of that religious insanity compounded with incestuous alienation—well, at a very early age I just took comfort in the fact that I didn't belong.

People have a *focus* on AIDS, but no one is talking about the twenty other *common* sexually transmitted diseases which plague mostly women.

I grew up in Rochester, New York, which is a fairly large industrial town. There's a ghetto of every breed in every corner of the city: bike gangs, gangsters, and hard boys—the *works*. I loved it.

But by the time I was 13, I knew I would get out of that reality. I knew that I needed to get out on the road and start experiencing what lay *beyond*.

♦ **V: Did the movies have any formative influence on you?**

♦ LL: As a young teenager I went to the drive-in movies a lot. One of the first films I saw was *Last House on the Left*—probably at age thirteen. And that was a good education—it's a small tale of psychotic revenge on three rapists who end up getting their own deaths served on a platter in a very grisly fashion. It was fascinating to me at the time—far more so than it is now.

But I think that music influenced me more—and writing. I was reading Freud, Sade, and Hubert Selby at 14 or 15, and those 3 writers probably influenced me the *most*—more than movies and more than music. Music influenced me to get out of Rochester and go to New York, because I saw and heard what was happening there at CBGB's and Max's. But reading those books—especially *Last Exit to Brooklyn* and the books by the Marquis de Sade—made me decide there was more to reality than the one I was functioning under, so . . . *time to expand*.

♦ **V: In Sade's books, did you identify with the males who are torturing the women?**

♦ LL: I could identify more with the philosophy behind Sade—that behind all the actions was *human or animal nature*. And that "nature" is the intrinsic driving force behind murder, rape, domination, fear, and insecurity. Because Sade, more than *anyone*, understood human nature. Even when he was exaggerating to the fullest of

his creative powers, he understood the basic *fears*. And he displayed them in horrifyingly graphic, exaggerated terminology, which made it obvious where they were coming from—every atrocity was excused by the fact that its origin was *man's human nature.*

♦ **AJ: What do you think *women's* human nature is?**

♦ LL: I think it involves nurturing, growth and development, and I think for the most part it's a very peaceful nature—when it's not pounded out of them, and when it's not perverted in them. Find me a woman that hasn't been perverted by the powers that be, and I'll show you one that hasn't been born yet!

♦ **AJ: You have a warrior mentality, but you also have grown beyond that. You aren't going to fuck over other victims, or derive sadistic pleasure in—**

♦ LL: —eliminating the weaker. I get more power from *empowering* weaker people than I do from obliterating them. It's the ones that *think* they're so strong that need to be obliterated. Why pick on the weaker?

♦ **V: Do you think that men wage war because they haven't really come to grips with death itself?**

♦ LL: Well, I have a quotation: "Men are so afraid to die that they have to kill everything in sight."

♦ **AJ: Exactly. Men are so *chicken shit*—they are so scared of death—**

♦ LL: —and losing control. And having to submit.

♦ **AJ: And the ultimate submission is to death—**

♦ LL: —a very natural progression, I might add. Thank god for *death!* It will one day be over—at least *this* version of it.

♦ **V: Do you believe in reincarnation?**

♦ LL: I don't really like the term "reincarnation." *Karma*—that's another tricky one. I think things are recycled to some degree—I think *energy* gets recycled. Reincarnation?—I don't know.

♦ **V: Well, maybe you'll be reborn—**

♦ LL: No. I hope to *not* be reborn, actually. I think I've reached the limit of my endurance for this reality. I would like to think this is my final life—that doesn't mean I feel it may have been my *only* one, but I would like to feel it is the *last* one.

What we do with our lives is basically squander as much of them away as possible, until we get so near to the finish line that we panic. But in my own personal life, I hope that *this is it*. I have no faith in reincarnation for myself in the future, and I would prefer it didn't happen, *thank you very much.* I look forward to the *relief* of death. I've never shirked it. That it hasn't greeted me at my front door yet is a miracle—I've left the door wide open.

♦ **V: But you don't tempt death, do you? You're fairly prudent.**

♦ LL: No, I've just lived in about 42 ghettoes in my life, where I was surrounded by maniacs of every dimension, from every walk of life. No, I do take precautions—I *do* wear clothes in the street. [laughs]

♦ **V: What do you think about women studying martial arts, self-defense, and handgun skills?**

♦ LL: Absolutely—more power to you. *Whatever it takes.*

Whatever it takes to make you feel better, and better able to defend yourself. Hand-to-hand combat and the ability to do so is an important issue, but more important is the ability to protect yourself from all the *other* traps that "they" set for you—the more insidious pitfalls. That's more important.

Men are so afraid to die that they have to kill everything in sight.

Of course, as violence becomes more predominant, one has to be equipped to face that reality, because it's becoming an urgent issue. It *is* civil war that we are living in. Just because one's safe little reality isn't confronted with it every day because of blind spots, blinders, and defense mechanisms, doesn't mean it's not right there. It's there. You're just safe *for now.*

♦ **AJ: Rape is up 50% over the last 10 years—even taking into account the fact that more women are reporting it.**

♦ LL: I think if more men started becoming the victims of rape—or castration—that might help redress the imbalance of sexual violence.

One of the points in my "Capital Punishment" speech was that since women only commit 13.3% of all crimes, they should have their own subways, their own streets, their own cities, their own countries, their own continents, and eventually their own *planet*—*yes!* Run by and for women. Just for a change—just to see if it makes a difference. I think that in the past there *have* been matriarchal societies that have been completely unacknowledged or unrecorded by "history."

♦ **V: In Bangkok, so many women complained of being harassed by men on crowded buses that they instituted buses *just* for women.**

♦ LL: Great. Excellent. Why should I be forced to mingle with the other 87% of the population?

♦ **AJ: What do you mean?**

♦ LL: Well, if women only commit 13% of the crime—

♦ **AJ: Yes, and that crime is usually prostitution or white collar crime or something relatively victimless. You certainly don't really have to walk down the street in fear of a woman—**

♦ LL: No. *Not yet!* ♦ ♦ ♦

Discography

TEENAGE JESUS & THE JERKS: various records including songs such as: *Orphans; Less of Me; Baby Doll; Freud in Flop; The Closet; My Eyes; Race Mixing; Burning Rubber; Red Alert; I Woke Up Dreaming.* On influential *NO NEW YORK* LP.

BEIRUT SLUMP: Try Me; Staircase.

LYDIA LUNCH: LPs: *Queen of Siam; Conspiracy of Women; Oral Fixation; Hysterie; The Uncensored Lydia Lunch; In Limbo.* Plus "The Agony Is The Ecstasy." "Twisted/Past Glas."

EIGHT EYED SPY: Diddy Wah Diddy; Dead You Me Beside

13.13: *Lydia Lunch; 13.13* LPs.

HARRY CREWS: *Naked in Garden Hills* LP.

VARIOUS COLLABORATIVE RECORDS with: Rowland S. Howard (*Shotgun Wedding*); Einsturzende Neubauten; Die Haut; Michael Gira; Lucy Hamilton; *No Trend; Birthday Party;* Thurston Moore; Clint Ruin; Don Bajema, Henry Rollins, & Hubert Selby Jr (*Our Fathers Who Aren't In Heaven*).

(Note: some of the above available from Widowspeak Productions, PO Box 1085, Canal St Station, NY NY 10013-1085. Catalog $2—make checks payable to "Lydia Lunch.")

Film & Videography

With James Nares (1978): *Rome* (1978). With Beth & Scott B (1978-81): *Black Box, The Offenders, Vortex.* With Beth B (1990): *Thanatopsis.* With Vivienne Dick (1979-80): *She Had Her Gun Already, Beauty Becomes the Beast.* With Babeth (1990): *Kiss Napoleon Goodbye.* With Richard Kern (1984-86) *The Right Side of My Brain, Fingered.* With Penn & Teller (1986-1990): *The Invisible Thread, BBQ Death Squad.* With Merrill Aldighieri & Joe Tripician (1988): *The Gun Is Loaded.*

(Note: *Fingered & Right Side of My Brain* available for $26 each ppd from: Richard Kern, PO Box 1322, NY NY 10009.)

Books

Adulterer's Anonymous, with Exene Cervenka. Grove Press, 1982.

Incriminating Evidence. Last Gasp, 2180 Bryant, SF CA 94110.

AS-FIX-E-8 (comics by Mike Matthews, Lydia, Nick Cave)

My Father's Daughter. Unpublished autobiography.

Film Script & Play

Psychomenstrum: The Case of the PMS Murders. Film, 1991.

South of Your Border. Play w/Emilio Cubeiro, performed NYC, 1988.

Wanda Coleman

A native of Los Angeles, during the past two decades Wanda Coleman has written two thousand poems, a hundred short stories and given over three hundred dramatic poetry performances. Her voice—exciting and hypnotic—has been captured on several recordings: *Twin Sisters* (with Exene Cervenka), *Black Angeles* (with poet Michelle Clinton), and most recently, *Black and Blue News* (produced by Lydia Lunch's Widowspeak Productions). Her books include *Mad Dog Black Lady* (1979), *Imagoes* (1983), *Heavy Daughter Blues* (Poems & Stories 1966-1986), *A War of Eyes and Other Stories* (1988), and *African Sleeping Sickness* (1990), available from Black Sparrow Press, 24 10th St, Santa Rosa CA 95401. Currently she hosts a poetry interview program, "The Poetry Connexion" on Pacifica radio KPFK. Wanda Coleman can be contacted c/o PO Box 29154, Los Angeles CA 90029.

◆ **ANDREA JUNO: You grew up in L.A.?**
◆ WANDA COLEMAN: Yes. I was born and raised in Watts. Then *all* of South/Central L.A. became Watts after the riots in August '65. Until 15 years ago I lived in that area.

I have some college, but college and I did not get along too well, so I dropped out. I had a hard time—I was taking workshops, and my lifestyle was usually working two or three jobs, including waitressing on weekends. I had two babies by the time I was nineteen, and they were being shuttled from one babysitter to another.

All of the problems that are "trendy" now, like child-care—see, I was *avant-garde* for that. How do you deal with childcare?—how do you build a survival unit? To survive, I was networking with girlfriends in "everybody eats when you have money" kinds of situations. When I divorced my husband at the end of the '60s, I was still thinking, "There's so much liberation going on—*of course* I'll be able to get a good job." Little did I know! I discovered I really had a hard time getting a job, especially since I wore my hair in a natural—
◆ **VALE: *White* people were getting naturals, then—**
◆ WC: Oh no they weren't! I applied for a job with a *black* employer who told me, "You're a very striking woman . . . but you've gotta do something about that hair!" [laughs] I never went back! And because I was working 2 or 3 jobs, my hair was too hard to maintain,

so I started wearing a wig. People will accept a wig before they'll accept your natural hair—even a *natural* wig, because the real thing—*authenticity*—is a threat.
◆ **V: What were your parents like?**
◆ WC: My parents were petit bourgeoisie. My mother was a domestic—she came to California from Oklahoma when World War II started and jobs opened up for blacks here. She worked in movie stars' homes, and in fact worked a year for Ronald Reagan when he was married to Jane Wyman—she quit when he wouldn't give her a raise! [laughs]
◆ **V: "Inflation—what's that?"**
◆ WC: Even *then!* [laughs] My father moved here from Little Rock, Arkansas in 1931 after a young black man was lynched from the church steeple. They just left the body hanging there. . . Some people with California license plates were passing through town; he offered them $15 for a ride, and they brought him to Los Angeles.
◆ **V: And he got a job—**
◆ WC: Well, his aunt was a domestic who also worked for Ronnie Baby as the washerwoman who would come do the laundry. She invited my mother to church and that's how my parents met.
◆ **AJ: I think people don't realize how recently black people were getting lynched—**
◆ WC: Well, it's still happening! Just like the drug

Photo: Olivier Robert

problem—no one tells you that the drug problem was the creation of the federal government from the start. Blacks were targeted and drugs were put into the black community *by* the federal government of these United States, and the drug problem didn't become important until it spilled over to the *dominant* culture. Then suddenly it became a problem, just as with *LSD*. And where did *LSD* come from? The *government*.

◆ **V: I saw a photo of a black man who had been lynched in San Jose (near San Francisco) in the '40s— not *that* long ago. I thought that only happened in the Deep South.**

◆ WC: Well, in downtown Los Angeles they lynched 9 Chinese gentlemen in the '30s. Ah—"America the Beautiful!"

◆ **V: There's a lot of hidden history—**

◆ WC: And you won't get it if you don't look for it— you're certainly not going to be taught it in *school*. [laughs] I remember being in high school in '64, taking World History and reading, "The negro race has made no major contribution to the history of the world." Uh—*right!* There's a whole lost history, and as a writer, I constantly think about the fact that no one's ever written, say, the history of Black Los Angeles... I've written 6 books and feel it might have been *16* books if I'd had the quality time to just do *that*.

◆ **AJ: That's how they keep you from having a voice—**

◆ WC: You're spread so thin trying to survive or make ends meet that you have no voice. This is true of women in this society, and particularly women with kids—I think it takes a *genius* to be able to write amidst this! Yet there are more of us than you think—have you seen the *Breaking Ice* anthology? There's 52 writers in there— most of whom *I've* never heard of, and most of them have 5 or 6 books out. And they range in age from 25 to 70. But it's hard for us to get in the mainstream of literature because our books are seldom reviewed, and we're seldom interviewed. This society has what we call the "Nigger of the Minute syndrome." Only one token nigger is allowed at any given time, regardless of regionality or differences in style.

It's strange, but in recent years there's been quite an increase in "artificial opportunities." All of a sudden you're in demand, but this demand is really tokenistic: "*Hey*, it's Negro History Month!" So the only time you'll get work will be during Negro History Month—the rest of the year you'll be ignored.

◆ **AJ: As if you don't have something to say about the human condition in general—**

◆ WC: Well, according to the gentlemen who put together the *Great Books of the Western World*—we don't. Whatever literary prizes that may be available to us are doled out tokenistically: you have to fit into a certain mold, you have to be *safe*.

◆ **V: How did you start writing?**

◆ WC: Even as a kid I tried to keep diaries, but I was so full of hate and rage that when I go back and look at them, they're nothing but bursts of *anger*—very little else. But my parents encouraged me; I had my first poems published when I was 13 in the local "fishwrap" throwaway newspaper.

I was the kid who always got an "A" on the Father's Day poem—I was sort of an egghead, but a *dumb* egghead! [laughs] I was always daydreaming and reading literature other than what was given me in school. At that time books were segregated—you had *boys'* literature and *girls'* literature. When I went to the library, I could read *Cheryl Crane, Nurse,* books by the Bronte sisters, and *Nancy Drew mysteries*—yes, *those* horrible things! But I wasn't allowed to read Sir Arthur Conan Doyle or H.P. Lovecraft—the boys' books. So I would have my *father* go to the library with me; I would pick out what I wanted and he would check the books out.

My father moved here from Little Rock, Arkansas in 1931 after a young black man was lynched from the church steeple. They just left the body hanging there. . .

Then I could read to my heart's content! And I was reading way beyond my years: when I was ten I had read the complete works of Shakespeare. I read Sir Richard Burton's *The Unexpurgated Arabian Nights*—in fact I had a gorgeous leatherbound copy of the *Arabian Nights,* but left it in the trunk of the car one night, then came down with encephalitis for two months (there was an epidemic going around) and while I was sick my father sold the car! It was *beautiful*—it had all these colored plates in it. And it was gone. . .

In high school I began reading the heavyweights: Nietzsche, Sartre, Heidegger. And my teachers started getting *upset.* One of them actually told my parents that these books were *bad* for me; that they were making me rebellious, and that my parents should forbid me to read them. By then I knew I wasn't getting a good education, because I had done all this reading. Also, I was on the debate team. So I would go from inner city black schools to white schools in Beverly Hills and look at other kids' books and compare them to what *I* was reading—and I *knew* they were getting a better education!

This was when the "white flight" was beginning—when whites were fleeing the inner city of Los Angeles and moving elsewhere. When we first moved to our house, the neighborhood was white, but by the time I had graduated from high school only two white families were left on my block—and they were old people. So the class became 80% black and 20% "others" (Latino, Filipino, etc) with maybe one or two poor, lower-class whites left.

In class there were so many ugly situations. I remember one time the kids called our white male teacher a homosexual (you didn't *do* that in those days), and he went *berserk* and proceeded to tell us how superior he was! I remember teachers getting beaten up by kids or parents or uncles because of some racial incident or slur—they would wait for them after class and beat the shit out of them, or destroy their cars. These were mostly white teachers.

◆ **V: After high school, you had two kids before the age of nineteen?**

◆ WC: Blame it on the Civil Rights Movement! [laughs] My first husband was a trouble-shooter for SNCC [Student Non-violent Coordinating Committee, a civil rights group] who came to Southern California with Jesse Jackson and Stokely Carmichael. He was a white guy who was part of Martin Luther King's inner circle; he had been in several early protest marches. He was from Georgia (and called himself a redneck), but he was a very unusual person—very *unique* for that time. He came out here for a fund-raiser and stayed.

◆ **AJ: So you were getting politicized then?**

◆ WC: I would say that he politicized me. Interestingly enough, his politicizing brought our marriage to an end—because I began to *outgrow* our relationship. I still wanted to be a writer for the "revolution," but I knew I was being treated patronizingly—the men didn't take me seriously. Because if you don't have something to offer—either sex or money—you're of no value for the most part . . . *still!* [laughs] The roots of this haven't changed.

Also, my father had given me a lot of ideas, even though he didn't have a college education—he had dropped out of school when he was eight years old. Nevertheless he taught me a lot about graphics, advertising and the media—I know how to dummy a newspaper, for example. He tried for years to get a black men's magazine going in the '50s, but Johnson Publications (who controls the circulation of *Ebony, Jet,* etc) stonewalled any competition.

◆ **V: —the black media establishment. How did they react to the emergence of the Black Panthers? Did they even cover this?**

◆ WC: Well, those publications have a policy: unless it's sanctioned by the white media—unless you're *recognized* or sanctioned by the pop culture, you're not going to appear in their pages. Because they're not about exploring or finding out about anything.

◆ **V: So for them the '60s never happened? The Black Panthers and SNCC were never covered in their pages?**

◆ WC: Only after they became big names and received national attention. My first husband and I were involved in "US" when Ron Karenga and his group [of black militants] were photographed for the cover of *Life.* There's a picture of my son in the magazine; I still have it. It's funny—my husband was so in tune with the *movement* that he was able to sit among people like Ron Karenga and Huey Newton—and he was *white.*

♦ **AJ: Those were exciting times—**

♦ **WC:** *Very* exciting, because I was living in two worlds. We were living in the world of the black militants, but we were also living in the world of the hippies. So we would go from *love-ins* to underground meetings plotting the overthrow of the government! My husband and I were on our way to becoming members of the *Weather Underground* when we split up. At the time we belonged to a para-military organization. We went from group to group (starting with the NAACP Youth Council) just getting steadily more and more militant. We had heard about the *Symbionese Liberation Army,* but decided to join the *Weather Underground.* Then I decided I wanted to become an artist—that was more important to me. So we split up—I decided I'd had enough of being *married,* anyway . . .

♦ **V: You'd begun to see inequities in the "revolutionary" underground?**

♦ **WC:** *Definitely!* Plus, there was a strong anti-intellectual climate—if you saw through somebody's game, you had to keep your mouth shut. You couldn't call them on it. There was a subtle group pressure to *conform to the party line.* You didn't ask questions—you didn't question your leadership, so to speak. And there was a lot of intimidation. . .

The drug problem was the creation of the federal government from the start. Drugs were put into the black community, and the drug problem didn't become important until it spilled over to the *dominant* culture.

If you really *looked* at some of these people . . . if you were bright enough to see through their "mac" [con game] and say, "Well, I don't necessarily feel like doing that; that doesn't make sense to me," well—! I'd always thought the Panthers were wonderful *theater,* but I didn't think they were *revolutionary.* But when they'd come into a room dressed in black leather and carrying those rifles on their shoulders—if there was any grumbling in the room, it would *cease* [snaps her fingers]—everyone would just snap to attention! So it was an exciting period. There was this feeling that, "Wow—we really *are* going to make a difference!" Little did we know. . .

We also spent a lot of time in Griffith Park at the love-ins. That was the other thing—the *music* was such a part of the excitement! We were always crashing concerts and doing things like jumping up on the stage. I remember when *Big Brother and the Holding Company* came to L.A. and did a concert in one of the parks, and I jumped up onstage with Janis Joplin and was dancing—me and my brother and a guy with a banana in his crotch—I'll never forget it! And they wouldn't push you off the stage; they would let you dance. You can't do that now. But back then you could get up onstage and then go backstage and get high with them, or whatever. And when you went to Griffith Park, the families (there were several "families" there, including the Manson family) would pitch tents, and you could go inside and sit and talk with them or share their food—it was great! Everyone was young and beautiful, and drugs were free, and it was a fabulous time.

We went to San Francisco during the Summer of Love. We had a '58 Studebaker convertible and one day we jumped in it and headed north to the Haight-Ashbury, in and out of crash pads and head shops—we just did the whole trip. It was a wonderful experience—like an endless series of parties and meetings—it was really *something* to go through!

It's funny, because I was going through all of this with one eye open and one eye wary—I was cynical even *then.* I felt that people were underestimating the enemy—and I was *right.* I thought a lot of the leadership was extremely naive, if not downright stupid. During the Poverty Program, they were handing out all this money, and it was like the program was designed to fail. People were being trained on obsolete equipment; money was being stolen right and left by young hotshot accountants (black or otherwise) who got in there and started ripping off the money, driving around in gold Mercedes while blacks and Hispanics weren't getting anything. These old, "churchified" preachers who didn't know what they were doing were getting paid to "teach" young people—it was all an immense disaster.

♦ **AJ: But now things are so much *worse!***

♦ **WC:** Of course! When you talk to a lot of blacks, they reminisce about how wonderful the March on Washington was (when Martin Luther King gave his famous "I Have a Dream" speech). Well, that march was supposed to be *violent;* it was supposed to be angry—not a giant *love-in!* What happened was: when the government found out that blacks were going to be furious, they got on the horn and contacted black leaders and told them to get the militants outta there. They got all these old "biscuits" like King to turn the march into a giant love-in. And that's one of the reasons things are the way they are now.

♦ **V: You called King a "biscuit"?**

♦ **WC:** I was never in his camp. I always felt that what happened in the South was fine, but that it didn't have universal application to all the problems that blacks face . . . that you had to use different strategies in other parts of the country, particularly in the Northern cities and out West where racism wears a different face and is much

more sophisticated . . . where people kill you with kindness—they'll be grinning in your face, saying "Oh, yes, brother!" while they're stabbing you in the back. But who was going to listen to a 19-year-old female? I had no power, no influence. Usually people would just look at me and tell me to shut up.

♦ **AJ: Now things are so bad that there's no hope of mobilization. Do you think rap music will—**

♦ WC: As long as we're dancin', we ain't fightin'! When blacks were rioting, a song by *Martha and the Vandellas* came on the radio: "Dancin' in the Streets!" I think that song was deliberately promoted by the government, during that long hot summer, to distract blacks from taking care of serious business.

Did you know we have never had a major black actor? Sidney Poitier and Harry Belafonte are not American black men—they're islanders. [laughs] They're from the West Indies; they're not American black males. And the ones that we've *had* have been comedians or comics. See, the clowns and the gangsters always have work. In the black community, those are the people who make the money—the clowns and the gangsters/sharks. Everybody else suffers.

♦ **V: What do you mean by gangsters?**

♦ WC: I mean just that. And you can make those appellations as broad as you want. By "clowns" (and I don't necessarily want to demean some of these people, but I'm talking about how they're viewed by the dominant culture): Michael Jackson would be a clown, Oprah Winfrey would be a clown, Bill Cosby would be a clown, Eddie Murphy would be one. These people are allowed to make money in the system and in the society because they're no threat, no danger.

♦ **AJ: And very rarely do you ever have a black male lead who's a sexual, romantic figure—**

♦ WC: Exactly. Here we are on the verge of the '90s, and they're censoring Whoopi Goldberg kissing a white guy out of a film—give me a break! But you have to remember this is *Hollywood*, the entertainment capital of the world. Women have made inroads in science, in politics, but they haven't made any inroads in Hollywood. It's the same old *same old*.

♦ **V: Women are sometimes film editors, but rarely directors—**

♦ WC: You have a few. . . And the men are hip to the game—if feminism becomes trendy, all of a sudden *they're* writing feminist scripts, too! [laughs] Blacks also have been tied into this "artificial liberation"—this illusion that blacks have *achieved* all of their goals—and women too! That's right. Therefore, whenever you have a spokesman for the so-called "black point of view" (there may be 5 different attitudes within the black community), they'll pick a *conservative* black.

Perhaps I'm particularly sensitive; maybe you could talk to somebody else black and they'd say, "*I've* never experienced prejudice. I've never experienced racism." Recently I went to hear a friend read at a punk rock place called the *Anti-Club* in L.A., and there were these jigaboo pictures on the wall. I don't know who put them up—a *black* artist could have painted them, for all I know—but I found them insulting.

The paintings were recent—they weren't old. I didn't need to see this shit, so I tried to ignore it. My husband's Jewish; he's from Brooklyn. I was trying to pretend I didn't see them, but finally he said, "Wanda, look at those jigaboo pictures on the wall!" I saw the owner, a French Jew, sitting by the counter, and I said, "Matt, if you want to file a complaint, go talk to the owner over there." He went over, and all of a sudden she couldn't understand English—kind of convenient, you know? [laughs] I was listening to him trying to explain, and finally I went over and said, "*Yes!* As a black person, I can testify to the fact that these paintings are *offensive*. In fact, they make me feel like getting an ax and putting it in the head of the first white person I see—*you!*" [laughs] The owner went into shock . . . then started snatching pictures off the wall! I mean—if I had put swastikas upon her walls, I'm sure she would have understood *that*. For her not to have understood—give me a break. Let's get real.

When I was a kid, my first experience of being called a "nigger" involved a white kid. My *son's* first experience involved a *Nicaraguan* kid—see what I'm saying? There's a real lack of understanding about: when you go to another country, you buy into whatever the *lie* is if you're going to survive there economically. People who emigrate to America buy into the lie of American racism, which means keeping blacks at the bottom of the society.

People emigrate here and their psyches are *whole*. They haven't been oppressed on that racist level. So when they come here, they don't *understand* black Americans—who we are or where we're coming from. And they're not going to get enlightened by our history books, psychology books, newspapers or TV. These people have no way of understanding us when they get here. So you end up with conflicts between communities: the blacks and the Koreans, or the blacks and the Vietnamese, or the blacks and the Cubans . . . as an outgrowth of this lack of information and understanding.

♦ **AJ: And of course the white establishment—**

♦ WC: —feeds off that and encourages it. In the '60s I would encounter people from Nigeria or Kenya or wherever, and the first thing they would say is, "We have been told by your government that we're not supposed to associate with you; otherwise they will cancel our visas."

♦ **V: Did they also feel superior because they were Africans?**

♦ WC: Yes—and rightly so, because they're coming here the same way a European would—they're immigrating into the country. They have been subjected to colonialism, but even colonialism did not erase their *culture*. Even South Africans have their identity as a tribal people—they didn't have their language taken away; they weren't forced to intermarry the way Aborigines were, or the way blacks were in the breeding plantations in the United States.

The victims are constantly blamed for being victims in

this society. Historians will tell you, "Well, you black people sold each other into slavery." But actually that wasn't what happened: one tribe might have sold an enemy tribe into slavery, but that isn't the same thing—that's *tribalism*. Whereas *racism* is a unique American product. Throughout the history of the world you always had one tribe, regardless of what race they were, fighting another. There was warfare, and one culture would absorb or cannibalize or be parasitic upon the other. To the victor went the spoils—that was the way of the world. But Black Americans are a *whole new animal*—we are unique in the history of the world. Our situation is not comparable to what happened in the West Indies, in Africa or in South Africa.

♦ **AJ: Your writing is giving voice to a stifled culture—**

♦ **WC:** If I had left L.A. for New York in 1969, I might be nationally well-known. But I had 2 kids so I had to stay here and make a living. I was invited to be a member of the first black delegation that went to China, when China opened up to United States citizens, but I couldn't go—I had to work.

♦ **AJ: So how did you manage to raise 2 kids and survive?**

♦ **WC:** I went without sleep! [laughs] I would go 2 or 3 days without sleep . . . and without the assistance of drugs, and I didn't drink coffee in those days, so it was really hard. And most of the time I wasn't eating. I would sleep on my break; I carried an alarm clock in my car and would put it on the dashboard and sleep in the car until the alarm went off.

♦ **V: But you managed to keep your writing spirit alive—**

♦ **WC:** When I was a child I was reading all these tomes by these so-called "great" writers, and every now and then I would stub my metaphorical toe on the word "nigger" or "negress." And the hunger was always there to present my world view, because *my* world view didn't exist—it didn't even exist when Simone de Beauvoir wrote *The Second Sex*. She wrote about women all right, but what she wrote didn't apply to *me*.

♦ **AJ: You felt that the Feminist movement omitted black culture?**

♦ **WC:** Well, I thought that it mainly belonged to rich white women who were not interested in *my* concerns—I saw that right off. What did I need to do—trade one oppressor for another? And they were using tactics that blacks had pioneered in the Civil Rights movement . . . that people from the Left had pioneered in the strong Labor Union movement in the United States.

♦ **AJ: So . . . what are some of your goals in your writing?**

♦ **WC:** For awhile I was writing for television, but finally I decided to leave the world of popular culture. I was on the staff of *Days of Our Lives*, and they got the Emmy award; then the writers got the ax, and I never went back—I disappeared and didn't keep in touch. And what did I want to do? I decided I wanted to be a

"literary" person, because I felt that's where the changes *originate*—the popular or "low" culture always cannibalizes the "high" culture. Also, working in television I got tired of being told what I could say and couldn't say—so I went to *books*.

♦ **AJ: Do you feel hopeless or enraged?**

♦ **WC:** My anger knows no bounds; my anger is unlimited. I'm a big lady, I can stand up in front of almost any man and cuss him out and have no fear—you know what I'm sayin'? Because I will go to blows. But when I get older, I'm not going to be able to do that, and with *my* temper—I'm going to have to start carrying a gun! And if I'm going to carry one, somebody's ass is going to be shot! Because at the rate things are going . . . I won't tolerate this bullshit (contrary to some of my colleagues who have mellowed with age). I'm not among them—yet. Maybe I have to go through some kind of biochemical change or menopause—I do not know! I'm trying to come to terms with this, because I'm tired of dealing with racial incidents on a daily basis. Why can't I just leave my house, go shopping, do my thing and come home? Why do I always have to deal with some bullshit?

As long as we're dancin', we ain't fightin'! When blacks were rioting, a song by *Martha and the Vandellas* came on the radio: "Dancin' in the Streets!" *I* think that song was deliberately promoted by the government, during that long hot summer, to distract blacks from taking care of serious business.

♦ **AJ: What do you think the future will hold?**

♦ **WC:** I don't know.

♦ **V: Don't you think things are getting worse?**

♦ **WC:** Well—times are tough. If you ask a young person today, "What do you want to be when you grow up?" the assumption is: you're going to live long enough to grow up; someone's not going to drop a bomb on you, or you're not going to be shot by a cop. I have a 12-year-old, and what is his future going to be as a black male in this society when a third of the black men in the state of California have records, have served time, or are serving time in jail. Now unemployment for black males is in excess of 60%. So what's the future? I don't know. All I can do is try to arm him—give him psychological and emotional armament, so he will be ready for whatever they throw at him!

♦ **AJ: You've got the warrior mentality—**

♦ WC: Because it's a war! Certainly we're being warred against. In my books of short stories, all the stories are about this constant self-conscious confrontation that happens the minute you meet a black person. Because in order to have any kind of constructive dialogue, there has to be a context. And often that context is music, like jazz or rap music—which gets to be a drag!

When I go somewhere like Atlanta, I get really excited because I am not used to seeing so many black people—I start staring! I go into a restaurant and it's amazing; I go into the street and the police are black—everybody who's doing things is black. You don't have that experience in Southern California. So for me, when I go to D.C. or Philadelphia or even Chicago, I get really excited—

♦ AJ: Because here you can never forget you're black—

♦ WC: And it gets to be a chore. Every time you go to a party, you're an *issue* just because you're *there*; I don't have to say a word. It's hard to have a good time! Even socializing on a minimal level gets to be a pain—why can't it just be a *party?!* But somebody always opens their mouth and says something wrong, like, "Well, Wanda—your people have sure made a lot of *progress*, haven't they?" And then I have to say, "Wait a minute. . ."

♦ AJ: They say that now?

♦ WC: Oh yes—in fact, that happened a month ago, baby—here in the 1990s! Ignorance yet abounds . . . And the other side of the coin is: I get tired of being "Wanda the Explainer." I get tired of giving people an education on racism—have my brain picked for free. I feel like saying, *Motherfucker*, if you can't handle it—tough! [laughs]

♦ V: "Read my books!"

♦ AJ: Do you get hassled for being sexually explicit?

♦ WC: [laughs] So far I haven't. If anybody's denied me anything, I don't know about it. I've gotten my share of grant money, because not everything is a diatribe, and not everything has four-letter words. I like communicating with mature minds, and you need a certain life experience to really appreciate the bulk of my work. So I don't talk to a junior high school audience without giving them a certain context. And I have enough work (I've written a couple thousand poems and a hundred short stories) to select from, so we can come to a real good understanding without having to blow their lids! I don't need to do that, nor am I interested in doing that, because I'm about *communicating.* I'm not about shock; if any shock is present it's the shock of *recognition* . . . or the shock of *understanding* which might just go with the turf. But I'm not deliberately out to just shock people—I'm not about being sensationalistic.

I want *freedom* when I write, I want the freedom to use any kind of language—whatever I feel is appropriate to get the point across. There's a piece in *African Sleeping Sickness* where I use very pornographic images, blatantly sexual imagery—I'm just downright *nasty* . . . but I choose that language deliberately, because I'm talking about a downright nasty situation, which is: my experience in literary workshops—how I was treated. I start out using the metaphor of a circle jerk, and it gets nastier from there. So I'm deliberately using sexual imagery, but I'm talking about writing poetry and my workshop experience as a poet. The subject matter is not really sexual at all—the imagery is!

When I moved to Hollywood, little did I know that it's now a hardcore ghetto! When I was working in the entertainment business, my associates were afraid to come here. I live right on the borderline between Hancock Park (wealthy homes with real mahogany and crystal and beautifully kept grounds), and a lot of drug activity—there's a heroin dealer down the street, and gangs. There are 80 different languages spoken here. To the northeast is the Armenian population; the Korean population is just south; the Chinese and Japanese are further; and there are a lot of Thai and Vietnamese . . .

The ghettos have changed a lot. In South-Central L.A. people are dying—sitting in their living rooms watching TV and catching stray bullets. So there's no haven, no sanctity—I worry about my mother living there. Because the new school of gangsters are sociopaths—they don't respect anybody. They don't care who you are: "Oh, *you* a great poet?"—they don't give a fuck. If they want your car and they got an Uzi and a bicycle, they're gonna make you get out of your car and give it up. If they think you have some money and you don't, they might shoot you because they're mad 'cuz they took their time to hold you up and you ain't got nothin'—so you're dead either way! There's no respect for anything.

♦ AJ: Did there used to be?

♦ WC: Yes, when I was growing up, gangs had their turf and they respected "civilians." They wouldn't shoot a woman unless she did something—stepped on somebody's toes—she would have to do something *to* a gangster to be the victim of gang activity. Now you don't have to do *anything*—just be in the wrong place at the wrong time, and you're in trouble!

♦ AJ: How did that develop?

♦ WC: We can thank the federal government for putting drugs in the black community. These young kids know that if they work at MacDonalds—they know the American dream is a lie ("If you work hard in this country, you'll succeed!") because they saw their parents do that—and look what happened! They know that you cannot count on a job being there for 25 years, and if you decide to retire, you cannot count on your retirement funds being available, because they may have all been lost on Wall Street, or turned into junk bonds, or otherwise been embezzled.

♦ AJ: But that's been happening in the black community forever—

♦ WC: It's happening to the whole culture now! And it *hasn't* been in the black community all the time, because before integration there was this big hope: that once the doors opened, we would be allowed in! Now that hope is gone—black people *know* their lives are of no value. Twelve-year-old black boys know that our government wants to fry them—boys my son's age. They want to put them in the electric chair or gas chamber or in prison for life.

You see, black people were believers back then—they're not anymore. They know the American dream is a crock of shit, because they saw what happened to their parents who were believers, who can't get insurance coverage (or when they *do* get insurance, they're charged unfair rates because they live in a certain community). Now they know it's all jive and bullshit; they know their lives have no value. And if their lives have no value, why should they value anyone else's lives? No matter what age they are—whether they're 5 or 105, whether they're a preacher or a pauper, if *their* lives have no value, no one else's do either!

> **Before integration there was this big hope: that once the doors opened, we would be allowed in! Now that hope is gone—black people *know* their lives are of no value.**

The generation before them believed that the white boy would let them play the game. Now we all know that the white boy has *no intention* of letting us play the game. And you cannot afford to wear gold chains around your neck if you're working at MacDonalds 12 hours a day. You know you will never make enough money to be driving a Maserati or an Excalibur or live in the Hollywood Hills. And you will never be sitting in the front row at Trump Towers watching the Mike Tyson fight if you're working at MacDonalds. And these young guys know it.

They also know that not everybody has the smarts to get a PhD or the money to buy that education. And education is being undermined left and right; the advances made in the '60s are being reversed: blacks have a higher dropout rate across the board. So on every level you look, where do you go? You can't even go to church anymore—church used to be *strong* in the black community. The preacher could actually protect a young man and keep him out of jail—he can't do that no more. There's no more dialogue; the preacher can't protect your ass anymore—*his* ass is being shot up, too! He doesn't get the respect from the community he used to get.

♦ **AJ: Were you part of a church when you were growing up?**

♦ WC: Yes. But these young people don't respect the church anymore—they'll shoot it up just as soon as they'd shoot up a liquor store!

♦ **V: There's a literary tradition celebrating (if that's the right word) black criminals or black underworld activity, by writers such as Melvin Tolson in the '30s, up to Donald Goines. How do you feel about the *Iceberg Slim* books?**

♦ WC: I got an autographed copy! I've got about 4 autographed books by him. I knew the real "T"—which we will *not* discuss today! [laughs] As far as myself—well, I consider myself in the tradition of *Western Literature!* [cackles evilly] W.E.B. DuBois is my man—he wrote *The Souls of Black Folk.* And even though the language is a little stiff and archaic, he's important because he identified our context: that we live in 2 worlds simultaneously. Everything in the dominant culture is ours also; there's this 2-way mirror effect: you can see *their* world, but somehow they can't see *yours!* So you have *your* world as source material, but you also have access to theirs. And they refuse to see your world because they consider *their* world to be the only one of value.

So you're bicultural—and if you're smart enough, you're bilingual. Because there's definitely a difference between writing with a black sensibility and what I call writing "white." And if you want to succeed in this culture, you learn how to write "white"—I mean I've written ad copy and done other kinds of writing; I can write about another poet's work without necessarily having to be "Afrocentric" or "Afrocultural." I'm able to do that, but I doubt if a white writer could read my work and divorce himself from his culture—that would be an impossibility! Because he wouldn't be bicultural.

I can criticize a movie or piece of fiction because I belong to both traditions. I'm affected by the literature I grew up with, which is: Edgar Allan Poe, Nathanael West, Nathaniel Hawthorne, Evelyn Waugh, Somerset Maugham, Albert Camus, Andre Malraux, Chekhov . . . these are all people I read, they're all my influences. I was privy to that literature; I read Plato, Aristotle, Kant, Emerson—all of them. But I also listened to the blues; I also know who my culture is. I read Richard Wright, James Baldwin . . . although I came to black literature *late* because I didn't have access to it until I became an adult.

If you ever want to read my biography, read *The Street* by Ann Petry—my biography's already been written. Do you know what it's like to discover that your biography was written the year you were born? You can probably find this book in the library—she was one of the first black writers to be treated in this tokenistic fashion.

♦ **V: Still, she got her message across—**

♦ WC: I don't know—you'd have to ask *her!* [laughs] I came across that book in my early twenties and it had a very profound effect on me—as profound as listening to Billie Holiday . . . or Nina Simone or Etta James or John Coltrane or Jimi Hendrix.

♦ **V: How would you context Iceberg Slim?**

♦ WC: Well, he does not give up as much game as you think he's giving up! He doesn't really give you the full

"T" in his books. I used to go to young black guys' houses and that's the first thing I saw on the coffee table: a copy of *Pimp.* Well, I read *Pimp,* and if you've had experience with pimps you know he ain't telling all the game. If you follow that book you might end up dead somewhere rather than as a successful pimp, because there's different kinds of pimp "macs" . . . and he lays down one, but that's not necessarily the style you might use if you were going to go that way.

I have yet to kill anyone—I have exhibited *great restraint!*

♦ **V: But you do respect him?**
♦ WC: I like the man; I met him. And I know some things about him that are not public knowledge, so—what can I say? I understand who he is—I have the proper *context* for him. Other people who read him wouldn't necessarily respect him. *Okay?* So because of that I like him. But I wouldn't consider him an influence on *my* work. And on my Top Ten list of black writers he would not appear—neither would Chester Himes, whom I *don't* like because of all of his shame; all his bootlicking; all his catering to white racist conceptions about blacks. *Cotton Comes to Harlem; Crazy Kill*—awful stuff! Even though the language and some of the descriptions may be interesting, nevertheless all that hatred is there and it's sick—from my point of view it's very unhealthy. And he was not a great writer by anyone's standards—black, white, or otherwise. He was a mediocre writer; he did his job—probably the best he could. I never met the man so I couldn't assess that, but what he has left behind, I think is awful.
♦ **V: But you don't feel that way about Iceberg Slim?**
♦ WC: Well, I can see how some people could evaluate him that way, but I've had personal contact with the man so. . .
♦ **V: How did you discipline yourself to produce a couple thousand poems and a hundred short stories?**
♦ WC: Just by *sheer force of will.* It's harder now than it ever was; I've never been able to have the luxury of a routine. There was a time when I could get up at 4 in the morning and my kids were little, but I've never had a lot of "golden time" or peaceful time—it's always been catch-as-catch-can. When you're poor you spend a lot of time standing in line and waiting for service—and it's usually not *good* service, either. Like getting your car fixed—you're sitting in the shop *cooling your ass.* So I use that

time constructively—I always have a book to read, or a book to write in. If I'm in the bank standing in line, I have a notebook to write in. That's how I do it.
♦ **V: How do you regard your sense of humor?**
♦ WC: My humor is a weapon. And as far as my taste goes—I went to see *Good Fellas* [ultraviolent gangster film] and I *roared!* To me that was one fucking funny movie—I thought it was hysterical. I was laughing; I was trying to control myself because I knew I was probably interfering with other people's experience—the audience was being horrified [gasps] while I was going, "Hee hee hee!" You know what I'm sayin'? So as far as my sense of humor goes—for a long time people told me I didn't have one, or that I was too serious . . . I think they just didn't appreciate or understand where I was coming from, or how my sense of humor operated.

I love irony—that's my favorite. I love satire. And when I laugh, I laugh loud, and long, and hard . . . and *mean!* Sometimes I can be a little sadistic: "Oh—did that hurt? Want some more?!" I can sometimes be cruel, but then again—I haven't been spared. So if I can dish it out, I can take it—and I don't dish out anything I can't take. . .

The pop culture in America romanticizes every bloody thing—when you live in a culture that can romanticize an ax murderer—what can one say? Give me a break! To me those are the true obscenities: movies like *Halloween.* Because to me that's part of the dehumanization process; to me that's an extension of what racism does. Because you're dehumanizing these people so you can just kill one after the other: these are not human beings who are falling—they're props in a movie! So you can hack them up, you can butcher them, you can have all this disgusting shit happening on the screen, and it *inures.* So that when you really see someone killed, it's not as exciting as they saw it on the movies. And usually not as gory, either.

A girlfriend of mine killed her old man—she served about 3 years in jail and was let out. I remember talking to her at the time, and she was absolutely amazed that what little she did could actually kill a person—there was no loud music playing when he was shot! Whereas the movies build up all this sound and drama.
♦ **AJ:** *Do you think you're angry?*
♦ WC: If you're sane and you're perceptive, you have no choice! Maybe the word "perceptive" has to be wedded to the concept of anger, because you have to be perceptive to see what's *really* going on—there are people who have blinders on, and who don't see it.
♦ **AJ: Have you ever seen anyone die?**
♦ WC: I have seen people in the process of dying, but I haven't actually been present at the moment of death. I haven't seen anyone killed, and I have yet to kill anyone. I have exhibited *great restraint!* ♦ ♦ ♦

Avital Ronell

Avital Ronell is an "ivory-tower terrorist" who has disseminated Jacques Derrida's work on "deconstruction" throughout the United States in an attempt to make his potentially subversive philosophy "mobilizable" . . . i.e., close the gap between theory and action. The first theorist to write a philosophic essay on AIDS before it had scarcely been recognized (1983), Avital has consistently investigated the implications of the emerging *technology of subjection* in articles on war, feminist philosophy, Walter Benjamin, Nietzsche, and in her books *Dictations: On Haunted Writing; The Telephone Book: Technology, Schizophrenia, Electric Speech;* and *Crack Wars: Literature/Addiction/Mania.*

The Telephone Book has been described as "the first political deconstruction of technology, state terrorism, and schizophrenia. It offers a fresh reading of the American and European addiction to technology in which the telephone emerges as the crucial figure of this age . . . her highly original, multifaceted inquiry into the nature of communication in a technological age will excite everyone who listens in." One of Avital's primary concerns is *language deviancy:* "To try to limit language is always a kind of right-wing desire. The idiom of Nixon was always, 'Let me be perfectly clear.' The idiom of any totalitarian use of language is always under the sign of absolute clarity. Life resists that kind of clarity—and it would be crushed by the attempt to pin it down to a single meaning. Deviancy in language is something that *doesn't* say: obey me, follow orders, imitate me—rather: *resist* me."

Avital Ronell was born in Prague and lived in Israel, New York, Berlin, Paris, etc before moving to the Bay Area. Currently teaching at UC Berkeley, she lists her principal interests as "technology, anti-racism, state torture, and electronic culture." Her books have been published in France, Germany, Japan and Spain. Recently she affirmed, "I think it's absolutely essential to resist the catastrophic shutdown of knowledge in America. America's being emptied of the *desire to know.*"

Part I

♦ ANDREA JUNO: What's "wrong" with feminism today?

♦ AVITAL RONELL: It's dependent on what *man* does. Feminism today has a *parasitical,* secondary territoriality, and if you respond to present conditions, you're subject to reactive, mimetic and regressive posturings. So the problem is: *how can you free yourself?* How can you not be *reactive* to what already exists as powerful and dominating? How can you avoid a *ressentimental* politics? Is it possible to have a feminism that is joyous, relentless, outrageous, libidinally charged—

♦ AJ: —humorous, ironic, with all the layers of privi-

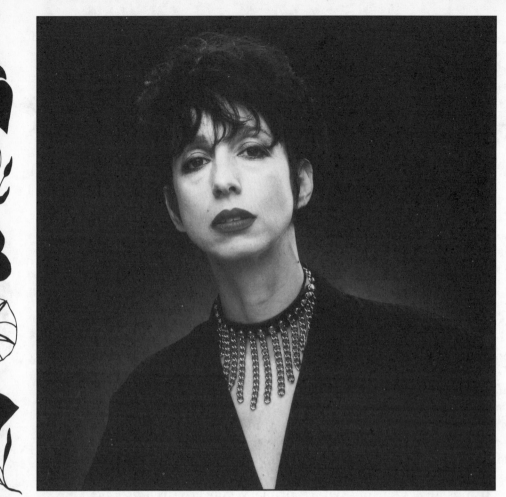

Photo: Bart Nagle

certain *metaphysics* onto which she's already imprinted?

♦ **AJ: For me, an example of the flipside would be Andrea Dworkin. Though claiming to be a women's liberationist, she's perpetuating an oppressive, status-quo stereotype: that women aren't supposed to be interested in things like pornography. Then ugliness intrudes—that repressive grimness that one thinks of as not fun or ironic—**

♦ AR: Well, the ugliness has to be taken seriously, I think, because it's part of a whole politics of demasking or denuding, and getting to a *Puritan* core—like the ban on makeup. All that is part of a *politics of self-presentation* which is still ruled by a *metaphysics* of self-presentation that doesn't consider current thinking about: artifice, technicity and so on . . .

lege that the male status quo has always enjoyed—

♦ AR: And do women have to be grim and humorless in their response to an admittedly appalling situation? This grimness isn't necessarily the most noble response; it's often fed by values of resentment and anger—

♦ **AJ: —with the male constructing the question and the female responding.**

♦ AR: That's why I was interested in telephone answering machines: how the feminine becomes a kind of answering machine to the call of the male metaphysical subject. So the first question is: Could there be a feminine intensity or force that would not be merely "subversive"? Because subversion is a problem—it implies a *dependency* on the program that is being critiqued—therefore it's a *parasite* of that program. Is there a way to produce a force or an intensity that isn't merely a reaction (and a very bad and allergic reaction) to *what is?* In other words, could feminism be a pointer toward a *future of justice* that isn't merely reproducing *what is*, with small reversals?

♦ **AJ: These are central, key concerns. Historically, revolutionaries seem to always end up being the new oppressors. How do you terminate this cycle? How do women stop being the flipside of the coin—and start a whole new currency?**

♦ AR: How can woman avoid being the flipside of a

♦ **AJ: I felt guilty even *using* the word "ugly"—**

♦ AR: Yes—one of my mentors, the French feminist writer Hélène Cixous, came to America years ago, and one of her first gestures (which horrified American feminists) was to point out what ugly shoes they wore. And this completely scandalized everyone! Hélène is an incredibly beautiful Egyptian lioness—she's splendidly dressed. Somehow the lines between pragmatic American feminism (of course, there are other branches) and French theoretical feminism were drawn along *eyeliner* marks: *artifice, seduction* (that a lot of French feminists still believe in; seduction as the power to create distance, to *dis-identify* with one's self, to mask and play around, and to perform different versions of oneself).

The whole power of *miming*—which makeup has to do with—would be an interesting history to trace, because women were always considered creatures of the simulacra who were fake or false—therefore not "readable" or reliable. So it's very odd for a European (with another notion of history than Americans have) to note this desire (which is a totally *male* desire) for absolute self-presentation without artifice, makeup, lying and deception. Now certain philosophers *revalorize* deception as a playful honoring of life's multiplicity, rather than as a subjugation of the lie to truth—

♦ **AJ: In most ancient magical myths, behind the**

masks there's so much power in the artifice—

♦ AR: I think that the artifice has often been on woman's side. And the rejection and *demonization* of the artifice is a very strange but basic gesture of American ideology. For me, feminism, as a perturbing *intervention* into *what is*, has to be very suspicious of *anything* that coincides with American ideology. For example, this propaganda about "sincerity" and "honesty" which the Right propagates, is always in the service of the greatest *servility* to the law, and *docility*.

♦ AJ: Of course, we should define our terms—

♦ AR: I'm just referring to the way "sincerity" and "honesty" are used in common circulation as American values—this myth (or mystification) that things could be presented without frames, artifice, or interpretation. This reflects an American nostalgia for an original state of things, that would be immune from copies . . .

In "The Critique of Violence," Walter Benjamin said something very curious: *Only* where lying and deception would be promoted as a sign of the flourishing of art and intersubjectivity, would there be a possibility for peace—this is very enigmatic. The minute lying became a problem of the *law*, and became affiliated with fraud, conflict was inevitable—

♦ AJ: Copyright as opposed to appropriation. If you're drawing something to look "real," you have to "lie," otherwise the perspective will appear distorted. Here, a deeper truth can become manifest only when one acknowledges there is no single "reality."

♦ AR: [laughs] Reality is so complicated, yet our culture wants to simplify it into one total (or totalitarian) truth. A lot of political movements still hang onto a single shred of truth as if it were "the" truth—this has to be abandoned. That's why one rarely uses the word "revolution" anymore—or rather, "*the* revolution." I think we're in a very *mournful* and depressed era right now, because all revolutions have disappointed us. The Third World, for reasons we understand, can no longer offer a model for revolution—

♦ AJ: Neither can the Communist example—

♦ AR: We have to get back to the basic question of: *Can there be a community?* A community that isn't based on fusional desire, and fascistic projects or goals (and their attendant dangers)? Even the so-called Sexual Revolution largely ended up fucking with women.

I think we're in a historical depression right now, because everything has failed so entirely. This could be a great moment, because we have to re-think everything: "Okay, we're at absolutely a dead end—an absolutely *devastating* impasse." Which means that one has to think one's way out of it.

One can no longer talk about simplistic polarities—we have to get beyond *oppositional logic*. In Europe, World War II started with a left wing revolution (the Communist-Bolshevik one) and a right wing Nazi (National Socialist—or rather *fascist)* one. Now, oppositions are shifting (West vs. East to North vs. South) and certain stand-offs have collapsed. If it's the end of history, we at least could note that, "Every end is a beginning," and that it's imperative (*morally* imperative in a new, intellectually fanatical sense, because we're being throttled) to really think this through, to take time out. We're certainly being *given* time out—*nothing* is happening now!

♦ AJ: Right. We're facing death. All the philosophical foundations we live by have to be re-thought.

♦ AR: It's not to be understood (with the optimism of the Marxists) as a "crisis"—they always say, "A *crisis*—oh, something good will happen!"

♦ AJ: Or like a *catharsis;* the Freudians love you to have a major catharsis so that you can then rebuild—

♦ AR: So it's not that kind of optimism—a crisis out of which a reversal will erupt. Nor is it of an *apocalyptic* nature where a *revelation of truth* will take place. This is why there's probably a great, pervasive depression, because there's no revelation forthcoming—*that's* the revelation! There's no sudden revolution or reversal to be hoped for (nor necessarily to be desired).

Also, what we're calling "Woman" has to be rethought, because first of all it's something that feminism has perhaps *unconsciously* borrowed or left uninterrogated; it's a *hand-me-down* that was inherited through our phallic legacy. Whenever anyone has tried to define "Woman," it has always been mystified and presented as a series of symptoms—as the Other to man. And this is something that has to be interpreted—if not rejected. We have to get beyond this inheritance. An inheritance isn't something you simply *ignore*—it's part of you, it's part of the *transmission system*. But you have to negotiate with it and recognize its history—where it comes from, what it imposes on you, what kind of a frame it traps you into—

Is it possible to have a feminism that is joyous, relentless, outrageous, libidinally charged?

♦ AJ: Like the label "gay," which is essentially useless since there are so many variants: from a Republican gay to a lesbian separatist commune member. On one level we seem to need these labels to mobilize and bring about "real" political effects . . . yet we must avoid the dogmatic traps those labels impose—

♦ AR: You're exposing political and real effects of sheerly *linguistic phenomena*—the way certain words are appropriated—their usage, circulation, and how the appropriation is often a *reappropriation*, which is to say that very often a word that tries to pin down an identity comes from an *Aggressive Other.* Very often this aggression is *accepted* (with a bit of irony), and it goes through many permutations. So *word usage* is already something (if one is attentive to it) that is extremely politically inflected. That's why the High-Rising of Illiteracy is a very politi-

cal problem in America. People are no longer reading, no longer speaking, no longer existing *in* and *as* language, no longer enjoying the *perversion* that an adherence to language always promotes. They're not being liberated into linguistic spaces that really *do* produce effects of self-transformation.

In the '60s, with one hand people were forming fists, but in the other hand there tended to be a *book*—preferably a philosophical book, whether it was Herbert Marcuse's influence—

◆ **AJ: Or Mao's *Little Red Book,* or Marx—**

◆ AR: Right. There was a rapport to the "book" which has now been *broken.* The fact that censorship right now is so powerfully deployed on language and general inscriptive usage is very important: *there is a desire to shut down the freedom that language always points to.* And it's a freedom beyond "transcendental essences," beyond the repetition of traditional images, values or aspirations. Language always has a random element, a secret track or rebellious provocation. *Language is not beholden to traditional truth value.* The fact that there's a growing *desire for illiteracy* is also part of a general libidinal political shutdown. And this is never mentioned (to my knowledge): the fact that the '60s was also a *reading period with a reading list*—actually, a *number* of (and a *proliferation* of) reading lists. There was a real power generation going on through the raising of philosophical questions—

The High-Rising of Illiteracy is a very political problem in America. People are no longer reading. There is a desire to shut down the freedom that language always points to.

◆ **AJ: Which was keyed to the reading of books—**

◆ AR: Now, even among so-called "intellectuals" there's a real hesitancy to mobilize a more philosophical or abstract idiom. There's an unfortunate distinction being drawn between "practical" and "intellectual" movements, and even though I don't trust intellectuals for one minute (whenever they mix into politics all my *psycho*-alerts go on) nevertheless I don't think there's a possibility for true change without some sort of very carefully drawn out *intellectual* surge—despite the saying, "Never trust an intellectual!" (or certainly, "a German with an idea!"). I don't know of any revolutionary instinct that hasn't been fed by so-called "abstract" notions. People who are distressed over what they call abstractions or theorizations are too impatient—

◆ **AJ: As Walter Benjamin said, "He who claims to**

be without theory is simply in the grip of an older, unacknowledged theory."

◆ AR: Right. I was at an international conference on feminism in Tokyo. Now I believe in making trouble—if women have any *duty* at all, essentially it's to be a pain in the ass. So I said: "Women have never invented anything." This shocked a lot of people. Then I said: "Women will never invent anything." Then I said, "Nor will there ever be a woman genius." And suddenly it seemed like: *Who was I?* Was this some Kabuki performance—was I just wearing the *mask* of a woman but was really a man? *What* was speaking here—what kind of outrage was being committed? Then I said, "This is *good news!*" Because this isn't something that women should aspire to—concepts such as "genius" and "invention" always have a single male signatory. *Geni*us is related to *geni*tals. Evelyn Fox Keller has shown how a woman's invention in physics can't be *received*—there's no "admission policy" for the discovery that a woman might make.

◆ **AJ: You mean "woman" as the label rather than the biological woman, because you do have the example of Madame Curie—**

◆ AR: She is the exception; the one self-poisoning sacrificial inventress—

◆ **AJ: Right. She's even denied heroic status because she poisoned herself with her own radiation—**

◆ AR: Exactly, the excessive—who also (obviously) worked with her husband. . .What I meant by the statement that a woman can't be a genius is: some women still aspire to be canonized or recognized as a genius. Recognized by whom? Historically, genius has signified a privileged relation to "nature" involving male subjects. Yet genius also tends to bear marks of Otherness—in Kant's third *Critique,* genius is considered a monstrosity of nature and a glorious aberration. Woman is *already* considered kind of monstrous—but not in this privileged, sheltered and sanctioned way that male genius has always been regarded. In a genuine feminist intervention what has to happen is a Will to Rupture—a Will to Break with these phantasms and divinizations. Women don't need a secondary and pious rapport to the possibility or goal of being recognized as a genius—

◆ **AJ: Male genius is typified by megalomaniacal denial, as in the case of a technology-worshipping nuclear power plant engineer who is incredibly unemotional *(Father Knows Best)*, and proclaims: "No, there is no danger. We have logically worked all this out." These men are worshipping technology as an escape from their own feelings/body/death. Since they identify with technology rather than humanity, the madness is: they think they can escape their own mortality—although the real madness is: the moment you separate from the body, you'll *die.***

◆ AR: That's true. The only "hope" for surviving your *deadline* is a separation from the body—the Christians figured that one out by negotiating an "afterlife!"

◆ **AJ: The male has been constructed as the head/ mind, while woman is the body . . . the emotional,** mindless creature of instinct.

♦ AR: I think that what's important now is to mobilize *hysteria* as a quasi-revolutionary force. Hélène Cixous insists it is an inherently revolutionary power: it intervenes, breaks up continuities, produces gaps and creates horror—refusing conformity with *what is*. Feminism could benefit from an *affirmation of hysteria*; hysteria as a response to what is unacceptable and intolerable in life . . . as a response to *emergency*.

Very often my women students report that when they start writing their PhD dissertations, their intimate friends begin to create problems domestically. Usually someone will say, "You're being hysterical!" And I say, "What's wrong with that?" If you read Freud, you find that creativity and hysteria are linked. Hysteria is stimulating—it's not to be repressed. And it's funny that women have *internalized* that *censorship of hysteria* as though it were an unwelcome disease . . . whereas it should be *welcomed* as part of the work force.

♦ **AJ: How many thousands of conversations have there been where the woman *knows* something's wrong and asks the man to open up. When he doesn't respond, she starts to "nag." Then the man reproves her: "You're just being hysterical; I don't want to discuss this now." Here the male takes the stance of holding it in, being autistic, and the woman, who is trying to elicit communication, becomes the scapegoat or is "hystericized" with a pejorative evaluation ("What's wrong with *her?*"). Yet the truth of the matter is: it's the *man* who has the problem—and the woman takes the heat!**

♦ AR: *Male autism* is possibly one of the biggest problems we face on every level of existence. And hysteria—including PMS which has a very genuine rapport to time and to repetition in time, communicates a rapport to death, an anxiety about Being. Let's digress for a moment. Women's bodies take out *monthly mortgages;* women have a *regular* relation to blood. Men—I don't mean to just produce binary oppositions, but this recent desire for a "bloodless war" has shown us that men's horror of blood has *got* to be dealt with. Here again Walter Benjamin already predicted that the desire for a bloodless war would take on all sorts of "divine" modalities, and now our high tech war is obviously a denial of body and bloodshed.

If someday I were to become Empress of the World (I am waiting for the call!) and could begin remaking the world, I would start with the relation to time, to finitude, and to the *blood* which separates the sexes. I would inject men with a monthly relation to their own finitude. The PMS syndrome—the tension, the despair, the relation to death, and the suicidal recognitions that take place—are not something I *exalt* (I've been tortured by it all my life). Yet at the same time I must say it's produced an understanding of Being that has ontological resonances—just the way you fade out periodically, and the fact that there's no refuge. There's a pain that's not strictly physical, but which never allows you to subtract the body from this sudden abyssal opening and exposure to your *limits*.

♦ **AJ: PMS provides a displacement from a linear, rational world. In some tribal cultures, during menstruation the women went off together into the huts; this was a time of spirituality, a time of going inward. Sometimes I feel that if I could just isolate myself for three days or so, then menstruation might actually be sort of wonderful. But the world imposes its obligations on you, forcing you to remain "external," thus causing all the negatives: irritability, depression, etc—**

♦ AR: What's interesting is that it *pushes* a remapping of relations; it provides a sudden disruption of any continuum. At Princeton my exams were scheduled for the day I would suffer most severely from PMS. So I had to go in and ask for a change of schedule, and the professor was extremely nasty, ultra-conservative—in other words, a "gentleman." He asked why I was requesting a rescheduling and I replied, "I have medical reasons" (which was the conventional euphemism). Then he wanted to know the exact content of these so-called "medical reasons" and I was surprised—he's a married man; couldn't he have guessed? But when I told him it was PMS (that I suffered enormously; felt almost deranged and wouldn't have mastery over the material) he threw me out of his office! Then a colleague said to me, "*Well,* are you going to regulate your entire life around this? You've got to get used to these impersonal schedules."

What we're calling "Woman" has to be rethought . . . it's a *hand-me-down* that was inherited through our phallic legacy.

Then I realized that one's life was organized around this kind of disruption, and I tried to "read" this "unreadable" event that recurs monthly, yet each time arrives as a *surprise attack* . . . which no calendrial mastery can adequately deal with. So a politics that might articulate this rapport to time and death would be very interesting . . .

♦ **AJ: The book *Fear of Women* by Lederer describes the relationship women have always had with birth, death and blood, and men's fear of the *vagina dentata*—the fear of falling into some fluid, mucous-filled death world. One counters this fear by keeping everything clean and sterile. The author also shows how women have been regarded like those *frauveldt* statues of the beautiful woman whose back reveals decaying, worm-eaten pestilence. This book makes some wonderful points, although the last third is unreadable.**

♦ AR: Recently I read an essay in which Derrida asked the question: "What is *exposed* in photography?" Then I read the *Commissioner's Report on Pornography* (prepared by Meese in 1988). Essentially it says that sex itself (as if there were a purity, a stability, an identity of "sex") is not a problem, no matter how it's performed or who conducts it. The problem lies in the *representation* of sexuality. Even legally sanctioned sex, once it passes into an inscripted form, is immediately pornographic. So, *what* is being censored . . . *what* is the problem here?

True feminism has to investigate & encompass biotechnics, biogenetics, & all fields of technology. A true feminism will stop being phobic about these areas, because it's crucial that women be involved in investigating, exploring and shaping the technological realities of the future.

The first question would be: what does a photograph expose? This is an ancient problem: the difference between form and content. And on one level Kant already liberated us from this—he said that that the content of a "work of art" cannot have a determinate value (i.e., have defined limits). It's only the *form* we should be attentive to, as we cannot judge the content. But what's happening here *is* precisely a judgment of content.

So, what does a photograph expose? It exposes, says Derrida, the relation to the law. What he means is that every photo poses itself as this question: *Are we allowed to view what is being exposed?*

♦ **AJ: This brings up the question of . . . take the example of being gay. In Yemen, sleeping with people of the same sex is very common; both the men and women do this (as long as they don't do it in the street and frighten the horses and children). Yet on another level there is oppression of women and homosexuals, grounded in very archaic customs. Also, before the labeling that emerged in the '60s in America, two "women friends" or "bachelors" could live together and not be subject to condemnation for their sexuality—yet their behavior was technically illegal and subject to repression. In both instances, society hadn't yet taken the "photograph" (or been labeled)—the representation hadn't been concretized.**

♦ **AR: This *Commissioner's Report* is very smart on this point: it says that the law is sending out "signals" about how you're *supposed* to behave; it's just sending out signals about what in censorship is *necessary*, and what it can let slide. It's not going to deliver a discourse, because if it were to take that risk it would find itself in a contradictory situation. This is like the paranoid world of Kaf-**

ka's *Castle*, where the castle (a metaphor for the Law) sends out signals which are very important, but "K" doesn't understand what they mean.

We have to ask, "What's the status of an *example?* How can an example cover how you're supposed to behave in every situation—take over the whole field? Is an example primary or secondary?" And in the *Report*, the example given is "procreative vaginal intercourse." Clearly, this sexuality needs to be interrogated! Because suddenly the law is saying that true sexuality is *vaginocentric*—the law has become a kind of *speculum* entering the vaginal area in order to legally sanction sexuality.

♦ **AJ: So *that* tells us what is legal? It's not even mentioning the phallus at this point—**

♦ AR: No. This is all about protecting art, protecting *women* (a "cause" which, as you know, came up again in this Gulf War).

♦ **AJ: And this Meese Commission was using the right wing fundamentalists *and* the Andrea Dworkin-type feminists to form a coalition—again, ostensibly to "protect women."**

♦ AR: Exactly. The whole question of protecting art is one that shows the extent to which Woman has become law's *symptom*. But I ask: Is woman an example, or the central field according to which sexuality has to be adjusted?

Again, according to this report, sex itself (as long as it's not publicly exposed) is absolutely outside the reach of this law. The "damage" comes when it *isn't* sex, but *representation*—sex must not in any way be inscribed or transcripted, and I quote: "The alleged harm here therefore is that as soon as sex is put on a screen or put in a magazine, it changes its character, regardless of what variety of sex is portrayed." Now this is interesting, because you could then say to them: "So homosexual sex *in itself* is okay, but if it's depicted, then it changes its character and it's not."

Every photo poses itself as this question: *Are we allowed to view what is being exposed?*

♦ **AJ: Essentially, their definition of sex is strictly heterosexual—**

♦ AR: Yes, but they're not saying that—this Report is from 1988 and they don't yet know that word! I continue the quote: " . . . And to the extent that the character of sex as public rather than private is the consequence here, then that, to many, would constitute a harm."

Here I ask, What constitutes private and public spheres with guaranteed borders? If the police intervene in the bedroom of a gay couple, then it's not clear when an image or an utterance ceases being private and becomes public. So the difference between private and public has to be reflected upon. If the law says that the problem is the representation *in public*—not the act itself—

♦ **AJ: In the case of *2 Live Crew* who were acquitted of obscenity charges, ultimately it was a matter of: "We don't mind if you have your black culture, as long as you don't *talk* about it . . . or put out a record!"**

♦ AR: Also, there's a whole logic of contagion involved: you might expose people to something that *contaminates by example.* Here we have the problem of mimesis: art is mimetic—it has to do with an imitation of reality, and even though art is fiction, doesn't it produce the *desire to imitate?* So it would be incumbent upon the law to think about mimesis and imitation—*what's imitating what?*

One of the destabilizers of art's private integrity is democratic reductionism to an average person. Because the Report refers to the "average person" and "community standards," and in the name of the average person (which art has never claimed to care much about), the law has permitted itself to *pornographize* art. In reality this shows a lot of *scorn* for the average person. The average person and community standards—really, these *legal fictions* are *unacceptable values* for art. Right now I have to say that I don't support a "culture of art." But I have to protest this situation in which we find ourself defending rights that should have been set in stone years ago. It is necessary to take sides with full *clarity.*

One great ancestor of this whole censorship delirium was the example of William Burroughs' *Naked Lunch,* which of course was initially censored. Before that, there was James Joyce's *Ulysses.* Here, the judge had let all his friends who were upright gentlemen read *Ulysses* in the privacy of their own bedrooms, and these were men (he wrote) who were not prone to sexual arousal in arbitrary and unacceptable ways. It was stunning when the judge proved in his argument that James Joyce had produced a novel which had nothing to do with sexual arousal, but which produced nausea–it only made you want to throw up! Then the judge declared that *Ulysses* was hereby admitted into the United States of America. This was such a sublimely grotesque moment.

But, I submit the law forgot how closely disgust and desire are linked! Bataille showed that a woman's genitals are frightening because they have the smell of death and all sorts of disgust that sexuality is linked to. But anyway, this *Ulysses* case revealed a charming but very disturbing form of legalization. Because one can imagine a society in which something that makes you want to throw up would *not* be considered legal. It's as if *Ulysses* were defended with an insurance policy, in that the law implemented a *self-installation* of censorship. Because if *Ulysses* produces these horrible effects, then it has already censored any *sensual* rapport to this book. However, the law never questions what *reading* is, what relation we have to reading, nor what *arousal* is . . .

♦ **AJ: This relates to the problem of the "natural" and the "artificial." The implication is that somewhere** there's a Garden of Eden where sex exists "naturally" (as long as we don't inscribe it or take pictures of it)—

♦ AR: And that's a very dangerous phantasm: that *pure sex itself* is a possibility, prior to any interference of language. Any reader of Freud would realize that these are *pre-Oedipal fantasies.*

What's important now is to mobilize *hysteria*—it's an inherently revolutionary power that intervenes, breaks up continuities, produces gaps and creates horror—refusing conformity with *what is.*

♦ **AJ: We have to constantly remind ourselves that the Nazi fascists were heavily into the "nature" myth—the myth of an "innocent" world, and that they also burned books. All this goes hand-in-hand with the fear of language, fear of artifice—**

♦ AR: Hitler said that "A true German woman does not wear makeup"—i.e., does not "inscribe" herself with makeup. The woman is supposed to be part of this "natural" world that hasn't been interfered with by cosmopolitan or "material" (i.e., Jewish) influences. Historically, the Jews have always been known as the people of the *book* . . .

♦ **AJ: We need to examine how the uncritical idealization of "nature" leads to the fascistic. Because to even think there is a world without language is delusionary—we *create* our world by language, literally.**

♦ AR: Allusions to "nature" are always secondary and a projection backwards—usually a very dangerous projection. All Edenic projections of plenitude have proven dangerous.

♦ **AJ: The hippies had a reverence for the "natural"; they had that idea of "Let's go back to the earth"—**

♦ AR: There are still hippies in Berkeley, of course, but they're largely scorned for their failure. Some of the '60s hippie initiatives still command some respect, but . . .

♦ **AJ: There were some wonderful things that happened, too: the courage, the enthusiasm, the righteousness to change the world.**

♦ AR: One of the major problems with the hippie movement is: *it couldn't reinscribe love.* Their concept of "love" still reverted to a Christian communion of love that still had a "transcendental" essence, and maybe that was their failure. As a matter of fact, it could be that historically love is no longer possible. In the Western world love has always involved the promise of eternity conjuncting with

Photo: Nina Glaser

derived some major pit-
falls; the pitfalls of many
historical revolutions derive from that idea of
"nature."

♦ AR: Feminism as a
force or intensity has to
disrupt all officially charted maps—it calls for the
remapping of relationships.
Everything has to be called
into question, including
the possibility of love. This
is a big, ambitious, crucial
project that breaks with
what is traditional or ossified. Therefore it can't
harken back to a "natu-
ral" state which you've
been rightly criticizing as
a very dangerous image,
fantasy, or nostalgia.

Just to get back, I think
that the failure of the hippies is still something that
we have to interrogate—
because something did collapse with their collapse.
And I don't know what it
is. I have no desire to *di-
vinize* them in any way, but
through their arising something was seen to be *possible*. They did articulate a
certain limit (or lack there-
of) of social being, and a
certain democratic spread-
ing of what they called
"love." They demonstrat-
ed a certain opening of
the libidinal economy
(and all that implies), and
a breakdown in *class*
differences. Their adher-
ence to Marcuse and
Hannah Arendt and even

terrestrial being. The hippies tried to render "love" transparent—wasn't that what they promised? And wasn't
that the word they destroyed, finally?

Also, they probably didn't take into account *narcissism*, which as a very violent reaction is what created
things like the '80s "Me Generation"—this re-narcissiza-
tion of the *polity*. That's why I suspect that the hippie
generation's failure was to embrace this Christian communion of love which hadn't yet been mediated by Nietzsche and the Will to Power!

♦ **AJ: To recap another point: it's in the idea of
"nature" and "woman as nature" where feminism has**

a certain reading of Heidegger and Freud was very
interesting, too.

What got busted there needs to be understood, too,
because now the grim reality of drug wars, the war on
art, the war on the homeless, and the war on the sick is
somehow the legacy of that failure. We don't have to
remind ourselves that Reagan was the governor of California at that moment, and that there's some sort of
belated relation to that repressed "revolution" that is still
being worked out by the *undead* presidents that we're
dealing with now . . . who are completely struggling
with *phantoms*.

◆ AJ: I often think about the failures and the promises of the '60s—so much was unleashed that we have to analyze. It's hard to get the whole picture, and see the forest from the trees. The hippies were exploring new frontiers and territories with no language structure. Drugs, Sex and Rock'n'Roll are perfect examples of an original intention to re-spark the nervous system—to shock new neural nets or pathways; new trains of thought through altered states. The lack of analytic faculties ("Hey man, don't talk so much, let's just listen to the music") resulted in communion (drugs, sex, music) without community. And that was a major failure.

If the Washoe Indians participate in a peyote ritual, it's to provide an experience of "communion" to bind the community together in a collective search for truths, insights, new language or poetry, and myths to integrate into the culture. But in the society of alienation that is America, if you take a drug, you get further and further away from the community, because this is not a communal journey with a shared language. The drug experimentor who becomes an addict doesn't find communion or enlightenment, but becomes sicker and more alienated from the community—stealing from friends, etc. So—how do you envision New Worlds which stimulate fresh inner perspectives? The promise of the '60s was to remap such a frontier community, but unfortunately the remappers came burdened down with the baggage of our linear-brained, alienated mind-set—

◆ AR: In *Crack Wars: Literature, Addiction, and Mania,* I was dealing with this promise of a sheer Otherness, a new frontier that didn't have an idiom yet. I dealt with the War on Drugs as a War on Creatures of the Simulacrum—I started writing it before there was a War on Art. And I argued that these are co-related; that there can't be a War on Drugs without a War on Art and in fact a War on every conceivable type of *fictional desire*—

◆ AJ: A war on dreams, a war on the imagination—

◆ AR: —on the *productivity* of the unconscious. I would say America's waging a War on the Unconscious . . . be it South America, or wherever.

◆ AJ: A war on whatever the construction of the "Body" is. This War on Drugs is so reprehensible because it's so hypocritical—

◆ AR: I was reading a German who wrote, "Leave it to the Americans, the true nihilists, to call it 'intoxicant', because it always has the 'toxic' prejudice in it. Why can't they have a more pleasant, ecstatically inflected word?" In America there's always that emphasis on the "clean"—it's a very obsessional, neurotic culture. That's why it always wants to clean the borders and frontiers and demarcate them clearly—

◆ AJ: Another Either/Or dualism: America has this shadow world of alcoholics, drug addicts, crack users—and fundamentalist Christian teetotalers who have repressed every impulse of the body. These are two sides of the same coin—one that's in denial of the body.

◆ AR: Absolutely. Did you notice that this censorship business is totally out of synch with the sexual politics of the nation—it seems to have started when the "TeleChristians" discovered their own sexuality—

◆ AJ: Rather belatedly, long after the '60s—

◆ AR: Remember when Jimmy Swaggart, Jim Baker and all the others were found to have these *secret sexualities*? They were forced to denounce themselves, and as a self-defense tactic suddenly they lashed out against *art!* Basically they shouted, "Where's the sexuality?" and then started locating it *everywhere*.

If someday I were to become Empress of the World (I am waiting for the call!) and could begin remaking the world, I would start with the relation to time, to finitude, and to the *blood* which separates the sexes. I would inject men with a monthly relation to their own finitude.

In the meantime we had punked out. It had been years since the '60s; we were no longer into sexuality—AIDS had been acknowledged, etc. We (meaning people who are "creative," on the "cutting edge" and all that bullshit) were completely divested from the notion of sexuality as that privileged force which could create the "revolution" and other new economies. Now, years later, these Christians have discovered their own transgressions—now that we're no longer in an Age of Transgression. So what's weird about all of this recent censorship hysteria is that it's totally out of synch—they're out of touch! Meanwhile we're "post-punk," cool and calm about sexuality—

◆ AJ: To us sexuality is no big deal, it's a vital part of life—so what? Whereas to a preacher like Swaggart, sex is still really "filthy"—something to be hidden and denied. And it's this denial which creates *true* perversion—his relations with a prostitute were pathetic. Apparently he didn't even penetrate her; he would hire her to dress really sexy—but mostly he got his rocks off yelling and swearing at her. That's so sick—

◆ AR: These exhibitionist Christians love to exhibit their repressed "love." They're totally promiscuous (because they love *everyone!*) yet they repress their sexuality.

◆ AJ: Have you ever watched those fundamentalist Christian TV broadcasts? Their confessional format is similar to that of AA meetings. All these Christians confess in livid detail: "I was a drug addict, child

molester, pervert . . . until I found God." If you watch this program you'll get an amazing dose of titillation with incredible detailing.

◆ AR: I have a friend who observed, "What could be more pornographic than a crucifix?" Here you have this virgin body that is totally S&M'd, wounded, bloody, crushed against a restraint and naked in pure offering — in a sacrificial ceremonial. What's *odd* is the widespread *non*-recognition of the completely S&M culture that Christianity has always embodied (even if the Protestant version is more austere and tries to get away from the voluptuousness of the suffering, self-flagellation and detailing of the sacrificial idiom, the purity of the pain that Catholicism insists upon). Nonetheless, at some point one has to confront its S&M origins, or at least try to understand the relationship of S&M to Christianity —

◆ AJ: Also, colonialism and imperialism has always been the legacy of Christian do-gooders; master-slave relationships and political oppression have always followed the initial, "friendly" intrusions of the so-called "missionaries" —

◆ AR: In this censorship controversy, *both* sides are active in the same "clean-up" project of art. Those defending art from the position of Freedom of Expression are *resisting* the excremental, improper, dirty, disgusting *necessities* of artistic expression. I think a lot of this is a question of *frame:* What are the limits of art? What are the formal restrictions? What constitutes art? What is obscene? All these are controversies over *property values,* it seems to me, or "propriety."

Basically, all cultures of art have depended on a "religious" thematic of *art as a transcendental essence.* They tend toward an aestheticized politics which historically we associate with the Nazi state. This has always been dangerous as it involves a politics of exclusion, a politics of "purity" following the logic of "natural" endowment, "natural" production of a national essence —

◆ AJ: Basically Hitler was an artist with a grand scheme for all of society —

◆ AR: So we should be infinitely suspicious of any "culture of art," because the most politically dangerous events have arguably always gone under the name of art and not politics.

◆ AJ: But let's define "art" — again, here's this problem of lumping together many different meanings into one limited word —

◆ AR: That's true: this has to be differentiated. One needs a situation in which one can, with infinite patience and suspicion, examine each word and its nuances, and locate the contested sites of subjectivity, of creativity — as we've been trying to do. For example, one must understand that art is the last "transcendental essence" related to creation. Also, art still embodies a notion of work which is *not* common labor — it belongs to a different kind of economy. That's why the granting body which grants the gift that allows the artistic "genius" to produce an economy that breaks the larger economy, is so crucial —

◆ AJ: Because this reinforces the myth of the artist as some inspired "genius" who doesn't even work — like a priest or something —

◆ AR: That's a crucial part of the mystification . . . You were saying that the "Either/Or" is a simplistic structure. Well, what we can't tolerate these days is the *Both/And* structure: a totally *inclusive* movement.

◆ AJ: In all of our would-be "revolutionary" movements, there are all these exclusionary distinctions made. For example, a lot of women who should be feminists aren't — because of Either/Or constraints such as the notion that if you're a true feminist, you can't wear makeup —

◆ AR: Absolutely. We were talking the other day about the astonishing lack of narcissism of our *body politic,* in that it thinks it could dispense with art —

◆ AJ: Lack of narcissism?

◆ AR: Well, for example, the French think it's crucial to their future that they be monumentalized by artistic innovation. In fact, every government in Europe wants to monopolize the best artists, in order to celebrate itself and constitute itself as an art work or a remnant of some sort of artistic insight. I was surprised to discover that America didn't feel that need. And I still don't know how to interpret this, unless there was a "transference of accounts" from art into technology. Maybe high tech is, for Americans, an *art form* — like Livermore Lab, Biosphere II, and the fighter jets that airmen often paint and name. Perhaps America has gone back to the very origins of art (which were in the *techné* or the artifice) by moving into technology —

Feminism as a force or intensity has to disrupt all officially charted maps — it calls for the *remapping* of relationships. *Everything* has to be called into question, including the possibility of love.

◆ AJ: I've often thought that — besides in art, real creativity and imagination is being expressed in science. Physicists and other scientists are truly reinterpreting how we view the world —

◆ AR: One of France's greatest philosophers, Jean-Luc Nancy, just underwent a heart transplant (and it's working). I saw him in France and our visit "scripted" like De Quincey's "The Last Days of Immanuel Kant" — not that I feel I'm Thomas De Quincey. Anyway, I visited him on August 2nd: the day Iraq went into Kuwait and the U.S. started its high tech fabulations. Hence, the coincidence in my life of what is too quickly called "good" and "bad" technology: the same time a friend got a new heart, George Bush set the mortality timer for the Iraqi people. Due to the technology behind both the "surgical" strikes and medical science, my friend's body is accepting this new and highly-philosophically-invested organ. It's amazing—apparently they find this to be among the *easiest* of transplants. Once completely drained, dilapidated, exhausted and visibly expiring, he's now (and I am fervently hoping this is not another empty promise) incorporating a youthful, vigorous heart.

I was feeling personally heartbroken and wounded . . . and when Jean-Luc had this transplant, I suddenly thought, "Okay, *I'm* going to have a transplant, and my old, wounded heart is going to be exchanged at the same time." I don't know what kind of metaphorical imperative I forced upon myself—I'm not saying that my new heart is absolutely resistant to new woundings or inscriptions, but I really got the sense that things are *renewable*—and I borrowed the possibility of renovation from a technological structure.

◆ **AJ: For me, a priority is the rethinking of the body away from an outdated Luddite, Thoreau-ean mythology which only conceives of technology as hostile to "nature." In the future our bodies will increasingly interface with cyborg technology. And it's this same Luddite mentality which only fifty years ago refused to consider the photograph as art. I think of Walter Benjamin's "The Work of Art in the Age of Mechanical Reproduction" and wonder about all the implications of the photograph—was the photograph "art"?**

◆ AR: In the case of Mapplethorpe, it's as if he (or his legacy) were clinging to membership in the art world. I've heard people lecture on his work, and they never let go of the word "art." Yet if that legacy would let go, a much more radical impulse could be communicated.

◆ **AJ: Society does not *want* to eliminate pornography. They want to keep it illegal, just like they keep prostitutes in the shadow world of criminals who can be controlled and whom they can profit from. And it's the status quo who are the johns. If they raise a fuss now, it's just to redirect the flow of money in their direction.**

If Mapplethorpe photos can just be clearly labeled "homosexual" or "S&M" and put into this "box," then there's no transgression; they cease being an issue. And the artists themselves aren't brave enough to ask, "What's wrong with pornography?" They just want to say, "No, this is *art!*"

◆ AR: Exactly—it's their vanity that's directing the fight. Because if they'd say, "*Art?*—I don't want to have anything to *do* with art! This is a *protest* against all art; against all the appropriations in the West that art has meant—"

◆ **AJ: Yes; aesthetics themselves are a form of elitism—there's this horrible fascism of aesthetics; about what is artistic and what isn't.**

◆ AR: These protesting artists are all somehow a little stupidly beholden to some *paternal metaphor* that legislates what constitutes "art" and what doesn't. And they still want to be *inside* this signified art—

◆ **AJ: Now there's a kind of postmodernist movement that takes very visceral, "unaesthetic" things from TV or "trash" culture (like a Jim Thompson novel) and incorporates them into painting, or whatever. And maybe it's bullshit for the most part, but at least it's inspiring people to buck the status quo and to reevaluate aesthetic fascism.**

> # I believe in making trouble—if women have any *duty* at all, essentially it's to be a pain in the ass!

I've always hated institutionalized "art culture," yet when this censorship hysteria began, I realized that grant-giving institutions like the NEA did spawn art galleries like the Kitchen in New York which put on the Annie Sprinkle performance that Jesse Helms attacked. And these galleries were manned by illegitimate offspring of the Academy—what I call "Trojan horses"—who simply exercised the values that society purports to uphold, such as literal "freedom of expression." These are the unanticipated products of a white male imperialist culture—the suburban '50s society had *no idea* it was producing a generation which would reject its own values.

◆ AR: What I think we're agreeing upon is the Both/And structure—*inclusive* movement. This kind of thinking is both low-tech (reproducing, copying things) and very high-tech in terms of analytical, laser-like interventions. Certainly our communication has to be more intricately configured; the people who have said, "Let me be perfectly clear" [Nixon] or "I'm telling a transparent and evident truth," have always been the worst types of power brokers . . .

You mentioned playing with language. The history of the pun is very interesting in this regard, because the pun was always considered "loose" or "on the loose": double-meaning, double-faced, and somehow always anally attached in the figurations and metaphorics that attended the pun. So the desire to repress double meanings is very interesting . . . and the promise (or threat) of one totalizing or totalitarian meaning is a very serious one. You're absolutely right to want a society that could play with language—there's something radically attractive about that; something that equally draws all sorts of repressive measures to itself. So the pun has always been slightly feminized, homosexualized, having to do with anal eroticism, being two-faced . . .

◆ **AJ: This brings to mind our dualistic Judeo-Christian structure of God/Devil, where God is all good and**

the Devil is all bad. In many other cultures where punning and wordplay predominate, there is a more integrated complexity of God/Devil, such as the trickster/coyote in American Indian mythology. In our society, what did the Devil become?—pure evil, to be cast out—not to be integrated. So what you're saying about the pun is perfect, because we threw out the trickster (as a creative integrated force) who speaks truth in roundabout, playful terms—

◆ AR: I tend to be associated with writing which is considered "morally wanting" because it indulges in wordplay. Recently I was routed through a whole discussion of "language abuse" (a strange displacement of "child abuse") as if language were something that one shouldn't push—that has something *pernicious* to do with desire. So there's a whole moral imperative not to play around *in* and *with* language, and to be "straightforward" . . . to be expressive in the most simple (or rather, simplistic) ways without artifice or rhetoric.

What could be more pornographic than a crucifix? Here you have this virgin body that is totally S&M'd, wounded, bloody, crushed against a restraint and naked in pure offering, in a sacrificial ceremonial. What's *odd* is the widespread *non*-recognition of the completely S&M culture that Christianity has always embodied.

There is such a denial of the rhetoricity or the inscription of what is said or done—as we saw in the recent censorship hysteria. A so-called "honest" language would involve (and you objected to the American abuse of the word "honesty") the *negation* of language. "Non-deceptive" language would have to give up figurality—in other words, deny its dimension of play and experimentation. I suppose we are returning in a circular way (how Joycean!) to questions of makeup, artifice.

◆ AJ: So—how does one formulate a politics of revolutionary feminism? Because feminism has to change—it can't be exclusionary to race, men, whatever . . .

◆ AR: By choosing woman as its fully-formed subject it's always had to receive reproaches of being partial and therefore not being about justice. *If feminism is anything it has to be a call—and a rigorous call—for justice.* As long as it excludes certain people, animals and even plants (I am thinking of Hegel's work on plant-life in the *Phenomenology*), it's not delivering its promise—

◆ AJ: And therefore it can never embrace a revolution for all of us.

◆ AR: One of the Japanese women at that conference said to me, "How can your abstract thinking ever lead to revolution?" And I replied, "I'm very sympathetic with your question—because I have to ask *myself* that every morning!" But in fact the most "abstract" notions are responsible for the most virulent and recurrent persecutions. The causes, motivations and justifications behind apartheid, the persecution of women, blacks, minorities and so forth is in the first place *abstractly determined*. And that continues to legitimate these aggressions—

◆ AJ: What's more abstract than saying what a "black" person or a "woman" really is?

◆ AR: All of these distinctions are based on Western metaphysics—therefore derived from so-called "abstract" systems of thought. So, a housewife who feels particularly depressed and wonders what is wrong with her is facing the question of *theorizing her predicament*. Precisely because we haven't found the answer and are only barely beginning to pose the question, we can't ignore the fact that this must have been institutionalized in very rigorous, systematic types of *discursive oppression*.

◆ AJ: Absolutely. And the more one delves into and *discusses* the underlying "abstract" assumptions that have oppressed life, the more one can map out strategies of what to do in *reality*.

◆ AR: I'm very often at odds with institutional feminists (or with institutionalized *forms* of feminism) because feminism as it's practiced (and it is diverse, yielding incredible knowledge, information and data) hasn't yet in the university fundamentally *perturbed the system*. In practical terms it's not providing any *new* guidance, any serious optimistic abundant "revolutionary" hope. It's just relocating the Woman as the specular mirror image of the Man. But considering the way neo-conservatives are attacking tenured radicals, deconstruction and feminism, at least feminism is part of a felt *provocation* to the right. Maybe this is one of those viruses that travel an as-yet unmapped trajectory.

In practical terms, feminism has to be granted regions beyond legal cliches—*equality*, to my way of thinking, *is not enough*. It's just not that desirable—it's a computation, it means "one equals one." I don't think that humanity can be computed in such an equation. The question that might be raised is, *"What does a liberated woman want?"* And I feel that, for example, my female colleagues tend to reproduce forms of autonomy and self-expression that are merely the counterpart—therefore parasitic—of "phallic" literature. They simply reverse certain values without fundamentally *displacing* them and perturbing the systems of power.

◆ AJ: That's a Male Question, based on the *a priori* assumption that you're the "Other." The male's not asking, "What does a liberated man want?" We need to reformulate the question, because what *is* necessary to ask, is: "What does the liberated *human* want on this planet . . . if we're to survive . . . and even *evolve?*"

Photo: Nina Glaser

Part II

♦ **AJ: Why have all "revolutions" failed?**

♦ AR: We've already said that traditional revolutions haven't worked—even the sexual revolution. And to do diagnostics, one has to enter areas that are not covered by the insurance of "political correctness." One has to posit theories that appear unacceptable or problematic— it takes the *courage of indecency* to figure out *why* things have been so massively defeated. Why is it that "revolution" as a signifier has seemingly been obsolesced? Let's review what has gone wrong, because it's very hard to admit: "Look, it *hasn't worked*—we've lost. Justice has lost."

Now what about "justice"? *Justice does not have a recognizable history.* We can't even point to a *moment* in history and say, "This is an exemplary or 'just' moment (or country or figure)." In fact, the figures of justice we have are rather frightful: King Solomon whose justice was instantaneous, prepared to cut the body of a child in half . . . Justice always has involved the reiteration of this cruel cut.

The problem is, first of all, to try to understand justice. Yet if we ask, "What is justice?" we find it is already contradictory—doesn't it always imply brutality, war, or a decisive "cut" (as in the case of King Solomon)? If "revolution" is *that which is to bring about justice,* why is it that we can't even represent what justice *is?*

♦ **AJ: In the '70s, Foucault, in the book *Power/Knowledge,* was telling a group of Maoists that the very structure of the court system already defeated the notion of justice. And the Maoists countered, "But the Chinese Revolution was just!" Well, we know in retrospect that China hardly became a society of justice— just look at Tienanmen Square! What are some examples that will make this idea of justice come alive?**

♦ AR: Of course there are examples of *heroic* justice, of selfless care. Nevertheless, justice does not have a recognizable history. Does that mean that justice cannot take place? That's possible—in Hegel's sense of history, *progress,* for example, is always brought about by *war.* War is the midwife to history. Here war had this meaning and value ascribed to it where *violence is recuperated by reason.* Now if our concern (whether it goes under the name of "feminism," "leftism," or whatever) is indeed to bring about justice, we need to think about where to locate it, what it might mean, what values it mobilizes, and what kind of violence in history it has depended upon so far.

♦ **AJ: I think people mostly think in terms of what is "unjust."**

♦ AR: And most utopian societies proposed in literature or non-fiction have been based on an *exclusionary*

operation . . . some regulative mechanism dependent on a powerful sense of what *cannot* take place in that "post-political" space. Such utopias may not be based on justice but on a naive notion of pleasure—or plenitude, where capital would be *so* present that it wouldn't be a problem. A utopia might even involve a kind of *transcendental* capitalism, for all we know. Different utopias have made claims for *pleasure* and a cessation of agony. But they've only rarely made their goal *justice*.

Now to get more down (or up) to earth: what about the prospects for revolution? Recently Eastern Airlines cut health care for the families of workers (while of course the top brass are still riding around in limousines.) Some employees have wives or husbands with cancer who need expensive treatment. And when interviewed, these workers said, "Well, I guess we'll have to *bite the bullet*"—in other words, let their spouses die! And I was shocked and perplexed by this *docile* response . . . by their interpretation of something so criminally unjust as a *destinal occurrence* . . .

♦ **AJ: Workers even accept pay *cuts* just to keep their jobs. Nowadays, the contemporary equivalent of a raise is: *not getting fired!***

♦ **AR:** One has to reflect on why *nothing* will incite people to become outraged. You may recall the Washington, D.C., riots caused by police brutality in the Latino community, when the city started going up in flames. I thought, "Now's the time for everyone to come to the nation's capital and join in solidarity; it's essential that this become a locus of public outrage." Of course, this idea didn't occur to *anyone*, whereas at least there was some mobilization against the Gulf War. It's as if Americans freeze when the time comes for local agitation. Even with people who are *in principle* mobilizable, a certain paralysis and blindness rules. These Washington, D.C. riots had the potential to evolve into something much more turbulent—and powerful—

♦ **AJ: Obviously, society's "control process" has nipped such potentials in the bud. It seems that the American people have an infinite ability to accommodate any abuse.**

♦ **AR:** At first glance what you see is an extremely depressed country—no one can "get it up" to deal with these things. But the question is also: *whom* do you address yourself to? What *locus of power* do you appeal to when authority is so diffused? There seems to be this *contagious complacency*—the populace seems tranquilized.

A crisis is supposed to provoke a *breakthrough;* it's supposed to reveal what's *wrong*. Unacceptable situations are finally no longer permitted. But the tolerance for alienation and political bludgeoning has become so great that, far from being recognized as an oppression, it's being somewhat uncritically applauded. Alienation has been *transvaluated*, in that David Lynch and others are now celebrated as "artists of the alienated." Here I'm including all the genres of the "Living Dead" movies—in general, the "post-punk culture." Americans are so deeply alienated that body piercing and tattoos might be some

of their greatest art works—the way forms of alienation have been translated and inscribed on the American body.

♦ **AJ: Actually, I think the people in our *Modern Primitives* book, who play with piercings and tattoos, were trying to form a community *against* the alienation.**

♦ **AR:** There's a *logic of the vaccine* at work here: If society appropriates alienation as something to be "read about," then the very condition of alienation itself (which could mobilize a widespread powerful reaction to it) is somehow, by this displacement, neutralized through an *anesthetized acknowledgment* of its existence. *Modern Primitives* involved a *playing* with forms of alienation and a radical embrace of artifice by which the body might be *regained*, rather than remaining in existential districts of *disavowal*.

♦ **AJ: In *Migraine,* Oliver Sacks gave the example of a genius mathematician who would be catatonic with depression for 4 or 5 days, then pass into a manic phase where he would be absolutely brilliant as a mathematician, then descend down into the depression phase again. As part of a "cycle," perhaps our current social depression is a prelude to some major breakthrough—**

♦ **AR:** I see your point, but my fear is that these cycles are subject to values that are becoming scarier and more *regressive*. (Also, what's taking place is the Death of Death, meaning the death of the *singularity* of each death.) If our "depression phase" was the Vietnam Syndrome, then the "manic phase" was the Gulf War: taking uppers, launching a million sorties, spending excessive sums of money for each piece of "collateral damage" and in general taking great libidinal pleasure in high tech destruction. This is the way America has regulated its cycles—with war.

If feminism is anything it has to be a rigorous call for justice. As long as it excludes certain people, animals and even plants (I am thinking of Hegel's work on plant-life in the *Phenomenology*), it's not delivering its promise . . .

We've had to regard all past "revolutionary" movements with a lot of suspicion because they've been reactive and dependent. Revolution so far has been based on an *oppositional libidinal potentiality*: if you wage a war against the war, it's always according to the same values. As fabulously as the Sixties may have liberated signs into the public sphere and offered certain possibilities, nevertheless this took place within the syndrome of the Vietnam War. What would be a genuinely affirmative movement that wouldn't merely be the excremental outcome or the dirty underside of some appalling power gesture? *That's* what I think about. See, all protest has been within the parameters of war and negativity—subject to the law of the father, to mere *transgression*—which is just not enough. Come on—we *have* to get out of this infantile reactivity!

What would it be to initiate an affirmative movement? To affirm certain values—not merely in protest and anger, but in almost *serene determination* because we've spent some time reflecting on things? Our methodology has been reactive—nothing has been affirmative. Is there the possibility of a genuine displacement, realignment, reterritorialization, that would not be so dependent on the very values we abhor? This would have to come from *feminine intensity*—I don't see where else it would come from.

To start thinking about, initiating and instituting a genuine peace (or "something") movement—again, we're stuck with words that are *paleolithic*. Yet we can't just coin new words each time we need new concepts; therefore we're stuck in a paleonymic linguistic trap. We saw this in the peace movement: the nostalgia for an idiom that was so rusty and obsolesced—nevertheless this is our predicament as humans. This is why I think *linguistic* revolution is the first order of importance—we need a language change, which means, among other things, we have to actively affirm *mutation*.

◆ **AJ: That's *key*. We have to open up our language to encompass many more complexities, because a simplistic language invites fascism. The word "love" is a good example: there should be at least 10 different words for the stages of a love relationship, with complex associations for each. Words like "peace" or "revolution" must be more action-inspiring—**

◆ **AR:** Kant wrote a text called "To Perpetual Peace," which begins by saying that in the first place, "perpetual peace" evokes a *graveyard* (as in, "May one rest in perpetual peace"). He inquires into a "genuine" institution of peace which wouldn't be dependent on war or negativity, and observes that peace treaties are completely in bad faith, because a peace treaty always implies that force will be used if there's a breach of contract; a peace treaty with another nation is already an admission that it's merely a *suspension of hostilities*. And Kant says, "This is not sufficient . . ."

◆ **AJ: Implicit in any "peace" treaty with Russia is spying and surveillance—visually and electronically invading and penetrating their territory to be sure of "compliance." There is a mistrustful and hostile legalistic underpinning.**

◆ **AR:** Exactly; Kant says that we have never known a peace that would be "perpetual." Recently Bush made reference to an "enduring" peace. "Enduring" (as opposed to "eternal") has a certain range, but it's clear we have *never* maneuvered toward "perpetual" peace. Kant makes this clear in an incredibly lucid way. He very ironically states that as a theorist he can fire his entire volley since no one cares what philosophers have to say—already he is in a warlike polemic! He also says that every government should consider having philosophers advise them, because there's never a danger that any philosopher will ever agree with another philosopher! So there you have the *guarantee* of a felicitous "anarchy," where thinking is continually taking place . . . where there will never be a "unification" of ideas, because philosophers disdain one another. Therefore thinking people ought always to be consulted—this, as you know, is a bit of a foreign policy to America!

What about the prospects for revolution? One has to reflect on why *nothing* will incite people to become outraged.

But you mentioned "love." I wanted to say something about the *right to love* and the *love of rights*. The invention of a new kind of "transformative grammar of revolution" would take us toward a relation to rights that would have as its basis an understanding of *finitude*, or loving the Other as mortal, fragile and finite. And this is what we as Americans have never been able to do; especially with our high tech ideology of progress in which everything is *infinitized*—you know what I'm saying?

◆ **AJ: When you say the "Other," who are you talking about? Anybody who's not your Self? Or are you talking about blacks, women, minorities—all the displaced people who are in the shadows?**

◆ **AR:** All of the above. Traditionally (historically and philosophically) the Other has been viewed from the position of a solipsistic (i.e., solely self-referencing) self. The Other is that which may or may not be colonized by the Self, but is viewed from the position of the self.

◆ **AJ: America used to believe in the notion of "progress": that technology would take us to Outer Space; that cars and houses and everything would continue to improve—basically that there would always be this linear ascension, which was essentially white imperialist evolution—**

◆ **AR:** And the problem with the concept of a "high tech war" is that it still hangs onto the ideology of progress, like: "We've made *progress* in our ways of destruction!" America is stuck in the denial of death—witness the preoccupation with health clubs, vitamins, "scientific" body building techniques, etc. If we refuse to recognize

and acknowledge the Other as *fragile*, destitute, mortal, and finite—*that's* when you start bombing the shit out of them! Does this make sense?

◆ AJ: **Yes—if we cannot deal with death, we end up *accepting* the incredibly artificial and objectifying language used by the media to describe the Gulf War—**

◆ AR: Like "friendly fire"—a full-on repression of death. The minute Americans see "live" blood, they freak out. They experience a denial of death which is absolutely *profound*—so that when death does take place, the vocabulary shifts to "collateral damage" (or a similarly abstract euphemism). America became really anxious when they thought there were Americans dead—but almost immediately this became translated into "friendly fire" which was within that syndrome of death denial. Americans cannot take blood—that's why censorship probably was absolutely necessary from the government's point of view. That's why the Gulf War had to be bloodless, precise, sutureless, high tech . . .

The question is: *Whom* do you address yourself to? What locus of power do you appeal to—when authority is so *diffused?*

◆ AJ: **The descriptions of this war were so hygienic and anesthetized. No close-ups of bodies have been published—no photos of napalmed children running naked and screaming down a road. Suddenly I flashed on the Nancy Reagan biography, which contains beautiful little details. She's typical of a certain generation of women, wanting money and glamor and clinging to an incredible denial of death. And when her husband almost died, she banished words like "assassination attempt," saying instead, "The 'thing' that happened to Ron Reagan"! What an outrageous euphemism, like: "I don't want to talk about anything bad." She refused to let anybody around her mention that "nasty" subject. And she is archetypal of that generation which came to power in the '50s.**

◆ AR: The Reagans are a very important prop or metaphor. When Barbara Walters interviewed them, there was one off-the-script question that was surely meant as a pleasant diversion—a moment of joviality at the end of a rehearsed interview. But it caught Ronald Reagan by surprise, and for me his answer was crucial. She said, "Spontaneously, I'd like to ask you what your favorite films are?" And there was a moment of panic because this was unrehearsed! Then Ronnie went, "Well, *Dracula* and"—then he had a memory lapse and gestured at the neck to Madame Reagan, saying, "You know—" and she replied, "*Frankenstein*, dear." And he said, "Yes."

For me this was incredible (precisely because it wasn't

rehearsed) that he should prefer the *living dead*, these mummy techno-monsters and vampiric figures. That was the most important statement in the entire interview—which is to say that he identified with these figures in particular. He certainly acted out a *mummified presidency*, and now Son of Reagan (Bush) is following in the footsteps of his predecessor trying to engender life through death—the death of social services, affordable housing, etc. Of course, the Bushes have a retarded child—Quayle!

The whole Bush family is extremely important, including the family pet, Millie the dog. When Bush was elected President, one of the first staged "events" was: Millie got studded out, so she could have puppies. And this was a major propaganda ritual which was all about proper breeding—it was a complete animal racism discourse. I remember telling people, "Watch their rapport to the dog, because here is where they articulate things that are taboo, that are unconscious." About 3 months later the dog's "autobiography" was released, in which the dog ventriloquizes the "family history." The positioning of the family pet and all of the incestuous Oedipalizations implied are topics for future discussion . . .

◆ AJ: **Some people think Reagan was a war hero—he thought so himself—but his only war heroism was in a Hollywood movie which was a bad '50s docudrama . . .**

◆ AR: That's why I think that interpretations or analyses that limit themselves to the *media* aspect of this war are inadvertently aiding and abetting that "bloodless" fantasy. We still have to figure out in what ways this war was part of the Western logos and a product of it. In other words, how is it that values of national sovereignty have been rehabilitated, and war *relegitimized?* Don't forget that Vietnam was a war that rendered war a shameful activity—it was actually a "lapsus" in the logic of Western metaphysics. The Gulf War *wasn't* just a media war—that's part of the "logic" fostered by *Nintendo* with its extremely regressive values; this war, like any war, inflicted barbaric, appalling ways of death. Postmodern readings of the war that limit themselves to its "high tech media aspect" may be interesting and merit some thought, but they are complicit with the "enemy"—

◆ AJ: **Part of our alienation and depression comes from the fact that we are so removed from blood, death—*realness*. I keep thinking that we didn't even see a real war—it was just a realistic cartoon. And no one can say they even *felt* it.**

We're so anesthetized by seeing violence on TV which is always done on this cartoon level, so no one ever feels the shock of what brutality really is. You're not feeling that pain, you don't smell that blood, you can't even mobilize your shock. And if suddenly this Rodney King video is aired and the police are really beating him up— you can *feel* his bones being broken.

I think we are so controlled by TV—is there any other culture that watches more TV than we do? In Europe they don't watch as much, do they?

AR: They will! I think everyone will have this strange displacement which is related to the post-political passivity and the loss of a public sphere. I'm sure that in a way, you are *trained* as a spectator. TV might be the greatest dispenser of tranquilizers ever invented; it almost certainly has a maternalizing function, no matter how violent it gets—

AJ: But it isn't "real" violence, like I said—

AR: Depends on where it hits you. Still, we like to eat and act out in front of it; we don't like to stop the flow of tranquilizing caresses—even if they tend to get a bit *rough.*

AJ: Only rarely does something "real" break through, like that Rodney King video. That was probably the first time we ever saw real police doing something so barbaric that a whole continent of people were mobilized into genuine outrage—

AR: And its timing was important; it was a partial allegory of the war. It was "wild," uncensored video. It showed the whole unleashing of police *force* on a single man of color, exposing all the attendant rhetoric of *racism* which was censored during the war. I think a lot of the response was the displaced response that would have taken place had the war shown its true violence. And in the "real" Gulf War, the spirit of the combatants imitated that of a football game or the Fourth of July . . . plus, they were bombarded by porno films before they soared into the sky. So they were in a state of transfixion by media—maybe it was that *addiction to media* that allowed them to do their "work." This is something we have to think about . . .

***

Justice does not have a recognizable history. In fact, the figures of justice we have are rather frightful: King Solomon, whose justice was instantaneous, prepared to cut the body of a child in half. . .

***

AJ: How does the Denial of Death relate to the failure of the feminist revolution?

AR: This is very problematic; it involves a rhetoric of *empowerment*—

AJ: That was a key feminist term which has now been taken up by Bush; everybody now says "empowerment."

AR: Yes, we haven't yet given up the "signifier" of power, the desire for power, or an understanding of power as desire. What I expect from "true feminism" is a complete breaking up of old orders of language and concepts and values . . . a *thorough* deconstruction of power. Instead, Phase One of the feminist movement still

aims to attain a certain level of power and equality, even though equality is simply not enough—it doesn't even *work,* based as it is on that strange computational notion that *one equals one.* But it's a reasonable start, given what we have to work with.

AJ: Does one man ever equal another man, or one man equal a woman? Who determines the *standard* by which the equality is judged?

AR: It's always in the name of "equality" and the democratization of values that outrages are perpetrated. Equality is not enough; it's an insufficient concept—but one we have to be very patient and careful in dismantling, because one would never want a rightwing backlash to take place while you're dismantling it.

It would probably be necessary to move in the direction of *fundamental dissymmetry,* which is to say that the Other is *destitute.* A responsibility without limits has to acknowledge the Other's fragility, susceptibility to death, and absolute destitution . . . so that one responds *not* to that barbaric yet powerful myth dominating our existence—which is that the Other will kill, mutilate, devour and destroy you. Because traditionally, the Other has been viewed as something that is threatening. It's this view which has to be neutralized.

A feminine displacement of values would tend to view the Other in its destitution, helplessness, and in terms of its mortality . . . then the Self would *necessarily* have a relation to *the Other in its full neediness.* The works of philosopher Emmanuel Levinas are a good place to start getting this together.

We can find examples of ethical concern in past moments of Liberalism—with Kennedy there was the Peace Corps. One can say, "Oh, that was colonialist *this* and *that,* appropriation . . ." but if one could momentarily halt those formulaic and tired observations, one could see this as a moment in American history in which a more *just* relation to the Other was being at least, with all the awkwardness of infancy, attempted. Here there was a relation to the Other's fundamental destitution; a sense of responsibility toward other countries.

AJ: Perhaps our momentary relation to the destitute Other stemmed from an Aristocratic inheritance: *noblesse oblige,* the notion that one was *obligated* to help those needier—

AR: And that position has almost completely disappeared; on every level of "being" and "political vision" it's simply no longer there. I mean we've changed from the War on Poverty to the War on Drugs—or more literally, the War on *Poverty* has changed into the War *on* Poverty (the homeless, the sick, the uneducated, and so on). For this war to have been successfully deployed, there had to have been a complete reversal of the previously legislated American relation to "the Other."

AJ: Americans no longer feel any obligation to any other culture. Behind the Peace Corps' "generosity" was America's ethnocentric belief that we were the "best" and richest nation on earth—and to some extent we *were* the richest. But we don't feel that any-

more—60% believe that the Japanese are economically superior—

◆ AR: We are becoming an underdeveloped nation; there's no doubt about it. But the change in attitude took place prior to our collapse as an empire. America's fabulation about itself, the "uppers" it took to feel good about itself, had to do with a certain discourse which has now been *completely* effaced: the discourse of the Statue of Liberty ("Bring us your poor, your tired, your huddled masses"). America used to get high on itself, thinking about its exceptional position as a generous and open space of sublime moral competence.

◆ **AJ: When growing up, I remember people felt superior to everyone ... mothers would tell kids, "Finish your plate; think of all the starving kids in China, or in Europe!" Now America's full of homeless people wandering around—**

◆ AR: There has been a movement from the neighborhood Irish cop that everyone is supposed to love, to a different kind of policing of the world. And I think this "responsibility" is making us feel profoundly depressed. Are people *truly* buying into this foolish, infantile yellow-ribbon-tying parade and circus of patriotism? I can't believe there's really much *affect* behind that—it's more like an avowal of total alienation.

◆ **AJ: Another factor is the death of the Space Program. Society's vast collective enthusiasm about this future high tech frontier just evaporated. I think this did a lot to whittle people's hope down.**

◆ AR: That was an extremely important event—the last surge of societal optimism that I personally felt. Because when that phallic *Challenger* exploded, it traumatized the entire nation. People were deeply shook up; suddenly this promise of a *perfect* (and morally unambiguous) *technology* was shattered *literally;* all sorts of future-oriented openings were shut down.

Perhaps the "trade-off" was "fair" (if one can calculate in this way—which is always obscene): seven people died; what were the consequences? Well, if this was indeed a metaphor for technological power failure, disappointment and *non-knowledge*, then its lesson for humanity was *indispensable*. People experienced great depression with regard to the *collapse* of that technology which was so sure of itself. It was to be this *pedagogical mission* [it had a teacher on board]; it would open up space to *civilian* passengers ... this was to be an extra-globalization of incredible technological frontier-busting. Instead, it was a very bleak *day of shock*. I thought, "Well, this will truly shake up any optimism about the great, so-called 'high technologies'!"

◆ **AJ: —which Reagan had already started to dismantle or divert to militaristic purposes. The last time the country bonded together for something that wasn't "negative" (not a war, not a crisis, not a death or wreaking of death) was the Moon Landing which kindled imaginations worldwide.**

♦ AR: "Community" and "bonding" open enormously important dossiers. *What about community?* There's been two possibilities so far: 1) the "community with a project," 2) the "community of lovers." Very often when the project (or ideal) turns sour, there is a retreat to the "community of lovers," where the lovers will bond and be at once "finite" yet making promises of "eternity"—offering each other the possibility of an infinity beyond the present moment.

Now let's take this slowly. Would it be possible to have a community without a "project" (by which I mean a *fascistic* project) or a real or even fabricated crisis? Let's assume as a working hypothesis that "community" is what we *need*—and I think that's true. Now, unless one wanted to be completely in some sort of psychotic isolation . . .

♦ AJ: I don't think humans want that. Babies die if they don't have enough personal contact.

♦ AR: There's a whole history of communities: religious communities, patriotic communities, fascist communities. As different as they are from one another, they all "guarantee" their bonding by some sort of communion or promise of communion, or a project, or a goal. Sometimes "community" is established in reaction to a crisis; but once the crisis is resolved, the community disbands.

Now, is it possible to have "community" without fusional desire, or without a project? Could there be a feminism that would establish community *without* "1-2-3-4-5" as its demands and goals (because once you reach your goals, that would be the end of feminism). I think this is a critical question: could there be "community" without an agenda, a project, a fusional desire.

♦ AJ: Most cults have an exclusionary bonding; it becomes "Us Against Them." Or a neighborhood tree-planting project will self-destruct once the trees are all planted.

♦ AR: The war produced the simulacrum (if not the reality) of community; an incredible simulation of "pulling together," supporting the "tropes" (as in tropism) and resuscitating all sorts of cliches that would allow a community to feel itself as something *vital*—that exists, that desires, and has power. Another catastrophe example was the earthquake, which produced a sense of community in the Bay Area.

Here we have to interrogate our desires: what is it about war that we *desire?* This is part of that "indecency" we have to confront, because we can't continue to consider war as an accident or simply unfortunate or inevitable. Clearly, there's something about *destructive pleasure* that has to be brought into focus.

♦ AJ: Perhaps, but in the Gulf War the "destruction" aspect was anesthetized and whittled away to nothing. We never saw (or experienced) the death or destruction. That war briefly provided the illusion of community, but that illusion has evaporated as people continue to lose jobs, and more "homeless" appear out of the woodwork everywhere . . .

♦ AR: Historically, the last systematic statewide attempt at community was communism. And with the failure of communism—I'm wondering what the after-effects or after-shocks will be?

♦ AJ: After the Russian Revolution of 1917 degenerated into Stalinism, a lot of Trotskyites, Marxists and assorted leftists in America still clung to their fantasies for decades. Even in the '60s and '70s there were still idealistic groups struggling toward that ideal of a Marxist "community." But now, with the fall of the Berlin wall, etc, it seems there are no more illusions of some "sweeping revolutionary force" to hang onto—

♦ AR: Also, what has been "let go of" is the illusion that the state is the site or locus for realizing or fulfilling the need for community. Today, for example, a state like "Kuwait" can exist *teletopically*—which is to say, "long distance," based on foreign circulation of its funds. It's not simply a locality in the old sense of what would constitute a state.

So in terms of "community," a truly thoughtful, demanding, relentless feminism would demand a re-charting of territorialities; the suspension of old-fashioned boundaries of what constitutes a state. In this regard technology is on our side, because it charts new spatialities. I don't want to sound like a cheerleader for technology, but what is required for the future is a remapping even of our *unconscious topology*. Therefore, no one in their right mind is even going to hope that the *state* will be the place where something grandiose will happen, community-wise. Nor are they going to expect *justice* from the state—nor from any typical (or stereotypical) and sclerotic institutional models.

All protest has been subject to the law of the father, to mere *transgression*. Come on—we *have* to get out of this infantile reactivity!

Earlier, I mentioned the "community of lovers." There you have a microcosm where justice is played out, ethics are revealed (there's always a question of wrongdoing—what is a "just" way of behaving toward "the Other" whom you love?)—

♦ AJ: But that's very narrow—a "community" of only two lovers?

♦ AR: Yes, but we don't have *that* many communities to examine. Since we're diagnosticians, the advantage of looking at the "community of lovers" is to see how it, in its many differential modes, promises itself justice, makes promises for a future, draws up contracts . . . plus the way it reveals "acceptable" excesses of violence (show

me a couple without violence), and extreme volatility.

Well . . . do we have models for what it is we want? Because it's no longer sufficient to merely *overthrow*. We have some models of elementary justice in mind that should be immediately implemented: universal health care, for example. But this certainly wouldn't be *my* only goal—it's nothing to get excited about because it's so primally *necessary*. According to Kant, freedom isn't a question; it is something that we are *given, granted*, as human beings. Freedom ought to be a given. Right now, however, society is in the emergency ward, and urgent measures have to be taken—but they're *not* being taken, partly because the fundamental question of "community" needs to be explored; it remains a question. *Then* you can *start* talking about "justice" and what one *really* wants.

◆ **AJ: And this goes back to the possibility of human revolution. So many things are almost forcing the breakdown and remapping of everything we think of in terms of "territoriality." Historically, we've evolved (if that's the right word) from the tribe to the city-state to the "country," all of which has paralleled the evolution of human consciousness. Now, (potentially) we're global information nomads, ready to wander the world at will without moving our bodies from our computer terminals. But we've yet to assume a "world citizen" identity which bypasses the conception of earth without those "sovereign" borders.**

◆ AR: I think "in-mixation" would be the rule, and this is precisely what freaks people who are still brandishing slogans of "purity" and all those racist notions of strict separatism. *Ice-T* noted that racism is no longer to be considered as the difference between "black" and "white" in America; it's now been reassigned according to other categories—such as the *conservatives* and the *non-conservatives*. I thought that was pretty accurate, in light of other global and more local realignments going on, which if they just repeat and reproduce the structure of *binary opposition*, are surely *not* acceptable.

◆ **AJ: I don't think they can be anymore.**

◆ AR: Exactly—and that's the hopeful possibility.

Part III

◆ **AJ: What would constitute a "feminist" revolution that would truly change the world? Right now, a big obstacle is the dogma involved in being "Politically Correct," which triggers feelings of guilt and repressed desire. "Revolutionary" groups often impose strict exclusionary guidelines for membership. For example, there are certain feminist or lesbian "guidelines" regarding: which clothes are socially acceptable, how you have sex and with whom, compulsory vegetarianism, etc. This becomes as oppressive as being in *grade school*—**

◆ AR: Somehow we have to find a *conduit* that will relibidinalize and realign our *hope*. We need a newly structured *horizon*. The problem is: how do you mobilize

people . . . while precisely allowing for deviations which may fracture the group? Right now we're in this genuine impasse. We see what has paralyzed and neutralized our desires and our political *engagement*. By cultural definition, women are not satisfied; Lacan said that woman's essential signifier is "encore"—more, more, more! So if there *were* an essence of woman, it would be *to demand more*. And Lacan linked this to the traumatizing fact that women can have multiple orgasms or even fake them, and that women are on the side of what Deleuze will later call "multiplicity; more; surplus." (Here I don't want to essentialize the biological model—nor to repress it.)

What I expect from "true feminism" is a complete breaking up of old orders of language and concepts and values . . . a *thorough* deconstruction of power.

What is the group psychology of the future? As the "community" or the *notion* of community disintegrates, we observe that the group today depends upon a mirroring of appearances; *this* identity or *that* ("black," "lesbian," "Chicano," etc) which is in part an artificial label. In psychoanalytic terms, it's all about the expansion of the ego which is multiplied and endlessly reflected, like a *narcissism*. The group demands conformity and uniformity so that the ego at its roots finds no opposition.

But I think what we have to find is the possibility of a *community of shattered egos*—if that's possible. Until now group psychology or military psychology (or any model for activity or action) has always been based on the "ego" (which is a male ego, and, as Freud insists, a male libido). This ego has to be *shattered*. And Woman under patriarchy has faced an inhuman choice: to do *without* an identity, or to identify with what she is not. So there has been no way of expressing her special needs . . . Woman has had to identify with what is only an *absence*.

Laurence Rickles has observed that the group member (which he identifies with a "Californian" or "National Socialist" ideology) wants to be "different, like everyone else he wants to be like"! The question is: how can we genuinely shatter the iron collar of group formations which demand conformity and uniformity? How can we truly transform group psychology without violently "appropriating"? How can *depropriation* (*not* being identical to others, or even *self*-identical) become a politically powerful and compelling force?

◆ **AJ: In order to have this shattering of the ego (which is more like *reconstructing* the ego) we have to put a stop to a certain widespread cycle of abuse. Basically we have a culture of severely dysfunctional,** abused people. The whole nuclear family upbringing keeps recycling these crippling patterns of child discipline and withholding of parental love. So throughout life there's this desperate conformity and self-denial in the hope of attracting the parental love that was never given. Most people are bleeding, wounded souls who think that if they join some group and look and talk the same they'll find what they've always searched for. This is a key fundamental cause to be grappled with.

◆ AR: Do you mean the abusive structure, or the wounding?

◆ AJ: The wounding. On a deep personal level, people have to want to break that ego shell, dismantle that armoring (that was formed in our very dysfunctional early upbringing) that keeps us from really being flexible in life—having humor, irony, desire and pleasure. In a society where people could actually feel true pleasure, there might be fewer problems. I see ego shattering as akin to going to the source of denial—the irony is that letting go and experiencing the source of pain paradoxically revitalizes the body and self to experience joy and life. Ego shattering to me would be breaking down on a very deep level to build up again with more maturity and pleasure. Obviously, this is simplistic, yet . . . wounded, emotionally immature and crippled people just replicate the same oppressions they were taught—the Women's Movement tried to articulate this.

◆ AR: The task for women is *unlearning* self-repression and reaching affirmation. How would that be possible? Everyone can probably identify the symptoms, although some people might resist that self-knowledge. Women are socialized to see more than one point of view at a time, and certainly to see more than their own point of view. Women are absolute *specialists* at seeing the view of the Other—whether it's that baby they might be carrying, or a parent or a friend, etc. And if this ability could be re-framed as a positive force, this could be extremely important.

We can't continue to consider war as an accident or simply unfortunate or inevitable. What is it about war that we *desire?*

I'm not saying that men don't have a rapport to the Other (in fact some of the best male philosophers have proven that they are obsessed with the Other). But with very few exceptions men have initiated movements of *appropriation* of the Other, colonizing the Other to the point of *annihilating* the Other. Whereas women are trained to try to clear abysses of difference without expecting to assimilate the Other in any "total" way. Trinh

Andrea Juno with Avital Ronell

Photo: Bart Nagle

Minh Ha has a term, "inappropriated," which I use in this way: that women need to be *inappropriate,* not appropriated, not proper or part of a property value that can be clearly delimited. An example that's *not* an example is our history. Women have always been appropriated—if they exist at all in the major systems of thinking and desire and discourse and action, they're begrudgingly lumped into "universality" or "humanity." If we're talking about "equality" one usually says, "Well, women are the same as men; that's why they deserve equal rights." Whereas it's never been the case that women have been given their *Otherness* (note that "been given" is already a *passive* verbal construction!).

◆ AJ: In history, in science, in art, women have always been appendages onto a male world. Even on a craft or folk art level, women's achievements were never valued, although this is starting to change—

◆ AR: We have to overturn all of that. Don't forget that democracy (based on this computational notion that "one equals one," or "equality") is fundamentally grounded in *fraternity*—derived from the French Revolution's "liberty, equality, fraternity." We have definitely integrated that heavy and inappropriate word into our notion of "democracy." I don't think that's an accident or a random incursion of historical negativity. The fact (and it *is* a fact) that this is a *fraternal* politics which we're still calling a patriarchy (we're taught in school that George Washington was the "father" of our country) has only recently been analyzed by Jacques Derrida and by Juliet MacCannell in her book, *Regime of the Brother.*

Now the "post-patriarchal" phase might be the *fraternal* one. And what's a "brother"? What's a "community of brothers"? Freud (and others) had something to say about this: a sister is *completely* secondary and derived from this fraternity of men. And this has to be analyzed—the fact that "one equals one" really doesn't cover the aberration that we're calling *woman*.

Until now, social forms and cultural needs have been structured according to concepts that in one way or another derive from the concept of the "ego." Since the 18th century the strengthening and the unifying of the *self* has been a major project of man. Here Freud pointed out a real *caveat*: Aggression has to be addressed. Aggressivity is *admired*, even exalted; it's a libidinal force. It's not something that can simply be discarded or phased out. Any true thinking about or remodeling of the "social" has to take into account the human grounding in aggression, which Lacan then explains in terms of "paranoid mappings of the maternal body."

How are you going to make the world safe for *true* deviance, true play, a genuine expression of aggression as desire, and sexual expression that displaces aggression? This is very difficult!

Aggression has everything to do with the conquest of space; it's primordial in that it is related to the infant's rapport with the maternal body and the sense of territory and conquest from having to be weaned from that first body. It's no coincidence that for centuries "country" and "cunt" have been linked etymologically; by Shakespeare's time this was already established.

♦ **AJ: In any future society or organizational structure, one cannot repress or eliminate violence or its expression, but one has to rechannel it into more constructive uses (in aikido, one can redirect an assailant's energy against them). In Bali, one of the most peaceful cultures on the planet—a place where art and life are totally intertwined—entire villages regularly stage dramas involving mock warfare and conflict; the violent impulses are channeled and integrated, so to speak, into more creative and "safer" outlets.**

♦ AR: First of all, we want to *expose* patriarchy and its mutant offspring, "fraternal order." Under that *undead* President, Reagan, patriarchy proliferated like a disease. But part of this "exposure process" which we have to undertake (and really think about) includes the way certain images of ecological balance and planetary unity are being exploited. Because any planetary, visionary projection tends to efface local differences which may exact difficult demands, intellectually and politically.

Now I'm not saying that we shouldn't engage in "local" activities like recycling; I'm saying that the *displacement* to the "ecological" (even in the case of eco-feminism) may be just a diversion from the "local" to the "whole"—

and "universality" is always a way to efface consciousness of what may be truly oppressive, to the detriment of genders, classes, races, and difference . . .

♦ **AJ: When Bush says a "New World Order," it's more in terms of Nazi fascism: one body of oppression wiping out all the diverse cultural expressions humans have evolved. But if we are to survive, we absolutely need a planetary "maturity" to be able to "come together" on a global level and yet not wipe out all the African tribes or South American Indians to exalt some sterile WASP ideal.**

♦ AR: I agree, but I'm just pointing out that most discourse about planetary unification is still a *male* discourse, is still an *exclusionary* one—and one which mobilizes the same logic of *displacement* we've seen before. Why do some of my students prefer to campaign on behalf of Greenpeace rather than dealing with the inequities of that Oakland ghetto next door? I'm talking about an actual *apartheid* situation where welfare mothers are injuriously deprived of dignity and funding. In general, my students who may be "PC" will far more willingly engage in "global" levels of activity rather than the immediate, local, face-to-face encounter with the "Other" in the next neighborhood. Their "global" discourse reflects the fact they see themselves as the cowboys who are on the "good" side . . . but I am very suspicious of the ideology of good guys who are going to rescue a kind of *entirety of existence* rather than go help the ghetto-dweller next door.

Ice-T noted that racism is no longer the difference between "black" and "white" in America; it's been reassigned to other categories— such as the *conservatives* and the *non-conservatives*.

There's a movement to *reintegrate* objects, things, animals and plants (which by the way I'm very sympathetic toward; I have never argued for the absolute strict difference between human beings and animals in philosophical terms; I love plants, mineral life, etc—I'm sure there has to be a new ethics about *justice to all life* on the planet) but I still find this "movement" lodged in a kind of *oppositional logic*. It doesn't seem that people are able to invest their engagement in both the black woman across the street *and* in saving the whales. Everyone's saving the whales while stepping over bodies in their own streets. This is a problem that really faces us now.

♦ **AJ: It's far easier—and less messy—to deal with**

an abstract whale halfway around the world than to actually involve oneself in the lives of people next door. We live in a superficial culture of denial—death denial is one of our societal underpinnings.

◆ AR: This is very important, because the Gulf War was played out in a mode of forgetfulness—as if the war didn't attack us personally. It was zoned outside of the American citizenry—the war was *out there, elsewhere*. This is a very dangerous schizo-relation to what happened—particularly because it is an effect of the projections of a very disturbed presidency.

◆ AJ: You're talking about human life being devalued into meaninglessness: the fact that perhaps 300,000 Iraqis were massacred in the span of two months. Fifty years ago we felt "morally right" when we bombed Hiroshima—yet when that bomb dropped, as a human response our culture was *shocked* at the horror. It's amazing that *now* we've so detached ourselves from human life to the point that there still is no mass comprehension of this death. So our relationships to other humans are very schizophrenic—we can invest energy and enthusiasm in saving the Amazon forest, but—

◆ AR: The Rain Forest and Save the Whales are all non-conflictual, uncontested sites. Madonna (or is it *Mac-Donna*, as a friend of mine says) can be for the Amazon forest, and who's going to be against it? Once again this is an example of a suppression of difference. Everyone *agrees to agree*, therefore in a larger sense there's a suppression of conflict. And this scares me; this "Let's all agree to agree" process. What can we all agree on—that garbage should be recycled? Or to Save the Amazon—of course we agree! But this is part of a numbing *politics of schizophrenic investment* usurping our energy to protest.

◆ AJ: I think people have suffered so much wounding and abuse in their childhood that they're incapable of maturity. So now the average marriage or even friendship lasts 1-7 years, at most. Consequently one never deeply confronts oneself or any other person. There's a continual erecting of ego walls, because if you drop that ego, you're going to experience some extreme pain of realization: the pain of our lives, the pain of our bodies, the pain of our planet, and the pain of our inevitable future death. Yet until you do that, you can't reconstruct a positive life. It's not "wiping the slate clean" so much as stripping down to an essence. But people are too scared to look at the pain in our world. The suffering of people right now is so intense, from AIDS victims to the rapidly increasing poor—there's no medical care, no schooling—we're rapidly retreating back to a feudal order where only the 10% who can "afford" a life will have it.

◆ AR: We're probably returning to a schizophrenic, "cold" society: what Levi-Strauss saw as the neo-savage world of parsimony, limits and the "end"—meaning not the end, but a world ending in sheer exploitation of man by man, brute force, and cover-ups.

◆ AJ: This coldness and cruelty is emerging in soci-

ety—yet it's nothing you can put your finger on. You don't have the satisfaction of pointing to precise, evocative Amnesty International images of torture in Chile that people can get passionate about—

◆ AR: Until now we've had one tyrannical gender's rule, and we have to ask questions about "post-patriarchy." And our discussion would include all the inflicting of epistemological damage to our language and culture. It would include displacing and overturning all these images that have taken up possibly *permanent* residence in the imaginary—for example: "God the Father had a Son Who"—*right*, the son just *popped out* of the virginal vessel who was completely *secondary* to that primal lineage. Our discussion would include all sorts of difficult overturnings—including turnings of one's *stomach*—because these subjugations are inscribed *very* deeply. To let go of these *fascistic* structuring powers of tradition (which keep you glued to the old pathways, almost genetically, so to speak)—we need the Will to Rupture. Because this will be a hard task: it's not easy to open up a space where the future will be something absolutely "Other" and "New"—not just a mutation or repetition or reproduction of the *past*.

Group psychology or military psychology has always been based on the ego (which, as Freud insists, is a *male* ego). This ego has to be *shattered*.

◆ AJ: Every past "revolution" has produced an authoritarian, guilt-ridden nightmare, with in-fighting and constant pressure to keep your desires down so you can be a good "PC" party member—

◆ AR: So when I call for ego-shattering politics, that means entering a Danger Zone!

◆ AJ: In a New Society, the *aggression* drive will be widely acknowledged and consciously channeled into more creative outlets, such as theatre or art. Because if you close your eyes, it's going to hit you over the head from behind.

◆ AR: As finite beings in a finite world, how do we break with what seems to be an infinite process of structuring and tradition that people (who pretend things are working just fine) are clinging to? The point is, as a body politic, we're *not* doing real well—

◆ AJ: Things now are like a manic St Vitus Dance—

◆ AR: Exactly. And feminism as a *movement of thought* is in a difficult position now, because Woman wants to be detached from universalizing propositions; doesn't want to be an essence that's fixed, or the projection or the

symptom of Man. If women are inappropriate, and can't be appropriated into a totalizing system, then you can't generalize. That's where we find ourselves.

How do women negotiate a contract with the future that would open up a "place" between the absolute singularity of each person, and a more general law or horizon of justice? One thing we've learned, at the end of the Millennium, is that we have *not* learned to be just. Why is it that justice, which was a project and a promise from the pre-Socratic era, could never be realized except as a *threat* ("We will bring this person to justice!" is a very violent promise)—justice itself appears as its own *negativity*. The question, "Why have we not learned to be just?" must co-appear with questions concerning why women, racial differences, class and economic differences are still a "problem"—a *world-wide* problem. Don't forget that the Gulf War was a *regression*—back to an absolutely male-dominated conference table.

◆ **AJ: This new fake tokenism issue about women fighting in the war pretends to be some breakthrough in women's freedom. This just exacerbates the confusion that people feel—**

◆ AR: That's a great irony, and it brings us back to the problem of group psychology. This is about the literalization of uniformity and conformity; about appropriation. For a woman to participate she has to be uniform with the "unisex" of the universal male. She hasn't yet been allowed to go to the killing fields, poor dear, but this is absolute reduction to the same sorry level of "equality." And this is exactly what we're opposed to.

Aggressivity is *admired*, even exalted; it's a libidinal force. It's not something that can simply be discarded or phased out. Any true remodeling of the "social" has to take into account the human grounding in *aggression*.

◆ **AJ: The funny thing is: the issue of whether women are going to be allowed in front line battles has been twisted into a question of "universal" (translation: *male*) height and measurement requirements—meaning that very few women will be able to qualify . . .**

◆ AR: The way women were appropriated by this war machine is a little scary, because via the female body they're now projecting *future* wars. This is one of the first times that we're actually "lightly" discussing future wars. World War I was supposed to be the last and total war: the "war to end all wars." World War II was a totally traumatic finality of war. Every war has had its articula-

tion of absolute *showdown*, Armageddon: "This is it!" Vietnam was: "No more Vietnams!" Every war has brought the promise of closure and the promise that war will end. Every war has been explicitly self-hating, explicitly shell-shocked by itself and its inability to contain its effects. And this Gulf War was to be yet another war of closure which would bring about a "New World Order."

Yet as the "closed" war it proclaimed, "In future wars *women* are going to . . ."—and this is absolutely shocking! This is a total *perversion* of women's life-giving potentialities: under the guise of "more freedom for women" to engender a discourse toward a whole new offspring of post-Gulf Wars?! I have never seen this before, because every war has looked into its own abysses with horror and has implored the higher powers that it be the last war; that it was necessitated by absolute *moral* instigation: *somebody* had to deal with Hitler, Saddam Hussein. . . .

◆ **AJ: This is the first war without any shocking images of human death or tragedy. The horrors and torturous deaths weren't reported in the American press. The European press revealed a few nightmarish news fragments, such as a report on these star cluster bombs whose fragments were so small they couldn't be removed, yet in a few days your body would be shredded inside! This kind of death isn't like Hiroshima, where you're walking along and suddenly you're vaporized. Yet there were no reports about these bombs in the paper. The much-touted "precision bombing" apparently was only a small percentage of the total bombing; it was a government PR scam.**

◆ AR: When the war broke out, the American rape rate rose dramatically. It unleashed this *libido* that was kept in its cage: this male ego libidinal force. In other words, the effects of this war were very far-reaching and will continue to open up incredible areas of disaster.

◆ **AJ: Yet despite all the apparent passivity everywhere, I think that people really do not like the state they're in—just being couch potatoes watching a numbing series of lies on TV. There are many people who would love to be involved in multicultural groups, in political action. We need a structure by which all these groups could be mobilized and allied—**

◆ AR: Well, we don't have the *access* code yet, and that's what we're trying to invent. People can always be *mobilized*—that's the tragic lesson of the 20th century. They can be mobilized to gas Jews, they can be mobilized to lynch blacks. This is partly why we're such a depressed couch potato society—

◆ **AJ: But these are negative mobilizations based on hatred and exclusion—**

◆ AR: But don't forget that when they are mobilized, it's in the name of a *positivity*: "one nation, one *Volk*." Even for the Gulf War, people were not mobilized to *murder*, they were mobilized to be on a *Mission from God*. Everyone from Madonna to Bush is on a mission from God—people are always putting forth the "call of mobilization" in terms of positive communion values. So we *know* that people can be mobilized, but we've been *holding our fire*.

How are you going to make the world safe for *true* deviance, true play, a genuine expression of aggression as desire, and sexual expression that displaces aggression? This is very difficult stuff, and this is where we find ourselves. Another problem is anger, because anger is a very strong, important, and "therapeutically correct" attitude. Most therapies want you to render transparent your anger as a moment in a larger healing procedure. And this has something to do with the promise of the future.

My students who may be "PC" will far more willingly engage in "global" levels of activity rather than the immediate, local, face-to-face encounter with the "Other" in the next neighborhood. Everyone's saving the whales while stepping over bodies in their own streets.

How was it possible for one gender to dominate the other so tyrannically? How was it possible that this war be perpetrated, that racism completely ravaged our unconscious and our conscious lives? It is possible that, at best, *we're all only recovering racists*. Perhaps we're so inscribed by these annulling, annihilating traditions that we're barely going to climb out of the mess we're in.

This is why I'm trying to summon up such an old-fashioned notion as the *will*. We know that the will to rupture, the will to break, might produce breaks and breakdowns. We have to examine how we can not be *condemnatory* while passing through the necessary mode of anger—not get *stuck* there. How can we *affirm* where we're going—affirm the multiplicity, the difficulties?

One question that's been raised is: could there be a "female" (or specifically "feminine") discourse? Here, the problem is that women tend to speak about themselves as if they *know* who they are. Yet there are so many unresearched areas of "non-knowledge" associated with Woman: for example, divination, witchcraft and other "occult" concerns. These areas of non-knowledge have to be liberated as they are crucial to Woman's understanding of who she "is." This is a delicate operation, of course. For the domains of non-knowledge are hardly gender-specific, and we want to resist the pernicious trap of expulsing women (once again) toward extra-epistemic orbits. Does one need to be reminded that women are also thoroughly capable doctors, professors, publishers, etc?

Yet another (though related) area of questioning in-

volves: how can we posit values *beyond* questions of sexual difference? Here we note that this already *assumes* a truly feminist *location*. Women are not the ones who initiated these values that are making women rightfully and justifiably angry. Here I call to mind Nietzsche's question: "How do we overcome our nausea about 'man'?" For Nietzsche, vomiting represented a *reversal* of assimilation by the digestive system (thus a reversal of dialectics and a way to attack Hegel); it was: "No, I won't assimilate this; I'm going to reject this. I want to puke out all the poison I've been fed by philosophy, by history, by patriarchy." This is why Nietzsche tried to invent what is falsely translated as "Superman"; the "Übermensch" is not necessarily a man—it's *trans-human*. And I submit that its gender is *not* clear, because the relation Nietzsche had to women and to Lou Salomé was so complicated. When Nietzsche was puking out Woman, he was puking out *Woman as invented by Man* (weakened therefore, and ravaged by resentment), and pinning his hopes on a *trans-human* that would have overcome misogynist inscriptions of woman.

♦ **AJ: So what does the "trans-human" mean to you?**
♦ AR: It's a bridge to the future—something posited *beyond* the values of sexual difference and the war of the sexes (always initiated by the conquering male metaphysical subject). To return to an earlier question, how do we displace anger—that anger which eats up your insides, yet must be positively valorized? Anger has to somehow *bypass* conflict without *suppressing* conflict—because a true conflict *does* exist. But how can anger come to term (and that is a feminine figure of speech: "coming to term.")? How do we give birth to that which will *succeed* anger—be the successor and the "success"?

When the war broke out, the American rape rate rose dramatically. It unleashed this *libido* that was kept in its cage— this male ego libidinal force.

♦ **AJ: The only way a woman can escape an abusive, misogynistic relationship is through full-fledged anger. Anger may also be the conduit by which women in general can free themselves from larger social oppressions.**
♦ AR: Anger must not be confined to being a mere *offshoot* of ressentimental, festering wounds, but must be a channeling or broadcast system that, through creative expression, produces a certain *community*. That image of a mythical, Medusan threat is wonderful—
♦ **AJ: Although historically, she's like a lot of these goddesses who became defamed, denigrated and vili-**

Photo: Jane Handel

tained in the patriarchal vocabulary while "juno" (term for a woman's soul) was lost. Yet how could Juno not be enraged when her (and all women's) roles had become so repressed and enslaved? Suddenly Juno is the "property" of Jupiter, inferior to him—of course she'd be mad and hysterical!

♦ AR: Hélène Cixous wrote *The Laugh of the Medusa*, which rewrites Medusa's face, or rereads it as laughter that is frozen through history. It's a very powerful work that opposes the whole "traditional" reading of Medusa as the castrating abyss that at once petrifies and wilts the penis.

♦ AJ: How could the Medusa ever have been interpreted as castrating? The Medusa is a very sexualized being inseparable from the earth and the body. Snakes—how phallic, sexual and libidinal can you get? Snakes are associated with kundalini energy which is very explosive and electric, producing a surge that clears away fog in the brain and invigorates the spine—it produces a rupture—

♦ AR: That's what Nietzsche insists upon: *to bury what is dead*. This is the difference between destruction and devastation. Destruction is that clearing away, so life can be welcomed and invited to flourish. Whereas devastation is the sealing off of any possible advent of the future.

When Medusa opens her mouth, this could be read as: the body begins to speak, to ulcerate, to protest in all sorts of ways from that "other place of latency" that speaks without fully knowing what it's saying. That voice may be considered "hysterical" because it makes no claims for "mastery," for knowledge, for ego knowledge or epistemologies. That voice "lets go" of language as it courses through the subject; the subject "ventriloquizes."

fied as the patriarchy took over—Juno being a prime example. In the lunar/matriarchal times she was a multi-dimensional goddess who encompassed a wide range of activities: Juno Fortuna, Fate; Juno Lucina, the Light; Juno Martialis, the Warrior—to name only a few. Also, every woman had a "juno," which was the name for her soul, just as every man had a "genius." When the solar/patriarchal societies took over the lunar/matriarchal societies, the goddesses became denigrated. Juno became the jealous, hysterical wife—a bitch-figure forever raving against her husband (Jupiter)'s lovers. Also, the word "genius" was re-

◆ AJ: Feminism has to remake the future as well as the past—

◆ AR: True feminism has to investigate and encompass biotechnics, biogenetics, and all fields of technology. A true feminism will stop being phobic about these areas, because it's crucial that women be involved in investigating, exploring and shaping the technological realities of the future.

◆ AJ: All of the implications of the coming bio-technological innovations have to be thoroughly analyzed: the test tube baby (and the ownership ethics involved), genetic manipulation, etc. As computers become more interactive with humans, how does our language change? What happens when Artificial Intelligence starts to have wider applications? What happens when a "machine" has the capacity to make judgment calls and to learn from its mistakes?

If we can conceive of the "inanimate" world (that very word betrays our *techno-racism*) as a continuum to our "animate" world . . . and "thinking machines" (cyborgs) as a continuum to our biological bodies, then maybe we can rethink who we are as gender, as man and woman—as the entire planet. Then there can be a global consciousness.

◆ AR: Historically, women have been associated with deviant forms of knowledge: sorcery, witchcraft, etc which are "the Other" to so-called "science." Even midwifery survived through the centuries as the Other to clinical epistemology. There's always been this Other to accepted bodies of knowledge which has been suppressed, ignored or simply not researched. There yet exist mysterious, uncanny technologies which have a secret relation to divination; which break up classical taxonomies of knowledge, and suspend what we *think* we know. Basically, all these dislocations are in the realm of the feminine.

Destruction is that clearing away, so life can be welcomed and invited to flourish. Whereas devastation is the sealing off of any possible advent of the future.

◆ AJ: What is the "feminine"? What is the "body"? Residing in the body are truths that have been sedimented over. In *The Man Who Mistook His Wife for a Hat,* Oliver Sacks wrote about aphasiacs who couldn't proficiently comprehend verbal language, yet could understand body language and intent very well. They were watching Ronald Reagan read a serious speech on TV which they couldn't comprehend linguistically—yet they were laughing hysterically because they knew he was lying. So what is that ability in us which can recognize when somebody's lying?

◆ AR: Certain women are worried about incursions of feminism into their "daily life," because they are afraid their tricks of manipulation will be *exposed*, thereby paving the way for *new* (and worse) kinds of oppression. Women's survival weapons have always been covert rather than overt, involving seduction rather than "open warfare"—

The question, "Why have we not learned to be just?" must co-appear with questions concerning why women, racial differences, class and economic differences are still a problem—a *world-wide* problem.

◆ AJ: Yet seduction, secretiveness and manipulation were a natural outcome of having no other options—basically, these were women's only power. Given a different environmental "set," a directness can emerge. I think these women's "tricks" really resulted from a self-perpetuating cycle of socialized abuse.

◆ AR: And this is part of being "hystericized" or positioned into a corner, whereby you become a "trickster" and perform tricks in your own theater of hysteria. This experience at staging tricks and sleights-of-hand is something that has permitted women, in certain situations, to become *escape artists*—escape-ologists, even. Because in an environment in which honesty and sincerity may lead to bodily harm—even death [e.g., Scheherezade in *The Thousand and One Nights*], one may be forced to take recourse in trickery.

◆ AJ: Honesty is a complicated word—it has to be incorporated into a paradoxical world view which exalts creativity, pleasure, fun and play. Honesty does not have to be synonymous with dullness or plodding simplicity. As humans, we can create a playful mythology and theater; as humans we have a need for creative play. Honesty and truthfulness do not "exclude" the playful use of masks, the playful use of artifice, the playful use of technology. In Huysmans' *Against Nature* the "hero" invents his own house, aesthetics, customs, etc. As evolved human beings, part and parcel of our identity involves manipulating this wonderful world. In Mexico people take tin cans and old newspapers and make beautiful, inventive artworks out of them; they create their own baroque, wonderful expressions of creativity. If we really loved the material world (which we don't), we would be creating art all the time with our lives. ◆ ◆ ◆

Kerr & Malley

British-born Suzy Kerr and American Dianne Malley met in 1986 and have been fighting anti-abortion forces both on the *street* and in their *art* ever since. From the time of their first collaborative installation in Buffalo, New York in 1987, they have endeavored to understand the roots of today's sexual oppression by researching women artists and activists in the past, then presenting their findings in installations or performances which utilize art, photography and text. They place the current hysterical attack on abortion rights in the context of the past two thousand years, arguing that the Christian religion has *always* had as its goal the *control of women through their sexuality*. A recent installation juxtaposed excerpts from the *Malleus Maleficarum* (the Inquisition's 1486 "Bible" used to condemn millions of "witches" to death) with similar texts culled from the tract published by Randall Terry's "Operation Rescue," the loose coalition of anti-abortion religious fanatics who have tried to shut down every women's clinic in America.

In the last five years they've organized over fifty installations and participated in numerous street interventions as well as lecture/performance presentations. Kerr & Malley can be contacted Shea & Bornstein Gallery, 2114 Broadway, Santa Monica CA 90404.

♦ **ANDREA JUNO: Your work is a mix of art, political activism and the history of women's liberation—**
♦ DIANNE MALLEY: We first started doing work that examined women's reproductive rights historically and then related this to current issues—a historical basis is so important to understanding any subject. People don't feel so overwhelmed and depressed when they realize that there have been attempts to control reproductive freedoms *all along*.

Our commitment sprang from the time we first began defending family planning clinics who perform abortions. Growing up in Philadelphia, I went to D.C. for numerous demonstrations where everyone who was putting their bodies on the line basically agreed with one another. But the first time we defended a clinic, we found ourselves face-to-face with the *opposition*—and that was an amazing experience that affected us a lot. That's when we both made a commitment to make our art deal with this.

Previously, we had already decided to relate the topic of reproductive rights to the persecution of witches in history. And at our first clinic defense, there was one gentleman who we've become very familiar with since—
♦ SUZY KERR: "Gentleman" is a little too polite—
♦ DM: That's true—*slug* would be more like it, he was physically *gross*. Anyway, he was barefoot, had a beer belly, carried a bullhorn, and had a straplike harness around his waist supporting this huge banner which read, "Witches, Lesbians, and Basic Idiots: Repent—No Choice Exists in Murder." (Another banner read, "Witches, Lesbians, and *Rebels*: Repent—No Choice Exists in Murder.") And he has a van, which is his Bible-thumping van—
♦ SK: Which at first was just painted a regular color like blue. But a few months later it had been painted white with orange, red and yellow flames rising to the roof, and slogans like "Jesus Saves!" and "You will perish in hell!" painted all over it—plus (of course) an

Dianne Malley & Suzy Kerr

Photo: Laura Aguilar

American flag. Nowadays he climbs up on the roof and parades around holding his massive banner.

♦ DM: When we first saw him, we freaked out because of the "witches" connection—we had no idea anyone would make it so *clear* for us! This clinic demonstration was in an area of Los Angeles which is primarily black, although most of the demonstrators were white. And they were very violent—their aggression was extreme. They would lock arms and break through your line, shoving and pushing you, screaming in your face—

♦ **AJ: What were they screaming?**

♦ DM: "Lesbian witch!" or "You're gonna burn in hell!"

♦ SK: People with rosaries would come and stand right in front of you and pray directly in your face—

♦ DM: —or try to encircle you. You'd be standing

arm-in-arm with a few others and suddenly you'd be surrounded by all these religious zealots praying with their rosaries. We saw people being "born again" right before our eyes—crying and falling down on the street . . .

♦ SK: And there were other characters—all men—thrusting huge color photographs of fetuses in your face, trying to shock you by how "awful" this is . . . that *this* is what you get when you murder innocent babies . . .

♦ DM: There were skinheads and "Bikers For Jesus," too—

♦ SK: People on "our side" got very paranoid because a lot of the opposition looked like us—it was hard to tell who was who, especially when the opposing side crossed lines to get to certain areas. We started using badges so

155

Anti-Abortion Demonstrators. Photo: Kerr & Malley

can go in or out. So the pro-choice people were trying to beat them to it. Sometimes the clinics can afford to hire security to keep the doors open, but it's still a battle . . .

♦ DM: There was a sense of real absurdity as well—some mornings people were defending clinics that weren't even open that day!

♦ AJ: **It's hard enough just being pregnant and needing an abortion, but to have to *fight* to get in the door—a lot of people couldn't even get in, right?**

♦ DM: Yes—and would you *want* to walk in? Even a determined person who believed in "the struggle" might still be afraid that someone on the other side would do something crazy—

♦ SK: Already, there's the assumption that every visitor is going in for an *abortion*. I mean—some of them go for very basic family planning services—

♦ DM: That's why calling them "abortion" clinics is off the mark—

♦ AJ: **When I was poor, a clinic was the only place I could afford to go to for pap smears. Basically, these fundamentalists are denying gynecological services to the poor community—**

♦ SK: These demonstrations always happen on a Saturday morning, because that income group can't afford to take time off work during the week. And we discovered that basically all the clinics that had previously performed abortions had *quit*—they were tired of being picketed and boycotted, and dealing with all the trouble that came with that. For most poor people, a private doctor is out of the question . . .

ACT UP has been great in pushing the pro-choice people to be more radical—instead of just *defending* rights that are slowly being chipped away, pushing to *expand* them.

we could really know who to listen to.

♦ DM: That first time, there was a long ramp leading to a basement. And I remember a mad scramble as people on our side jumped ten feet down to get to the door first—so *they* couldn't block it. All this must have inspired absolute fear in anyone actually planning to go inside for services.

♦ AJ: **Well, the fundamentalists' agenda is to keep women who want an abortion *out*—**

♦ SK: Right—their tactic is to get to a clinic first thing in the morning and block all the entrances, so that no one

♦ DM: These anti-abortion demonstrators would go to one clinic, decide that maybe they weren't going to be able to shut it down, get in their cars and hit somewhere else. On a few Saturday mornings, by 11 AM we'd been at four sites—it was really a zoo. One particular demonstration led by Randall Terry [anti-abortion crusader] was really intense—when we finally arrived, there were twenty cops surrounding him, just to protect him. The media were all there, and the whole street was closed off. But now they don't hit in L.A. anymore.

♦ AJ: **Because of your work?**

♦ DM: Yes, and that of other pro-choice people—particularly the ones who always get up at 5 AM, which we don't always do!

Pro-Choice Demonstrators. Photo: Kerr & Malley

Anti-Abortion Demonstrators.

◆ **AJ: Can you describe these anti-abortionists?**

◆ SK: For the most part they're very mainstream, white, lower-middle class, slightly lower income, lower-educated people from the suburbs—*away* from wherever it is they're protesting. They're people who feel threatened by the increase in Black, Latino, and Asian populations. These demonstrations are usually organized by their churches, and they come out in mass groups—it's like their "work picnic."

◆ DM: And they bring their children—many times it's a "family affair."

◆ SK: And they're predominantly male—there's a lot of young *single men.* Many are "Born Agains" rather than churchgoers who grew up with a religion and maintained it. It's all part of this "conversion" syndrome, and their minds are *very* simplistic. Even though you're instructed not to argue with these people, you can't help it, because they start baiting you and so you start to argue back—

◆ DM: And you try to use reasoning and find out there's no use—neither side is ever going to convince each other of anything. But we all do it! You think you're going to affect that *one* person—

◆ SK: Of course in *their* minds, pro-choice people are sick deviants because we're all gay! Or so they think—especially since ACT UP became involved, because *they* brought in a large, conspicuously gay population that is very good at organizing these things. In the fundamentalists' minds you're corrupt, you're a prostitute, you're a slut—there's no room for the concept that a "regular person" might get pregnant and need an abortion.

◆ DM: Speaking of ACT UP—they've been really great in actually *being there* in numbers, and in pushing people

to be more radical, because the pro-choice people basically only *defend* the rights that are being chipped away, rather than push to *expand* them. And they're consistent—you see the same faces there regularly.

◆ **AJ: Well, they're also dealing first-hand with genuinely *intense* issues surrounding Death . . . For awhile, after the '60s, it seemed like we could progress toward deciphering even deeper concerns related to sexism and other aspects of liberation, but now things are going backwards. What are your thoughts on this?**

◆ DM: Historically, we began relating the basic pretexts of the *Malleus Maleficarum* (also known as "The Witches' Hammer"; it was the Inquisition's "Bible"used to condemn witches to death) to the premises in Operation Rescue's manual. The wording, the quotations, and the whole ideology turned out to be remarkably similar—

◆ SK: Both were based on the notion of being "God's soldiers in the fight against Satan." The Operation Rescue manual was written in military terms: first you receive training to be a soldier, then you go out on the front lines as part of the *troops for God.* The *Malleus Maleficarum* is more complex; its context is the Inquisition, with God's soldiers carrying out the fight against Evil and Satan's influence. And the way the Inquisition defined and pinpointed what was evil was based on very superficial, surface signs on women, especially old women—

◆ DM: —as well as anyone who had connections to reproductive services or health; basically anyone who had any folk knowledge of medicine—

◆ **AJ: During the Inquisition, male doctors attempted to assert their authority and get rid of all the midwives—**

◆ SK: And there were other, deeper implications having to do with *economic power*—when a witch was tried and executed, all their property and goods were confiscated. That's why—after they'd used up all the "real" witches, so many "regular" people were condemned. And I think that underneath the right wing fundamentalist movement are similar issues involving economic power, plus race—basically, they are unable to accept a changing world order.

Reproductive rights have nothing to do with *morality*— they have to do with business, economics, medicine, and who really controls it all.

◆ AJ: **Their activity is rooted in a deep racism: that we don't have enough *white* babies— that we're getting too many black and Chicano babies. What percentage of these anti-abortionists are non-whites?**

◆ DM: They're at least 85% white. However, in Los Angeles you will find Mexican-Americans coming out in church groups, singing hymns in Spanish—

◆ AJ: **Well, the white instigators know that the media would like to see that.**

◆ DM: Absolutely. They've done a lot of Outreach; they're very conscious of making it *look* multicultural.

◆ SK: We went to a rally Operation Rescue staged on the steps of City Hall, and *all* the speakers were white. A couple of women stood up and testified about their experiences as "political prisoners" (which is now how they refer to jail time served for blocking clinic entrances— *that's* a political prisoner?!) One of the women had thirteen children and was expecting her fourteenth. In her speech she urged the crowd to go back home and procreate, because, "We need more soldiers!"

◆ DM: She was unbelievable. "God" had told her she should have 15 children, and even though she was having morning sickness that day, God had *willed* it and she was going to give her talk. She *literally* told people to go home, fuck, and have babies—it was really scary.

What's most frightening is all the ways reproductive rights in this country are being chipped away *right now*. People have focused on the issue of abortion and access to clinics, but meanwhile other rights are evaporating, such as the right to have access to RU-486, or to have a midwife. For black women in many rural areas of the South—there's no doctor available if you have no money.

The state of health care in this country is outrageous. I think that for most black communities the agenda is still healthy babies and not abortion—that's why you still see less people of color in the pro-choice movement, and this is not being addressed. And it's outrageous that RU-486 is not available in America, particularly since USC [University of Southern California] was the major place where research was conducted—and that was stopped. There are so many problems, really.

◆ SK: It really pains me that our actual rights are being diminished. Unfortunately, there's been a nasty shift in people's perception of women's role in breeding—

◆ DM: —like arresting mothers who are on crack. The powers-that-be view women as merely *carriers* for the child. We saw this huge billboard of a baby born from a crack-addict mother that said, "Don't take drugs if you're pregnant." (So if you *aren't* pregnant, it's okay?!) But that's the shift in the psychology.

◆ SK: We've been really horrified by people our age (twenties to mid-thirties) who have become quite right wing in their thinking, like: "It's okay for *other* people to have an abortion, but *I* would never have one." That's a radical shift from the late '70s when I first became aware of these kind of issues.

◆ DM: Also, Health Care should be a Number One priority in this country, because without that, everything is affected—AIDS, reproduction rights, etc. It's amazing—I was listening to a speech by Martin Luther King which could have been written *yesterday*. He was saying how the war in Vietnam was a *War on the Poor*—

◆ AJ: **There's been such a shift in people's *expectations* across the board. I grew up in the '60s and '70s convinced that you could never turn back the clock; that abortion rights were *secure*. But now you see hesitancy and confusion in women—**

Underneath the right wing fundamentalist movement are issues involving race and economic power. Basically, they are unable to accept a changing world order.

◆ SK: "I'm all for women's rights, but I'm not a feminist myself!"—that's the other line you hear all the time now. Or, "Of course women should be paid equal money, but—ugh, these *feminists!*" As though economics and liberty were completely unrelated! The right wing is really successful at keeping all these issues separate, so there appears to be no unifying philosophy or overview. It's not surprising that people see AIDS as quite separate from reproductive rights, environmental issues, and so on.

◆ AJ: **Also, economic issues are not perceived as being fundamental—**

◆ DM: As though the Gulf War had nothing to do with economics—it was all about "defending freedom."

♦ AJ: The issues of reproductive rights and our health care system are *about* economics—it's totally class warfare—

♦ DM: We've tried to examine reproductive rights in relation to how States use them to further militaristic and imperialistic aims. And it's amazing—

♦ SK: Historically, women's reproductive rights have always been given or taken away to increase or decrease population growth, especially after major wars. In France in the early '20s or Germany during World War II, abortion was illegal be-

Photo: Kerr & Malley

cause the population had been decimated and they needed to replenish it immediately. On the other hand, in this country sterilization has been used to control the growth of certain ethnic groups such as Puerto Ricans—

♦ **AJ: That's another major issue that's downplayed. Even in San Francisco (which supposedly is an enlightened city) if you speak Spanish or if you're black, one of the first questions you're asked is, "Would you like to be sterilized?" But that's *never* mentioned if you're white.**

♦ DM: Absolutely. And it's not easy to find historical records tracing any of this. In the past there have been some odd situations: for example, the Black Panthers were very much against some reproductive rights because they were emphasizing the idea of "power in numbers." It's depressing to see how both the Left and the Right have used reproductive rights *against* women.

♦ SK: In America, there's an underlying assumption that there shouldn't be many black (or Hispanic, etc) women having children because they don't have the *intelligence* to figure out what's best for themselves, and they don't have the economic resources to raise these families after they've had them.

♦ DM: The Soviet Union provides a really clear-cut example of reproductive rights being given and taken away according to the whims of the State.

♦ **AJ: I read that essentially there is no birth control over there. They have these metal diaphragms that don't work, condoms that break easily, but the prevailing attitude is: "It's just a woman's body—they can get an abortion." So they have hundreds of free abortion clinics—most women will have ten abortions in their lifetime. They've taken things to an opposite extreme, but it reflects the same repressiveness—**

♦ DM: Exactly. You have the "freedom" to have a hundred abortions—but you're still just being controlled

and manipulated—at the mercy of the State.

♦ **AJ: And in both the East and the West there's a continuing dearth of feminine medical knowledge— does anyone fund studies of PMS, or P.I.D. (pelvic inflammatory disease) which kills literally thousands yearly?**

♦ DM: Right. At UCLA we've been researching the history of medical illustrations that depict abortion, giv-

Kerr & Malley's artwork—inspired by the photo above.

159

ing birth, caesarean sections, etc. And they're very revealing. Then we moved on to examine certain women in history who had been abortionists and had been persecuted for their activities. We discovered Madame Restell, who was an abortionist in New York City throughout the latter half of the 19th century—

Dr. Madeleine Pelletier, an abortionist, dressed in men's suits and had short cropped hair, but actually was never known to have lovers of either sex. Her theory was: society did not grant an ambitious woman the flexibility to have an autonomous sexual identity.

◆ SK: Her real name was Anne Loehmann. She started selling abortion pills by mail order. Of course they didn't work—none of those pills did at that time. They all contained a combination of ingredients that made you so sick to your stomach, you would probably go into shock! These pills were in principle similar to other early self-abortion methods: drinking coffee containing bits of lead, eating ground-up black beetles, or ingesting mercury compounds . . .

◆ DM: We began compiling lists of methods used historically to induce abortions. We did an installation with photographs arranged in the shape of crosses, with phrases like: "jumping off chairs," "throwing yourself downstairs," "a basket of yams"—all these "techniques" that we found reference to. The title of the show was "Milk of Another Woman," a method which *guaranteed* an abortion!

Anyway—Madame Restell became very wealthy and opened an office in Manhattan. After finding out that the pills didn't work, women would come in for a more conventional treatment—be jabbed inside and have an abortion that way. Her downfall came about because she flaunted her wealth; she bought a carriage and horses and rode around New York dressed in her finery—

◆ SK: She was arrested several times but managed to avoid being sentenced until she was entrapped by Anthony Comstock, who made a citizen's arrest—

◆ DM: Anthony Comstock was the early 20th century equivalent of Randall Terry. He was a self-appointed moral crusader who inaugurated the Post Office obscenity laws. He collected thousands of obscene drawings and photographs—he even went into art schools and confiscated any nudes he found. Of course abortion was his biggest target, but anything relating to birth control was also attacked. As a result Restell and others who had

active mail-order businesses became in violation of the law, because through his efforts birth control was declared "obscene." And Comstock's law literally wasn't taken off the books till the 1970s, so we see the effect one zealot can have! He personally made the citizen's arrest of Madame Restell, posing as a man who wanted some pills for his wife.

◆ SK: And she ended up committing suicide rather than facing trial and going to prison for the rest of her life.

◆ DM: This was when the medical establishment began taking medicine out of hands of lay people and legislating all sorts of laws against abortion and birth control, where previously there had been none. Historically, this is another instance of how reproductive rights have nothing to do with *morality*—they have to do with business, economics, medicine, and who really controls it all.

◆ SK: The other woman we focused on was Madame Pelletier, who was born in France in 1874 to a very poor family. Her parents had a grocery business, and she had to quit school at the age of eleven. Nevertheless, she managed to educate herself; she became the first woman doctor in France, while simultaneously becoming involved in politics—

◆ DM: —which were socialist, anarchist, Marxist— she was really radical.

◆ SK: She published journals and attempted to influence political elections. She started writing novels to express her beliefs, then decided to *practice what she preached*—so she became an abortionist.

Dr. Madeleine Pelletier believed in the necessity of violence to further her cause. One of her favorite quotations was, "Feminism can never go *too* far."

◆ DM: She was really amazing-looking. She dressed in men's suits and had short cropped hair, but actually was never known to have lovers of either sex. Her theory was: society did not grant an ambitious woman the flexibility to have an autonomous sexual identity. She preferred comrades who were not bothered by the illegality of her activities—

◆ SK: And she believed in the necessity of violence to further her cause. One of her favorite quotations was, "Feminism can never go *too* far."

◆ DM: She was active alongside other suffragettes and political organizers throughout Europe then. But after

Dr Madeleine Pelletier, 1874-1939. *faiseuse des anges (maker of angels)*, 1990
Kerr & Malley, Karl Bornstein Gallery, Santa Monica, CA

she started practicing abortion, she was arrested. When she went to trial at the age of 50, she had already had a stroke and half of her body was paralyzed, so the judge deemed her unfit to stand trial and incarcerated her in a mental asylum where she died.

♦ SK: One of her novels is *The Education of Girls* which she wrote in French—it hasn't been translated yet . . . She was really amazing.

♦ **AJ: What are you working on now?**

♦ DM: We want to deal much more concretely with the relationship between reproductive rights and States' control to further their militaristic and imperialistic gains.

♦ SK: We recently did a silkscreen print diptych utilizing two found images: a mass graveyard in Northern France from the first and second World Wars—just rows and rows of crosses over the unnamed dead, and a second image of Nazi soldiers goose-stepping. These were overlaid with a medical illustration of a woman giving birth—

♦ DM: —or having an abortion. It's from the waist down, and her legs are being pulled apart by men's hands (you see a hand, a bit of cuff from a white shirt and a suit jacket) . . . there's at least four sets of arms in the picture—

♦ SK: And these huge forceps are going into her womb,

which are being pulled at by hands labeled "A," "B," "C," etc. And a rope is attached to the forceps at a diagonal like it's going across the whole room, tied to a post and pulling down—

♦ DM: That medical illustration was very telling!

♦ SK: Then we found an amazing illustration of an angel—but a warrior angel—who's emptying a basket down onto Earth of babies who are being born as soldiers—they already have on little helmets and uniforms as they float down! It's the wildest illustration.

♦ **AJ: Do you think there's a link between the resurgence of anti-abortionists (and even anti-birth control sentiments), and the revival of the warmongering mentality?**

♦ SK: Yes—add to that the inability to address AIDS, too, because all of this is outside "traditional family values."

♦ DM: "48 Hours" [TV Show] filmed a whole day in boot camp which ended with a Marine's wife giving birth. A man in a white surgeon's gown turns around and underneath he's wearing fatigues. And before they even show what sex the child is, they say, "It's a boy! We'd love our son to be a doctor or a lawyer—but maybe he'll be a *Marine*, like his dad!"

♦ **AJ: Another thing I wanted to talk about was: you**

gain a real sense of power when you mobilize and actually get some results—you *did* help push the fundamentalists out of L.A. People feel so helpless most of the time—they don't think their actions can affect anything—

♦ SK: I think people immediately get a sense of accomplishment. But then there is no political party in this country which you can become involved with to take things *further*. This absence is discouraging—people's energy, motivation and interest just dissipates. So a mobilization *can* accomplish something, but it's very short-term because it's dependent on new people continually turning out in massive numbers.

We want to deal much more concretely with the relationship between reproductive rights and States' control to further their militaristic and imperialistic gains.

♦ DM: What's most discouraging is how our abortion rights are being chipped away at by people we elected who *claimed* they were pro-choice!

♦ SK: You can elect someone to power who says they're pro-choice, but then they will assign money to programs as they see fit.

♦ AJ: Well, it's a fallacy to think we're in a democracy, because it's *not* a democracy—the vote is mind-controlled by ad agencies hired by corporations or other monied interests (and it's not like we can elect the corporate heads who have a direct effect on our financial, environmental and daily life). For decades there's been a pervasive sense of *powerlessness* which has had a snowball effect. Yet people still can effect change—just the *threat* of NOW boycotting Idaho potatoes (when they were about to pass that law repealing abortion in Idaho) changed things totally around! I think the Women's movement was strengthened by that.

♦ DM: One hopes that in the '90s people have awakened from the sleep of the '80s. Another problem is that a lot of people who were active previously aren't sure what to do anymore. I hear people saying, "No more demonstrations—that's not working!" A lot of people want to do *something*—but they don't know *what*.

♦ AJ: That's the problem—the control system is so savvy. It's like the Pillsbury Doughboy—no matter where you punch, it just absorbs the shock. It's true that demonstrations in front of the federal building against the Gulf War really have become part of the status quo landscape. But still, people *need* a sense of empowerment, because right now America feels like those communist countries where apathy and lethargy reign, because everyone knows the government is so corrupt . . .

♦ DM: Some pro-choice people have felt such intense hatred and violence toward anti-abortionists that they've had to reassess their own deepest philosophical bases. Recently someone remarked, "You see these people week after week and you're ready to *bash* their heads in! How do you channel that anger?" A lot of people are at a loss as to how to deal with this—

♦ AJ: That feeling is common to *any* "Dispossessed Others." If you're black, where do you channel the daily dose of racism you encounter on every level? And as a woman, you're constantly being buffeted—

♦ SK: There's a certain glamour to demonstrating in public that attracts people—the emotional *rush* that comes from being in a big crowd. But it may be more productive to do something like speak out at your local Board of Supervisors' meetings, because so few people bother to turn out for them. And because that seems more like drudgery, it's very hard to commit to it.

♦ DM: But I think demonstrations *are* good—if they do nothing more than motivate the people who attend them. When I was in school, attending a demonstration could be a *high* that sustained your morale for months afterwards!

♦ AJ: How do you see the future?

♦ SK: Political content has come back in a serious way into artists' work. Meanwhile, the system of government, corporate and foundation funding of the arts is being eroded very fast.

♦ AJ: Things are getting a lot tougher; things are going to be really bad *soon*.

♦ SK: We need more politicized art, and I think the place for it is not in the galleries but in publications, TV and movies. Because people do not go to galleries. You can do Outreach until you're up to your ears, but people don't relate to it—it doesn't touch their lives.

♦ AJ: Do you have any hope?

♦ DM: I have hope (tentatively), but it may not be because things are getting better. I just happen to be an optimist.

♦ AJ: Yeah—against all reason!

♦ DM: I have hope, because I do see issues being discussed, debated and questioned. I think women *have* to align their struggle with the struggle against racism—which in turn is connected to all these other struggles, like ecology and economic justice. And I think enough women now are at a point where they aren't going to let any of these issues just *disappear*. There are enough scholars, researchers and historians uncovering crucial women's history who know how important their work is for the benefit of the next generation. History that is never reported and never read, just doesn't exist! ♦ ♦ ♦

Sapphire

Sapphire is a New York writer whose poems and short stories describe tragic, intense and unforgettable experiences . . . while not abandoning a sense of visionary hope. In performance her presence is electrifying as she reads with a clear, beautiful voice. Her classic poem "American Dreams" vividly evokes the nightmare of our contemporary social landscape, while "Mickey Mouse Was a Scorpio" skillfully interweaves icons from our common childhood with the reality of incest trauma.

Sapphire lived in Los Angeles, San Francisco and elsewhere before moving to New York City. Although she has been published in several anthologies and poetry journals, her uncompromising writings deserve much wider publication. Sapphire can be contacted c/o PO Box 975, Manhattanville Station, NY NY 10027.

♦ **ANDREA JUNO: What are some of your themes?**
♦ **SAPPHIRE:** My peom "American Dreams" delves into the *mutilation* that society makes us go through—the "never being good enough" syndrome—which is also called the "addiction to perfection". That's what surgical alteration of people's bodies is about: you have an ideal in your mind which you keep trying to achieve by the most destructive means—you cut off a piece of your nose, or insert some silicone in your cheekbones. Watching someone like Michael Jackson totally alter his face in search of an "ideal" forces you to question this society.

Somehow there's a basic premise set up in people that they will never be good enough. Lifetimes are spent pursuing the perfect body and the perfect face. This just seems so sad in the light of more pressing concerns: that on the brink of the destruction of Western culture, people's energy would go into trying to obtain the perfect *nose*. It would be nice if this would just happen and be done with, but—Michael Jackson has had hundreds of operations; this is something ongoing—

♦ **AJ: It's also a WASP ideal. Michael Jackson wants to be one of the "Brady Bunch," eliminating all traces of his blackness—**

♦ **S:** Exactly; it's all related to *deep self-hatred*. This keeps a lot of people's energy and creativity *sapped*. The very forces that could be harnessed to fight fascism and imperialism are being drained off into "fitting in" and "being

accepted." And really, what this is about is *being loved*—trying to find love through achieving this ideal. Yet this ideal is nothing that reflects you or could *ever* reflect you—if you're black, you can never be white! And if you're a female, you can lift weights forever and still look like a woman—so for all your energy to go toward trying to achieve maleness is sad. Not wrong—just sad. Because there's so much else to do.

♦ **AJ: People have internalized self-hatred and they don't realize how alienated they are from their true selves, their creativity and their power. We're all getting mowed over—**

♦ **S:** It's all about *power*. If you love yourself, then you don't give your power away to people who hate you and want to annihilate you. I think that's what *healing* is about: finding that person buried inside us who can stand up to oppressive authority.

♦ **AJ: Let's talk about your background—**

♦ **S:** I was born to an army family in Fort Ord, a military base near Monterey, California. My early childhood was spent on army bases in California, Texas and Europe. I was eleven when I moved to South Philadelphia with my mother; my father went back to Germany and stayed there. Living on army bases was alienating enough for white children—but for a black child it was *very* alienating. This lacked the benefits of middle-class alienation—I wasn't in the suburbs getting a great edu-

Photo: Chris Buck

cation. The whites in the army were underclass/working-class whites (they weren't middle-class), and the blacks were people who couldn't make a living on the "outside"—they'd joined the army out of desperation. There was a real feeling that people were in flight from economic deprivation of all kinds.

It wasn't a "Be All You Can Be" mentality; it was for people who had been beaten by society and now just wanted some economic security. Very little was available culturally; it was a *Donna Reed/Father Knows Best* ambience—I remember not being exposed to anything *real*. I grew up during the birth of Tupperware and TV—just real shallow bullshit. We lived in a little house that was part of a G.I. housing project.

At the same time I had no illusions about America—

here I was in the heart of fascism. My father would leave the dinner table saying he was going out on "war maneuvers" just like other fathers might say, "I'm going to do some work at the office." Beyond my school playground was a mock battlefield; while school was in session the Army would be practicing field maneuvers and war games! Every week we had to rehearse diving under the desk in case of enemy attack—shit like that! So I grew up thinking that's just the way life *was:* that tanks rolling through the village was normal . . .

◆ **AJ: This was in the '50s?**

◆ S: Yes, I was born in 1950. Besides Fort Ord, I lived on an army base in Germany. After the War a lot of working-class Germans, desperate for jobs, came into soldiers' homes to dust and clean—our housecleaner was

MICKEY MOUSE WAS A SCORPIO

the night was no light,
black.
he came in
light cracking the night
stuck in the doorway
of dark
deep hard.
my father,
lean in blue & white pajamas,
wild ignorant farm boy
throws my pajama bottoms
to the pigs,
grabs me by my little skinny knees
& drives his dick in.
i scream
i scream
no one hears except my sister who becomes
    no one cause she didn't hear
years later i become no one cause it didn't
happen
but it's night now & it's happening
a train with razor blades for wheels is riding
thru my asshole
iron hands saw at my knees
i'm gonna die
i'm gonna die
blood, semen & shit gush from my cracked ass
my mother comes in when it's over to wash me
glad not to be the one,
she is glad glad
satanic glad.
she brings her hand up from between my legs &
    smears shit, semen & blood over my mouth,
    "Now she'll know what it's like to have a
    baby," she says.
drugged night so black
you could paint with it,
no moon no stars no god
the night stick smashes my spinal cord
my legs,
bleeding bandages of light,
fall off,
let me go
let me go
don't tell me about god & good little girls
i want to live
i want to live
my cells crack open like glass
my bells are tolling for me
my name disintegrates in the night
God's a lie

this can't be true
M-I-C-K-E-Y M-O-U-S-E
mother is house (we have a nice house, California
    ranch style)
brother is the nail we drive thru your heart
do it
do it to her brother
M-I-C-K-E-Y M-O-U-S-EEE
mouse is in the house
running thru
my vagina
& out my nose.
saucer eyed buck tooth child
Betsy Wetsy
brown bones
electrocuted.
Tiny Tears
that never dry
hop scotch
hickory dock
the mouse fell off
the clock,
the farmer takes Jill down the well
& all the king's horses
& all the king's men
can't put that little girl together again.
crooked man
crooked man
pumpkin eater
childhood stealer.

Excerpt from AMERICAN DREAMS

One time when I was a little girl living on an army base
I was in a gymnasium & the general walked in.
& the general is like god or the president, if you believe.
The young woman supervising said,
"Stand up everybody! The general's here!"
Everybody stood up except me.
The woman looked at me & hissed,
"Stand up for the general!"
I said, "My father's in the army, not me."
& remained seated.
& throughout 38 years of
bucking & winging
grinning & crawling
brown nosing & begging
there has been a quiet
10 year old in me
who has remained seated.
She perhaps is the real American dream.

a Nazi. Both my parents had been in World War II, and we had books describing the horrors of the camps which I had read as a little girl—I'd learned how to read early. For whatever reasons—perhaps because my parents were *wholeheartedly* economic victims—there was a facade of belief which they played out to the end; a certain kind of patriotism. Of course there was no talk of dissent.

Nevertheless, there was a deep "place" in them that didn't *believe*. I remember being sent home from the First Grade because I wouldn't stand up for the Pledge of Allegiance. On the way home I was preparing myself for a beating—certain things you got beat for (for example, my mother put all this energy into making dresses like those bitches wore back then on *Father Knows Best* and the *Donna Reed Show*, and to mess those up meant a beating). I was an impulsive talker, so to get a note sent home that I wouldn't stop talking also meant a beating.

Deep self-hatred keeps a lot of people's energy and creativity *sapped*. The very forces that could be harnessed to fight fascism and imperialism are being drained off into "fitting in" and "being accepted."

I was walking home very slowly, knowing I was going to get beaten for not reciting the Pledge of Allegiance . . . but when I got home, as trivial and petty as my parents could be, my mother read the note and didn't say *anything*. Then my father came in (he was a regular rage-aholic) and the two of them whispered . . . and nothing else was said! I went back to school the next day and still didn't stand up, and the teacher didn't bother me. So, in all of their nothingness, in all of the damage my parents did, and in all their oppressiveness, in some way they made a space for me to be this *rebel!* Given who they were, they should have *killed* me! It was kind of like: letting that part of me *live*, because they had killed it in themselves. So on that issue, they left me alone.

I remember another time me and my siblings (we were all raised Catholic) sat down and decided we were no longer going to attend church. Again, I was waiting for a beating. I hadn't yet realized that my parents were *dysfunctional*; I still thought that getting a beating for breaking a glass "made sense." Anyway, we came in and announced, "We don't want to go to church anymore!" and to my surprise, my father replied, "You have an absolute right not to go to church anymore"—he was talking like a liberal or something.

So in some kind of way I wasn't *totally* destroyed. I guess that's the nature of a dysfunctional family: on the one hand, they tried to kill and destroy everything I was; and on the other hand, they—in little pieces—gave that back.

◆ **AJ: Perhaps they recognized, in a way, that they were fodder. You have to be very courageous to go against society—**

◆ S: Especially without any support. I'm sure people around them weren't saying, "War is wrong," but somehow I feel they *knew*, and that must have contributed to their self-hatred—participating in a system like that. My mother never told *me*, but one time she was talking to my ex-lover about when America dropped the first atomic bomb, and how the Army had lied to them. So in 1986 when my mother was dying of leukemia, I asked if perhaps her cancer was related to being exposed to atomic war games in the '40s when she was in the army. She lay there for a minute and said, "I just really don't know. They never told us the truth about *anything*." Later I put it all together: no one in our family had ever had leukemia—yet out of nowhere came this leukemia that killed her.

For the first 10 years of my life, my parents were functioning under severe "post-traumatic stress." My father had been incarcerated as a prisoner-of-war in Germany (I never got the full story). He and my mother married in the army; I know that after Germany fell my mother had to guard Nazi prisoners, then she got pregnant and went straight from active duty into '50s Fantasyland with these bouffant dresses, trying to raise kids.

◆ **AJ: Was your father brutal to your mother?**

◆ S: Later I found out that he had been, but I never *saw* it. We were one of the few black families on the base. My father had distinguished himself in the War, and he and my mother really played out a role. My mother is a beautiful woman and very social; they did a lot of entertaining—there was a lot of *front* going on. Later she confided, "He beat me." Even though I didn't see the beatings, I did see a coldness and distancing, a ridicule and disdain she displayed toward him. I never saw any brutality, but now I know it existed.

My father played the role of the "good parent," but he had been abused by his parents and he passed this legacy on to me. Also he was a split personality and could change abruptly—while we were going for a "drive in the country" he would suddenly turn into a monster. And my sexual abuse happened when I was very young: there was no fondling or touching—it was a brutal rape, and then it was like it had *never happened*. It was very war-like.

Have you ever read *The Courage to Heal* by Ellen Bass? It's a book for rape survivors, and in the back are personal testimonies. I read them all—you know how you're always looking for your own story? I really couldn't relate until I came to one woman whose father had been a Colonel in the Army. They had lived a "normal" life (whatever that meant; everything was "peachy-keen") until one day he came up to her room (she was 3 years old; catatonic expression on her face) and raped her. He was a surgeon. He split her body apart, and then without anesthesia, sewed her back up . . . left the room, washed his hands, and *said it never happened*. Denied it 'til the day he died, and life went on "as usual." And that was similar to my experience. Some women describe their abuse as a "relationship": on-going, "Daddy's little girl," with ice cream and presents almost to adulthood. But mine was really a Dr Jekyll/Mr Hyde thing in the middle of the night. And *nothing happened*; it was a lifetime of denial for my father. He never ever on any level copped to what he had done.

♦ **AJ: This was all part of a cycle of abuse.** *He* **was abused, so he abused you. Incidentally, "pedophile" wasn't even in the dictionary until recently . . .**

♦ S: All I can say is: the level of awareness I had to ascend to, in order to accept what had happened, was *consummate*. He and my mother divorced; I lived with him afterward as a teenager, and he never bothered me. Nothing ever happened again. So: Number One, he was a real pedophile—I understand that now. And that's not a common pattern among black men:

Photo: Chris Buck

to focus on the under-six-year-old. (My sister also had memories of sexual abuse, independent and separate from mine.) I first began to suspect my father had abused me when I wrote my poem "Mickey Mouse" in which I felt *compelled* to use the word "pedophile" in connection with him. And this revelation is part of the reason why I trust my *writing* so deeply! I believe in it, because that's when the memories first surfaced—from the writing.

When I'm writing, I know what lies are—I know that Bush and all these "leaders" are murderers. Other times

it's almost like I'm shoved back into being a little girl, having to smile, function, and go along with the murderers—hold hands with the perpetrators. But when I'm writing, I *know* that they've dropped napalm on little children in Iraq and that they've polluted the water for centuries to come and that the earth will never be right again. *That's* when I know the truth—when I'm writing. But the rest of the time, life looks like my family in photos from the '50s. We had a new Chrysler, wall-to-wall carpeting and life looked pretty good, *except . . .*

this man came into my room at night and almost killed me . . . then left, and the next morning we had pancakes for breakfast.

Early childhood experiences shape the way we look at the world. Many times I've had to descend into the *heart of darkness* or plunge deep into the heart of society in order to seize some dark truth or insight. Other times, I'm back chewing bubble-gum or whatever, so it hasn't always been a consistent, clear view for me. But when things get clear—it's through my writing. When people tell me my writing's *powerful* and that it *goes to the core*— that's what they're talking about. The rest of the time my mind can dwell in a world of illusion, but that other side is pretty strong, and it keeps pushing me *through* the illusion.

To me, more than any other time, the '50s was the *world of illusion*—just horrible. In no other era had such pallid and ugly denial existed, where the men came home to these women on tranquilizers, and these houses with lawns, and forgot all that *war.* And World War II was an ugly war—yet they were able to couch it in righteousness—able to shift the burden of the holocaust onto the Germans, rather than look at what *we* did.

The '50s were simply the biggest whitewash you've ever seen. And look what it produced—that's where Reagan and Bush came out of. That's what I grew up in, and a lot of that informs my writing: "Mickey Mouse," "American Dreams," and even a recent poem like "Rabbit Man" is still coming out of that era: trying to see through water all the way down to the depths where truth dwells . . .

◆ **AJ: We all know we're being lied to; that's why people love your insights—**
◆ S: Unless they blatantly misunderstand me, most people are appreciative of my work. I wrote my "Wilding" poem about an incident which took place in October, 1988, where 40-50 black and Hispanic males were running through Central Park attacking people. They attacked a guy on a bicycle, they were throwing stones at people—a male rampage was going on. They came across a female jogger and raped her and beat her almost to death—evidently when they found the body, three-fourths of her blood was gone, her skull had been fractured— they thought she was going to die. She's *still* brain-damaged; she has double-vision so that for the rest of her life when she looks at someone, she sees two people; when there's two people, she sees four. And her memory is never going to be right, even though she returned to her job. But she survived because of her *will*—she was supposed to die; these kids evidently meant to kill her.

I felt there was a lot of denial on both sides, so I wrote a poem about that. I felt some black people were denying that these kids were murderers: it *didn't happen*, it was false arrest, they were jacked-up, they're making "too big a thing of it"—just all kinds of weird denial like that—
◆ **AJ: Because there *is* a racist interpretation there—**
◆ S: Exactly. And people do get arrested falsely for all these things. Yet somehow this just wasn't the case here.

Of course, within the white community there was a refusal to see these young males as children, a refusal to see them as human beings. They kept calling them "dogs" or "animals" because that's much easier than thinking, "Here's a human being who's been so damaged by society that at 12 years old he's a murderer." If you call him an "animal," then he's totally responsible for his behavior: "He grew up in a vacuum; he has a genetic coding that makes him crawl on 4 legs and bark," as opposed to: "he was a little baby, just like that jogger was a little baby once, yet by the time he was 12 his life was so *nothing* that all he had was rage, anger and the *urge to kill*." So those were some of the operative thoughts in that piece.

Early childhood experiences shape the way we look at the world. Many times I've had to descend into the *heart of darkness* or plunge deep into the heart of society in order to seize some dark truth or insight.

The first time I read this poem was to a group of black mothers with children who had been in jail. I thought they were going to crucify me; I thought I was setting myself up to have rotten eggs thrown at me . . . but they were very quiet and very appreciative—I was really shocked. Interestingly, the few people who ever gave me static about this poem were people totally removed from it—I remember a couple of white women coming up to me and saying, "We just think that poem's horrible!"
◆ **AJ: Like, "Don't talk about horrible things!"**
◆ S: Yeah. But whenever I've read it to actual *people* who could've been involved in something like that, I've never had people go into nutsville or denial. I was trying to enter into the heart of this darkness, but a *living* heart . . . and just present what I had seen. As a poet I go where my heart and soul takesme; I still may not have a totally accurate analysis of all the class issues within the black community—maybe people can nitpick one or two things. I remember Audre Lorde commenting that I needed to do a deeper analysis of "the mother" . . . but in general the response was: "Go with it—go *further!* You're on the right track!"
◆ **AJ: You were taking on the persona of a "wilding" boy in a very honest way. There was a lot of brutality there, but the attackers were human beings. Was it cathartic for you to look at the world through their eyes?**

♦ S: It was *necessary* for me. Number One, I couldn't view this group like I did my father/victimizer. I was viewing them through the eyes of a woman old enough to be their mother; at the time I was teaching kids their age. I was looking at potential lost and denied; I was looking at kids who—there was no doubt in my mind, *would* do something like that. I couldn't distance myself the way people "downtown" could; I was liking the horrible little sexist bastards. Some of them I was even *loving;* I could see why a few mothers needed so badly to say, "Not *my* son!" I could see what was good in them, and I could see them being destroyed by the culture they lived in.

This was very different from looking at adult black men, because I was realizing that adult men (black or otherwise) have a *choice.* Children *don't* have a choice. As a child, once the pattern of victimization is in you—unless you have therapy, or unless you are one of "God's Chosen" (some children have awareness at a very early age, but most don't), then you are a victim. There was no other way I could look at those kids but as victims—victims who were *killers.*

I think I was able to enter into this subject with empathy. When I was writing, I could feel myself *running*—I was feeling what is denied women. Here's this white middle-class jogger who's "free" to run through the park, and here are these black males who are free to run through the park . . . yet very few black women are going to leave Harlem and go running *anywhere*, because we wouldn't even make it to the fuckin' park—you know what I mean? So *I* didn't have what either of them had, but I could feel it—that joy of just running.

And I could feel the camaraderie of that gang (50 of them), with the moon full in Scorpio that night. I could just feel them throbbing and running . . . the joy of blood on their hands—it wasn't like a judgment or anything. And the feeling was: knowing that *I* could have done that, too. It just so happened that the nature of my "acting out" as a teenager did not include that type of thing—and I'm not a male.

♦ **AJ: And as a female you're not even given that form to express yourself in—**
♦ S: If I had tried to get out there and run, they would have raped *me*—I would have been the first rape they discarded at the corner, before they went on to rape their "real" love. But . . . I could feel it. I wasn't looking through a microscope; I felt I'd merged with them—that while I was writing I *was* that kid; I *was* that anger; and I *was* that jogger. That's what I was trying to do.

♦ **AJ: This is an incredibly healthy process that women need to do: to be able to really *understand* the feelings of their oppressor, their enemy. Because in the setting up of these polarities, power is given to the oppressor. Both parties—victim and victimizer—are diminished by this scheme. So it's important to work yourself out of either identification.**
♦ S: Exactly; that freezes you in your victimization. And that's what I think is so powerful in Alice Walker's work (*The Color Purple*). She refuses to freeze black people into a

victim role; her story shows how we play all roles.

These are *roles*, that's all. We are people and we will play out these roles. As much as those children learned in one role to be a victim, and went on to play out their other role as victimizer—neither of them is necessarily *who they are.* They're not animals, they're human beings who chose a certain way to deal with their oppression. For me, one of the ways out of oppression is to find *all* of my selves. And part of myself was this Oppressor.

That was when I came out of denial: when I realized (and I had blocked it for years) that when I was a child I was going to stick a lit cigarette up a cat's ass. I thought: "So this is *me? I'm* into peace; *I'm* a pacifist; I'm into *talking it out."* And if this is what *I* was going to do, no wonder my father did what he did. And my father had been through two wars, not one: World War II and the Korean War . . . under fire, in the trenches. So—*of course he did it.* There's nothing else a person who's been subjected to that type of stress can do. That's part of why rape is encouraged on the battlefield—rape and drugs are encouraged. That's part of how soldiers can deal with the stress of battle. Yeah—my father *did* that—
♦ **AJ: The military eroticizes violence and killing—**
♦ S: Exactly, and they view their own death as a big, heroic orgasm. Finding that darkness in *me* made me able to clearly see it in other people.

Incestuous abuse is the *underpinning* for our culture— this is what we're built on. *We're a rape culture.*

♦ **AJ: As a child you were doing a symbolic act; weren't you also raped in the ass, too?**
♦ S: Exactly; it was a *repetition* for me. When that happened to me, I had no frame of reference—anal sex had not been part of my sexual behavior; it was like it was *coming from nowhere.* And not only was I going to penetrate this animal but I was going to *violently* penetrate it. Now why didn't I think to tear its legs off, or chop its head off? Why did I automatically proceed to *that* behavior? Well, I really do believe that the *compulsion to repeat* is not just psychological—it's almost coded into your neuroreceptor senses, and on a certain trigger you will act out that behavior again.

So, it was really *freeing* to see what I was doing; what had happened to me. I realized who I was and what I was capable of doing—I was just a woman who had been raped, and this was what I would do to a fucking *cat.* So what would a man do to a *woman*—you know what I

Photo: Chris Buck

er than the other slaves?" and somebody would say, "Because the Master's your daddy!" Then you might get an extra lump of sugar at Christmastime, and by the time you're 14 and have some breasts, here comes daddy to *fuck* you!

One of my great-grandfathers was a slave. In the '90s, most black people are 5 or 6 generations out of slavery; I'm three. My father's father was a sharecropper who evidently was psychotic—all the other people would be out there doing their slavery routine, but my grandfather would be out there receiving visions from "God" (not "good" visions, but visions telling him to go hit someone over the head). He brutalized his family; he wasn't all there.

♦ **AJ: Of course, how could anyone enslaved have**

mean? Society is not even *for* abusing animals, but they are for abusing women, and they tell men, "This is your property; do what you want with it."

Now it's easier for me to see things like that and understand that we're a culture built on this type of abuse. I don't go anywhere and listen to women and think that they're lying; I believe it is only 40% who remember their child abuse ... and far from what we're taught (that this tears the family apart), actually it seems to hold it together! So we have this archetype of the incestuous or dysfunctional family: the alcoholic father coming home from working in the factory who rapes everybody ... Incestuous abuse is the *underpinning* for our culture—this is what we're built on. *We're a rape culture.*

I'm also working on how for black people, this incest dates back to slavery. From the very beginning, the Master would come and fuck the "bitch" and she would have the baby, and later he would come back and fuck that baby. However he was able to dissociate himself, nevertheless the *child* knew: "That's my daddy!" Maybe the child would look around and ask, "How come I'm light-

Photo: Chris Buck

been "all there"?

♦ S: So, early on: instead of the pattern his neighbors acted out (womanizing or alcoholism), madness was part of my heritage. This was a direct result of some kind of *invasion*. When people talk about slavery, it took me understanding my life around gay people to realize how

170

one-sided the picture was . . . to realize: "Hey, if the Master was strolling through the field and spotted Caledonia and told her to bend over, how come he didn't tell Otis to bend over too?" Men were being raped, too, but you never hear about that—it's what they cannot cop to.

Now I believe that just as many men were raped as women. And there is nothing else to do with such behavior but *act it out*. Both of my brothers—and they were very oppo-

Photo: Chris Buck

site—acted this out. One is dead, but he was the scape-goat, the madman—he became schizophrenic and dysfunctional, but he was very beautiful and very talent-ed. And the other brother literally went on to make $100,000 a year playing football; I can turn on the TV and see him. He was the one who had everything; he graduated from Stanford with honors, got an engineer-ing degree and went on to play pro ball, have the "pretty little wife" and buy into the whole fantasy. He was at a dinner with the Mayor and they were giving him an award for—you know, being a "good negro" and piling up all these "social achievements"—and the police came and arrested him for rape!

His whole hero image crashed in '87. My next door neighbor knocked on my door with a copy of the *New York Times:* "Have you seen the paper—James has been busted!" I said, "What?!" I *knew* he was a misogynist, but he was the Father's Son who had recreated the pretty picture of "the Nuclear Family with the Three Cute Little Kids."

I had *heard* things but hadn't wanted to hear them. One time the sister-in-law of the brother who died (well, they were never married) said something odd about one of James's children taking off all her clothes and acting out something bizarre sexually. And I thought, "NO—it can't be happening with *Mr Perfection!*" But then he got arrested for this rape. He had enough money to buy his way out; it involved a white woman. As racist as this country is, he was able to be acquitted—this shows the power he had even as a black man. He had the best lawyers, and his stu-pid wife was there—she's an ex-beauty queen, a Vanessa Wil-liams type. She was standing by her man [meek voice]: "I know my husband didn't do that," (this is on TV) "I know that he would *never* do that. The night of the alleged . . ."—you know, lying for him and everything.

But another sister had told me that on the night of the offense,

Photo: Chris Buck

James was gone! The wife had told some woman that she was at home playing out her "enabler" routine, making costumes for her kids for some party and wondering where James was. So he *did* it! I don't know all the details of the actual case, but one of my goals is to find that woman and talk to her. Because nothing but the truth breaks the cycle; nothing but coming out of denial and copping to "who you are" and "what the fuck did you do?" breaks the cycle of lying—nothing else.

I feel that my father's death is allowing the *male* part of me to live!

I understand my brother even went to therapy—he has that kind of money and mentality—but it was a "put-himself-back-together" kind of therapy because the team had sold him. It was the trauma of "not being on the team" and maybe not being a millionaire anymore. So the therapist put him back together so he could rise back to the top: he's risen, he's healed his career, and now all the people who were against him are for him and they realize that maybe they made a mistake and he could *never* have done that—you know, he did *that* kind of "fixing," but nothing on the order of admitting, "Yes, I *did* it."

◆ **AJ: In a way he'd already made a bargain with the devil: buying into the nuclear family and all the "straight" societal values—to be a *football player?!* To be that, you have to deny so much of your creativity and your uniqueness—**

◆ S: He's like my father; part of him is so dead, and part of him is so vital and alive. What I find with a lot of perpetrators like my father is: they have a deep *fear of women*, and this manifests itself as *a fear of death* and a *fear of aging*—all this is deeply imbedded in our culture. Fear of the natural process of death and getting old and power dissipating is accompanied by fear of female blood, gore, and the dankness of earth . . .

I feel that the way my father and brothers reacted to this culture was with an exaltation of the "super-dick" that is actually very *impotent*. Later in life I found out that with adult women my father had been impotent most of his life. I don't know how I was conceived, but I must have been—because I look like him. Also, my mother is extremely small and passive—very tiny. I remember she looked up at me after we had been separated for many years, and I said, "Gee, I never knew you were so short!" Shocked, she replied, "I'm not short—you're tall!" Since she was very doll-like and diminutive, maybe that had something to do with my father's attraction to her. Anyway, I would hear over and over again that he was impotent; that he couldn't function with women. So I

think it's very interesting—that in terms of his maleness, his interest in athletics, his hatred of homosexuals, hatred of anything weird and his extolling of male myths in general, he wasn't even a fucking "man" by his *own* definition.

◆ **AJ: So many exhibitors of male bravado are impotent or premature ejaculators . . . or else literally do not get much pleasure from sex—to them, this is an act in which they are trying to conquer the thing they fear . . . How did you decide to write?**

◆ S: For years, while I was attending various colleges, I was constantly bouncing between these two identities: "I'm a writer!" "No—I'm a dancer!" But the writing kept getting stronger; this was what I was being asked to do—being *paid* to do. No one was paying me to choreograph or to dance, yet people wanted to hear the writing. That made me take myself more seriously.

I mean—I'd always taken myself seriously in terms of telling the truth as I saw it, but I also realized that I had a gift as a performer. And I was astute enough and had enough integrity to know that I didn't want to use that charisma to mask *bad writing*. I was able, just with the cadence of my voice, to clean up a bad poem, but I realized that I wanted to be able to really *write!* I didn't want to get out there and just "sell it"; it's much more wonderful to get out there and sell work that's good! I didn't have a formal education in writing, but I started to put in the time to try and develop a craft.

◆ **AJ: The academic system perpetuates narrow formalistic approaches to writing, whereas real creativity involves remaking *everything*, not emulating other people. Society really needs a better language system—**

◆ S: —a *symbolic* language. We've tried to make everything concrete to the point of our death: "Can you *prove* it?"

I'm not trying to be another Shakespeare or Henry James—I'm trying to find the blackest, bloodiest, female-est form of expression I can!

◆ **AJ: And it's so obvious that the system emphasizing linear scientific thought has not worked.**

◆ S: They don't want *us* to understand that *they* understand their system doesn't work! And that their "theories" are just that: unproven hypotheses. They have sold us their theories. Most people never fully realize that much of the so-called "reality" that's sold them is based on thoughts that are not even *true*, yet we can literally be locked up in nuthouses for not accepting "reality" as it's presented to us. But I don't want their language; I don't want their linear male "murder mind." I'm not trying to be another Shakespeare or Henry James—I'm trying to find the blackest, bloodiest, female-est form of expression I can! I'm not aiming to be as good as a white man; I'm aiming to find the *Heart of Darkness*, the very thing they've tried to suppress . . . which they claim is ugly and valueless, then spend half their time imitating and murdering—I'm trying to find *that*. That's what I value.

There are things I *must* do. Jung said something beautiful: that his fate was merely to *find* his fate and follow it. I feel this is what astrology does for me; it's not like everything is clear, but I use the insights from astrology to try to determine what it is I'm supposed to do.

◆ **AJ: I've studied astrology for 15 years. It's a very deep and rigorous subject which seems to integrate humans into the fields of experience, and maintain an elegant empirical system as well.**

◆ S: There's joy in finding your fate and submitting to it. Besides studying Western astrology, I want to study Egyptian and Mayan astrology. And fundamentally, it's all about accepting a force greater than myself—which is what white male culture has refused to do. They have said, "We are God; we are over Nature." Not "in conjunction with," not "at the mercy of"—no, "We are *over* Nature." There is a part of astrology that says, "God is *over* us, and *in* us," and I love that. That's true power to me. We've inherited a lot of ways of thinking which—once we realize the bigger picture—we can discard. We hold on to a man because we think we'll die without him—like I thought I would die without my daddy, even though he was *killing* me. But once we let go, a new life appears in front of us—this pasture of green grass—and we just have to go for it! So at the age of forty, that's how I see myself: as a child running through a field of flowers, being born again!

Now I feel I'm strong enough to go back to college and get a Masters Degree in writing; that I can stand up to "the father," go through whatever it is that faces me, and still have my integrity. I want to do the work, the discipline—I want to "train" almost like a boxer prepares for his calling.

◆ **AJ: Maybe you'll reclaim authority from the white male power structure as a confirmation of your own self-sufficiency—**

◆ S: Exactly. In other words, the father can't destroy me anymore, because I don't identify with that authority. It's interesting: the day my father died (we hadn't had a relationship for 20 years), I started to *take control* of my life. I began making arrangements to pay off these debts—I realized that I was *free*.

Most black women grew up in female-dominated families, but I grew up in a male-dominated household (which is not the norm). My father controlled the money; he controlled the transportation—to this day I feel ashamed that I don't drive (he took me everywhere). But literally the day he died I started looking in the phone book for driving schools; I called this financial planner; I started to take control of my life. Not that I hadn't been doing this before; I had been putting my art out there and

paying my own way for years, but never totally *letting myself take care of my self*. Because I had been taught that *someone else* was going to do that for me. It had never occurred to me to do those things for my *self*, because I had never seen my *mother* do that—she had been taken care of. She had played out a role as a very passive, weak woman . . .

I feel that my father's death is allowing the *male* part of me to live! My female self is alive—sometimes I feel it's *too* alive for this culture—but it hasn't been able to move forward in the world the way I've wanted it to, because my *male self* wasn't there. But now I feel I'm becoming a whole person—not *overnight*, but. . . So that's where I feel myself at, now: that I'm going to take this healing deeper, beyond just detailing the victimization and telling the truth about it. I feel I'm moving toward *regeneration* . . . transformation of this pain into full human *be-ing*. Society cuts off your limbs and leaves you a "human torso," but now I feel that "starfish" quality: that you can grow new limbs—that's where I'm at now.

◆ **AJ: Most people never even get that far; they're totally crippled on all levels—**

◆ S: Most people live for 50 or 60 years as the living dead.

◆ **AJ: Do you define yourself as a lesbian?**

◆ S: I do. I don't run from that; I embrace that definition of myself—even though I have loved men and maybe will again. I don't define myself as a bisexual or heterosexual; I'm just a lesbian. There are straight people who go with gay people every now and then. My sexuality has never been that rigid or boxed in, but the minute

I loved a woman, I knew I didn't want to run from that fact. And that meant proclaiming I was a lesbian; accepting the term "lesbian" and defining it for myself. Just in the same way that I was shocked (after living all my life as a black person in the United States) when an African told me I wasn't really "black"—that black Americans were something else—like *hybrids!*

♦ **AJ: What do you mean?**

♦ S: This African told me that he was a "real" black person—"pure" . . . and that as far back as time began his ancestors were black. I know that one of my great-grandmothers was white and another was Indian—nevertheless, I don't define myself by *his* definition; the lightest-skinned black person is "black" to me. The Supreme Court proclaimed: If you have 1/32 black blood, you're black and you have to remain a slave!

Now, several women have come up to me and said, "I am a 'real' lesbian—I've never had sex with a man; I never will have sex with a man. I live on a commune in Oregon, and we are working toward the eradication of all men—we are going to drown all male babies in wells. And you—you're just a bisexual *slut* and a *whore;* you are not a true lesbian." But I can't let *them* define lesbianism for me any more than I can let this African define "black" for me: by *my* definition I am a "lesbian" in that I have loved women and will continue to love them sexually, politically and spiritually—it's very much a political statement for me, it's not the rigid limitations of some kind of biological choice, like: "I *only* sleep with women."

It's not like I ever felt like an *imposter,* but I need to start defining what I mean when I say I'm a "lesbian." I think this will help give other women room, too, like: "If this is how Sapphire defines herself as a lesbian, and she lives as a lesbian, and she takes flak as a lesbian, then "lesbianism" is much broader than this other conception." If I were a *heterosexual,* I wouldn't define my heterosexuality that old, narrow way. I require a much more open and freer identity, so it's not like walking some narrow line where if you ever deviate (whether it be into celibacy, or a relationship with a man, or whatever) you're no longer a "lesbian."

♦ **AJ: There's a real empowerment in reclaiming negative terms that society has conferred on oppressed groups. But it's sad when some lesbians or blacks then apply the most rigid definitions and constraints, because then they become exactly like their oppressors— particularly in the area of sexuality. Very few people in the world are any one *thing.* These are *societal* definitions anyway—in reality we are so much more of a mix.**

♦ S: Exactly, and I'll never find *all* of who I am if I have to go by other people's definitions. A big part of dealing with my incest trauma had to do with a long protracted period of celibacy. And some people actually had the nerve to comment on this—it made them uncomfortable! Because . . . they weren't able to "place" me anywhere— if I wasn't actively involved in a sexual relationship, how would they define my sexuality? Because *their* sexuality

was defined by the *act* with not a lot of theory behind it: "This is who I'm fucking. I'm with a man now, so I'm 'straight' . . . Now I'm fucking Susy, so I'm a lesbian." If I wasn't fucking anybody, then I was a nothing—a *no-sexual.* It was really hard for me to be in that space, because a part of me knew that what I needed to heal myself was celibacy. And there was a part of me that craved social *acceptance* (on some level it must be important to me), even though I hate to admit it!

We hold on to a man because we think we'll die without him— like I thought I would die without my daddy, even though he was *killing* me.

I think it's very hard to be anything other than what this culture tells you: which is to be passive and to be in a relationship with a man . . . or to be in a relationship with a woman that *recreates heterosexuality.* But to be some type of "free" sexual being—even if it means *not* being sexual—is more than most people can handle. And part of my struggle comes from defying my father, even though I didn't have a relationship with him as an adult. Yet from him I got ideas about male and female sexuality: that the woman was supposed to *be there* for the man; there was something wrong with the woman who withheld herself; that she was frigid or sick, and that this was *wrong.* So when I was being celibate, I had to fight a part of me that still didn't regard myself as a sexual being *deserving* of getting what *I* needed instead of just being there for *other* people.

♦ **AJ: Society tells women they're just a part, not a whole; to be fulfilled they have to be "part of" somebody else.**

♦ S: Yes . . . For a long time I didn't write about sexuality because I was writing so much about abuse. Then I got a call from a woman who said, "Sapphire, I think I'm going to have a baby; come to my birth." And we weren't really that close; she was a closer friend with my ex-lover. I remember saying, "Look, I have a *tai chi* class this morning, but thanks for inviting me." I was on my way to the class when something like a bolt of lightning hit me: "Go to this birth!"

So I went. It was at a birthing center, not a home or hospital, and I was assigned the job of cooking. The mother had once been at my house when I'd made this split pea soup she really liked, so she asked me to make some. So everybody's running around while I'm in the kitchen making soup and I hear, "The pains are coming!" Then the midwife calls to me: "Come here and hold her legs!" And I'm right there holding her legs apart where the doctor is supposed to be, watching this baby come out, and of course, it was the most wonderful thing I've ever seen. I'm feeling all these emotions and I don't know what I'm feeling, but all of a sudden I go home and start making split pea soup. Later on that night I sat down at my desk and wrote two of the strongest erotic stories I'd ever written, combining them with a woman's journey through the South (I've never been through the South) and Blues music.

One story, "Looking for Robert Johnson," featured a woman my age who was doing research on the blues down South, finding these older black people and draining the life out of them like researchers do. She meets a man who has known the famous blues guitarist and starts asking him all these nerdy questions. Suddenly she asks, "Were you there when your first child was born?" (In other words, she discovers what she really wants to find out about is about *life,* and that somehow she's missed it in the city.) Then the two of them have this affair which is very healing for her; they share one night together under a full moon and she's convinced she has become pregnant. (At the time I was thinking, "Am I ever going to have a baby?") Then she goes back home . . . and her period starts. In the process of crying about her period starting, she gets her voice back and begins to *sing.* So this encounter brought her a *gift.*

Further on down the road she meets an older woman who also knew Robert Johnson, and has a sexual relationship with *her.* Then she asks, "Can I stay?" As intimate as she had become with the man, there had been no question about wanting to stay or be "his woman"; she'd wanted to have this experience and to heal herself, but not to *bond.* But she asks the older woman if she can stay, and the woman says, "No!"—she has to return to her work.

I think that witnessing that birth inspired in me an eroticism and a power of narrative which was a harbinger of where I could go in my writing. I think when you pass through these healing experiences, you feel hope—as opposed to: "You're permanently damaged and you're going to remain so forever—"

◆ AJ: —as if life is static and not in flux.
◆ S: Exactly. So these two stories I wrote were kind of a *way out,* affirming that my sexuality is a *choice*—I can be with a man or a woman. As in the story, I *chose* to be with a woman, because that was where the woman got the greatest gifts. When I was dealing with the man, the woman wasn't in the picture. I didn't leave him just to be with a woman; I left him to continue on down the road—you know what I mean? It wasn't a rejection of him for a woman, it was: whatever it was I got from him, I got it and then moved on.
◆ AJ: I think women have to have a very strong community if our planet's going to survive. And we can't tolerate separatist labels—
◆ S: I feel that way, and I'm gathering more courage to voice that view. Because the *other* view has been so strong;

it's been there to kill you. Sometimes, when I would hear this more "limiting" version of lesbianism, I would feel so *killed in silence* that I would just have to shut the fuck up. . .
◆ AJ: It's so sad when groups of "Outsiders" fight amongst themselves.
◆ S: There have to be more of us who refuse to *give in* to rigid definitions. It's interesting: I've worked in the sex industry and have done a lot of writing about this. When I would identify myself as a lesbian, this would upset people—this was *not* work lesbians were supposed to do. But I found out that the industry was *flooded* with gay women; every other woman I met would turn out to be a lesbian—yet we couldn't *talk* about it. I went to England and my performance piece, "Are You Ready to Rock?" had a lot to do with that. I would give a reading and afterwards I almost couldn't take it: people would come up to me and confess, "I was a prostitute." "I was a go-go girl." And these would be the squarest little English things I'd ever seen! It was like this horrible secret—even more so because they were *gay.* They had broken the taboo about sleeping with women; they felt they were "whores," too, so this guilt had been pushed deep down, down and down . . .

When you take an individual like Twiggy and hold her up as an ideal, you're holding up *death.* This is not what it *is* to be a woman, and to hold that up for people who can never be that is to hold up hate!

◆ AJ: Society controls you through whatever you're ashamed of—
◆ S: So when we release the shame we discover a new source of power: "What's wrong with this?"
◆ AJ: In previous eras, blacks used to be ashamed they were black. Whereas the shame should have been directed toward white society's racism—
◆ S: Exactly; shame involves buying into a value system that does not *belong* to you. For example, that whole dogmatic condemnation of prostitution—I get angry when other women define "prostitution" for me; it's like "blackness" which needs to be defined by black people. I was telling a transsexual: "I'm not here to define your reality; *you'll* have to do that. But until you do it, other people will do it for you. Edward Albee will be there to write about it for you if you don't write about it for yourself."

I feel that because there's such a denial of women's economic reality, many women think that other women

are free *not* to be prostitutes (or whatever the degrading economic role in question is). Lesbians also share this kind of snobbery—that's why there's so much denial about the sex industry in the lesbian community. Yet where do we *get* economic autonomy?

We have not created an economic base in our community that provides jobs for women. So to survive, a lot of lesbians have to leave their lovers, get out and go-go dance, and come back to be a "butch." This is what you have to do to play out being a "man" with your woman; and the denial of that is a way to deny our economic powerlessness. It's too painful to admit that with all our "enlightened" attitudes, we're no different—we're subject to the same pressures as other women: *to make money.* All of us can't be construction workers; some women *have* to get out there and take sexist jobs. So there's still a lot to do in terms of just *unveiling shame and giving it back!*

Sometimes in my writing I've felt I was *re-victimizing* myself by exposing so much! But I know that I hadn't done anything wrong and had nothing to be ashamed of; that I *wasn't* re-victimizing myself—it just *felt* like that. The reality was: I was handing back shame that wasn't mine.

♦ **AJ: We're trying to heal a wound, but the wound has to be uncovered and exposed first. Those of us who had horrible sexual experiences with men in our youth—why should *we* feel ashamed? *They* should be ashamed. And this can be extended to all areas where society makes us feel shame—**

♦ S: Can you imagine waking up in the morning, looking in the mirror and not liking your nose? But we accept that it's *common* to wake up in the morning and hate your nose, your thighs, your this-and-that . . . What kind of culture is this: where we can't love how we look?

♦ **AJ: To think that somebody as emaciated as Twiggy could be a physical ideal!**

♦ S: That's a worship of death, in a way. When you take an individual like Twiggy and hold her up as an ideal, you're holding up death and the antithesis of what femaleness is. This is not what it *is* to be a woman, and to hold that up for people who can never be that is to hold up hate!

♦ **AJ: You cannot split the Mind from the Body—**

♦ S: —without grave consequences: "We're building our house next to a nuclear power plant. What do you mean: there's radiation in the air? What are you talking about? We have a great life. No, we would never move; we trust the government's reports entirely. We *trust* our government." Well, you'd have to be totally *insane* and out of your mother-fuckin' mind to believe that—but many people do.

♦ **AJ: The entire culture's based on denial: "You can cut down the rain forests and don't worry about it, we'll patch it up later."**

♦ S: "There is no karma; we can replace the land with asphalt; there's no problem." This is massive denial.

♦ **AJ: Basically, all you can do is reclaim your creativity and put it out to the world, and try to heal. We**

refuse to forever remain the *walking wounded*—

♦ S: Exactly; I refuse to accept that image of myself. I refuse to see black people as a race of victims anymore; I refuse to see women—half the world—as victims. We have been victimized—that's what we have to open up and heal from—but I'll be damned if I admit to being a victim. I'm a *survivor.* I lived. That was part of what my father dying meant for me: I *outlived* the motherfucker. I am a survivor. And what I am ultimately about is: to live. I'm moving out of *death worship.*

This culture wants us obsessed and addicted—they don't want us joyful and happy. What kind of culture *is* this—that breeds materialism, misery and depression?

I think I used to be unhealthily narcissistic—romanticizing death and suicide and mourning. I saw myself as a victim; I had my victim fantasies, and of course, sometimes life would fulfill them for me—you know what I mean?

♦ **AJ: But that's the process: you may find yourself there for awhile, but then you move on. Now you're a warrior—**

♦ S: That's what I see, too. Part of my process is to go all the way down and delve into my deepest depths. The other part of my healing involves eventually coming into the light—not just the examination of darkness.

This culture wants us obsessed and addicted; they don't want us joyous and happy. The tarot card of the sun with the child naked and joyful—well, I feel I deserve that, too! Whether I get it at forty, fifty or whatever—I deserve that kind of joy. I see animals happy; why the fuck can't *I* be happy? And by happiness I don't mean "having everything." What kind of culture is this that breeds materialism, misery and depression? How come I can't be happy? I think that's part of healing: not just saying "I survived; I made it," but somewhere finding an *ecstasy* in my heart.

♦ **AJ: And communicating that to people is a power: taking that personal pain, drawing out the poison and putting it into an art that speaks for all of us—and in the process, healing yourself. I think the Donna Reed types in the nuclear family are certainly not happy— that's a very difficult act to pull off—**

♦ S: I think Donna Reed died of cancer! She was the *stoic type;* I think she smiled every day under chemotherapy and denied the pain while she cheerfully fought it. She went out like a real Donna Reed! ♦ ♦ ♦

Kathy Acker

Born in 1948, avant-garde novelist Kathy Acker hung out in New York with the FLUXUS group and underground filmmakers in the '60s. At Brandeis University she studied with Herbert Marcuse, following him to UC San Diego. Back in New York she studied with Jerome Rothenberg and hung out in the early punk rock scene while writing art criticism, book reviews and prose pieces. Her libretto, *The Birth of a Poet,* was produced as an opera at the Brooklyn Academy of Music.

In the past two decades Kathy Acker has written thirteen novels, whose sexually explicit language, multiple personas, plagiarism and sheer linguistic inventiveness embody a subversive sensibility: *The Childlike Life of the Black Tarantula; Florida; I Dreamt I was a Nymphomaniac Imagining; The Adult Life of Toulouse-Lautrec; Hello, I'm Erica Jong; Kathy Goes to Haiti; Blood and Guts in High School; Great Expectations; Don Quixote; My Death, My Life, by Pier Paolo Pasolini; Empire of the Senseless; In Memoriam to Identity* and *Hannibal Lecter, My Father.* During most of the '80s Kathy lived in London and Paris. Currently she lives in the Bay Area and teaches *performance* at the San Francisco Art Institute.

◆ ANDREA JUNO: How has sexism affected your life?

◆ KATHY ACKER: *All things are sexist!* Pornography is sexist, books are sexist, magazines are sexist. For many historical reasons, there is this fear of sex—in women. It was a big step when women said, *"We'll start making pornography; we'll take over those areas."* It's fantastic that women are doing this! And men just can't deal with it—that's what all this recent censorship is about: the men are freaking out!

◆ AJ: In your writing, an inversion of gender sometimes occur where you become the male role. Can you talk about that?

◆ KA: Actually, it's different in different books. In early books, the characters (to the extent that they were "characters") changed gender a lot: I never got "his" and "her" right! And the dumb reason was: I just didn't remember, I didn't care, it meant nothing to me. Until I met Sylvère Lotringer [*Semiotext(e)* editor], I didn't understand a lot of the reasons I wrote the way I did. I did things without any theory—I did whatever just seemed

intuitively "right." But I think the reason was probably my *hatred of gender* . . . a hatred of the expectation that I had to become my womb. My hatred of being defined by the fact that I had a cunt. And as a kid I really resented the fact that I couldn't be a pirate! There were these great lesbian or bisexual pirates who would disguise themselves as men—like Annie Bonney, whose gender was only discovered after her death.

◆ VALE: How did you actually lose your virginity?

◆ KA: I grew up during the days of the Double Standard, so you weren't supposed to have sex, but what happened was: all the boys we dated (who went to boys' schools) would go to Europe and get seduced by older women, then come back and seduce *us.* I was easily seduced—it didn't take much! I was 13.

My parents were so anti-sex that they never gave me any sex education—how I avoided getting pregnant I'll never know. I remember the time this boy and I were fucking in a cemetery. I was having my period and he thought he had taken away my virginity, so he got all romantic. I couldn't tell him otherwise, because he was

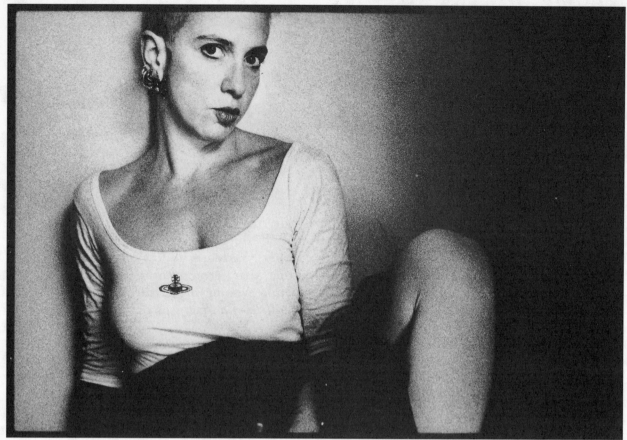

Photo: Chris Buck

really into this High Romance of Virginity! But that was my first orgasm—right away I understood: "Wow, this is what it's all about! *Shit!*"

When I started going to college, it was cool to fuck, because that was the beginning of the hippie days. So then I had no guilt whatsoever—I mean, my girlfriends and I would go out *prowling* every night. We'd pass 'em on to each other (``You have him next!''); we had charts of the lengths of cocks; we were *really into sex!* One girl, Susie Sampson, was the only virgin in our freshman class. So we all decided: ``Susie, you gotta lose it!'' The guy was picked, they got along okay, and during her first time she got gonorrhea!

◆ **AJ: Now AIDS has changed everything.**

◆ KA: Oh god—my first roommate at college ran an orgy in the room. I think her father was a trustee so she got away with it. She covered the whole room with green carpet and mattresses and it was like *orgy-time!* I moved out after 3 weeks because I never knew who was going to be in my bed, and it was hard to study. She had a dog named "Magic" who just *loved* genitals (both male and female)—she had trained it with pieces of meat. You'd be sitting at the dining room table and—all of us had holes in our blue jeans between our legs so that Magic could go from person to person. I guess those were the good old days . . .

◆ **V: When did the pill come in?**

◆ KA: I started taking it in college. Abortions were *illegal* in those days—there was one doctor in Philadelphia and we all used to chip in whenever somebody needed an abortion. I remember hearing horror stories of illegal abortions: women taping irons to their bodies and throwing themselves down flights of stairs, and then they'd have the baby in traction! Of course, there were countless coat-hanger stories.

◆ **V: Didn't you work in the sex industry?**

◆ KA: When I was in San Diego I worked as a stripper. There were these 3 clubs in San Diego and you went around in this pink Cadillac from club to club. They're burlesque clubs, you do your act, and you don't have to serve drinks or talk to customers. You would dance, get off stage and into the pink Cadillac and be driven to the next club; you would go around and around all night. So you'd spend all your time with the other girls.

Those were the days when everyone did drugs; these women would take anything—the most amazing combinations. I wasn't a big druggie, so I was always ending up having to work hard at the end of the night, because someone would be passed out. Anyway, these women would tell great, incredible stories—especially once the drugs got going. So what I did was: I copied them down. But I didn't want to be like a sociologist, so I would retell them in the first person, then put in some of my dreams. I had all this text consisting of these great stories plus my dreams—there was a murder story; some things were pretty wild!

◆ **V: Were you ever married?**

◆ KA: I was married twice. The first time I got married because that was the only way I could get money from my parents. But it didn't *mean* anything; we were hippies—I was 19 years old. The second time I got married was because I'd lived with this guy for 6 years and thought I was dying. I had this lump in my breast and the doctors said it was cancerous, but it turned out to be just this cyst.

Actually, getting married fucked up the relationship. It was sick, because before we'd had kind of a good relationship worked out; we'd lived together for six years. We didn't have sex anymore; it was just a family thing, we both had our lovers. So I just thought we'd be *partners*—besides, our families expected this. But after we got married, he got jealous of my lover—all that baggage came in. So now I think it's a bad idea to get married—besides, everyone starts treating you like this "couple."

◆ **AJ: When you first started getting tattoos, was this as an expression of reclaiming the body?**

◆ KA: Well, when I first got tattoos I did so because I just thought they were so beautiful . . . Tattooing seemed to be a real form of art—an *amazing* form of art, because it's art that's on your flesh. So you have a certain relationship to the artist that's very close—it's magical, really.

Some people see me as a bit weird because I have tattoos and I'm a woman (you know: if a woman has a tattoo, it's supposed to be a very delicate little one that's hidden on her breast or somewhere; you're not supposed to *do* these things). I guess I thought, "I'm old enough—I can start doing what I want. I'm over the age of beauty anyway, so what the hell!" After the age of 30, you're not supposed to be "beautiful"—so then you can start having *fun!*

If, every day I thought about all the things I'm not "supposed" to do because I'm a woman, and all the ways in which I'm not supposed to be—*I couldn't exist.* What I've done is: I've buried all that in my mind. And there's an amazing strata of anger in me—when it's touched, it just comes ripping out! So I don't think about tattooing as a way of asserting control over my own body—although it obviously *is*—because I can't touch that anger every day. It's not that I dislike men—I don't at all, but I dislike the fact that because you're a woman, you can't do things . . . that the word "NO!" is the very first word you learn and it's burnt in your flesh.

◆ **AJ: I think most women really have to deal with that bedrock of rage and anger.**

◆ KA: Well, we were taught to channel anger, rage, feelings of insecurity—to channel what would-be "negative" energy *masochistically*. We were taught not to do it *directly*—not to go out and hit someone, for example—but to do it so we'd hurt *ourselves*. And that's a typical feminine ploy to deal with power . . . in a way it's because you *don't* have power, but you're *looking* for power.

◆ **AJ: At the same time this gets inverted when you make a beautiful artwork on your skin—**

◆ KA: I think this is a bit how art is created. Julia Kristeva has written a book, *Powers of Horror*, about this: art doesn't come from a gesture that resembles one man going to hit another man; art comes from a gesture of power turned against itself. She calls it "ejection": when you take that emotion and turn it *in* on itself—which is what tattooing does, or what women do. And I'd say women are almost "natural" artists—we're just trained to do that over and over, so we have an amazing sense of beauty. And we decorate ourselves; we constantly walk around the world finding patterns of sensuality.

Makeup isn't frivolous; it's another form of art. And what we've done with our bodies is a form of art throughout the ages . . . yet it's always been put down. Whatever we do—that we learn how to dress well, or decorate our bodies a certain way, or walk a certain way . . . that we learn how to be elegant and charming and how to please people—all this is ridiculed, yet it's a form of art—a very high art! Again, I think a certain range of feminists have been scared by this, so they say, "Oh god—I won't wear makeup." And that's absolutely ridiculous.

◆ **AJ: Underlying all that is the *denial of the body,* the denial of what women have excelled in. Going back to your tattoos: how do people react to them?**

My first roommate at college ran an orgy in the room. She covered the whole room with green carpet and mattresses and it was like *orgy-time!* I moved out after 3 weeks because I never knew who was going to be in my bed, and it was hard to study.

◆ KA: Most people tell me they like them. I've never gotten anything negative from a guy . . . only women. I think it's the women who are more scared, because what women have done is to internalize this bad girl/good girl distinction, and out of fear say, "I've got to be a good girl; I'm not going to be a bad girl." So *they're* the ones who really get down on the so-called bad girls. I think women are really scared of taking control of themselves, and the men—well, there seems to be some crisis; the men seem to be absolutely *floundering* about: "Should they be strong? Should they be weak? How should they act? Maybe it's better to hide in a hole." Men don't know what to do at all—they don't want to appear to be the macho pigs they *are*. So everybody's walking around in fear these days, because the roles are absolutely not clear anymore.

Now in the battered wife relationship, it seems to me that to begin with: something is done to the woman

against her will. Usually it's in a situation of dependency—there's economic dependency, or children—for whatever reasons, she feels she can't leave this man who's been beating her. So she *takes it*—she does not leave at that point. But this is definitely against her will; she's not *asking* to be beaten. And when you're in a relationship (it doesn't even have to be one in which you're being *hit*) where the other person starts doing bad things to you, but you're scared to leave the relationship, you can start to think that *pain is pleasure* . . .

I dislike the fact that because you're a woman, you can't do things . . . that the word "NO!" is the very first word you learn.

We're very adaptable. It's well-known that some of the Jews in Auschwitz adapted to the concentration camp, which is probably as hard a form of adaptation as you can do. Some women who are in a situation which is terrible for them don't see a way out, so they adapt. And one way to adapt is: to find pleasurable what is not, because you can't live in total pain all the time. Even physically, if you undergo a lot of pain, your endorphins will switch around and start interpreting it as pleasure. Or you'll just numb out . . .

Look—I don't know why various people want pain. I think there's a huge number of reasons. Let's say we divide "sensation" into: pain and pleasure. Everyone thinks they understand why you would want pleasure, but not pain . . . but pain can be *interesting*. First of all, when you body-build, in order to really build you have to go through pain—you *burn*. If you don't burn, you don't build. The first time I burned, I wanted to run away, but my trainer said, "No! Just go *through* the pain." And I learned how to relax and not fight pain, and I think that's not a bad technique to learn. In certain tribes, rites of passage (when you go from one stage to another) involve a great deal of pain. That's another kind of pain, and that would be to physically shock you into another level of awareness (I've never done a rite-of-passage, so I don't know). There's a quote from Nietzsche: "That which does not kill you, will only make you grow."

I don't know how to talk about a utopian world. We live in *this* world and there's a lot of suffering. If you learn how to deal with physical pain, maybe you can deal with what's really much greater pain. Now if we're talking about an S&M relationship—the ones I know about are just *play*, really, which means if there's some pain it's "scratch pain"—little razor blade cuts which every kid does, a little play with dangerous weapons—*toys!* We're

not talking about huge amounts of pain. And I'm just talking about my own experience; I know that many people have done other stuff—there's a realm of S&M relationships that are very dangerous. But I think there's a way in which you play with what you most fear in order to learn how to deal with it—that's one thing you do. Another thing is: you're curious about your body—how will your body react to this? And it's not only just pain, it's also how you react in terms of being *controlled*. So you play with various areas.

Sexuality and play are very close, and when people start repressing and denying that play aspect, it's absolutely silly. I used to be terribly scared of cigarettes and fire, and this German boyfriend said to me, "Look, Kathy, I'll show you a game German kids play." And what they do is, they take lit cigarettes and just toss them back and forth from hand to hand. And they're doing it so fast that it doesn't burn. But I was frightened out of my mind; it took ages before I'd trust him enough to play this game with him. So I think it's all very complicated . . .

♦ **AJ: There's a continuum between pain and sexuality. Even "normal" sex includes biting and scratching.**

♦ **KA:** Well, my body is such that—it's very personal, but I have a tremendously overactive clit that can almost not bear to be touched—I'd prefer to be touched on almost *any* other part of my body than to have my clit touched! So the average man who wants to be a non-macho pig wants to go down on you, right? But I go, "Don't do it; absolutely do *not* do it! Spank me, do anything—here's a whip—but do not go *near* that!" Now that's not like I'm some victim or I'm being submissive; this is *my* body—I've got a weird body! [laughs] That's what I mean: sex is so unique from person to person. And from what a lot of my girlfriends tell me, I'd say about 50% of them don't cum from being fucked. No one's ever gone into this one, like: *how do you cum?* And if we talk about all the different ways we have to play, what we have to do to cum, what really gets us off—all this is *forbidden*. Yet this is the realm of pleasure!

♦ **AJ: And there's that continuum between pain and pleasure—**

♦ **KA:** That's what I mean: it *hurts* me to have my clit touched. Whereas if I get spanked it doesn't hurt as much, and I'll cum much faster! That's just the way my body is.

♦ **AJ: If you let a person spank you, can someone accuse you of being traditionally submissive?**

♦ **KA:** No one who knows me calls me submissive; just people who read my books get on this track: "All the women are so submissive." Well—not really! [laughs] A typical scenario goes: some guy wants to go down on me, and I go, "Don't do it! Don't do it!" And they feel very hurt, because guys now have this grand thing in their mind that if they do this wonderful thing of going down on you, you should be eternally grateful, and how can you deny this to them—it's as if you told them they had a small cock or something. I try to suggest, "Why don't you spank me a little?" and they go [gasp], "I couldn't do something like that!" And I go, "Oh yes you could!" "Oh no, I can't!" Here I'd say I'm not being submissive at all! I'm trying to make *them* submissive to what *I* want, and trying to figure out how to connive them into doing precisely what I want.

They always say the masochist is in control, and to some extent that has to be true. Because if the masochist isn't controlling, then it's rape or some horror story or it's a crime. I once asked this German boyfriend, "Why does a sadist *do* it? I don't get it. Why does anyone want to go to all that trouble? I get off so much more than you do. You don't get any pleasure out of this. What do you get out of this? What do you like?" And he said, "It's the tension." Yet the masochist is controlling that tension—there'd be no tension otherwise.

This boyfriend just loves situations of more and more tension. And it's not like I'm controlling—he's controlling, really. It just gets into this incredible amount of tension so you don't know *who's* controlling; you just keep pushing the situation so you can get the most tension out of it. It's like you set up an area of play and you just see how far you can go. Then it gets a little addictive so you have to stop, because it can get a little dangerous. It's like playing, "Let's go out into the street and see if cars will run us over!" It's kids' games, and I'm just a big kid; I've just never properly grown up. So I like motorcycles, I like kids' games. I don't really see this as being submissive at all. If we play a game about being submissive, it's just to get the tension going . . . to see how far everybody can get pushed. You do that in friendships; you push each other and see how far you can go.

Photo: Jill Posener

♦ **AJ: Here one word is covering two *very* different situations.**

♦ **KA:** Actually, submissive women freak me out; I like women who know what they're doing . . . I guess everybody makes a choice, somewhere down the line: that they're going to abide by society's rules and hide in their nice suburban house and do just what they're told and they're not going to step out of line—and maybe, just *maybe*, they'll be "safe." (I don't know what they'll be "safe" for, however.) My father made this type of decision; I saw him get a heart attack and suddenly he realized that he wasn't safe—he was about to die. He had done everything by the rules and it hadn't done him a goddam bit of good . . . he had *nothing* to hold on to. Because he didn't have any values—all his values were the values of society, they weren't his. There was nothing *in* him.

I think the other choice is: to find what your value is . . . to find who you are and where your energy is, where your ground is, where your guts are, where your centers are—however you want to put it. People are searching for their centers (be they centers of pleasure, pain, whatever) but really in a way it's a search for "god." And in this search—that's when someone starts being interesting, and stops being like jello. There are various ways of going about this search for "god."

Those of us who don't want to split the mind and the body go through ways that are considered abnormal, and

play is definitely an area where you can investigate certain things with some realm of safety. Because you've seen various artists who have died in this attempt—and you *don't* want to die! But it's a dangerous search, obviously, because there aren't many guidelines. I think that's what we're really talking about, and I don't want to take sex away from that. But really, it's all about this *search*. And we're being denied it by our repressive society.

♦ AJ: **It's about facing death, which your father couldn't do—**

♦ KA: Yeah! We're all going to die; that's the one *given* we've got. We know it, but what we *don't* know is what this life is about!

♦ AJ: **We try to keep the mind/body together and not have that repressive split. Because in order to get illumination you cannot deny the body.**

♦ KA: Well, there were ways in which nuns and monks denied the body in order to get farther. I think there's a way in which the energy comes up another way, but that's very radical . . .

A gay friend of mine said something interesting to me. I asked her if she differentiated between gay and straight women, and she said, "Yes, women who are gay are really outlaws, because we're totally outside the society—*always.*" And I said, "What about people like me?" and she said, "Oh, you're just *queer.*" Like—we didn't exist?! [laughs] It's as if the gay women position themselves as outside society, but meanwhile *they're* looking down on everybody who's perverse! Which is very peculiar. . .

In a relationship where the other person starts doing bad things to you, but you're scared to leave the relationship, you can start to think that *pain is pleasure* . . .

♦ AJ: **This happens a lot to outlawed minorities, who try desperately (in a denial fashion) to gain some sort of acceptance. In the tattoo world, there used to be almost this hatred of piercing, because the tattooers were trying to make tattooing "respectable."**

♦ KA: Everyone makes these arbitrary "definitions" in order to establish how "straight" they are.

♦ AJ: **It was like:** *"Tattooing's pretty normal . . . but god forbid you have a pierced nipple!"*

♦ KA: When I used to work as a stripper, all the strippers didn't want any whores in the club, right? So these 3 transvestite whores came in one night, and the strippers were screaming: "Get them *out* of here; we don't want women like that in here! We're *good* women!" [laughs]

♦ AJ: **You're still damned—you may as well be as outrageous as you wanna be!**

♦ KA: Well, I'm not much of a moralist that way. I have a friend who's always getting lipo-something, or getting her face changed—she does that. But tattooing—to me, it's a form of art and I'm dealing with a tattooer who's putting his/her art on my body. Whereas if I got lipo-whatever, it would be to conform to an image that's presented in *Vogue* or *Cosmopolitan*. A lot of women my age are heavily into dieting—to me that's another form of that lipo-stuff. They're basically anorexic. Whereas I eat like a pig, but I body-build—so I don't eat *enough*. I can't stand surgery—it drives me nuts. I once had a little cyst in my breast taken out, and I said, "*Never again!* Even if I get cysts in my breasts—I don't care!"

I saw this film by Jennie Livingston, *Paris Is Burning*, about Puerto-Rican and Black queens who dress up to be whoever they want, and they have contests. By my standards it was very radical, because they'd want to be the richest man in the world, or they'd want to be the head of the Pentagon, or they'd want to be a fashion model—there was no irony, it was like Postmodernism without the irony. They wanted to be just whoever they wanted to be without any politics or idea of "Left" or "Right" or whatever. And they went in and sort of showed off; they did these kind of *Vogue*-like dances [like *Vogue* models going down a runway]. It was hot!

When interviewed, some of them said, "Listen, we know that in this society a gay black man is a piece of shit, and a gay black man isn't anything, so we've done this because we know this is how we're going to get what we want. This way I can be anything and people are finally going to accept me because I'm going to be famous!" I mean, they weren't dumb. And if plastic surgery were like that—I can see it. It's the sense of *play* that I like—I like the art, I like the play, I like the extremity of it. But just women going around getting their thighs skinny so some guy'll fuck them—ugh!

♦ AJ: **We're talking about two different things. If you really are obsessive and have this creative idea to remake your body, then doing it *by any means* (lipo-suction, facelifts) could be a creative art form. But most people have actually *given up* their creativity, so this kind of remaking of the body is used for societal control. Sometimes a woman might like her breasts, but her husband *doesn't,* so getting breast surgery is not even for *herself—***

♦ KA: —they're like puppets or zombies. These PR Queens who were doing the *Vogueing* were definitely searching; they weren't puppets . . .

♦ AJ: **The key factor is the motivation behind it, that searching—**

♦ KA: The difference between the liposuction/anorexic behavior of certain women, and women who get tattooed or do every extreme body modification, is: the first class of women are just looking to come as close as possible to certain norms that they've internalized. They've taken an image out of a magazine or they've taken a number of images and thought, "This is how I should look; this is how I should be." Whereas the second class of women are actively searching for who to be, and it has to do with *their own pleasure*, their *own* feeling of identity—they're not *obeying*—they're not obeying the normal society. They're looking—it's very different. And when you look, you know you're "failing," you know you're "inferior." You're inferior because you're *looking*; there's always something *missing*. And it's *interesting* when there's something missing—it's *not* interesting when people think they're "gods" in that very stupid way. It's interesting when there's suffering there, and people are full of feeling, and they're full of life, and they're constantly making choices.

♦ **AJ: There's something moving about people who are really searching: who have the honesty to face up and admit, "I am inferior." It's a continuum: facing inferiority, facing death, facing who you are . . .**

♦ KA: Yeah! All of us have had these choices. I mean: you could have married and had a nice suburban house and two dogs and a cat and three children (or whatever they have these days). But you've made the decision not to do that.

Photo: Dona Ann McAdams

♦ **AJ: Another thing: liposuction and facelifts are very different from going to a tattoo artist. Getting a tattoo is a participatory experience. It is not like being anesthetized and flopped on a table like a cadaver who has just given up her body and soul for a period of time to this medical "institution"—usually a *male authority figure*—and getting plastic padding inserted underneath your nipple. And liposuction is far more painful; for months afterwards you feel "wrecked," you can't exercise, and you have to keep your body wrapped up. Surgery is pretty serious; it takes about 6 months**

to fully heal.

♦ KA: You're really messing your body up, then. I hate pain!

♦ **AJ: Okay, if you hate pain, how does getting tattooed feel to you?**

♦ KA: I hate it! It's not a high for me to get tattooed; I just love the tattoos! My idea of a good tattoo is one that doesn't hurt while it's being done. I'm really not into the pain of tattooing. It's one thing to control 2 or 3 minutes of pain, but after an hour of pure pain I think, "Fuck it!" A tattoo that takes 20 minutes—that's a kind of high. But 2 hours—forget it!

It's one thing to play with pain in an S&M context where: you play with things you don't like because you're scared of them. I really hate pain, so when I play with it I'm just seeing if I can endure it. It's like building muscle: you see if you can do another repetition. And I really have this thing about: "Go another step! Just go farther! Just go over another hill—there's another hill. Just go one little step farther!" I love doing that sort of thing. But if something gets *boring* and it's just about repetitiveness or unpleasantness . . . if you're tattooed for 2 hours, all it is for me is unpleasant, and I'd rather not feel it. Because there's no play there, I'm not learning anything—

I think you'd agree there are various things in us—not all of which are kind, gentle, and tender. But you can explore these things without becoming a mass murderer . . . without causing *real* damage, without turning to *real* crime.

♦ **AJ: Can you talk more about rites of passage?**
♦ KA: From what I understand, a rite of passage means a real change; you go through intense trauma or intense modification. The nearest I experienced to that was when I studied with a Korean Zen Master for about a year and then did a 3-day session with him. That was probably the strongest experience I've ever had in my life! Basically, we just sat in a room for 3 days; we didn't do anything (although we got up and went to sleep in the evening. I don't like to talk about these things too high-falutin' because of people's reactions). And at the end I had an interview with him. It felt like he just put his hand into my mind—literally! It *was* the most incredible experience I've ever had; the most radical. Is that a rite of passage? I don't know. I was very high afterwards; I was walking into cars—nothing happened to me, I was totally safe, but I wanted to come down, so I called him up and asked, "I'm too high—how do I come down?" and he said, "You're supposed to enjoy it! Oh—go get drunk!" So I went and got drunk, and that took care of that . . .

We don't have anything in our society that allows us to do a rite of passage *communally*; we do everything individually. Our own search is all done individually; now and then we might tell each other about it, but we always have the feeling we're being a bit "outside" the society when we tell each other. I mean, ecstasy—be it sexual (or some other kind of orgy) should be taking place somehow in our "community"—and it's not. *Our society gives us nothing.* We have no rites of passage—we

have *nothing*—nothing that gives us any wisdom, that gives us any way of dealing with death, that gives us any way of going from one stage in life to another, or even telling us what a stage in our life *is*. We just grow up and earn money and have babies! And *work!* A holiday is degenerated from what should be ecstasy into sort of *Club Med!* We don't have any language with which to talk about these things.
♦ **AJ: That's why we're tripping over words all the time—**
♦ KA: Yeah! And then we make up these activities— tattooing and piercing—which is the nearest we get to a rite of passage. I mean, it's our way of doing it—that's what we're looking for.
♦ **AJ: Looking for what?**
♦ KA: Well, we're looking for a society that allows us *the fullness of what it is to be human,* I would think—it's hard to know because I've never been there! But I read about societies in which ecstasy and joy and certain areas of sexuality are venerated (not just in individual situations— or maybe it can be even individual experiences that go further). And: a whole range of feelings—really, a *fuller life!* I keep thinking: what we know of as "life" is so thin and juiceless and boring, frankly—we're ground into nothing before we even start out! I mean, take tattooing (which has been denied us for so long): it's beautiful, the colors are gorgeous, the images: if you have the tiger on you, you have the spirit of the tiger in you—that's *something:* to find out what it is to be an animal! We forget everything; we forget all of this!
♦ **AJ: Really, what we're talking about is: the quest for creativity, the quest for illumination—**
♦ KA: Well, I think that's what we *want!* We don't want to just work like *dogs—*
♦ **AJ: Or live on the surfaces of life.**
♦ KA: A "normal relationship" is usually a surface thing where you wake up and say to your husband, "Hi, honey!" and have breakfast together and bitch a little and at night get into bed and think, "Oh, I gotta fuck *again.*"
♦ **AJ: But there's also a societal control process to get rid of creativity in people, because that can be very dangerous: people exploring creativity, then taking power in the world.**
♦ KA: I guess there's always this argument about whether humans are naturally good or naturally have evil or very destructive things in them. Obviously we have some destructive urges in us. The feeling is that humans aren't totally good; they have to be *controlled* or else their violent destructive natures will come out. There are also libertarians who argue, "Humans are good; it's society which is repressive." I think you'd agree there are various things in us—not all of which are kind, gentle, and tender— readers of de Sade and Genet would probably agree on this point! But I think you can explore these things without becoming a mass murderer . . . without causing *real* damage, without turning to *real* crime.

One way of exploring these things is through *art;* there are various ways of doing this. We have to find out how to have a community where the highest priority is to explore these different paths—to find out what it is to be human—and yet not wreak total havoc on the society! How can we have this freedom, so that society's not repressive, and yet it's not a society of mass murderers! And I don't think it's worthwhile making the problem too simple—I think if it were simple, it would have been solved long ago!

♦ **AJ: In Western society, the body tends to be identified with women and children and with uncontrollable forces of "nature" that are dangerous—therefore they have to be repressed.**

♦ KA: It's like Nietzsche's "Myth of the Eternal Return": you can view the world without "god" as "demonic" (in which *you* make the "demons" or the "horrible" forces of the body). Whereas: if you simply *accept* the Eternal Return, then the body becomes the area of joy, and you value life and you value all the changes and all that is in flux. So, how we can institute a society where that search is both individual and collective at the same time?

What society has done is: tried to make the search simply individual; also, label those individuals who are searching *with their bodies* as "weird," "evil," "freaks," "queer"—whatever words you want to use. But we could proclaim, "We're normal!" because we *are* normal! It's normal to love your body; it's normal to *have* a body; it's normal to see through the body and feel through the body. And during ecstasy, the body and the soul are united. So that's where the discussion about S&M ends up, really—

♦ **AJ: —and any discussion about body modification as well. We don't have a community; there is no communion; we're doing this individually . . . and yet there are attempts at making extended families, little communities—among many tattoo people there's certainly a bond.**

♦ KA: And among certain artists there's a network that's been going on . . .

♦ **AJ: And this network has to support individuals in their search for self-knowledge—**

♦ KA: Of course! You get through trauma by re-living the trauma, be it in fiction or in play. You don't get through trauma by *burying* it and not saying that it happened. If your attitude to "evil" or to something bad that happened is to just say, "Oh no, it didn't happen"—to shove it away—that just throws away an opportunity to grow. So if you want to say, "Women are totally equal to men; how can you say that women are submissive?" (in other words: you can't be a feminist if you say women are "submissive"), that's just shoveling it underground. Of course women are submissive: they've been *trained* to be submissive—that's the problem! And we get nowhere by not announcing the problem! It's like when black people decide to use the word "nigger," it's terrific in a way. We should take the word "submissive" and write it on the sky!

A woman who does a cutting on herself and lets her-

self bleed a little is hardly as unhealthy as a man who beats up his own wife. What so-called "normal" people do is so disgusting, that—! Someone who deliberately puts a few cigarette burns on their body is so much more healthy—well, at least they're trying to deal with it—

♦ **AJ: The body really is the only thing that you can control, and if you put a mark on your own body, it will heal—at least *you* own it.**

♦ KA: I used to cut my wrists, and I didn't do it just to die. I think (if I can remember the emotions) it was like: "Look, this incident has really hurt you—just look at how it's hurt you, and stop it right now!" It was a moment of *self-confrontation;* a way of telling myself, "Cut it out!" Or else, I'd do this to freak out somebody: "Look how you're hurting me! Stop it right now!" So this probably was not the most direct way of dealing with it, but . . .

There's a story about James Chance—he did a gig at a Mafia club in New York. Afterwards he asked to get paid and they said, "Fuck you—we're the Mafia and we're not going to pay you!" So he took out a razor blade, and they took out their guns ("Is this guy going to go for us?") and he just held it to his wrist and started cutting . . . They were so freaked out that they just threw the money at him and yelled, "Get outta here!" ♦ ♦ ♦

Valie Export

A Viennese radical performance artist well ahead of her time, Valie Export was one of the first to use the female body to critique the male gaze. While working in the same environs as the Viennese Aktionists, she formulated her own philosophy, expressed as "Feminist Actionism." For the past 30 years Valie Export has produced Body Art, performance actions, photographs, screenplays, films, installations and important theoretical and historical writings such as "The Real and Its Double: The Body," and her manifesto, "Aspects of Feminist Actionism." Currently she divides her time between Vienna and Milwaukee, where she teaches in the film department at the University of Wisconsin.

♦ **ANDREA JUNO: Where did you grow up?**

♦ **VALIE EXPORT:** I was in an Austrian convent until I was 14. I was quite obsessed with religion and thought of Jesus as the man I really *wanted*. I liked making confessions, even though I had nothing to confess, because this was so exciting. I thought sins were good—they meant to be *against* something, so I made up fantasies to confess.

After that, I went to an art school. I was married for 2 years, had a daughter, then I divorced. I went to Vienna and continued my studies in design school: painting, drawing—this was 1960. At that time Ernst Fuchs and Hundertwasser [members of the Viennese Fantastic Realist Group] were really prominent. I met a group of Viennese poets (the Wiener Dichter Gruppe) and a bit later met the Viennese Aktionist group and saw their performances.

At that time I did drawings and painted a little. I was interested in Constructivism but wanted to work in new mediums, so I started working in photography and "expanded cinema." With expanded cinema I wanted to liberate celluloid from its constraints—to free celluloid from plots and objects. I wanted to expand the boundaries of the image, so I asked, "Where does the image begin? *A priori* with the mirror, or on the screen?" What was important to me wasn't the *materiality* of the image, but its shifting significance—liquidity in running water, its reflection—the *light*.

♦ **AJ: Describe what you were doing—**

♦ **VE:** At that time I was experimenting in different media. For example, I poured colored waters and liquids into a mirror and projected this onto a screen, creating all kinds of abstract patterns and moving images in *reality*, not mediated by celluloid or through the camera—

♦ **AJ: But what were some of the *ideas*?**

♦ **VE:** The main point was to question the materials, question the medias, question what could be done in art, question the society. In other words, question what the "aesthetic of art" means. Second, was to integrate how society reacts to these questions. Third, was the political message—art was not done to *please* society. In those days this kind of activity was called *Anti-Art*, or *No-Art*. This was not art that bourgeois people could look at and feel satisfied with. Art was a political tool to react against society, or what we called the "Establishment." The goal was to build up an anti-aesthetic of art, an anti-ideological art.

In my expanded cinema performances I used mostly the Body, along with media like film, photography, video and "reality." For me the Body was the most important material: it showed my identity or my non-identity. I started asking what identity means: "Where is my bodily identity? Where is my mental identity?" The body was an artistic tool to communicate my feminist points of view: "What does it mean to use the body?" I was concerned with the relatedness of: the Object, the Image and

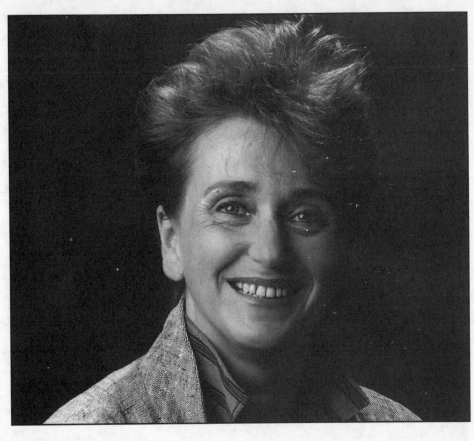

its Meaning. The body is a territory for itself, for society ... for the private sphere as well as the public sphere. It's a territory where the self-portrait and portraits of society affect or determine one another.

In my body performances I tried to make my body "inhabitable" for me — I wanted to create or produce what I would consider an "inhabitable" body. I wanted to suspend the ideological dogma of the body, and to make clear the relationship of inner reference to outer reference. The resistance that reality offers to the ego always reveals the power of the ego's *utopia*. I knew all the paintings by Surrealist women; my favorite painter was Dorothea Tanning; I also liked Leonora Carrington and Kay Sage. I knew how they used the female body: to disappear, to be transparent, or to be "decoded" (they didn't use that term then).

I felt it was important politically to use the female body to create art. I knew that if I did it naked, I would really change how the (mostly male) audience would look at me. There would be no pornographic or erotic/sexual desire involved — so there would be a *contradiction*.

My body was the most important tool; I felt it was important politically to use the female body to create art. So when I did my performance work, I usually did it naked. I was concerned with the male *gaze:* I knew that if I did it naked I would really change how the (mostly male) audience would look at me. There would be no pornographic or erotic/sexual desire involved — so there would be a *contradiction*.

For example, in 1973, I put a large plate of melted wax on the floor and arranged electrical wires in the shape of a man in the wax, then I laid naked in the outline. My body heat molded the wax around me into my shape. I was naked, yet because of the danger in the situation I was not "provoking" the men in the audience.

In 1968 I did a performance called the "Touch Cinema" at a street fair. I had strapped on a box enclosing my naked breasts, with holes that spectators could stick their hands through. I said, "This box is the cinema hall. My body is the screen. But this cinema hall is not for looking, it is for *touching* — it is tangible." I went out on the street and announced, "This is the 'Touch Cinema.' The state doesn't allow pornography, but *you* can feel free to experience the 'Touch Cinema' — but only for 13 seconds. However, when you do this, you will be seen and watched by everyone." So whoever came up and participated was interacting with the "screen" by touching it.

In Vienna I had won a prize for my film, *Ping Pong*, which countered the idea that you're never "free" when you're at the cinema — you always have to react how the director tells you to. If the director wants you to laugh or cry, you *have* to do it. So my film showed dots appearing which you played with as in a game of ping pong — it was a game between the director and the participant/consumer. This was a kind of "theoretical" film; it forced interaction with the screen — you "had" to play with the screen.

Then I was supposed to show my new film — my "Touch Cinema." I went onstage with my "box" and described what my new cinema was: that the audience could participate. I said that this was a feminist film, a "mobile film,"

Body and street action performance, "Touch Cinema," Munich, 1968.

Photo: Werner Schulz

and that you should come participate, and that *you will be seen* when you do that (that was the interesting point: that everybody could see you while you touched the

I strapped on a box enclosing my naked breasts, with holes that spectators could stick their hands through. I said, "This box is the cinema hall. My body is the screen. But this cinema hall is not for looking—it is for *touching*."

breasts). This actually was a very strong experience because, while participating, everybody stared into my eyes and I stared into theirs—everybody was *afraid*, really, during the encounter. A small riot broke out with the

audience shouting, "This isn't *cinema*—this is *nothing!* This shouldn't be allowed!" People started to fight, the lights were turned off, and the whole audience started chanting, "Export Out! Export Out!"

♦ **AJ: But did people actually touch your breasts?**

♦ **VE:** Yes, but not very many because then people started to fight onstage. They *hated* this contradiction: that the object of desire is standing in front of them and you *can* have it—but you have to *do* something for it. You're not in an intimate sphere now, you're in a public sphere and *that's* where you can have it. So I offered my body in the way *I* wanted to.

♦ **AJ: It's so wonderfully confrontational: for a man to have his object of desire so "boxed in"—defusing any erotic potential—**

♦ **VE:** The newspaper declared, "We cannot burn witches because it's forbidden now, and we cannot burn celluloid because it doesn't burn well, so we also cannot burn Valie Export." The next day I repeated the "Touch Cinema" on the Munich streets and people liked it—they thought it was really great. Fathers with kids did it first, then let the children do it. Mostly men participated, but a few women did, too. The police were standing there and they just laughed. This was reported in newspapers and magazines as a joke; it was even incorporated into a movie.

♦ **AJ: This is an amazing experiment—**

♦ **VE:** Mostly it was against the state notion of sexuality; it was a political action for sure. I used cinematic terms: "It's a cinema hall, and the body is the screen which you can touch. You will be seen; the gaze will be on you." And it was a political action to do this on the streets.

♦ **AJ: How did other performance artists react?**

♦ **VE:** Most of the men didn't accept it and were against me—they laughed at me or said, "That's feminist shit," or, "There's no need for that." I didn't have support from men or from women. Other women didn't like me because what I did was too "suspect" for them: to use my own body, to be naked in front of an audience, and to get the audience involved in what you're doing. So I had a lot of enemies—female enemies, too; they really hated me when I did that.

At the time I was divorced; I was independent, but in the midst of this group of Viennese artists. I never participated in an *Aktionist* performance because they had a different concept, but perhaps the most important thing was the feeling that everybody was in revolt against the status quo. The climate in those days supported everybody, including me.

I performed and called my performances *Media Aktionism*, because I used media—this was the great difference

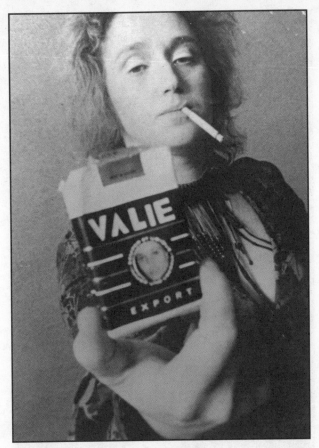

Valie Export cigarettes

"Genital Panik," 1969

between me and the Viennese Aktionism. What I did was a kind of "feminist" *Aktionism*, using the body but in a different way than they did. When I worked with the body, I used it as a code or a sign, in a semantic way—I never used it in a spiritual way or a biological way.

I was born in 1940, and in the '50s when I was curious about sex and the body, people would say, "Don't talk about that! I hate that!" This was a post-Nazi Austrian society, which really hasn't changed much from the way it was before World War II. I wanted to react against the rules and the order of society with its notions of how you "should" be; and against "art." So it was always "against" or "anti" behavior. But later on I realized that this had something to do with the time when I grew up. I used religious materials occasionally in my work, in protest against State Authority and Church Authority, and I discovered how much my identity was involved or invested in this society, and how I have to *change* . . .

I did one performance which is an example of how you can really change the male gaze (or cannot; I don't know!) . . . use the naked body as a sign, as a code; put something in a new context. I put a glass window on the floor next to some broken glass. I rolled my naked body on the window and the audience was very quiet. Then I rolled on the broken glass and the audience started yelling at me to *stop*, that they couldn't stand seeing this, that it must hurt—they hated it! I wasn't bleeding because I used very small panes of glass; this wasn't masochistic. It was a "context variation": I was using the same material

Body Sign Action Tattoo,
Frankfurt, 1970

Photo: Gertraude Wolfschwenger

that I wanted to live on my own, not in a close relationship. I wanted to make my own decisions and be responsible for myself. Since my divorce I've lived alone; it doesn't mean I don't have relationships, but I don't want to ever again have this feeling of *dependence*.

Maybe this was the goal of human beings from the very beginning: to kill themselves. Maybe the whole nature of the planet is summed up in the one word: *suicidal*.

I did a performance with a dead bird in which I poured liquid wax over this bird and over my hands. But in my description and photographs of it I said I had a *living* bird. So everybody thought I killed that bird—I did not; this was trick photography. This was also an example of the fact that photography can lie; that representation can be a *fake*. And this inspired a huge campaign against me; I was labeled an animal-killer, a witch, and a *feminist!* I lived alone at the time and felt that no man was behind me to defend me. Some people called up and said, "We're standing right in front of your door—we're going to break in and kill you now!" I called a friend to come over. Then, when I got more threatening phone calls, he picked up the phone and got a different reaction entirely—*then* the callers asked why he was with this *terrible woman*. But when *I* picked it up, they said they wanted to kill me or "do something" to me—kind of pornographic threats.

People put signs on my door and I got a lot of letters with skulls and things like that on them. I had to change my phone number. But I knew that if I had had a man behind me, the threats wouldn't have been so terrible—"having a man around" made a big difference.

◆ **AJ: A woman acting as a free agent is far more**

Stills from the film *Man & Woman & Animal*, 1973

in different contexts—first I used normal glass, then broken glass. And I used my body to "research" what the difference was, for this kind of analysis of the male gaze.

◆ **AJ: But wasn't the audience horrified because of the implications of the glass cutting a naked woman's body and producing blood—**

◆ **VE:** That was the purpose: to change the male gaze. The man can see you naked . . . yet he cannot see you the way he *wants* to see a naked female body.

◆ **AJ: How have your personal relationships evolved?**

◆ **VE:** At that time I lived alone. It was a conscious decision. I was married for two years and figured out

threatening to people. And if you're with a man, the implication is that you're some man's problem; *you're* not the problem. The man is the intermediary.

♦ VE: So if you live alone you can gain a lot of power in that men really are afraid of *you*.

♦ AJ: And if you lived with a man you would actually be more protected, but it wouldn't be *your power*—the power would belong to the man. That's the bargain women make.

♦ VE: I had to live alone, because if I do something and some man is behind me, it means *I'm* not really doing the real truth. If you live alone, it's more courageous. I didn't live alone just to *consciously* be more courageous, but when I live that way truth seems stronger to me—stronger than when you live in a "family way."

♦ **AJ: For the past 20 years you've lived alone?**

♦ VE: Yes. Sometimes it's hard, but I think it's more honest, more true for me. My art became more congruent with my life.

♦ **AJ: Don't you think life and sexuality are more conservative now then in the "wilder" '60s and '70s?**

♦ VE: All around it's much more conservative. Right now I'm working on a script involving a transsexual gender-crossing. This is very interesting, because then you don't have an identity of only one sex. For me, the

"Erosion," Body—Material—Interaction, Amsterdam, 1970

problem is: how to act and react in society when you have this gender-crossing. If you're no longer "female" or "male," should your life be determined by your biological gender? Whether your relationships are man/man, woman/woman, or heterosexual, there should be a kind of interaction between *all* the genders. So for me this is a main point: to have *both* female and male qualities in myself. My identity in society should not be determined by gender—therefore, society should be *changed*.

♦ **AJ: I'm very enthusiastic about the notion of**

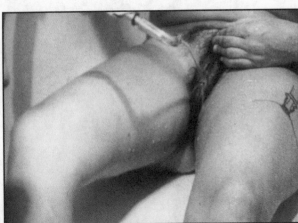

191

Body Action, 1973.

gender-blurring and subverting traditional gender roles. This is one of the key liberating ideas of our time. For several thousand years we've had a biological imperative to multiply and fertilize the earth with very structured gender identities—men "seeding" and women bearing the children, but now with overpopu-

Body Action, 1973.

lation that's positively suicidal—

♦ VE: That's why I want to work out this gender paradigm toward an inter-gender model: *not* to be determined by this dualism, *not* to be determined by this gender in which I may have been born biologically, but *instead* have this gender-crossing.

♦ AJ: How would one define being female or male, anyway? Where do you see our world going?

♦ VE: If it goes like it's going, a lot of people will be killed. This Gulf War was not a *real* killing war; it was a small *exercise* in how to do that. If our planet proceeds, it means a lot of minorities will be killed by the majority, because the majority think they have the *right* to do that—and they *want* to do it. And not only kill by bombs, but by denying education: not giving people the right education, so they cannot really grow, and have to live in inferiority and slums. In Peru there's an epidemic of cholera—it's easier to let the disease kill them, just as AIDS is killing people in Africa. A lot of people will be killed in the next decade, but this doesn't mean that the planet really will survive. People not only are killing people, but people are also killing the planet.

We're in a state of permanent war, however you turn around. The planet has *always* been at war; war has never stopped. Even if you have peace, peace is just part of the war that never stops.

♦ AJ: At least war makes it clear what's really going on, whereas during "peace," death, cruelty and destruction are going on everywhere anyway.

♦ VE: Maybe this was the goal of human beings from the very beginning: to kill themselves. This is very cynical, right? Maybe the whole nature of the planet is summed up in the one word: *suicidal.* Because the urge seems too strong now. I don't know how to change this.

♦ AJ: I think the only way we can change things is to delve deeply into our most underlying philosophies and original myths—they're responsible for what's going on now—

♦ VE: The planet is dying—the time is over. This could mean it goes for 200, 300 or even 500 more years, but maybe not. It's not because of the atomic bomb—that's not the threat now. It's the "human being" *philosophy*—

that's the underlying structure that's making the planet die. Because this structure has yet to change.

◆ **AJ: But that's where I have a glimmer of hope, because a handful of people are trying to analyze all our belief structures, from the bottom on down** [laughs] **. . . Even though the planet resembles a train going a hundred miles an hour with only a couple more feet of rails left before the cliff!**

◆ VE: Yes, so I don't have so much hope. We don't exactly know the whole history of this planet, but after a certain point the human being changed into a suicidal being whose only goal was to create suicide. That's terrible, but that's the way it seems to be. Maybe an intense consideration of the problem of cross-gender could help us break up our rigid belief structure. But maybe the group of people who want to consider problems like this is too small. Although—who knows what *determination* can accomplish?

◆ **AJ: In gender-blurring, certain gays and lesbians really are *"pioneers"* of the new world—**

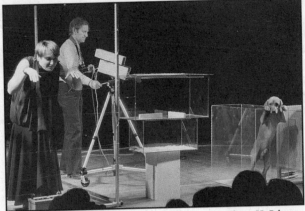

Photo: M. Schuster

Restricted Code Performance, Munich, 1979

> **An intense consideration of *cross-gender* could help us break up our rigid belief structure. The "phallic society" is *dead*.**

◆ VE: They give hope for the future. The "phallic" society is *dead*. It's still alive, but only because everything hasn't been destroyed yet . . . it can only work as long as there's something *left* to destroy!

◆ **AJ: And in the United States, schools are closing—that's shocking; it's so barbaric. I think there's an underlying agenda: to make the U.S. as much of a third world country as possible, so life will be like it was in the feudal age where only 10% of the population had the money to get educated.**

◆ VE: As I said before, their intention is to deny education—or give the *wrong* education.

◆ **AJ: We're exploring the liberation and enlightenment that comes from having the *tools of education* to liberate ourselves creatively, because only through *creation* are we truly alive to create new thoughts—and they want to stamp that out. . . Are you connected with other female performance artists?**

◆ VE: Mostly filmmakers; sometimes also performance artists, and more with females than males. But I'm not in a group with anyone. I stopped doing performances because I thought if I *repeated* something, then it's not really "true" anymore. My special theme was feminism, but

after 10 or 12 years doing performances I felt I had said it all. I had to take the next step, so now I do mostly filmmaking: feature-length films and avant-garde short films on video and celluloid. These days there are a lot of good films and videos dealing with gender issues or with "anti" issues—whether it's filmic language or political issues or a video about AIDS.

◆ **AJ: Can you talk about your tattoo?**

◆ VE: I felt that my body is skin, but it's also a page. And I drew something on my page—my own drawing, my own sign, my logo, and it stays there forever, and when I die it's over. I got it in '71.

◆ **AJ: Your tattoo is shocking because it seems so contemporary—very few people conceived of an abstract black-and-red design back in '71. Did you say it was also a garter belt? It looks more like an abstract representation of one, and that's very pioneering. What did this garter belt mean to you?**

◆ VE: It's a symbol of the fact that you have these stockings and this *kind* of erotic paraphernalia . . . and it's also a symbol of a definition of a woman that's now obsolete. Because the garter has to do with a kind of stockings which are connected to a certain definition or identity; that you belong to a certain "type" of woman. But now that's over; you have your own identity. So it's like carrying around an old historical antique with you—

◆ **AJ: But that tattoo marked a changing point for you?**

◆ VE: Exactly, it's like a vestigial tail. I have this tattoo, but when I die I won't need it anymore—it's over with. And a vestige refers to something that takes a long period of time to change. The guy who tattooed me refused to do the design the way I *really* wanted, which was to have a snake wind around my back up my shoulders and onto my cheek; he said, "If I did that, you could never get *married!*"

◆ **AJ: Some people use tattoos as historical markers, to mark time—**

◆ VE: So you can look at your body when you're sixty, and see all that's gone on in your life. You can remember all these significant events . . .It's true . . . ◆ ◆ ◆

Susie Bright

Susie Bright is the best known lesbian sex writer in America. She was editor of the pioneering feminist erotica magazine, *On Our Backs* (whose editorial policy proclaims, "Entertainment for the Adventurous Lesbian!") and *Herotica: a collection of women's erotic fiction.* Known as the "X-rated intellectual," she has packed theaters across the country with her workshops, lectures and lesbian safe sex demonstrations. Some of her articles—delving into rarely discussed topics such as vaginal fisting—have been published in her recent best-seller, *Susie Sexpert's Lesbian Sex World.* Besides writing five books, numerous articles, X-rated film reviews (for *Penthouse Forum*), and appearing in a dozen TV, film and video productions, Susie has given some classic sex-educational presentations—particularly, "How To Read a Dirty Movie," which was illustrated with sizzling film clips. Susie Bright lives in San Francisco with her daughter, Aretha. She can be contacted at 3311 Mission St. #143, San Francisco, CA 94110.

Part I

♦ **ANDREA JUNO: Tell us about your background—**

♦ **SUSIE BRIGHT:** If you knew what it was like to be ten years old in 1968 in Los Angeles, I shouldn't have to explain further! My family was influenced by the counter-culture and the politics of the '60s. At the time I was going to a parochial school, and my parish girl scout troop collapsed because of *Beatlemania*—this was when John Lennon was saying the *Beatles* were more important than Jesus. In meetings, all we wanted to do was play *Beatles'* albums and scream and get sexually excited until we peed in our pants!

It was a time when people were dressing up as hippies for Halloween. Reagan was the governor of California, and I was so vehemently against his administration, his treatment of student protestors and his attitude toward the Vietnam War that I did my own neighborhood campaign. I used a crayon that Crayola has now discontinued—"Red Orange"—and made several posters against Reagan's election campaign, signing them, "Concerned Citizens of California." I made about 9 signs and couldn't spell "Concerned Citizens of California" right, even once! I stuck them surreptitiously on people's mailboxes.

My parents lived outside America during the '50s and then returned. They were very interested in the Civil Rights movement and the Beatnik movement and the Folk Music movement . . . all of the *questioning* of the U.S. establishment which was taking place in the "all-American way"—my parents were not the most radical people on earth. As the "counter-culture" grew, I felt very affected by it in a revolutionary way, like: *something was very wrong here.* It's no accident that by the time I got to high school and started meeting radicals and underground newspapers and socialists and Yippies and acid-dropping freaks, it was right up my alley—I had been waiting to grow up to be part of that group.

I wanted to change the world; I wanted to be in a big circular waterbed with all my friends, sharing the "Bohemian" ideals of sexual freedom and imaginative social welfare.

♦ **AJ: There was something in the air then; changing the world was not disconnected from changing sexuality in the world—**

♦ **SB:** If you're raised Catholic, you get a lot of very explicit information about the "Do's and Don'ts" of sexual morality. And if you're up for questioning any of it, you're going to have a field day! When I started masturbating I didn't even know the *word* until years later. I thought the devil had gotten inside of me, but I was

somewhat accepting of that—like, there wasn't a whole lot I could do about it. One thing I *did* do was: I stopped going to confession, because I couldn't imagine talking about this to a priest. The only people in the church I could relate to were nuns who were taking off their habits and letting you see their hair for the first time, organizing anti-war *masses* outdoors with painted banners.

At that age, if there was a God, it was Mom—and my mother was divorced. She would never take communion because she'd been "excommunicated," and she was really mad about that!

♦ **AJ: Why—because she had been divorced?**

♦ **SB:** Yes! Consequently she would go to church with me, not take communion and make sarcastic remarks about the priests the entire time. So I was getting these mixed messages: even though we went every Sunday,

she was always making fun of the church and its hypocrisy. She would tell me stories about when she was little and you were never supposed to look at your body, and how patent leather shoes would reflect up your dress and reveal something . . . and how the nuns put talcum powder in your bath water so you would not see your body as you were bathing. She told me these stories to show how silly and stupid these ideas were.

However, when it came to talking about sex itself, my mother was shy. Once I was listening to the *New Lost City Ramblers* sing about when God discovers that Adam and Eve have pinned fig leaves over their genitals. I asked, "Mom, what does 'pinning leaves' mean?" And she turned really red and couldn't tell me. The next day she gave me a little pink book called *A Baby Is Born*. She wanted me to have a scientific, rational approach to sexuality so I wouldn't be scared by it like when she was growing up,

Susie's first performance, Berkeley, 1963

ground can be used to justify a person becoming a deviant, a pervert, or a Bohemian. If I said, "I came from a white-bread, 2.5 children WASP family," then my rebellion would be a "textbook example." Yet if I had "liberal" or divorced or otherwise unusual parents, that also would explain why "she became the raving queer she is today"!

♦ **AJ: You can twist anyone's background to support any theory you want. Like you, I grew up in the '60s and think something very special happened then that to some degree I'm lamenting, because the next generations won't have that feeling that you can *change the world*. I think this generation feels so defeated that they don't realize they have the right to get outraged; they're just *surviving!*

♦ SB: I know; that feels really sad. It's funny because those of us who were influenced by the radical politics of the '60s—*we* were rejecting everything. We were rejecting a two-party system; we were rejecting the nuclear family; we were rejecting "job security"—all these things that other people had embraced as part of the future. We had optimism; an attitude of "Why the fuck *not?*" We felt we would "Bring the War Home" to this country; that political issues were meaningful, organizable and that you could *do* something about them. In the '70s by the time I was old enough to participate as an adult, I thought the movement was over. But compared to what's happening now, it was *thriving.*

Yet things have come quite a ways since I came of age sexually. The Gay Liberation movement grew, sexual minorities of all kinds began making their presence known (both in erotic and political ways). That's very exciting. Traditional left politics never knew what the hell to say about sex (except, "If it's under capitalist society, it must be bad"). Plus, our culture is so easily titillated by sex that it's hard to get beyond the shock value.

I think people *are* interested in doing art or political work on sexual issues—they want to have a sense of humor *and* they want to seize the state! They want to turn things upside down, but they refuse that pedantic approach that politics had before. Now they insist on the necessity for beauty; they want a sense of the surreal; maybe they want a sense of the spiritual; maybe they want a sense of the visceral. They just want a multi-dimensional approach to social change, and sexuality is so complicated that it really spits in the face of people who want to dogmatize their political issues.

♦ **AJ: How did you start to identify yourself as a lesbian—or do you?**

♦ SB: I started identifying with all kinds of sexual fantasies by just reading about sex. I didn't have any sexual experience at all—not even a kiss; not even holding someone's hand. It was just me and my sexual fantasies and my masturbating (although all that was very powerful) until I was 16.

My first sexual experience was with a man and a woman, and in one afternoon I went from no kissing to *everything!* I was very pleased with myself, and also felt this was an omen that I was bisexual (to me, "bisexual"

but she couldn't *talk* to me about it—so she gave me a book.

My parents gave me the gift of reading. When I was a kid, the only thing I got punished for was reading *too much*—I got my books taken away, because I wouldn't do my chores. Reading introduced me to a lot of grown-up ideas at a young age. Also, my mother was (and still is) very theatrical and loved to dance and *make-believe*, so I always had a big bag of clothes, high heels, pearls and hats to dress up in.

We moved a lot. Not having any continuous real-life friends, I had a major make-believe world. I had my sack of clothes and dolls and that was my only consistent social life: my little world. I would put on these little exhibitions and performances. My mother was my only dependable audience, and she loved that. Lots of moms want their little girl to learn to dance and sing and make music and just be "Little Miss Vivacious"—my personality was potentially that, anyway.

I often wonder about the question, "What's your background?" because either a normal or an unusual back-

was more of an anthropological than a political term). I was aroused by both the man and the woman and felt comfortable with both. I was so overimpressed by the "first-timeness" of it all that I really can't say what specifically stimulated me; I was just excited to be doing something. It all felt like the most natural thing in the world: to kiss *her*, to kiss *him*—to be with two people at the same time. I had my utopian dream then: I imagined that everybody was bisexual . . . and that if everyone would just get over their "hang-ups," we could all be having such a good time!

Then I became introduced to lesbian politics and the idea: "Why be with a man when you can be with a woman?" And there were all these reasons why. Now I completely disagree with the notion of having *reasons why* anyone goes to bed with anyone else, because my attractions have led me down so many strange paths with both men and women that there are no rational justifications or explanations. This is a perfect example of people trying to mix linear-brained politics with sexuality. Even though it was stimulating to ask: "Why do you feel you need to be with a woman?" or "Why do you need a man's approval to be an exciting, successful woman?" Politically, those questions were very arousing, but sexually, they didn't necessarily ensure *gratification*.

♦ **AJ: This is a key issue: taking a political stance, yet not being dogmatic about the varieties of sexuality which defy facile categorization—**

♦ SB: I was seduced by the feminist ideal of lesbianism—it made perfect sense that a woman would know best how to please and care for another woman. It was appealing because of course I loved women; women are fantastic; and anything that promotes women and loving women is *where it's at!* So those ideas were very easy to embrace. I enjoyed confronting the way I'd been raised to be a "wife" or "mother" . . . how I had been invested with certain notions of "femininity" that didn't fit me, and that I was longing to throw off my shoulders. I was *happy* to rebel. At the same time I was having affairs with women that didn't follow any particular lesbian-feminist prescription, but I wasn't taking myself to task for it: this was *life*. I had my political ideas and tried to incorporate them into my personal life, but when they didn't fit I lacked the insight to understand *why*; I needed to grow up a bit.

Sometimes I think, "What else could I do?"—I was 16. I still don't understand myself, and now I'm 33. Because I was too young and too scared to go to bars (I didn't know anything about gay bar life or the old gay world), the only lesbians I had contact with were women who all wore a certain "uniform" and carried a certain set of politics—and that's what I thought "lesbian" was. I didn't know any gay men whatsoever.

There was so much excitement uncovering the things we were fighting for, that I didn't stop and think, "Why is it that at my underground newspaper every woman involved in this collective has slept with each other, and none of the men have?" [laughs] For a long time I never really paused and thought about that; I just loved my group and was very loyal to them.

I'm proud of the fact that I was a member of the longest-lasting high school underground newspaper ever published in this country: *The Red Tide*. It fought a very important court case: the right of high school students to publish anything without prior censorship (just because they're minors), and I was the plaintiff in that case (it wasn't settled until long after I was out of high school). We won, although in a practical sense the victory was rather hollow, because ever since I graduated, high school students have more and more become prisoners in a little cage . . .

I wanted to change the world; I wanted to be in a big circular waterbed with all my friends, sharing the "Bohemian" ideals of sexual freedom and imaginative social welfare.

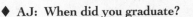

♦ **AJ: When did you graduate?**

♦ SB: I would have graduated in '76, but I left a year earlier. By that point I had joined a *grown-up* socialist organization which had come out of the "New Left." Our plan was to merge the student movement with the working class movement . . . to organize important unions and industries until we could do like the "Wobblies" had done, and force a General Strike!

So in the mid-'70s I got a solid, first-hand introduction to trade unionism. It was hard to just attend *high school* when I was on the ground floor of starting a teamster rank-and-file group—at five o'clock in the morning I'd be leafleting every teamster bar in L.A. county. Then I'd get a bundle of *Red Tides* and distribute them to other high schools in the district (because we had our *own* politics: "Narcs in the Schools!" or our "Gay Liberation" issue or our "Free Palestine!" issue—*whatever* was going on, we had something to do with it). I'd get to school around 9 AM and be *exhausted*. The idea that I was just supposed to sit there and discuss something like Alvin Toffler's *Future Shock*—I thought, "Are you kidding me?" I had a taste of influencing *real life* politics; I was writing propaganda on important issues of the day, and didn't feel like writing term papers on "Caste Systems in India." I was in Marxist study groups 3 nights out of every week, and didn't have time to participate in high school *bullshit*—so I left.

I wanted to start *Red Tides* all over the place. *Red Tide* was in Los Angeles and we joined forces with this incredible group in the Bay Area called the "Contra Costa Socialist Collective" which was formerly the "Red Polar Bear Party." It was a group of kids at St Ignacio Valley

High School—you never know where some band of radicals is going to emerge—but these kids turned things upside-down there. They did guerrilla actions against tract homes, they did environmental zap actions before *Greenpeace* was even on the scene—

♦ **AJ: These were** *high school kids*—

♦ **SB:** Yes, and a lot of us were living outside our parents' homes in communes—high school student flophouses. I left home when I was 17; I was lucky in that my father encouraged me. Some kids ran away and others—well, their families didn't *care*. We were busy little bees; after joining forces with the Contra Costa group, we decided to branch out to the Midwest. Realizing we were predominantly white, we wanted to have a more multiracial organization, so a group of us moved to Detroit and started the first *Red Tide* to hit the urban Midwest.

That was really incredible: you'd write about everything unfair going on in your high school—from the non-union lettuce in your hamburger to the fact that the principal was expelling anyone who wore a hat because it meant they were a gang member . . . to lies told in U.S. History class about black history or Indians . . . to criticizing the sexism in the school—you name it. We critiqued how some of us were being trained to be janitors or to be unemployed, while others were being tracked to go to college.

People *are* interested in doing art or political work on sexual issues—they want to have a sense of humor *and* they want to seize the state! They want to turn things upside down, but they refuse that pedantic approach that politics had before.

♦ **AJ: It's amazing that high school kids could do things like that. I remember when I was in high school we stopped school for a day to have a moratorium against the Vietnam War. I don't think that would happen nowadays—**

♦ **SB:** We had a high school strike against the war! We brought Jane Fonda to our high school in '73 when she was fresh out of Hanoi, and her talk was so intense that after the school bell rang and they yanked her microphone, a whole group of us just walked out of school to a nearby park to continue doing a *teach-in* against the war. And this was when Nixon was in Cambodia.

Our high school administration was so angry that they said the only way Jane Fonda could speak was if we had an "opposing view." So Bob ("B-1 Bomber") Dornan (one of the most successful right wing politicians from

Southern California) came to speak, and basically his position was, "Bomb Hanoi!" He and his wife were raving lunatics. We were attracting a lot of attention, and Ron Kovac (the Vietnam vet against the war who wrote *Born on the Fourth of July*) and other members of his veterans' group showed up. They were right in front in their wheelchairs heckling Bob: "Look at me, bud—I served in this war and *I* don't agree with you!" And Dornan's wife lost it—she started beating on these guys in wheelchairs with her purse! That kind of stuff I just don't see happening in high schools anymore. . .

We had "Women's Week" which was our alternative to the "Girls' Week" that was sponsored by our idiotic girls' dean (who was a dyke, of course). The *Red Tide* women got together with all the other feminist union women and formed this women's group. We decided we wanted a birth control information seminar, a lesbian panel, self-defense classes, a Holly Near concert, a "Women's History Day" . . . all to counteract the "Powder Puff" football cheerleading brigade and the "Mother/Daughter Bake Sale." And we did all that!

This was before I ever thought I would have children—at that time I didn't think it was "right" to bring children into such a shitty world. I knew people couldn't believe that *teenagers* could be this politically active and intellectually aware, and have the brains and the know-how to pull these things off—yet we did. This whole idea of the *empowerment of young people* was no small thing to me; we did it and were very effective, very powerful. From that point on I was very excited: working with young people and knowing the potential that's just *sitting there*—they have an enthusiasm that—when you get older, you just can't recapture ever again.

So . . . four of us white kids from California went to Detroit to organize an all-black chapter of the *Red Tide* in the inner city schools—this was in the '70s when Detroit was the first city hit by the Recession. And we weren't doing a "Just Say No" campaign—we danced and fucked and smoked dope all the time! A couple of us were the most talkative and best-informed about the "politics"—the rest were better at making small talk and selling dope! The combination of the two would bring people around—both the ones who were ideologically attracted, and the people who went, "Hey—cool party, check it out!" But the combination worked. It was a very exciting group of people in a much more repressive environment than Los Angeles.

I remember when we had a Midwest "teach-in" for high school students on *apartheid*—before that became a household word. We arranged for some wonderful speakers from South Africa to show up, and planned all kinds of other events. In order to provide an excuse for kids to get out of home, we printed these fake forms advertising some liberal "YMCA" kind of program, but in reality the kids were coming to our *Red Tide* anti-apartheid symposium. At the end of the day everyone was tired out and came to my house to have spaghetti.

Like I said, we were a pretty hard-partying group, but

at this point everyone was so pooped they were just lying around on sofas waiting for the spaghetti to get cooked. All of a sudden there was a hideous pounding at the door—it was the *cops!* I was trying to gather my wits about me; the police were so angry and violent—it was obvious that, to them, something was a really big deal. I stepped outside the front door and asked, "What's going on?" and they sneered, "None of your fuckin' business!" They were swearing at me and being really abusive—it was one of those events you need a video camera for.

I asked, "Why should I let you in my house without a warrant?" and one of 'em took my arm and twisted it behind my back, pulled his gun on me and said, "Open the fuckin' door!" So I opened the door, feeling responsible for everyone sitting inside (who ranged in age from 13 to 20). And I saw the fear in the cops' eyes and realized that they weren't afraid of me the way I was afraid of them. I was afraid of their guns and of them assaulting us, but they were afraid because we were an interracial group of young people just sitting around peacefully—and they couldn't comprehend that. Somebody had called them because they saw black and white teenagers sitting together in a living room—*that's* why they had come.

Then they blustered, "We have information that you are holding a kidnapped police officer inside!"—yeah, *right!* Luckily, because it was such a totally innocent situation, I think even *they* saw that their fears were overblown—there was *nothing* going on. But it made everybody—the whole establishment in Detroit—very upset to see this group of black and white teenagers just socializing (and organizing) together. This caused the most incredible sexual terror and security panic. And this kind of social reaction happened over and over again—this raid was just the most *violent* manifestation of it. The police went away after ordering our group to

Susie (right) just out of high school with best friends Kim Anno (left) and Rebecca Hall at a Pro-Choice Demonstration in Los Angeles, 1978.

disperse. Of course I got in a lot of trouble because it wasn't my apartment—it was some older grown-up's, who was not too pleased at the turn of events during our "spaghetti dinner."

◆ **AJ: What happened after the Detroit organizing group?**

◆ SB: Well, our teamster organizing in particular was successful—so successful that it split apart the group and I was expelled!

◆ **AJ: Why?**

◆ SB: It was just *horseshit*. We didn't know what to do with the success we had with the teamsters—we had created a rank-and-file group that set into motion the first national strike in the history of the teamsters, as well as a union reform group called "Teamsters for a Democratic Union." People were arguing about the best way to approach this. Some felt we should fit in with "mainstream" teamsters as much as possible—therefore every-

one should sew an American flag on their jacket, get married and listen to Country & Western music and sort of "put on the dog" to impress these "working-class" people. Others felt that *those* are not the teamsters who are interested in socialism or revolutionary feminism or sexual liberation or fighting racism—the kind of people who support that are young people, part-timers, blacks and women. So there was this real "What approach do you take?" quandary.

Success was looming large—in fact, I would say that success was what broke up the group! At the time it was over issues that in retrospect seem very petty now. But I think the break-up had to do with *not knowing how to handle success.* Everyone had put this "trust" in one central body and thought that we all agreed with each other—but we *didn't,* really, and we didn't know how to cooperate and work with our differences.

I found out *everybody* has some kind of gay history—either gay people in their family, or they've had a homosexual experience.

I had to get out of Detroit because politically it became really ugly—I was part of the "opposition" and I had to leave. So I went to Kentucky where busing had started only the year before, and the sole white people defending the black community were Communists. When I arrived in Louisville I was taken to a house where someone greeted me with, "Well, you're gonna need *this!*" and handed me a shotgun. I asked, "Where should I keep it?" and the reply was, "I'd *sleep* with it if I were you!" Like: *Welcome to Louisville!*

When the group broke up, the guy who'd given me his shotgun was on the other side. When he came over to take back his gun he was so tense—I know there was this tiny part of him that wondered if I was going to blow him away—we'd been fighting so passionately. And when I handed him the shells (which let him know that the gun was empty)—well, all the blood just drained out of his face!

After that, I talked to my dad and said, "All right, I guess I'll go to college." I didn't know what to do; my world had been broken apart. Being in this group had been so intense, like being part of an ultra-ultra cadre; there were some "cultish" aspects to it, where you think you could never fuck anyone outside the group, or that nobody on the "outside" could possibly *understand* you. And it was terrible—when the group fractured, a lot of people felt very debilitated and depressed.

♦ **AJ: The '60s had that sense of community and**

trust. When it ended, a lot of people felt abandoned. Suddenly it was like: "You're on your own now!"

♦ SB: Right. So I went to college in Southern California and sought refuge in Women's Studies and Theater, and it was very exciting because it turned out I was in one of the most radical Women's Studies departments in the country, with rootin' tootin' lesbian feminists. Even though my Marxism made me critical of some of their positions, I needed this; I needed a good dose of something other than what I'd been feeding on.

It was exciting to see that commitment and expansion. This was a time when the Feminist Women's Center was beginning in Los Angeles, and we were doing the whole "Do your own speculum," "Do your own birth control"—"Do your own *everything!*" We were exploring "the Body"; self-help groups were really popular, and self-defense classes were really popular. This was right when Andrea Dworkin's anti-pornography "issue" had started to become known. But it hadn't completely dominated the women's movement yet; other things were in the air.

In theater class, the very first collective project we did was on lesbianism, and I was the only person who actually had some lesbian experience. That was my first experience as "Susie Sexpert"—I knew something that nobody else knew; I had *hands-on* experience. This show was particularly memorable because of the prettiest girl in the cast—a blonde princess, the only one among us who had had the perfect romantic sexual awakening with a man on a sailboat and a sunset. The rest of us had experienced more squalid initiations—one person had been raped, someone else had done it in the dark and hated it . . . but hers sounded "picture-perfect." Yet she became the biggest dyke in the entire group!

Years later, "Mary" is still the most committed dyke I know—right up there, a Kinsey "6." Everyone can empathize with the excitement of bringing someone "out" for the first time or being someone's "first." And I was the first woman she ever kissed! She had the reaction everyone wants when you kiss someone for the first time: she fell back on the sofa, turned bright red and her eyes rolled back in her head. She let this incredible sigh come out and breathed, "I've never *felt* anything like that before." She could barely catch her breath, yet all I did was kiss her! I felt like Prince Charming waking up Sleeping Beauty; it was a devastating experience.

In Long Beach, which is on the edge of Orange County, I was attending a college which was a little hotbed of radicalism. I worked as an extra in Hollywood movies, and also was in an experimental theater group called the "Frankenstein Theater," doing "demolition derby" versions of Greek myths. For money we would act out Mark Twain stories at senior citizen nursing homes and insane asylums. I was "The Jumping Frog of Calaveras County" at every funny farm in Southern California.

This was when the Briggs Initiative in California was being promoted. Briggs, a conservative Republican, was trying to outlaw anybody in the public school system who would say a decent word for gay people. His position was: if you were gay, you should be fired; and if you support people who were gay, you should be fired. This marked the birth of "Gay Power" as we know it in the state of California, because people started coming out of the closet and demanding that the public know who the gay community *was*. For the first time I went from door-to-door saying, "Hi, I'm gay. My name's Susie and I want to talk to you about this initiative and why you should vote against it."

This was a very powerful experience for me. I had hundreds of conversations with different individuals, and found out that *everybody* has some kind of gay history—either they have gay people in their family, or they've had a homosexual experience themselves. So this is an issue that anyone can talk about. That was a big change for me; in terms of issues gay politics and gay liberation provided a much bigger framework than the lesbian-feminist scene I had been exposed to. And I got introduced to bar life for the first time, and working with gay men, and all this was much to the better in terms of my understanding of sexual politics and a sexual liberation philosophy. I began to realize that the sexual liberation message had something in it that feminist theory didn't have, just as feminist theory had something that Marxist theory didn't have. So I was piecing sections of theories together—

◆ **AJ: What does feminism lack in terms of sexual liberation?**

◆ SB: Well, feminism is a discussion of gender and oppression based on the premise that men are "better" than women. Feminism's position on sexuality is: women have a right to control their own bodies; women know what is best for our own bodies; our sexuality is as powerful and lustful as a man's; and our sexual integrity is right "up there" with a man's. This might be a legitimate feminist "take" having to do with an idea of equality (not sameness, but prerogative, initiative, dominion, power—and control, too)—

◆ **AJ: Back then, the Andrea Dworkin-types were very influential in the feminist movement. You were a pioneer in bringing porno and erotic issues out into the open—**

◆ SB: The Separatist point of view put *patriarchy* as the core issue the world revolves around, whereas the "Sexual Liberation" message was about differences based on sexuality; the idea of undermining a sexuality based on procreation and the maintenance of the nuclear family. It went further, in not just *criticizing* the fact that stereotypical sex roles were restricting, but advocating that sex roles had erotic possibilities if you *subverted* them! Eroticism gave a spin to some of feminism's lessons, and that made a lot of sense to me.

I knew that from the time of the suffragettes, feminism had always been split between—well, Emma Goldman's a perfect example when she said, "It's not my revolution if I can't dance to it!" (and here she was clearly talking about fucking). Now we can read her love letters and learn that she had "G spot" ejaculations and was bisexual

and was *this* and *that* and that she loved sex; she felt part of her sexual politics was to embrace "free love"! When I read her memoirs I thought, "Nothing has changed—I feel exactly the way this woman does! I am a free love enthusiast!" That's what they called it then; that's where I'm at now. She was promoting a very strong, exciting vision of women's sexuality.

On the other hand, there were always feminists who in the old days were epitomized by Carrie Nation; she felt that women were moral guardians and that femininity was a Vice Squad! Sexuality to her was "male"; and maleness was almost equated to a *rapist mentality*. And that idea really appalled me, because it took all the sensitivity and diversity and power behind what drives masculinity and femininity and just reduced it to really ugly, ugly stuff.

In every culture, whatever is taboo gets *eroticized*. In this country, it's black-white relations, incest and rape. Any taboo subject is often a well of sexual dynamite.

◆ **AJ: Well, Andrea Dworkin's conception is similar; when she teamed up with the fundamentalist Christians against porno—**

◆ SB: If you understand that Andrea Dworkin is the reincarnation of the Marquis de Sade, her whole thing makes sense! She's a severely repressed sadist. I just have to say: read her novel *Ice and Fire* as a companion piece to Sade's *Justine*, and you'll realize that they are the exact, same story: a woman who tries to be virtuous, who tries to do the right thing, and what happens? She gets fucked in the ass in a really mean way, over and over again. Not in a nice way, but in a mean way! And when I read in the *New York Times* that Andrea Dworkin has a special place for dishes that her partner hasn't cleaned properly (so he can re-scrub them), I thought, "This is all too clear and too painful! Why isn't everyone noticing this?"

Recently I compared myself to Andrea Dworkin, because she's the one other person in America I can count on to look at any situation and locate the sexual politics. I really appreciate that about her: the fact she finds the sex in *any* issue. She has a radar for the masculine/feminine, top/bottom confrontation in life, and you can bet she'll find it. And her research is brilliant. Of course, the two of us deviate in terms of what we consider the outcome or conclusion.

For example, she wrote an article on Israel for *Ms.* magazine. She talked about growing up Jewish; her early feelings about Zionism; her departure from it; visit-

Virgin Machine, a film by Monika Treut.

ing Israel. And then one thing she talked about (that no other travel/tourism writer would ever discuss) was: pornography in Israel. I was fascinated—I want to know *everything* about pornography all over the world. She said, "They don't have porno magazines as such; it's more a part of everyday life. It's in magazines you can pick up anywhere." And she revealed that popular symbols, styles, locations and props recall images of the holocaust, citing "Trains, showers, long dark tunnels, very skinny women, weirdo doctor-nurse garb"—she had this long list of "evidence." Essentially she was describing a *Night Porter* scenario of all these different elements that one might call *holocaust fetishism* (an eroticization of the holocaust, but not in a blatant way). Then she went on to say how much this *sickened* her. I'm sure that what she observed is quite true, in terms of those images.

Where I go from there is: I see that in every culture, whatever is horrifying, whatever is beyond sane social comprehension—all that is considered "taboo" gets *eroticized*. In this country it's black-white relations, incest and rape—everything that is beyond "typical" understanding. Any taboo subject is often a well of sexual dynamite. Sexual taboos involve catharsis; they are not about butterflies and daisies and pretty walks along the coast (those are all very "nice" and you might have great sex involving any of those) but typically our most powerful fantasies have to do with images that are dominating,

violent, unequal, and cruel . . .

One could have these fantasies and perhaps feel insecure about them, like, "Am I a cruel person?" or "Do I believe in these stereotypes and prejudices? Do I support these fears that manifest themselves in my fantasies?" And you may get to a point where you feel quite confident and say, "Well, as a matter of fact I don't." I'm sure that for people who find themselves sexually moved by some of the awful history of the holocaust—it's quite a contradiction to deal with; you can't just sit back and think, "Why am I, a Jew, turned on by any of this? How can I be? Am I self-loathing?" Although—that's one way to handle it.

Another way to deal with this is to feel confident about what you believe in, your understanding of history, and your sense of right and wrong, and realize that your sexual fantasies are not some kind of *McGuffey's Reader* on how to live—they're *sex*. And sex takes anxiety and prohibition and all these things we become numb or rationalist or linear with—sex takes them and just rips them out of your clit! It handles that kind of material in a completely non-rational manner. I'm not *surprised* that holocaust imagery would be the hot porno topic in Israel, anymore than I'd be surprised that religion and history and war in any culture you visit has had a tremendous impact on the sexuality and what is considered "exciting" and "titillating" in that culture.

◆ SB: For over two years I wrote a column called "The Erotic Screen" for *Penthouse Forum*. It was a nice opportunity. *Penthouse* had a "radical" editorial staff at the time who loved *On Our Backs* and decided they wanted to include a video column. They asked me, "Would I take a crack at it?" I was nervous at first, because I didn't know a lot about video, and I was very critical of what I knew to be *out there* so far. Not for those typical Dworkin-ite reasons, but for my own.

I felt most porn videos were mediocre and they condescended to the audience; they were supposed to appeal to your sense of guilt and your assumption that all such videos are "crap, but I'll get off on it anyway." Most of them were completely oriented to what the male raincoat-wearer is supposed to be preoccupied with. They were *insulting!*

I didn't have a VCR so I had to go to adult theaters and watch them, and I made some incredible discoveries. In these disgusting stinko theaters, every once in a while on the screen something would happen that would just make my mouth hang open. Sometimes because it was so sexy, and sometimes because it was moving or consciousness-raising in a way I could never have foreseen. I treasured those little moments, and was thrilled to have the opportunity to write about them.

I quickly realized that I was not able to give "erection-ratings" to movies and write in a facile way about what was being ground out of the porno factory that week. It was much more interesting to write essays about *life* and use pornography to illustrate my point. So if I wanted to talk about war or guns, I'd talk about pornography where all the women carried high-powered weapons. Or if I wanted to talk about prostitution, I'd include some porn movies that had that as a theme. If I wanted to talk about incest, I'd talk about incest on the screen.

Sometimes I'd do behind-the-scenes stories, like the father-son relationship in the porn industry which I believe is the heaviest family bond in American business! I know stories that would break your heart. My favorite one is about the young man I met at a porno convention who was selling gay tapes; he looked like a young street hustler himself. I began talking to him and he said, "Yeah, I'm in business with my dad." I said, "No kidding! How'd that come about?" He said, "Well, I didn't know my dad growing up; I was raised by my mom and never saw him. I got in a lot of trouble; I got into drugs; I joined the Navy but kept fucking up so they kicked me out.

"I ended up in Hollywood hustling and doing bullshit scams. There was this bar that catered to rich, soft queens looking for people such as myself. One night I walked in and saw this blonde, balding guy at the end of the bar. I went over to talk and he took a special interest in me; he kept delaying me. He didn't go for what I thought he was going to go for; he kept wanting to talk, and kept looking at me in this *very strange* way. He kept drinking and I kept drinking and I was getting really bombed when he pulled his wallet out and said, 'You're my son!' and showed a photo of me that was taken before I joined the navy.

"He said, 'Your mom's been sending me pictures of you all these years. I have pictures of you and your siblings.' " Well, the son *freaked;* he tore out of the bar and went on a bender for a week because he just couldn't deal with it. But at some point he came to and went back to that bar and sure enough, there was his dad . . . who asked, "Do you want to go into business with me making gay porn movies?" The son answered, "Yes," and that was all she wrote.

I soon discovered that fathers and sons are very important in this business. *Family* is important, because the family are the only people who support you and love you and know you as human beings instead of as "pornographers"—which is how the media views you. Customers, after all, have no sense of "you." Pornography exists in such a twilight zone that the only people who see you for who you are, is your family. So there's this embrace of one's children that's really powerful.

There is no commercial child pornography, **period. That's just been the battering ram of the right wing to close down 1) legitimate sex education of young people, and 2) the whole media of eroticism.**

When I had my child, Aretha, no one sent more sentimental greetings and bouquets than my friends in the porn business. They were the ones who were like the Italian grandparents—they just went bananas. They would say, "There is nothing more precious than your children." [laughs] And that's part of the reason they get so upset about accusations of child pornography—because they're *parents*. They're very protective of their kids.

◆ AJ: Is there child pornography in—

◆ SB: *There is no commercial child pornography,* period. That's been used as a hideous "pink herring" or something! Every despicable act that humankind has thought of is probably on videotape somewhere, now, and it doesn't have to involve a child for it to be ugly. Really sick things have happened and sick people have profited and gloated and god-knows-what over them. But these things that really spark our sense of horror and evil are *not* really available on the commercial market—you just can't walk in and get them anywhere. And that includes child pornography—that's not something that has *ever* been readily available.

On the other hand, this country is so sex-negative that a book like *Show Me* was virtually run out of the country. The photos showed little children, young adults and

adults in the nude; it showed genitals, bodies and differences between men and women; what men and women look like when they make love; what a pregnant woman looks like, etc. This was a children's book which was produced in Scandinavia—

♦ **AJ: I saw it; it was an incredibly humanistic, almost New Age presentation—**

♦ SB: Very New Age, yet it was hounded out of this country. I know I started having sex when I was a teenager; I know that sexual feelings among children and young people are very powerful and vital, and to say that they don't exist is appalling! It's just as appalling as an adult exploiting a kid's sexual inexperience and lack of power. It's sick to be *ignorant*—people get taken advantage of because they're ignorant. So when people say "child porn" to me, it means nothing but *political rhetoric*—because in practical terms it simply doesn't exist.

An individual's story about someone using or abusing a child—that *means* something to me. But don't talk to me about "kiddie porn" because that's just been the battering ram of the right wing to close down 1) legitimate sex education of young people, and 2) the whole media of eroticism. When progressive-minded people (erotic artists, whatever they call themselves) are trying to create new words, pictures and ideas and bring diversity, creativity and quality to this medium, it really hurts us to have critics and nay-sayers saying, "Well, we don't know if we can buy this; after all, *you may be child pornographers!*" That kind of instant condemnation terminates discussion; there's nothing more to say once that label has been dropped . . .

In porno movies, why does the man always cum on the outside? What's the point—I *believe* he came!

♦ **AJ: So what are some of the discoveries you made?**

♦ SB: I learned that pornography employs a language of directness that is like four-letter-words: it shows everything without comment. It's like, "Here it is. People try to color this a certain way, but here it is. Here's a cock and a vagina jumping up and down on each other. This is what sucking looks like. And this is what somebody's big fat butt looks like." It's all *right there;* it doesn't try to make it be anything other than what it is.

It's like yelling "Fuck!" in a crowded theater—it's a language everyone knows but no one wants to admit to. What's hard to understand about porn movies (when you're new to them) is: there's all these *rules* that you begin to realize are *de rigueur*—that on the face of it doesn't make any *sense.* Why do they have a certain kind

of sex act in the first five minutes? Why do you see the same sex acts in the same positions over and over? Probably the most famous question is, "Why does the man always cum on the outside?" What's the point—I *believe* he came!

Some of these "rules" are like vestigial remnants from the early days of porn: "they're *really* doing it; this isn't simulated; see, he's having an orgasm, there's the cum—*see, see, see* . . ." All they needed was to throw a wet hanky at you! These "rules" for a "successful" porn movie bypassed certain basics: good acting—who cares? Good script—who cares? Women's sexual satisfaction—who cares? None of this was that important.

Nevertheless, you do have real people having real sex in these movies. You also have directors who work in this medium for a lot of different reasons. Some of them want very badly just to make movies and are using this genre as a way to work. Others are sick of the hypocrisy in Hollywood, plus they want to *say something* about sex. And *those* kind of directors and actors who were more sincere (as to their own sexual energy) I would find fascinating to watch; I'd really look forward to watching them and I'd become their fan.

I began to develop some ideas: "A lot of feminists want to know: What do women *want* out of erotica?" And there is a certain "list" of requirements, such as: we want to see women cumming. That's so far ahead of everything else on the list, it's hardly worth it to get into anything else. I would rather see women getting turned on and cumming and seeing the look on their faces as they come down from their orgasm—I'd rather see *that* than almost any of the other criteria on my list, like: "Nice looking people," "nice looking location," "inventive dialogue," "meaningful plot"—all that I could take a bath on if I could just really vicariously *live* through the woman's sexual arousal.

But the question is not just, "What would women like to see?"—it's what *everyone* would like to see. I think there's a gross *underestimation* of what the male viewer would be interested in. I mean, after you've seen a few pussies and a few breasts—after you're over your "nudity threshold," well, there's more to it than that. At first you may just be amazed to see the act being done, but then that gets a little *wearying* . . .

I remember a group of us gals from *On Our Backs* were in Times Square for the first time. We'd heard that in New York City it was legal to show men and women having intercourse on stage, and we wondered, "What did that look like? How would they perform?" So we went to one of those huge sleazoid showplaces where they have hundreds of booths with seemingly all pre-op transsexuals behind door number one, and a dyke with a whistle around her neck supervising the entire floor, and a headliner somewhere who's doing a striptease number, and peep show movies, and it's all organized around taboos and voyeurism and seeing body parts, and this is what the big hit is: *talking dirty.* We're having a field day; we're the only women in there . . .

Susie with Christian Mann, one of her mentors in pornography.

Photo: Honey Lee Cottrell

♦ **AJ: Was the place sort of sticky?**

♦ SB: They have lots of janitors with mops who are constantly running in and cleaning up. Some guys clean up after themselves, and some don't, you know . . . but these mop-up crews keep pretty busy—at least in the better places they do. When I first started going to adult theaters I had this *fear of fluids*. But it wasn't as bad as I thought. Some places have this unaccountable odor—I don't know *what* causes it!

Anyway, we finally found the room with the male-female love act. Five of us went in, and there's a small circular stage about 6 feet in diameter, with folding chairs that aren't even unfolded leaning against the walls. The room is painted black. We got the folding chairs out and sat down. It was cold—no heat in the room. A few other men trickled in. It was dead quiet except for us talking—that's one of the things I *hate* about porn theaters: you're not supposed to *say* anything—even carry on a normal conversation.

♦ **AJ: Why not?**

♦ SB: You're supposed to be in your own private world. The unwritten law is: "Don't let anybody intrude!" and "Don't bring the real world into your private fantasy world . . . just let everyone be all by themselves; imagine it all alone, with no laughing, no giggling, and no gossiping"—and that's just not *fun!* I was always the person who would be reacting out loud in a porn theater,

whereas everyone else would be so deathly quiet, except for the occasional "heavy breathing thing"—but even that would be quite subdued.

So . . . the first song came on. I was used to striptease being a variety act in that something different happens with each song, in terms of how many clothes come off or what the dancer reveals. This sleepy, soft, round, plump black woman came out who reminded me of a koala bear. I thought she might be *really tired*—but perhaps that was her way of being sexy. Slowly she took off her clothes to one of those Marvin Gaye "Fuck me, baby" songs—and that was all right. Considering the setting, it was pretty sensual.

Then the guy who had taken our tickets walked on-stage, dropped his pants (but left his shirt and Nike shoes on), and the woman started sucking him. I realized that this was partly to show off an oral sex act, but also to get him hard. The ticket-taker had a nice build, but it was rather distracting that he hadn't taken his clothes off for us, the same way she had. Then, there was this *critical moment* when he got it up, and she *quickly* scooted into a position where he could slide it inside her. There was a little bit of pumping and then all of a sudden (it seemed to happen simultaneously) he pulled out *soft*, and the song (it was a record) went *scratch!* Someone just *boom!* lifted the needle up, the lights went on and the show was *over!* Basically: he lost his erection, they yanked the song

off, and the show was over. The harsh fluorescent overhead lights came on, so all of us girls got up, the male pulled his pants back on and started being the janitor/cashier again.

We left wondering, "What kind of a love act was *that?*" We're lesbians—I'm sorry, we were dissatisfied. So we gave the guy a hard time: "Hey, we wanted *more* from you! You have a nice body but you didn't *do* anything with it! You didn't even bother to take your clothes off. There was no foreplay, no grace—I mean, all of a sudden you lose your hard-on and the show's over?!" And he was completely mystified by our criticism; he just said, "Well, what can I say? You do 7 shows a day—you're just *tired!*" And I'm sure he *was* tired. But you can see that this whole set-up was designed around the idea that "Now you're going to *see* it—and it's going to be 'shocking' or 'lurid' or 'gross' or 'outrageous'!" Not: "This is going to be a *truly erotic experience.*"

When I first started going to adult theaters I had this *fear of fluids*. Some places have this unaccountable odor—I don't know *what* causes it!

♦ **AJ: Do you think it was erotic for the guys sitting in the audience? What was their reaction?**
♦ SB: Mute. I don't know. The first time I ever saw a photo of people having intercourse it stimulated me—it was both scary and exciting. But it didn't take long before photos of body parts in certain positions had very *limited* arousal potential. I mean they're *okay* as an opening, but I want more. And I get angry that just because something like this has been *forbidden* to me, it's supposed to provide enough excitement for the day?!

I'm much more excited by something that gets me on a *lot* of different levels. I'm not trying to sound high and mighty—I mean, I've used pornography as a vibrator sometimes. There've been times when I go, "Get out the 'All Anal Action' tape and let's watch it!" and just focus really hard on certain pictures and get my own fantasy machine going to just supplement all the other atmospheric elements I might want . . . and *get off* on that. There's a place for that that's sexually legitimate. It's just . . . what's so frustrating about commercial pornography is that it doesn't have a lot of aspirations, it doesn't have a lot of ambition, it accepts the stigma and the Twilight Zone that porn is put into.

In some ways I fully expect Hollywood, rather than the pornographers, to be the ones that bring explicit sexuality back to the cinema, because it's the independent directors in mainstream movies who are demanding more. They're the ones that got "NC-17" instituted, and who say, "I'm not going to change my whole script and my whole idea because some Puritan thinks I can't show this in my movie!" And they're right!

♦ **AJ: There seem to be different erotic "requirements" for men and women. If this cinematic formula hadn't worked so well for men, wouldn't they have changed it?**
♦ SB: I think men don't speak up and demand what they want. I think men accept this Faustian bargain: that they can have all the sexual entertainment and thrills and chills they want . . . but only if they agree to keep their mouth shut and accept guilt and shame. There's the underlying guilty thought that: "If they were a *better person*, they wouldn't need this. They must be *awfully lonely*; they must be awfully ugly; they must be awfully insecure to have to resort to this *terrible vice.*"

So it's like being a cripple. The product is designed for cripples, and the audience is treated in this most patronizing way. But I don't buy that; I think, "There are plenty of men who are looking for something more"—I meet those kind of men all the time. I met them when I worked at the "Good Vibrations" store selling vibrators, and I met lots of them when I was writing my porn columns for *Forum*. There are plenty of men who, without shifting their masculine point of view, will ask for what women are asking for.

I can't tell you how many letters I get from men saying they want to see women cum in movies—*of course* they do! If you like it in your life, why wouldn't you want to see it in a movie? There's nothing as exciting as feeling that your partner is *responding* to you. There are lessons to be learned from gay men's porn, which has been a better-made and more sophisticated product overall. Of course, many tapes are total crap, but because gay men place a higher *esteem* on porn as both sex and cinema, there have always been more ambitious artists involved in it, and more respect for what it's all about. Yet those lessons have been lost on straight pornography.

♦ **AJ: Is there good porno now?**
♦ SB: The people who are trying to produce more and give more are so oppressed by the political climate that they can barely operate. For example, *On Our Backs* can't get the minimal distribution that any braided rug manufacturer could get for their products. We're denied loans from banks because they say the nature of our business is "corrupt." Can you imagine a *Savings and Loan* telling us something like that?! You can't get a credit card or fire insurance because the nature of your business is "corrupt"?!

♦ **AJ: You've actually been told this?**
♦ SB: Yes—everyone's been told this! Part of the reason porn became so insular, and certain publishers bought their own printing presses, etc, is because of problems getting material printed. So I end up back with my Marxist viewpoint: "Freedom of the press belongs to those who own one."

So, when you have "institutional" pornographers being so conservative and disinterested in innovation (they've had a formula that has made them a certain amount of money and they're not really interested in changing) and then you have the mainstream that disdains *sex*—well, the *innovators* find themselves in a really difficult position because they're told that what they're doing is quasi-legal, is socially ostracized, and that in just trying to do "normal" business you're going to be cut off at every turn.

I mean, how many people have asked me, "What's a smart, attractive, talented person like yourself doing in this business? You'll ruin your life!" And I know what they mean, because to some people being involved in the sex industry is like pushing heroin (although I think heroin pushers have a better time of it!). I feel sorry for those of us in the sex business who are trying to do something new. Because the public has such an urge to say *No*—to be critical and say, "Well, this isn't what I had in mind!" or "I just don't find *anything* you do sexy at all!"

I really could care less what people *don't* like about a porn movie—do you know how easy it is to turn to any stranger and say what you *don't* like in a porn movie or sex story? It would take quite a bit of vulnerability on your part to turn to someone and say, "This excited me!" *Then* you would have to reveal something about yourself. All our lives we've been hearing pejorative opinions on sex, and no one has even 3 minutes to talk about what they *do* like about it.

◆ **AJ: Are you working in video now?**
◆ SB: Well, my old partners in *On Our Backs*, Nan Kinney and Debi Sundahl, were interested early on in creating lesbian-made videos because they didn't exist. The two of them are responsible for a small crop of new movies in which the actresses can be identified with lesbian culture and authentic lesbian sex. That's really thrilling, but these efforts are tiny. More and more books of women's erotic short fiction are coming out, but that's just a beginning—there's so much more material.

When I edited my essays on lesbian sexuality into a book, *Susie Sexpert's Lesbian Sexworld*, I had to laugh because so many of the topics I included are not mentioned in print anywhere else in the world. I mean: there's nothing written about vaginal fisting—why? People have been doing it for years—why don't they *say* anything about it? Why did I find myself being the first "lesbian" mother-to-be talking about sexuality and pregnancy in an open and honest way? It blows my mind. I wanted to read everything under the sun when *I* was pregnant, and I could not find information about sex and pregnancy except advice like, "Well, if you don't feel like having sex, we completely understand" and "After awhile, the missionary position will become difficult." Or, "Perhaps you might raise the subject of oral sex with your husband, although he will probably throw up when you mention it!" I mean, this is all so sex-negative—I hate it! So my work's cut out for me.

◆ **AJ: When did you start *On Our Backs*?**

◆ SB: Debi Sundahl started *On Our Backs* in 1984, and I contributed my writing and sold ads for the first issue. The second issue I became the editor.
◆ **AJ: Where did the title *On Our Backs* come from?**
◆ SB: In its classic sense, *On Our Backs* is sort of the perfect expression of how subversive sex is, because having sex is about the only time you get to be on your back *and* calling the shots. Usually when you're on your back somebody's got you at a disadvantage. But sex is so wonderful: because positions and situations that might be *unfortunate* to be in (outside of a sexual arena) can be very powerful and exciting when they're in a sexual setting. So *On Our Backs* is kind of a humorous, tongue-in-cheek reference to the power of being on your back and getting fucked, and how fabulous it can be!

It was also an ironic rebuttal to the feminist slogan, "Off Our Backs!" A feminist news journal called *Off Our Backs* has been around for years; I read every issue and still have piles of them saved up. *Off Our Backs*, unfortunately, took a very classic Dworkin-ite anti-porn position and really ruined their sexual politics as a result of it.

There's nothing written about vaginal fisting—why? People have been doing it for years.

◆ **AJ: What's *your* slogan?**
◆ SB: "Entertainment for the adventurous lesbian!"
◆ **AJ: *On Our Backs* contains such irreverence and humor and fun and pleasure mixed with some very serious deciphering of power inequities . . . Do you ever get shocked at how this country has devolved since the '60s—slid backwards in terms of sexual consciousness? How do you analyze what's going on?**
◆ SB: Earlier we were talking about this nervous breakdown among radicals in the '70s where those of us on the inside suddenly felt isolated and alienated from everything. All of a sudden we couldn't take "consensus" for granted. As for the ideas we initiated in the '60s and '70s—well, we never did convince the whole country that we were "right."

Those of us who were genuinely interested in "breakthroughs" have become more and more sophisticated. We've brought new people in who didn't have to go through all the prior stages (and in some cases we've lost a few). But our evolution has had unanticipated results—I mean, who would have guessed how popular vibrators are today? This doesn't show up on any kind of Gallup poll as an index of sexual openness in this country, but it is!

Meanwhile, people who objected to '60s radicalism and '70s New Age ideas have also become more sophisticated. At first they may have just been taken aback and

Susie pregnant, with Lulu in back.

Photo: Honey Lee Cottrell

thought it was all some sort of horrible generation gap, but both sides have come a ways, and have developed constituency and ideas and analysis and a far-reaching social agenda. It used to be, "You young people are getting out of hand!" (like, you're questioning things and in general just being 'naughty', but when you grow up you won't feel like this anymore.") But these people grew up and some of them got even more *out there*. Then the people who were critical had to say, "Well, obviously it's not just a matter of being 'naughty'; we have *ideological differences!*" And this is what I miss about no longer being in *Red Tide:* really intelligent people would sit around and talk about ideas all night long until we came to some incredible (or dismaying) conclusions. I don't have those kind of discussions anymore. I miss my *study groups—*

♦ **AJ: I think we all do! I think that's a widespread problem now: we all miss the dialogue, the conversation, the getting together in cafes and hacking out topics 'til dawn over espresso or god knows what, and really having the community to talk things over.**

♦ SB: I don't feel pessimistic in the sense of "We lost!" because we *have* made gains. On the one hand there's this phenomena of pornography being persecuted by the federal government to an insane, unbelievable degree . . . but on the other hand you have sex movies readily avail-

able in any mom-and-pop video store (although big chains like Blockbuster who only carry "family" videos are killing these little stores—*don't patronize them!*). Those two realities exist side-by-side. You have tremendous homophobia along with an unprecedented presence of gay visibility that is unbelievable. And the more outspoken sexual life is, the more you're going to hear the thunder and the lightning. The "enemy" isn't going to admit, "Oh, gee, I guess we were wrong!" There is going to be a confrontation.

You have the social phenomenon of something like AIDS which creates a context for anal sex to be talked about on the 6 o'clock Evening News, and for people to have to negotiate and speak about sex in a way that isn't a '50s prom date sensibility. Things are changing in technology and medicine, in our lifestyles, in women's independence and *enforced* economic freedom—now, whether you like it or not, you have to support yourself. These sexual issues are not going to be suppressed—they're just going to get more and more *livid* and *vivid*, I think.

Today in the paper there was an article about how rap music is being diluted (its politics, its lyrics), and how Vanilla Ice is a perfect example. They say his lyrics are about women and partying and getting high. But I read some of his campy lyrics about "Check out this girl/I take her home/she shows up in handcuffs and tall leather boots . . ." and thought, "There you go—it's that fabulous S-M consciousness that's sweeping the nation!" There's not a sitcom or popular song around that doesn't contain some tongue-in-cheek humor about kinky sex!

Kinky sex is so popular now . . . one stop at Macy's lingerie department tells the whole story! There's a lot of playful embracing of sexual hi-jinx . . . people aren't necessarily calling it "S-M" and proclaiming, "I'm into leather sex!" and joining leather clubs and going the whole political nine yards, but there is this openness about sexual subjects that we've never had before—at the same time they're being condemned.

Something like the *Meese Commission Report* is the perfect example: I masturbated to that report until I just about passed out—it's the filthiest thing around! And *they* know it! They made bondage a household word; everybody knows what bondage is now because of the Meese commission—you read all about it in the papers. The right wing's tactic is to titillate—show you the thing they want you to get mad about—thus triggering your shame and guilt feelings but discouraging deeper, contextual analysis. Well, that works with some people, but for other people it's like, "Hey, *check it out!*" They're amused, intrigued—whatever, with the result that it then becomes an open subject instead of a closed one. While on the one hand we're having attempts at censorship that are ugly and hard to believe, at the same time the list of topics that one *cannot* discuss seems to be getting smaller. Certainly sexuality has become a wide-open issue to be talked about. And it's no longer just doctors or professors pontificating—the hottest new "product" is amateur home porn videos.

◆ **AJ: But is just talking about sex equal to sexual liberation?**

◆ SB: When topics like safe sex and sexual risk are on everyone's mind before they hop into bed with somebody, that's a sign of the times that shows sexual fear— but it also shows that these are topics everybody feels free to bring up. The fact that anyone can rent a porn video and take it home without guilt implies a democratic notion that *everyone* can talk about/express opinions about sex, not just academics or authorities. . .

The right wing mind-set thinks: if you put a certain image or thought out, everyone's going to take it *one way;* that somehow everyone's going to have a single, identical reaction. And that accusation gets put to "pornographers" all the time. If you show a picture of two people fucking—then *ohmigod*, the whole social fabric's going to unravel, and people are going to do hideous things to each other!" I really hate that kind of belittling of basic intelligence. So talking about any taboo topic, especially on a popular culture level, must have *something* to do with liberation, because the more diverse points of view and contexts and interpretations that get expressed, the more the idea of authority in any area of life gets shattered . . .

◆ **AJ: Are strict definitional labels of gays and lesbians (as important as they are for a political move-**

ment) also a trap within the gay community?

◆ SB: *Yes*, I find that to be true. Declaring that you're gay is very important for a Civil Rights movement, because you have to be able to identify yourself and announce what freedoms you seek. The problem is: we want the privileges that heterosexuality bestows—legally and socially, in terms of recognition and empowerment, plus being able to have your *family* recognized—that's what it's all about. And—to not be discriminated against—just a basic anti-bigotry, pro-fairness message. So in that Civil Rights sense, calling oneself "gay" is very important.

But when it comes to describing *who you are*, what your erotic identity is, who arouses you, what your sexual life has been all about—then saying you're "gay" becomes more and more meaningless as every minute passes. The more people who come out of the closet, the more meaningless it becomes. We can't just say, "Oh, we're all together here on a yellow submarine." That's like me being in my little socialist group and thinking that we all felt exactly the same way about everything. How stupid! Yet that's a common sentiment in small gay communities: a really intimate—*incredibly* intimate—feeling. Usually people never feel that way except when an earthquake comes—then suddenly everyone identifies with each other—but oppressed minorities feel like that *all the time*. And that feeling gets shattered when your group gets too big, and the differences become better-known.

In some ways I've come full-circle from my early idea that everyone was bisexual. Now I don't believe everyone is "an equal mixture of this and that"—an equal mixture of masculinity and femininity. I think sex has a spectrum like the color spectrum, and that it isn't as important to say "I'm red" or "I'm yellow" or "I'm green" or "I'm purple" as it is to shatter stereotypes and misleading information.

> **I've come full circle from my early idea that everyone was bisexual. Now I think sexuality has a *spectrum*. . .**

When it comes to sex, people telling me what they "are" means less than nothing—they might as well say they're a Communist or a feminist as to tell me that they're gay—I have no idea what that means anymore. It was supposed to mean something *sexual* at one point; it was supposed to mean something *political* at another point. If you're a woman and you tell me you have a powerful attraction to another woman, and describe what you did in bed with her, and how that felt to you that night—well,

Photo: Jill Posener

on a kind of "Be Here, Be Now" basis I can understand or empathize with that experience.

I can also see what the gay community as an *oppressed* community has created, because every oppressed community always has the best culture going on—the best music, the best clothes, the best parties! To overcompensate for the fact that we are denied more boring parts of legitimate life, we prosper in the illegitimate and the imaginative parts of life—and that's exciting! I like that heritage—it's very powerful. And lots of so-called straight people are just dying to be part of that aesthetic, that sense of humor, that gay "thing" that is just so irresistible and attractive. Instead of being "possessive" about it and saying, "No, you can't come in; you have to be gay, and gay means A, B and C," I think we should display more *largesse*:This is ours; we created it; it's very powerful; it's very attractive; and people who understand the point of view or the aesthetic or the 'Bohemian' qualities of it should be embraced. And whatever their sexual life is will hopefully add to it all.

So . . . these kind of discussions are one thing, and talking about a woman's right to control her body in countries where women are considered entirely and completely second-class, is quite another.

♦ **AJ: You have to reclaim what society's taken from you, and that means reclaiming the labels used against you, from "bitch" to "slut" to "dyke" to—**

♦ **SB:** Sure—that political power of language is very important. But let's change the context for a minute. If I'm looking for a sexual partner and someone tells me she's a political lesbian, this is absolutely meaningless to me in terms of whether I'm going to have a good time with her, or find intimacy with her. I mean—we might be able to have an interesting *political* discussion, but that's not necessarily going to translate into an erotic infatuation. And this in itself has become a political issue: the

idea that you can expect a certain kind of "sexual life" from someone because of what they call themselves in front of the "establishment." Like, "I'm in Queer Nation!" Well—*so what?* Politically that means a lot to me, but sexually it's misleading—I'm not sure what you mean by that. Does it mean you're uninhibited?—if so, I suppose that's pretty good! But I honestly don't know what it means. And it's very difficult to talk about what's at the core of our sexual identities. Because there's probably not a group or movement around that totally speaks for you—that you can wholeheartedly join without reservations, and create a political platform. Sexuality's still quite personal.

I remember an old study group in which we had this long Lenin lesson on "bending the stick" . . . how you have to take a certain position to an extreme for awhile, not because it's the "true" position, but because it has to be done in order to end up in a "middle" or "correct" position. It's very important to put forth a "community" idea of being gay—I've contributed to that; I've worn the "Dyke" button to make that point. And now I find myself bending the stick in the opposite direction and saying, "Labels are misleading; they encourage false assumptions, and are not a very sensitive or accurate way of talking about sexuality. Don't try and pin *me* down. I have lesbian sex, but to call me a 'lesbian' doesn't mean a whole lot anymore."

Of course, no one wants to be called "straight" because that just sounds like the squarest thing on earth—no matter how fiercely you may be attracted to the opposite sex! Since I'm single, people always ask me, "What do you think your next partner will be: a man or a woman?" And I'm always hoping that my friends will ask me some really brilliant question that'll help me in my quest to find love and romance. But *that* question is so disappointing—because I've never fallen in love with anybody just because they were a man or a woman! That's never been *up there* with what got under my skin. I suppose people are trying to help me "narrow it down," so they know where to put my "personals" ad or which club to send me to—like some sort of efficient matchmaking device. But that depresses me. I feel most at home with people sexually who enjoy the distinction of masculinity and femininity; who don't want to merge it or blend it all into some kind of bland soup. If there's any sexual politics that I identify with in my cunt right now, it's *gender-fuck*—that probably appeals to me the most.

I'm always threatening to get out of the *lesbian* magazine business and into the *butch-femme* magazine business—there really should be a magazine for people who are attracted to butches, and another for people who are attracted to femmes. Sometimes this just seems like the classic way the cake is cut: instead of having to endure all these letters from people saying, "Oh, everybody in your magazine's too hard and cold and masculine for me," and other people saying, "If you show one more woman with lipstick, I am going to throw your magazine into the trash." Let's just make it really *simple* for the whole world, and say, "You want to look at this kind of person—here you go. You want to look at their opposite, here you go."

For me, sexual tension means masculine and feminine confrontation and confusion—that's what's exciting. For other people "top" and "bottom" scenarios are the most important kindling—what starts the fire. And others will insist that "warm, sunny days on the beach" are the kindling for their sexual desire—but I don't believe it! Because *I* like making love on the beach more than anyone—I like all those "vanilla" activities a lot, but that's not where my sexual taboos are at. That's *too* nice!

Some people wish that nice things were what pulled all of our sexual triggers (and some nice things do—I mean *tenderness* is an aphrodisiac to me), but you wouldn't feel all the soft and tender things if you didn't have something else to compare them to. They wouldn't have the *cachet* and the charged meaning they have if you didn't compare them to their opposite.

Part II

♦ **AJ: Can you talk about Good Vibrations?**
♦ **SB:** I was working at Good Vibrations, the feminist sex shop in San Francisco, after I left college in '81. In college I'd been very fortunate in that I'd gotten in on the last "experimental" year of a university (UC Santa Cruz) that was reorganizing itself back to "the three R's." But previously it had offered a wide latitude of studies for student investigation, and I'd told them, "Look, my major is Sexual Politics." I had spent my last two years of school mostly living in San Francisco working in different political groups, and the focus of these groups was more and more on the politics of sexual liberation inside the gay community. How did we talk among ourselves about sex? What did we present to the straight world about sex?

There were a lot of battles between people who felt that gay civil rights would be ruined if we put our sexual liberation message *out there* (we'd ruin our chances for acceptance from the mainstream) . . . and other people who said, "If we don't bring out Sexual Liberation now, we're going to be cornered later on." And sure enough—this was already happening: different aspects of the gay community were being labeled as "bad" and other aspects as "good." People who had sex in the park were

bad and should be disowned; people who had leather sex were equally disreputable. It was OK to be gay—as long as you were sexually bland, and as unprepossessing as possible.

> **I masturbated to that *Meese Commission Report* until I just about passed out—it's the filthiest thing around! And *they* know it!**

♦ **AJ: That's just transferring conservative, status quo values to—**
♦ **SB:** Yeah! The idea was to convince straight people that we eat just like you do; we comb our hair; we go to the dentist; we do all these things just like ordinary people—to try and make us seem less like monsters. But gay will always mean *sex* to the public, and for gays to not acknowledge this sexual perspective seemed crazy to me. I was very interested in us *not* dividing ourselves between who were the "good" gays and who were the "perverts." At first this was more from a political position, but as time went on I realized that I was more of a pervert than I was some sort of Middle-American "gay mainstreamer."

So I started meeting other people in the Gay History Project here—all sorts of artists and activists who were interested in sexual liberation. *Samois,* the lesbian SM group was just starting, and absolutely every lesbian who was at all interested in sex was joining up. However, interest in SM was almost secondary to just plain being interested in *sex* and wanting to be in a pro-sexual environment—because the lesbian social milieu had for so long been unsexual. Discussion of fantasies and erotica had been pushed under the bed way too long. And *Samois* was this huge breakout—an *extreme* breakout—and it polarized the community very quickly.

You also had people talking about "butch" and "femme," which meant that talking about masculinity and femininity was rearing its little head (instead of everyone being in this androgynous mudpile). Suddenly people were talking about "differences" and "opposites attracting," and the excitement and importance of having a sexual or erotic identity—we all didn't want to just look and act like Mister Potatohead in bed.

All this was going on when I left college. Like everybody I knew in San Francisco, I didn't have a job and was having a hard time finding work. One of my idols, Amber Hollibaugh, broke up with her girlfriend who was another idol of mine, Honey Lee Cottrell. Honey Lee worked one day a week at Good Vibrations. And she was so unhappy about her break-up with Amber that she left California, and I got her job working one day a week. Honey Lee had sold me a vibrator at Good Vibrations

a couple of years back and it had changed my sex life forever—I was very pleased to be working there. The owner, Joani Blank, had started the store as a way for women to be able to buy things like vibrators that would help a woman reach orgasm, without having to go to a sleazy adult shop. You could be in a *women's* environment.

The shop was very tiny and nobody knew about it. If I had a couple of customers come in all day, I felt very lucky. But what was great about it was: people would come in and talk at length about their sex lives with me, perceiving me to be an expert—even when I was very new on the job. And I just ate it up! I read every book in the place, and I would talk and talk with people—I was so grateful they would be candid enough to describe their sexuality to me. And I could see that I had a talent for communicating about sex, that I was at ease discussing *anything*. I wasn't judgmental—I mean, the last thing a sex educator does, is say, "You WHAT?!" When somebody describes their fantasies you listen—that's one of the best things you do: you *listen* and you accept that how people feel and fantasize is "natural." The whole idea of "perversion" really doesn't fit into my point of view. There are people who don't have compassion or empathy for how others feel, and who tread on other people—that's what the issue of *consent* is all about. But there's nothing that anyone would think of erotically that would shock me, or that I would think is harmful.

♦ **AJ: To even have a concept of "perversion" is to subscribe to the Christian belief that the body is evil. Christianity defines "perversion" as any sex that isn't for procreation. Anyone with any liberation—gay, lesbian, feminist—has to re-evaluate *desire* in the body. And it becomes no longer a question of what's "perverted" or what's not.**

Joani always thought the vibrator addiction paranoia went straight back to the fear that hair would grow on your palms if you masturbate too much. *There's a tremendous fear of liking sex too much.*

♦ SB: Well, when I started working at Good Vibrations there was very little for women to read . . . about the sexual feelings we have. There were a couple of books by Nancy Friday about women's fantasies, and I read them and realized, "My god, I do fantasize; it's just that these things are so naughty and taboo I didn't even admit to myself that I *thought* these things." There were a

couple of old books by Anais Nin like *Little* Birds and *Delta of Venus*—and that was *it*. There was no *modern* women's erotica; the only thing that was contemporary and by women was *Samois'* book, *Coming to Power,* which was about a specialized topic. Women were really upset to come in and not find any women's erotica—because there *was no* women's erotica. At this time the store was only selling vibrators, a few other sex toys, and a handful of books.

♦ **AJ: I went there in '79 and was so impressed that I wanted to make a film documenting it. But then I left school. It had a little museum of antique vibrators—**

♦ SB: People would always look at the museum first if they were really nervous, because anything from the *past* doesn't seem as threatening as something that's happening right now . . . that you might actually *use* in your sex life. But I tried out some of those museum relics in the try-out room and some of them worked splendidly.

♦ **AJ: That's right; there was a "try-out" room, too!**

♦ SB: That's probably the mark of a successful sales clerk at Good Vibrations: being able to convince someone that they can go use the try-out room and nothing terrible's going to happen—I'm not going to peek through the keyhole, and they'll be able to walk out and not have everyone burst into laughter or *stare* at them. It's hard to tell someone what a vibrator feels like if they've never felt it; it's like asking, "What does milk taste like?" You have to try it. And in fact, the sensation is so strong you can feel it through your clothes. Only once in six years of working there did I ever see someone just come into the store, disappear into the try-out room, and come out 20 minutes later. That *floored* me! This woman just "dropped in" to have an orgasm—then left.

My mouth was open, because usually people say, "Okay, all right, I'll *try.*" And they run into the try-out room and all they're doing is touching it to their pants for two seconds and going, "Oh, that kind of feels nice," and then they run back out. But to have someone actually *luxuriate* and moan behind the door—that was unbelievable!

♦ **AJ: Was she moaning?**

♦ SB: Yes.

♦ **AJ: By the way, did you make a sale?**

♦ SB: Oh no! She was a total *user.* She just came in, used my try-out room, and *left.* But this fits people's fantasy of what it's like to work at Good Vibrations. One time I had some underground comix folks including the late Dori Seda come in—she was this wild girl who looked exactly like Olive Oyl out of the *Popeye* cartoon. She said, "I want to do a shoot here—will you close the store? It's gonna be this scenario where this girl comes in to try out the vibrators, and the vibrator clerk ties her up, and then there's a whole bondage scene, and . . ." She was so goofy, I really wanted to do it! And sure enough, Robert Crumb and his assistant and the girl models came in and we did a "photo funny." I got to do the vibrator bondage since no one else really knew what they were doing, and I said, "This is what people think goes on here every day of the week"—and of course it doesn't; it's much more serious.

Actually, people often come in really concerned: something is *not* right with them, and they feel very secretive and isolated about what worries them—when in fact everyone has about the same five concerns! With women, the top question is: "Why is it so difficult for me to orgasm?" Either they never have, or they can only have it under certain circumstance, like, "I could only do it with Harry," or, "I could only do it with my shower massage," or, "I could only do it with *this, that* and the *other* thing." And this means that people are afraid to try something new, are afraid that it won't work, or are afraid that the vibrator *will* work and then they won't be able to have an orgasm any other way.

But there is something really wonderful about orgasm, which is: the more you have it and the more different ways you have it, the more versatile you become! And it's hard to change; you really do cling to one particular pattern that will give you pleasure. But to find another way by which you can achieve that same satisfaction or even *greater* satisfaction—this only opens your body up to break the habit again and again. People who change their eating habits notice this too: at first it's so hard not to eat the same things, but once they start experimenting, then they want to try more and more!

◆ **AJ: We have such a paucity in our language about how to discuss the body and orgasm. There is that myth about the vibrator: that you'll just get addicted to it—**

◆ SB: Well, Joani always told me that she thought the vibrator addiction paranoia went straight back to the fear that hair would grow on your palms if you masturbate too much. *There's a tremendous fear of liking sex too much.* When we make love, as much as everyone wants to cum and see stars and feel the world turn, we *resist* intense sexual experience more than we embrace it. And it's very difficult for us to *let go.* The idea of "letting go" makes people think they're just going to *lose* it—they won't get up and go to work the next day. I think that sexual repression really is key to the work ethic: the idea that if you pleased your body, you wouldn't be compelled to bring home the bacon, or wax the floor anymore—all those things that you make yourself do because you *have* to. And I think that in a romantic love culture, we sometimes have brushes with that, because often people will have a romantic experience where the rest of the world blacks out and you can't concentrate on anything else— you're in such a state of euphoria. With masturbation you don't have that "romantic" part, but you certainly do have a euphoria and a satisfaction and a *lack* of inhibition that is incredible.

◆ **AJ: Well, if people really were loving or revering their bodies, and really enjoying themselves with or without a partner—this would probably change the world. People would think twice about going to a job they're totally alienated from . . . You were saying there were about 5 things women want—**

◆ SB: Well, orgasm is the Number One thing for women. One of the most intense cases for feminism is: not being able to orgasm is not a man's complaint. (I have yet to meet a man who couldn't achieve orgasm.) And to think that so many women can't . . . and to think about what that means—to have never experienced a sexual climax in your life?! To me that's worse than getting 59 cents to the dollar; it just shows how women are divorced from their sexual capacity, and how passive our lives are supposed to be. On any given day in Good Vibrations— that could make me *cry.*

I wanted to tell why vibrators were the best thing that had happened since sliced bread!

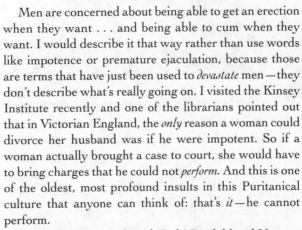

Men are concerned about being able to get an erection when they want . . . and being able to cum when they want. I would describe it that way rather than use words like impotence or premature ejaculation, because those are terms that have just been used to *devastate* men—they don't describe what's really going on. I visited the Kinsey Institute recently and one of the librarians pointed out that in Victorian England, the *only* reason a woman could divorce her husband was if he were impotent. So if a woman actually brought a case to court, she would have to bring charges that he could not *perform.* And this is one of the oldest, most profound insults in this Puritanical culture that anyone can think of: that's *it*—he cannot perform.

I started *On Our Backs* with Debi Sundahl and Morgan Gwenwald because there was nothing for lesbians . . . because lesbians are so invisible. But truthfully speaking, there's nothing for *anybody.* There's very little sexually *meaningful* literature for men or women, gay or straight—for any sexual persuasion. There's only a few precious things—most of which have been censored or forbidden at one time or another. There's only one book for men, *Male Sexuality*, by Bernie Zilbergeld—*one* book, and he did this in the '70s—about the demands this culture puts on men for work and sex, and why this screws men's sex lives up. I would think there would be a *million* books on this subject—and there's *one.*

◆ **AJ: What about *The Joy of Sex?***

◆ SB: That was horrible! I can hardly believe that was such a popular book. You can open up any random page, read one of the questions, and want to bury your head in shame. The author, Alex Comfort, is the guy who said that lesbians don't fuck, they don't do penetration—it's essentially the same as that book in the '60s, *Everything You Ever Wanted To Know About Sex But Were Afraid to Ask.* I remember being in grade school and hearing about that one . . . somebody had tried to steal one from their

Susie with Honey Lee Cottrell

Photo: Mariette Pathy-Allen

parents' bed-table. That turned out to be filled with inaccurate information—same thing with *The Joy of Sex*. It was a great marketing ploy—to promote something to mainstream American couples answering questions about your sex life, and it certainly promoted the idea that sex was a wonderful thing to have—but it was filled with inaccurate and prejudiced information.

♦ **AJ: What about Dr Ruth?**

♦ **SB:** She's contemporary, and also she doesn't publish books. She's a celebrity. She's another subject.

This is another subject, but women would come in to Good Vibrations and say, "My husband doesn't want to have sex with me anymore, and I think it's because my vagina's too big." This is another complaint that would send me into a total *rage. Everyone*, including women, knows much more about male genital anatomy than they do about female genital anatomy—in fact when I give talks to groups of lesbians, first I show them a picture of a penis just to *orient* everyone, because everyone knows what a penis looks like, but people don't really know what their clitoris or vagina or clitoral structure looks like—that's why when something comes along like the "G Spot," everyone thinks it's some kind of joke—because they don't know what women's sexual organs look like. If we *knew*, we wouldn't be so ignorant and say so many bigoted, stupid things.

First of all, a vagina is *not* a hole that comes in various

sizes; it's a *potential* space, and it's closed all the time. Its vaginal walls are muscles, and when something enters it, it opens to receive *just that much* and then closes again. People act like it's a pinball machine that you throw something in and see how long it takes to come out. And you can have strong muscle tone or weak muscle tone.

During childbirth you use incredible muscles to push that baby out—I mean, that's quite a feat. Childbirth is the biggest sex act of all—having just had a child, I can talk about this. And afterwards, you might want to do these exercises called *Kegel's*, which somebody originally thought of as a remedy for urinary incontinence—for women who were having a hard time controlling their bladder. But they also strengthen your vaginal muscles . . . and this is the same muscle that squeezes when you have an orgasm. So actually, having lots of orgasms will also improve your muscle tone! When you squeeze off your pee when you're going to the bathroom, that's a *Kegel*. You can do them all the time and they will improve your muscle tone and they will make you more orgasmic. In fact if you do 20 in a row, you'll realize that you've made yourself wet, and that you feel slightly aroused—it automatically does that.

But the idea that you should do these exercises because your pussy isn't tight enough is crazy. Most of the guys who bring that up—if the truth be known, that's not what their problem is in terms of getting turned on or getting off—but it's an effective way to stop arguing about having sex. In other words, maybe he wants to get his cock sucked. Maybe he wants to get fucked in the ass, or maybe he wants to fuck his wife in the ass. Maybe he has homosexual fantasies. Maybe he feels weird about her body in general since she had a child. Maybe something about seeing her as a mother has changed his fantasies about her—who knows?

♦ AJ: These attacks are usually about a man's lack of honesty regarding what he truly desires. Usually this is a whittling-down attack to make the woman feel bad—it's about control.

♦ SB: It's a very effective way to ruin your sex life! And it's the same thing if a woman tells a man, "You can't satisfy me because your penis is too small." That's like saying, "You can't satisfy me because you have red hair," or " . . . because you're only five-foot five." If the "reason" has something to do with your body, there's not a whole lot you can do about it.

♦ AJ: It's basically dishonesty about the fact that you have problems in the relationship with that person, and can't directly communicate.

♦ SB: So it's this dead end maneuver . . . Also, women would come in and ask, "I heard that using *ben wa* balls will help strengthen my vaginal muscles." Well, *ben wa* balls are the pet rock of sex toys—they don't do *anything!* If you put them inside you, you'll forget they're there—again, because the vagina's a potential space. It either hugs them or it doesn't hug them; they either sit there and you forget they're there, or they fall out and—! Whatever they do, they give you no sexual pleasure.

So I say to women, "If you want to practice exercising *and* have some fun at the same time, use a vibrator and make sure you're having an orgasm at least five times a day!" or, "Get this dildo; you might enjoy using it, and practice hugging and squeezing the dildo as you're playing with your clit (or whatever you do to get off)." And when I start talking to them in terms of, "If you really want to *do* something about this, you're going to have to start *cuming* more often," this just blows out their whole "My boyfriend doesn't want me anymore!" preoccupation because I'm talking to them about *their* sexual pleasure. And initially they didn't come in because they wanted to have orgasms—they came in because they felt bad that their lover had rejected them—

♦ AJ: They felt self-denigration instead of righteous indignation over the fact that *they're* not being satisfied—

♦ SB: Some of the questions that would walk into the store wouldn't even be said out loud; they'd be kind of *silent* questions. We had a big controversy with the owner, Joani, who didn't want to have dildoes in the store because she was so exasperated with everyone adoring "the phallus"—she just wanted to get the phallus out of her store entirely! And I had to say to her, "Look, I've got lesbians banging down the door for dildoes! I know that's not supposed to be what lesbians want, but that's

just because we've accepted this dishonesty that there's nothing physically pleasurable about fucking—and there is! It's very stimulating; people aren't just doing it because they've been "brainwashed by the patriarchy"—it feels good! And some people have these gender-bending fantasies—who knows what everyone's reasons are, but they want them." Joani and I would laugh a lot about the fact that *I* (supposedly the radical lesbian) was taking the pro-dildo position, and *she* (the suburban straight housewife—she's not *really,* but she likes to pretend) was taking the reverse. But eventually that gave way . . .

A real common event would be: the lesbian couple that would come in the store and start circling closer and closer to the cupboard displaying the dildoes and the harnesses. And it was usually up to me to "break the ice" and start talking about them in a very normal way, because a lot of people are there buying something like that for the first time. Also, if you buy a harness, it's obvious you're going to experience this *make-believe* of having a cock—and usually when you first put one on, you burst out laughing! Or you cover your hands and you blush—you feel so silly. Nevertheless, just to have something *dangling* from you in that part of your body is an extraordinary experience.

And then to begin using it with your lover—at first it's awkward, because you don't have any sensation in the plastic, so it helps to be really familiar with your hands to begin with. Accept that the first time it's new, it's embarrassing—mostly because of your own inhibitions. Once your inhibitions are down and you're not either having performance anxiety (that you're not going to do it "right"), or feeling, "What kind of a woman am I—strapping on this enormous lavender cock?" Once that's done away with, you could start having a really good time!

I feel sorry for any man who has never been penetrated—again, it's that *fear of intensity.*

♦ AJ: In your lecture, "How to Read a Dirty Movie," you showed a film clip of two women with a dildo that was very hot—

♦ SB: *Sexcapades,* with this older woman producer and this younger woman actress on the casting couch.

♦ AJ: There's something very liberatory about the blurring of (and playing with) gender identities. You have these two feminine women going in and out of "male" roles; the older woman's saying, "You bitch, you bitch, fuck me!" and the younger woman with the dildo strapped on is playing the "male" role. Some-

thing in us is released (in the sense of a desire system) that is challenging to our fixed notions—

◆ SB: Lee Carroll is dirty-talking Sharon Kay through her first dildo experience. And the way she instructs Sharon to use the cock—stroke it, fuck her, tease her with it (all these things that she wants)—in a sense she could well be instructing a *man* to do the same thing. Not all men are that sexy with their cocks—in fact, I think too many of them take their sexual identity and their masculinity for granted. Of course, when women start playing with masculine sexual energy, well—first of all it's taboo. But once you start playing with it, it had *better* be erotic—it's not part of our "natural" body, so the only reason to use it is to turn yourself on . . . learn something about yourself you didn't know before . . . put yourself in a different sexual position than you would ordinarily be in.

My first attempts at SM were more like a *Laurel & Hardy* film than either evil *or* liberation!

The same thing (regarding dildoes and harnesses) would also happen with a lot of men-and-women couples that would come in. This is what I call one of the biggest secrets of the last two decades: the popularity of anal sex has become *outrageous*. And this despite AIDS which has really dampened a lot of anal sex interest in the gay community, but among men and women it's incredibly popular—particularly with men who want their female lover to fuck them in the ass. And they're always very shy when they come in, too, and need extra-special attention, because . . . of course for a man to say he likes anal sex—to be penetrated—well, socially the stigma is: he's saying that he's really not a man, that he's effeminate—so then, *what is he?* Of course, most of the men who want to get fucked put out a very "masculine" facade—they're not the kind of person who walks into a room and you say to yourself, "I know that man wants to get fucked in the ass!"—I mean, you would *never* know!

The stigma attached to this is just a stupid prejudice; in fact, being entered by somebody is a very *profound* psychological (as well as physical) experience. Submitting to someone else's fingers or cock and letting them fill you up is really intimate—who wouldn't like that? I feel sorry for any man who has never been penetrated before, because they haven't experienced something sexually that's *so* powerful—again, it's that *fear of intensity*.

For a woman to say that she likes to be fucked in the ass doesn't have anything to do with homosexuality. No one would think you were a lesbian, or think you were any less of a "woman." It's more like: "you're cheap and

easy and fast and don't have any morals and anybody can do *anything they want* to you—you're trash. You would let somebody touch you in such an unladylike way—ladies aren't supposed to be interested in that kind of thing." So, that about covers the top ten concerns at Good Vibrations.

◆ *AJ: How did you start* On Our Backs?

◆ SB: As I was saying, all the staff at Good Vibrations were painfully aware of the lack of contemporary erotica for women, and the lack of any literature for lesbians—literature which emphasizes sexual identity. Lesbianism had become a political stand, not a sexual preference, and it was time to bend the stick the other way.

First we had *Samois* who put out their book, *Coming to Power*—political essays and erotica, including the first lesbian story I ever got off on reading: "Girl Gang Bang." That story did *so much* for me—I was beginning to think I would never be able to find a "home" in a lesbian erotic scenario, but thanks to that story I did! Now previously, when I lived in Los Angeles I had been doing theater, and all my friends would be trying to win an audition for a Burger-King commercial—that's what theater was *about* in L.A. But when I came to San Francisco, I discovered that you could have the most obscure poetry reading in the world and people would come to it! You could do performance art and total strangers would come see you and appreciate your work. So I was in heaven. I put on this show called "Girls Gone Bad" which was very controversial at the time. I think about what we did—we talked about Catholic school, we read from pulp novels, we wore lingerie and tore it off—now all of that would be just so much Madonna-videos-under-the-bridge, but at the time it was really exciting!

What this show was really about was a contemporary take on the "damned if you do, damned if you don't" rivalry between madonnas and whores, and what happens when women speak frankly about sex and defy the prejudices and the sexual script expectations. I loved doing that show. (This is embarrassing to admit, but so often my sexual adventures have begun with, "Oh, I read this in a book," or some other *intellectual* idea I want to try out. Sometimes I think I'm very unoriginal; I have to *read* about it before I get the idea.) Anyway, after reading what *Samois* was putting out and hearing these debates about SM, I went to my lover and said, "We have to *try* this, because I have to find out whether it's evil incarnate (like some of my friends say) or whether this is the new sexual liberation."

Actually, my first attempts at fetishistic SM were more like a *Laurel & Hardy* film than either evil *or* liberation. At Modern Times bookstore I had been reading some of my poetry where I talked about threatening my lover with a knife in bed (erotically). Somebody heard me reading these poems and a few days later I got a letter saying, "Hi, we're two gals starting a magazine called *On Our Backs* . . ." When I read that I burst into laughter because I knew *exactly* why they were making fun of the feminist newspaper *Off Our Backs* which had been denigrating the sexual voices coming up in recent years. This particular paper had been condemning all the discussion about SM, butch-femme, kinky sex—saying this was "wrong" and "anti-feminist." And here were a couple of women starting a magazine that turned that title on its head.

They said they really enjoyed my poetry—well, can you imagine? My poetry was so obscure that out of all twenty people who heard it, I couldn't believe I would get a letter like that. And it continued, "Would you like to submit some of your writing?" So I sent in some erotic work I had done, and also offered any help I could give. I had been doing "commie" papers, underground papers, trade union papers and other radical propaganda since high school—I knew a little bit about how to make it happen.

Eventually I called the phone number on the letter and asked, "What's up? I've been waiting *every day* for you to publish this magazine!" And they invited me over to meet them. When I did, I realized they were new to all this. They had some great material, but no money. The first contributors to *On Our Backs* included people who are some of the most popular lesbian writers today. I think about Joan Nestle's story in that first issue; about Tee Corinne; Honey Lee Cottrell did our first centerfold—a take-off on *Playboy* which we called "Bull Dyker of the Month." I did my first "Toys For Us" column because I wanted to tell why vibrators were the best thing that had happened since sliced bread—there were a lot of really great contributions to that first issue.

One of the founders, Debi, was a stripper. She knew so many gay strippers that she said, "Let's have a 'Lesbians Only!' strip show to raise money for the first issue"—and that's exactly what we did. I sold ads to everybody I had met through Good Vibrations; we sold advance subscriptions to people on the *Samois* mailing list, and Debi organized this incredible strip show. The first one was at the Baybrick Inn, a lesbian bar here, and the second was at Caesar's Palace, which resembles a lost Havana nightclub.

It was so much fun having those shows—the strippers were so excited to be performing for women. And the *women*—it was like taking kids to Disneyland for the first time, because women are not accustomed to gathering together for a *lustful* purpose . . . to be enjoying something *sexual* together—that never happens with women. (It happens subliminally when you're with other girls at pajama parties, but not on purpose!)

Then we took our first issue to the Gay Day Parade and hoped it would sell enough so we could pay the printer the other half we owed—and fortunately it took off.

◆ **AJ: So this struck a real nerve in the community?**
◆ **SB:** It was incredibly popular. In terms of the variety that can be found in the lesbian community, the lesbian feminist press reflects a very minority point of view—there probably has never been a press which is so *prescriptive* rather than *descriptive* with regard to whom it's

addressing. By and large this press said [about us], "They're racist, they're anti-Semitic, they're anti-feminist, they're woman-hating, they're sick, they're objectifying, they're demeaning"—we were called every name in the book! Or, people who were being "objective" would like *one* thing in our magazine but tear apart everything else. Nevertheless, the reaction of your average-dyke-on-the-street was, "Give me one *now!*" Obviously lesbians were starved for some kind of *sexual* recognition.

We started discovering things we hadn't been realized. For example, before *On Our Backs*, you rarely saw lesbian faces in print unless they were *dead*: a photo of Gertrude Stein. You just didn't see pictures of contemporary women who were gay. But in *On Our Backs* that started happening on a regular basis: you could look at all these different girls and say, "Migod—she's gay and she lives in Iowa!" (or wherever). Secondly, there was no national lesbian magazine—there was nothing that lesbians all over the country could connect to and read, that was like *On Our Backs*. Also, our production standards were wildly slick compared to anything that had come out of the lesbian community before.

There's always been this talk that lesbians don't have as much money, but it's not like lesbians as a whole are below the poverty line. That isn't the reason the lesbian press never had anything that looked professional or slick . . .

I finished a lecture and someone asked, "How come you dykes are all so fat and ugly?!"

◆ **AJ: I think that's true of a lot of fringe groups: basically, they internalize and perpetuate their own ghetto-ization.**
◆ **SB:** Working on *On Our Backs*, you had to learn how to become a journalist, a graphic artist, a business person—which is always shocking to artists and revolutionaries who don't think of themselves as having much going in the left brain. You don't think of yourself as a *business person*, you think, "I'm trying to smash the state and destroy sexual inhibitions!"
◆ **AJ: Taking responsibility is important, regardless what you do creatively. Our society is so full of these sick dichotomies: either/or syndromes where either you're a sterile business person, or you're a creative nut who can't function—**
◆ **SB:** *On Our Backs* offered a voice for a lot of incredible talent that had no place to be expressed before. I also found that my columns, "Toys For Us" (in which supposedly I was dispensing sexual advice: I might visit a lesbi-

an community in Chicago and describe what it was like, or tell about how I got pierced, or write about fisting) turned out to be "milestones"! I mean, no one had ever written about vaginal fisting before, and they still haven't—to the best of my knowledge. There were so many things to write about. I'd always loved to write but had never had such a devoted and diverse audience as I found in *On Our Backs*. And what I learned at Good ·Vibrations talking to people about sex, I channeled into this column. I found I could use humor to make everybody let their hair down about issues that otherwise no one would talk about.

Don't you shudder if somebody calls you "straight" because they see you with a man? The fact is: *nobody* wants to be "straight" anymore.

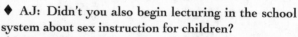

♦ **AJ: Didn't you also begin lecturing in the school system about sex instruction for children?**
♦ **SB:** I always did that. Some of my friends who worked in the public school system were instrumental in setting up programs where "Dick and Jane Homo" come to sex education class and talk about themselves (both in high school and college). Here, essentially you're laying yourself open to anything anybody wants to say, because in general young people won't hold their prejudices back. Plus, you tell them, "Please don't try to be polite." So if you've finished your lecture and someone asks, "Well—how come you dykes are all so fat and ugly?" instead of saying, "Well—I never!" and stomping out, you have to stand there and reply, "Do you think *I'm* fat and ugly?" (When that happened, for a second I was so crushed.)

But what that student asked reflects a fairly common prejudice: that the reason women turn lesbian is because they're too fat or ugly to attract a man. "If you have to turn to women, you must be so unattractive that a *man* wouldn't be interested in you." On the one hand, women who are lesbian aren't worried about whether their pussy is too big or not, or whether they're blonde, or whether their bust is big enough—lesbians do not impose the kind of sexual demands or pressure that straight culture puts on women. That's a very pleasing and comforting part of lesbianism—not to always have to think your makeup's on trial, in order to find a partner. But . . . lesbians are just as attracted to beauty as anybody. And we certainly have our standards about what we do or don't find attractive . . .

I remember I had this book from the '40s which gave "secret" insights into lesbians. One chapter contained

this sentence: "Some of the most beautiful stars in our Hollywood galaxy are secret lesbians." I always *loved* reading that sentence, because the other side of the dyke who doesn't get her hair styled, doesn't wear makeup, and has a beer gut . . . is that: many lesbians are totally entranced by beauty and glamour. Some people call them "lipstick lesbians," but this has been going on a long time—Greta Garbo was one of the most beautiful women in Hollywood; so was Marlene Dietrich—all these women have passed away now, so we can *talk* about them. But just imagine who the *contemporary* stars might be who are bisexual or gay, and the answer to that students question is both 1) you don't comprehend the diversity of lesbians; how many different kinds of women they are, and the different kinds of "looks" they're into; 2) is the idea that: if you aren't into men, you must not have any personal aesthetics or care about your looks? (Do I have to mention that the person who asked this question must have weighed 200 pounds, didn't comb his hair, and wore really ugly, mismatching clothes? It was like the pot calling the kettle black—that was an outrageous question.)

So I did lectures; I kept doing my performance art, but more and more just getting out the next issue of *On Our Backs* was the performance—I didn't have time for anything else. We went from quarterly to bimonthly; we created the idea of a lesbian pictorial. When we started out, there were three women who had done lesbian erotic portraiture: Honey Lee, Tee Corinne, and Morgan Gwenwald—and that was *it*. We put together pictorials of couples or single women, sometimes in a documentary style or sometimes to create a fantasy. It was thrilling—we were looking at every gay and straight men's magazine to see, "How do you lay out a pictorial? What's a pictorial all about?" and we were also completely rejecting the "standards" for those pictorials. Our women were very diverse and individualistic in their looks, and we were very excited to see the reaction to these women.

I remember with Honey Lee's centerfolds, "Bull Dyke of the Month." She got 3 responses: 1) the people who wanted to call her up in the middle of the night and talk dirty; the people who had found their dream dyke. 2) people who asked, "What is this ugly dyke doing in the middle of *On Our Backs?* I'm so disgusted. If you want to know what a good-looking woman looks like, I suggest you look at *Penthouse.*" And that was a very strong lesbian reaction: "I do not like looking at butch women, thank you very much. This embarrasses me; I don't identify with it, and get it out of here!" 3) (and this happened mostly among lesbian feminists) women who would say, "Wow! This is really great: to show a woman who is not the conventional pretty babe. But it doesn't turn me on, and I don't know *what* I'm supposed to do."

This sounds so young and innocent now, but a cornerstone of lesbians exploring sexuality is: we had a political point of view informed by feminism about how "we should accept ourselves, and love ourselves." And then, when we had to talk about our fantasies and what turned us on—well, granola didn't necessarily turn us on! Even though that was what we ate in the morning, that isn't what we wanted to look at pictures of. And to this day, this issue still bothers people.

♦ **AJ: It bothers people who really want *Playboy* types?**

♦ **SB:** Some of them might have wanted *Playboy* types; some of them may have wanted James Dean—who *knows* what they all wanted?! Honey Lee's centerfold was erotic but it was also making a point: you could enjoy the "political" point and not get *off* on it, or you could get off on it *and* enjoy the political point. It was startling to realize that a lot of women weren't accustomed to looking at pictures with an attitude of *subjectification*. People would say incredible things like, "How can I look at this picture and masturbate? For all I know, this woman might be a *racist*. She might be a child-beater. She might be a *meat-eater*. She might be mean to her cats. How do we know what she's *really like?*"

This is like the foundation of an education in the arts, or when you grow up as a child and learn about what's "real" and what's fantasy; what's "pretend" and what's "not pretend." You can look at a picture and imagine anything you want; it doesn't matter who the person in the picture "is" or what they "really" do—that's beside the point. I think part of our consciousness knows that very well—but there's part that's *troubled* by it. I think this issue comes up for our models who aren't professional. Almost all the models who posed for *On Our Backs* were amateurs, first-timers, who had to learn and realize that people would look at that picture and imagine anything they pleased. That's very difficult for a newcomer. And if you're a feminist, it's even more difficult because there's this idea that someone is going to "exploit" your image and think something about you that you don't want them to think!

♦ **AJ: We have a whole phallic Judeo-Christian mind/body split culture that also is very afraid of creativity. Creativity, fantasy, eroticism, playfulness, artifice, and all the arts are interconnected to social change or "revolution." A lot of women who should be involved in feminist/planetary revolution aren't, because of the pressure of "Who's more feminist than thou?" Or, "If I actually have desire that's not 'politically correct,' then . . ."**

♦ **SB:** As *On Our Backs* developed and I began to travel and meet people in other cities that read the magazine, I started to realize that this ideology that people call "politically correct" was maintained by so few people—the ideology itself is hypocrisy. These few people (who couldn't even live *up* to it) were the only ones who even believed in it; meanwhile, everyone else could really care less. I mean, if a person isn't being sexually open, it's not because some important lesbian is telling them they can't—it's because of very simple, powerful inhibitions and taboos you've had since you were a child. Which is a much more honest depiction of why people aren't more *out there* about their erotic identities. It isn't because of

peer pressure within a politically dogmatic milieu; it's because your mama told you not to do it—and that's the bottom line.

I think about all the silly things I didn't do when I was first sexual because I thought they weren't "politically correct." I remember not fucking my girlfriend because that would be "patriarchal" and "objectifying" her. I remember the first time a man ever spanked me in sex—I had an orgasm and I remember thinking, "Ohmigod!" As soon as he had stopped, I pulled myself up in a very pristine way and said, "Don't you ever, *ever* do that again!" and made this little note to myself that "he was probably mentally ill." This was *after* my orgasm! Now I'm so embarrassed—I wish I could write him a "Thank You" letter now (but who knows where he is?): "I'm sorry—I was so wrong, you were so right!" And I was objecting to that because of peer group pressure. When I really think about my most serious resistance to sexual exploration, it isn't because of the things I learned in the '70s from my political idols, it's because of my Catholic Girls' School education, and the kind of little girl I was brought up to be.

The first time a man spanked me—I had an orgasm, then said, "Don't you ever, *ever* do that again!"

♦ **AJ: I believe we have to position ourselves outside of the society for political gain and strength and mobilizing, such as taking on a lesbian moniker for political reasons: proclaim "I'm a lesbian!" or, "I'm gay!" or, "I'm in ACT UP!" or whatever. But when we get to areas of sexuality and desire, what do we want a revolution *for*? It's to have a more enjoyable life.**

♦ **SB:** I've come full circle on these labels. At first I was so angry about lesbianism being devoid of any sexual content, but now I feel that to tell someone you're "lesbian" or "gay" says so little about what your *sex* life is about that it's almost useless. I'd rather just have it be a *political* label now. I can't believe I've come that far. When I was 16 I remember being very excited when I got my first "DYKE" pin. I wore it to a demonstration and I wore it to school, and I fucked both boys and girls. I did that then and I do now. Putting a "DYKE" button on challenged all those people who thought that I was straight (they *never* think there's a gay person around them); it challenged their idea of what a dyke "looked like" or "was"—and this was worth *every second* of it! I'd do it a million times over. This was an example of a political statement that I couldn't possibly regret.

As far as finding women I was attracted to—I'm not attracted to all lesbians; I'm not attracted to all women.

You know what I'm talking about—there's this thing: "Well, if you're *gay*, it's a wonder I haven't ripped your clothes off!" Just as homosexuals are supposed to be compulsively attracted to anyone of the same sex . . .

♦ **AJ: That's such a homophobic attitude: If you're a lesbian (or gay), you sexualize the world. Whereas we don't assume that every straight woman wants to fuck every man that walks by. Somehow with gays there's the myth that you're not only assumed to be "available," but also "desirous" of anyone else who's gay.**

♦ **SB:** You have to be a nymphomaniac—yes! So of course it's helpful to be able to say you're a lesbian, or introduce yourself as a lesbian as a shortcut, because lots of times it's not appropriate for you to say, "Here's what my erotic identity is all about. It won't be in one word; it'll take a paragraph or two"—*if* you can even describe it at all; it's hard. Lots of times it's largely unconscious; most people haven't given it a lot of thought. Everyone's supposed to be straight; boys are supposed to be attracted to girls and want to do a certain thing in bed (and vice versa), and to deviate from that at all puts you in a "queer" category.

I can't think of another subject that binds people together as clearly as *sex*.

To tell people about the Kinsey scale, and that we're on a continuum from 0 to 6, and that most people are not 0's or 6's but are somewhere in the middle—that's one thing. But the other thing is: *why* is that so unpopular as a way to describe people? In fact, the labels people use (lesbian, gay, bisexual) depending on the time, place, bus stop you're sitting at, and words you use, mean a lot more than who you fuck.

For example, a recent issue of *Bay Times* reported this raging controversy about bisexuals in the gay movement. One fellow who was just being very candid said he thought men who called themselves "bisexual" were really saying that they liked men and women—but they like women a little bit *better*. He qualified this, "Well, maybe *some* people don't mean this, but that's what everyone understands you to be saying." And I thought that was a good observation on his part: that when we call ourselves these various names, we're not speaking "clinically" or being understood clinically; we're being understood with whatever's in the *air;* whatever our peers are deciding this label means politically and culturally. Language can be very frustrating!

I remember for my 1990 New Years Column I decided I wanted to be like Jeanne Dixon or Andy Rooney and make all these predictions and demand that people start

"Doing things for the '90s!" And my Number One demand was: "Do not tell me what you are, tell me what you *do*. Because your labels mean nothing to me anymore."

I remember when I would tell people I was a socialist; it was totally hopeless—what the fuck does that mean anymore? If you tell somebody you're a "feminist"—very little meaning is clear. Labels only work when there's about 5 people who are using them—as soon as anybody else starts agreeing with you and using that label, it becomes more and more meaningless. The thing that's so funny about the gay movement is: the more people that come out of the closet and say, "I'm queer and I'm proud and I'm out of the closet and I could give a damn what anybody thinks about me anymore!"—the less "inclusive" our gay label becomes. And there's kind of a *mourning* of that passing, like, "Gee, we all used to be in this family and know each other so well, and understand what we could expect from each other, and now we can't do that anymore." You can't assume that the gay person sitting next to you shares your political point of view, or your family background, or your sexual interests.

♦ **AJ: We have to have a different structure if we're going to survive as a human species. Can't we conceive of a gay or lesbian movement that would include "straight" people?**

♦ **SB:** But the fact is that *nobody* wants to be 'straight' anymore. Don't you shudder if somebody calls you "straight" because they see you with a man? Because you don't *feel* straight; you feel you're much more complex than the word "straight" would indicate to anybody.

♦ **AJ: To somebody like Jesse Helms we're all going to get locked up anyway. The question is: how do you have a revolutionary movement that's inclusionary rather than exclusionary?**

♦ **SB:** A sexual liberation movement, in order to be truly integrated and at its most powerful, would be a movement that *already* took gay civil rights for granted. And as long as there is institutionalized homophobia and gay discrimination in terms of jail, housing, jobs, marriage and all that—as long as that exists, the sexual liberation movement is going to be *stunted*, because those things are so important—they're like a big boulder lying on top of everybody's face—you can't breathe.

The people who are most interested in the sexual liberation aspect tend to be people who are living in Bohemian communities where they aren't often faced with the State sticking its morality up your ass, right? It only happens every once in a while, where suddenly we realize, "Ohmigod, my partner just died and I'm not being allowed into the hospital!" Then, when things like that happen to you; when you've been totally out of the closet for *years*, your mind is blown! You can't *believe* you're being treated like this, because that's not where you're at intellectually, and nobody you know *socially* is like that.

When we're among ourselves and we're writing and talking and discussing, we feel like, "Oh, give me a break—I don't care about the Equal Rights Amendment." Our mind and our sexual desires and our sophistication about our culture has gone 'way ahead of fighting Jesse Helms; we're on another planet! And it's hard to be patient—I get exasperated with the mainstream gay political movement because being out of the closet is such *old* news to me. But when I travel, I can see how much of an issue it *still* is for so many people for whom that just isn't possible. When I go to Arkansas to speak, they don't even put the word "gay" or "lesbian" on the flyer advertising me because if they did, none of the gays or lesbians would come! Because no one would want to be *seen* going to an event that proclaimed "gay" or "lesbian" on the leaflet—that's how crazy things are!

This is difficult for me to accept: the fact that I'm more interested philosophically in sexual liberation and in pushing artistic boundaries than I am in joining the Democratic party and trying to get Mr XYZ elected. That's not my bent politically or artistically—I don't want to do that. Yet I know that my chances for a really broad sexual liberation movement are hampered by the fact that basic civil rights are not, and have never been, secured.

♦ AJ: I keep thinking that the crisis is so deep in this culture, and the polarization between the rich and the poor so deep, that in order for any dispossessed groups to make any ground, we're all going to have to band together somehow. It was so disheartening to read recently how blacks pressuring for Civil Rights legislation were so upset about gay and lesbian demands— it's like, the resources are so scarce that all the disenfranchised groups are fighting each other over these pathetic crumbs. Then, of course, the power structure wins. Take your typical white WASP Republicans—they are very bonded together; they don't have much in-fighting. So how can all us dispossessed create a place where we can all work together?

♦ SB: Well, sex is a great common denominator. I've had people come up to me after my talks and ask if I felt that some of my observations about men, women and sex roles only pertained to whites, or to the middle-class, or to an "American" point of view. It's funny because I thought, "If you knew me and the way I grew up—Irish-Catholic working class, but education was a big deal— and the kind of schools I went to, and the kids I grew up with . . . then *yes*, a lot of my observations come from that point of view." But women's sexual oppression, unfortunately, is so worldwide that there's really no one who could get up and say, "Well gee, with the way *I* grew up as a woman I couldn't possibly relate to the kind of sexual oppression *you're* talking about." Forget it! I'm crossing that barrier because women have more in common about sexual denial and invisibility than we have differences. I can't think of another subject that binds people together as clearly as *sex*. That's been essential and key to my work. Everyone I meet who tells me something about the way they grew up and their sexuality is letting me in on *another piece of the puzzle.* ♦ ♦ ♦

Books

Susie Sexpert Vol II
Herotica II (editor)
Susie Sexpert's Lesbian Sex World
Herotica: a collection of women's erotic fiction
How to Read a Dirty Movie: essays on erotic film & commercial pornography

Periodicals

On Our Backs (Editor, Summer 1984-May 1991)
Penthouse Forum (Film Columnist; Contributing Editor)
Young Lust Comic: 20th Anniversary Edition (Co-Editor)
Good Vibration Erotic Video Library Catalog, 1989-present

Articles

"Masculinity in the 90s," *Esquire* Oct 1991
"Lesbians in the 90s," The *Advocate* Jan 1990
"1968-1988, 20 Years of Erotic Film," *Forum* Jan 1989
"Contemporary Women's Erotica," *Lambda Rising Book Report* 1988
"When Women Talk About Sex," *Utne Reader,* Fall 1988
"Profile of Chris Rage," The *Advocate* Sept 1988
"The Bloom in Women's Erotica," *Whole Earth Rev.*Fall 1986
"Safe Sex Behind the Green Door," *Forum* 1986

Classes/Lectures

"Reading, Writing and Rethinking Erotica" 1-Day workshop
"How To Read a Dirty Movie," a film clip/lecture presentation
"Politics of Sexuality," a semester-long program, UC Santa Cruz
"All Girl Action: the history of lesbian eroticism in Hollywood, hardcore and alternative cinema," a film clip/lecture presentation
"Sex in Public Erotic Expression, Censorship, and Sexual Repression," lecture
"The Bloom in Women's Erotica," lecture
"Reading, Writing and Rethinking Erotica," sex-writing workshop ("Learn how to write a killer orgasm scene. . .")

Television, Video & Film

Phil Donahue Show, May 1991
Gay & Lesbian Erotica in the US, BBC Documentary by Clare Bevin, Fall 1991
People Are Talking, talkshow produced by Nina Sullivan, 1989
News at 10, special documentary feature on women's erotica by Abby Sterling, 1988
Peril or Pleasure: feminism & pornography, video by Andrea Torrice, 1989
Stripped Bare: women in the sex industry speak out, video feature by Caitlin Manning, 1988
The Virgin Machine, feature film by Monica Treut, 1988

Articles & Interviews

have appeared in *Playboy, LA Weekly, SF Chronicle, Rolling Stone, Mother Jones, SF Examiner, Toronto Globe & Mail, Frisko* magazine.

Quotes

For the psychoanalyst, *ignorance* and *fear* are not two separate things. There's an ignorance that exists *through* fear. We hide certain things from ourselves to defend ourselves against them. With sex, this is precisely the case. — **from Pasolini's film,** *Love Meetings*

I know nothing that is beyond the reach of the human mind — except truth. — **Lautrèamont**

Love is not Happiness. — **Lautrèamont**

The spiritualities of male and female mystics were different. Women were more apt to somatize religious experience and to write in intense bodily metaphors; women mystics were more likely than men to receive graphically physical visions of God. The most bizarre bodily occurrences associated with women (e.g. stigmata, incorruptibility of the cadaver in death, mystical lactations and pregnancies, catatonic trances, ecstatic nosebleeds, miraculous inedia, eating and drinking pus, visions of bleeding hosts) either first appear in the twelfth and thirteenth centuries or increase significantly in frequency at that time. The body, and in particular the female body, seems to have begun to behave in new ways at a particular moment in the European past. The question is: Why is this so? — **Caroline W. Bynum, "The Female Body & Religious Practice in the Later Middle Ages,"** *Zone*

The Surrealists handed out leaflets in the streets before every new project and assured everybody that they, too, could be artists if they would only release the hidden creativity in their own unconscious minds.
— **Helena Lewis,** *The Politics of Surrealism*

Men created civilization in the image of a perpetual erection: a *pregnant* phallus. — **Phyllis Chesler,** *About Men*

Our modern society is engaged in polishing and decorating the cage in which humanity is kept imprisoned.
— *Enlightened Anarchism*

Pleasure is nature's test, her sign of approval.
— **Oscar Wilde**

A woman, especially if she have the misfortune of knowing anything, should conceal it as well as she can.
— **Jane Austen**

Disobedience, in the eyes of anyone who has read history, is man's original virtue. It is through disobedience and rebellion that progress has been made.
— **Oscar Wilde, The Soul of Man Under Socialism**

There is no surer way of subduing and oppressing the woman than with repeated pregnancies. The demands this makes on the woman occupy and wear her out till she cannot make any demands for herself.
— **Dr. Hedy Porteous, Sex and Identity**

ARE MEN REALLY THE ENEMY?
(1) When I am yelled at in the street I am (a) flattered (b) annoyed (c) astonished (d) sure I have been recognized.
(2) When I am yelled at in the street I respond by (a) lowering my head and walking quicker (b) smiling sweetly and nodding (c) addressing myself to the specific content of the yeller and replying appropriately (d) pretending it was not I who was yelled at and that I am not in that place and that he is not real and I am not real and thus simply extracting myself from the situation.
(3) Most rapes are committed by (a) women (b) children (c) men (perverts) (d) I am unable to distinguish rape from ordinary sexual relations.
(4) If I could do away with anything I wanted, the first thing I would do away with is: (a) the family (b) the state (c) private property (d) menstrual periods (e) all of the above. — **RAT women questionnaire (NY underground paper taken over by women in 1970)**

All the pursuits of men are the pursuits of women also, but in all of them a woman is inferior to a man. — **Plato**

No healthy male is ever actually modest. His conversation is one endless boast — often covert, but always undiluted. — **H.L. Mencken**

To build a revolution it is necesary to break all your interior chains. — *graffiti,* **May '68**

The weakness of their reasoning faculty also explains why women show more sympathy for the unfortunate than men. — **Schopenhauer, "On Women"**

How can a revolution be made without executions? — **Lenin**

Becoming masculine does not involve simple "imprinting." One has to *dare* to do certain activities which are dangerous and can be painful. There is nothing automatic about fighting. — **Norman Mailer**

Revolution must happen inside us before it is achieved in reality. . . A cop sleeps inside each of us — it is necessary to kill him! — *graffiti,* **May '68**

Action must not be a reaction but a creation . . . Speak to your neighbors; open the windows of your heart . . . Mind your ears, they have walls . . . We are reassured: two and two no longer make four. — *graffiti,* **May '68**

When men and women agree, it is only in their conclusions; their reasons are always different. — **George Santayana**

Being a woman is a terribly difficult task, since it consists principally in dealing with men. — **Joseph Conrad**

Don't liberate me — I'll do it myself! — *graffiti,* **May '68**

According to Fred Lawrence Guiles' biography of her, *Norma Jean,* Marilyn Monroe's agent told her in 1946: "I have a call for a light blonde — honey or platinum." In this world, women may be ordered like steaks: well-done, medium rare, or bloody. — **Angela Carter,** *The Sadeian Woman*

Free love — as if love is anything *but* free. Man has bought brains, but all the millions in the world have failed to buy love. — **Emma Goldman,** *Marriage and Love*

Where is the ebullient infinite woman who — immersed as she was in her naivete, kept in the dark about herself, led into self-disdain by the great arm of parental-conjugal phallocentrism — hasn't been ashamed of her strength? Who, surprised and horrified by the fantastic tumult of her drives, hasn't accused herself of being a monster? — **Hélène Cixous, quoted in** *Surrealism and Women*

God recognizes as freedom only that which is extended to *both* sexes and not to one alone. All the seeds of social abominations such as savagery, barbarism, and civilization have as their sole pivot the subjection of women. — *Design for Utopia,* **Selected Writings of Charles Fourier**

It is upon women that civilization weighs; it is for women to attack it. — *Ibid*

Among theologians, lawyers, and philosophers, discussion of women was almost always linked to marriage. Thinkers seemed unable to imagine a social role for unattached females. This psychological blind spot is one way to explain why a disproportionally high number of accused witches were widows and other unmarried women not under the rule of men. — **Joseph Klaits,** *Servants of Satan: The Age of the Witch Hunts*

Can man be free if woman be a slave? — **Shelley**

By 1600 advanced medical opinion, spurred by improved understanding of female anatomy, led most leading physicians to discard the Platonic image of the *migratory uterus*. . . "Woman's unnatural, insatiable lust," as the medically learned Thomas Burton put it, was proverbial, and her well-known capacity for multiple orgasms prompted the belief that she habitually exhausted and ran down her mate in satisfying her carnal appetites. — **Joseph Klaits,** *Servants of Satan: The Age of the Witch Hunts*

Mae West's sexuality, the most overt in the history of the cinema, could only be tolerated on the screen because she did not arrive in Hollywood until she had reached the age of menopause. — **Angela Carter,** *The Sadeian Woman*

An astonished eyewitness at Salem recounted how the Puritan Cotton Mather publicly exposed and fondled the breasts of a seventeen-year-old girl as she lay writhing in a fit of ostensibly demonic possession. — **Joseph Klaits,** *Servants of Satan: The Age of the Witch Hunts*

Art is the most intense mode of *individualism* the world has known. — **Oscar Wilde,** *The Soul of Man Under Socialism*

The male is completely egocentric, trapped inside himself, incapable of empathizing or identifying with others, of love, friendship, affection or tenderness. He is a completely isolated unit, incapable of rapport with anyone. . . He is a half-dead, unresponsive lump — consequently he is at best an utter bore. . . Eaten up with guilt, shame, fears and insecurities and obtaining, if he's lucky, a barely perceptible physical feeling, the male is, nonetheless, obsessed with screwing; he'll swim a river of snot, wade nostril-deep through a mile of vomit, if he thinks there'll be a friendly pussy awaiting him. He'll screw a woman he despises, any snaggle-toothed hag, and furthermore, pay for the opportunity. Why? — **Valerie Solanis, S.C.U.M. Manifesto (Society for Cutting Up Men)**

In the barbarian order it is necessary to brutalize women, to convince them that they have no souls, so as to dispose them to allow themselves to be sold on the market and shut up in a harem. — *The Utopian Vision of Charles Fourier*

The anarchist is the observer who sees what he sees and not what it is customary to see. — **Paul Valery**

There is a permanent conspiracy against anything that is original—that's what you have to get inside your head.
—**Flaubert, letter to Louise Collet**

Although they are housed on her person, from the moment they begin to show, a female discovers that her breasts are claimed by others. Parents and relatives mark their appearance as a landmark event, schoolmates take notice, girlfriends compare, boys zero in; later a husband, a lover, a baby expect a proprietary share.

—**Susan Brownmiller,** *Femininity*

Civilization, that great fraud of our times, has promised man that by complicating his existence it would multiply his pleasures. . . Civilization has promised man freedom, at the cost of giving up everything dear to him, which it arrogantly treated as lies and fantasies. . . Hour by hour needs increase and are nearly always unsatisfied, peopling the earth with discontented rebels. The superfluous has become a necessity and luxuries indispensable.—**Isabelle Eberhardt (***The Life of Isabelle Eberhardt* **by Annette Kobak)**

Do not waste your time on social questions. What is the matter with the poor is Poverty; what is the matter with the rich is Uselessness.—**George Bernard Shaw**

There can be no doubt that, historically, psychosurgery has been used predominantly against women . . . women are more than twice as likely to be subjected to lobotomy and electroshock as men. "The fact that she is returned to being a satisfactory housewife and mother is again typical of psychosurgery studies. Not only have the vast majority of patients been women, but the two most in-depth pro-lobotomy studies have already told us psychosurgery is much more effective on women than men, because women can more easily be returned home to function as partially crippled, brain-damaged housewives, while there are no social or occupational roles for partially crippled, brain-damaged men."—**testimony of Peter Breggin before Senator Edward Kennedy's Subcommittee on Health in the U.S.,** *Congressional Record*

Knock hard—life is deaf!—**Mimi Parent**

The goal of sexual repression is to produce an individual who is adjusted to the authoritarian order and will submit to it in spite of all misery and degradation.
—**Wilhelm Reich,** *The Mass Psychology of Fascism*

In Lancaster, Wisconsin, in 1982, Grant County judge William Rinecke sentenced Ralph Snodgrass, twenty-four, convicted of sexually assaulting the five-year-old daughter of the woman with whom he lived, to only ninety days in jail, because the girl was "an unusually sexually promiscuous young lady. No way do I believe that Mr Snodgrass initiated sexual contact."
—*Boston Globe,* **February 11, 1982**

When we consider the phenomenon of witch burning in Europe, we know that for every man burned at the stake as a witch, thousands and thousands of women were burned. Women were burned at the stake, accused by men, tortured by men, tried by men and executed by men.—**Jeffrey Masson,** *A Dark Science*

Men never do evil so completely and cheerfully as when they do it from religious conviction.—**Pascal**

All the statistics—whether they come from feminists, or the *Los Angeles Times,* or the government—are frightening in their implications: one in three women, before the age of eighteen, will be the victim of sexual assault. If we add to this figure rape and sexual harassment, there is hardly a woman growing up in our society who, at some time in her life, will not be subjected to unwanted sexual aggression.—**Jeffrey Masson,** *A Dark Science*

Women's Studies are a force that could revolutionize the very structures of knowledge . . .
—**Jane Gallop,** *Reading Lacan*

Political revolution will come about through *sexual liberation* and therefore *through the liberation of women.* That is why contemporary societies, under pressure of public opinion, are only making a show of liberating woman and tolerating the kind of sexuality that is not much more than a safety-valve.—**Jean Markale,** *Women of the Celts*

I have never been attracted by fecundity. It is the refusal of utility: participation in the continuity of the species is an *abdication.* In order to have children, a humility nearly inconceivable in the modern world is necessary, a brutalized passivity or a mad pretension. . . Myself, I know that I belong with the idea of Lilith, the anti-Eve, and that my universe is that of the spirit. Physical maternity instinctively repulses me.—**Leonor Fini**

People wore eyeglasses for 4 centuries before a London optician named Edward Scarlett thought of attaching them to ears in 1730.

If two people who are attracted to each other by pure friendship wish to conclude brotherhood, the man and not the girl first proposes it with the words, "I want to have a sister now." She agrees. In the presence of many others they mutually cut a small wound in the palm of their right hand, near the thumb, and suck each other's blood. They have then become brother and sister "as of one belly." Now they must always stand by each other in all matters, the brother must protect his sister. Valuable gifts are mutually exchanged. Even prostitutes behave tenderly, modestly and with consideration towards such blood brothers. I repeat, coitus between them is out of the question, it would be like incest. Such blood brotherhood can take place only between members of two different tribes, e.g. the Kikuyu and the Nandi.—*Voodoo Eros*

This is a government of, by, and for a bunch of *assholes*. Men in government butt-fuck whoever gets in the way of their war games, their head trips, and their death trips. Life is all about getting fucked—as in *over, up*, and *with* . . . I would inspire terrorism, assassination and sniping—but I'm not a politician.—**Lydia Lunch**

◆

Do away with the motive and you do away with the sin.—**Cervantes**

◆

I am not interested in policing the boundaries between nature and culture—quite the opposite, I am edified by the traffic. Indeed, I have always preferred the prospect of pregnancy with the embryo of another species.
—**Donna Haraway**, *Primate Visions*

◆

Animals have personalities like people and must be studied.—**Walt Disney**

◆

It is specifically the permanent tension between construction and deconstruction, identification moves and destabilization moves, that I see, not as uniquely feminist, but as inherent to feminism—and to science. Both feminist and scientific discourses are critical projects built in order to *destabilize* and *reimagine* their methods and objects of knowledge, in complex power fields.
—**Donna Haraway**, *Primate Visions*

◆

Life as human technological being is evolving toward the point at which the only energy on earth will be nuclear energy, the simulation of the sun . . . The humans are practically out of the picture already . . . Humans are the witnesses and agents—selective milieu—of an evolutionary mutation which will cancel us out or hold us in reserve with "nature" as slaves to the nuclear machines we will have synthesized to replace ourselves as "masters of the earth." This calls for consciousness and something more, but what?—**Peter Canning, "Here Comes The Sun"**

◆

Only since the 18th century have there been special clothes, games, and even books designed just for children . . . Childhood thus developed out of the printing press. Only since the 18th century has there been a special children's language. Part stammer and part squeak, part private code, even that idiom of transference love—baby talk—dates from the point of the printing-press child's emergence.—**Laurence Rickels, "Subliminalation"**

◆

As de Sade has demonstrated, pleasure—the pursuit of pleasure—emerges only within the alliance between imagination and conventional sign systems: the body is but the *limited analogue* of a pleasure that always comes from another place always held in place by *machines*.
—**Sigmund Freud**

◆

Americans admit they're liars: 91% tell pollsters they lie regularly, and 7% say they'd kill for $10 million.
—*S.F. Examiner, 4/29/91*

There is a crucial difference between the criminal and the outlaw. The criminal is a perverse rebel who acts out *against* the law, a subnormal person who is unable to care enough about others to bear adult responsibilities. The outlaw is a supranormal individual who cares about others too much to accept the limitations on *eros* that are imposed by normal life. Thus the outlaw quest moves *outside* and *beyond*, not *against* the law. While the rebel is merely rejecting the established, the outlaw is motivated by a quest for autonomy, self-government . . . *not* rooted in any undigested psychological need to rebel, but in a passion for justice, dignity and freedom. The trans-moral conscience of the outlaw is the inner voice of a universal community struggling to be born.
—**Sam Keen**, *The Passionate Life: Stages of Loving*

◆

All naming is already murder.—**Lacan**

◆

To me naming is about empowerment. It is also a source of tremendous pleasure. I name everything—typewriters, cars, most things I use—that gives something to me. It is a way to acknowledge the life force in every object. Often the names I give to things and people are related to my past. They are a way to preserve and honor aspects of that past.—**bell hooks**, *Talking Back*

◆

Freud discovered that truth manifests itself in the letter rather than the spirit—that is, in the way things are *actually* said rather than in the "intended" meaning.
—**Jane Gallop**, *Reading Lacan*

◆

Lacan teaches that language speaks the subject, that the speaker is *subjected* to language rather than master of it.
—**Jane Gallop**, *Reading Lacan*

◆

The function of representation comes to grief when words lose their connection with things and come to stand in the place of things—in short, when language represents itself.—**Mark Poster**, *The Mode of Information*

◆

In [a better] world, children will not be taught epics about men who are honored for being violent, or fairy tales about children who are lost in frightful woods where women are malevolent witches. They will be taught new myths, epics, and stories in which human beings are good; men are peaceful; and the power of creativity and love—symbolized by the sacred Chalice, the holy vessel of life—is the governing principle. In this world, our drive for justice, equality and freedom, our thirst for knowledge and spiritual illumination, and our yearning for love and beauty will at last be freed. And after the bloody detour of androcratic history, both women and men will at last find out what being human can mean.
—**Riane Eisler**, *The Chalice & The Blade*

◆

There are no positive terms for a strong, sexual woman. Whore or slut do not equal *stud*.—**Holly Hughes interviewed by Rebecca Schneider**, *TDR*

No fewer than 74 million women alive today have been subjected to female circumcision. In the worst cases they have had their labia and clitoris scraped or cut away and their vaginal opening stitched up with silk, catgut or thorns, leaving only a tiny opening for urine and menstrual blood. After the operation the girl's legs are bound together to ensure that scar-tissue forms and the condition becomes permanent. Later, when they marry, these females suffer the pain of having their artificially reduced orifices broken open by their husbands . . . A side-effect is a high number of deaths and serious illnesses caused by the unhygienic conditions under which the operations are performed. — **Desmond Morris, *Bodywatching***

The publication of *International Archives of Body Techniques* would be of truly international benefit, providing an inventory of all the possibilities of the human body and of the methods of apprenticeship and training employed to build up each technique, for there is not one human group in the world which could not make an original contribution to such an enterprise . . . It would also be a project eminently well fitted for counteracting racial prejudices, since it would contradict the racialist conceptions which try to make out that man is a product of his body, by demonstrating that it is the other way around: man has, at all times and in all places, been able to turn his body into a product of his techniques and his representations. — **Claude Lévi-Strauss, *Introduction to the Work of Marcel Mauss***

The society whose modernization has reached the stage of the "integrated spectacle" is characterized by the combined effect of five principal features: incessant technological renewal, integration of state and economy, generalized secrecy, unanswerable lies, and an eternal present.
— **Guy Debord, *Comments on the Society of the Spectacle***

The future can only be anticipated in the form of an absolute *danger*. It is that which breaks absolutely with constituted normality and can only be proclaimed, *presented*, as a sort of monstrosity.
— **Jacques Derrida, *Of Grammatology***

Whoever fights monsters should see to it that in the process he does not become a monster. And when you look long into an abyss, the abyss also looks into you.
— **Nietzsche, *Beyond Good and Evil***

Women who want to be equal to men lack imagination. — *graffiti*

[Fashion is] a kind of machine for maintaining meaning without ever fixing it; it is forever a *disappointed* meaning — but it is nevertheless meaning. Without content, it then becomes the spectacle human beings grant themselves: of their power to make the insignificant signify.
— **Roland Barthes, *The Fashion System***

When Eve was created, Satan rejoiced. — **Mohammed**

Is it not commonplace nowadays to say that the forces of man have already entered into a relation with the forces of information technology and their third-generation machines, which together create something other than man: indivisible 'man-machine' systems? Is this a union with silicon instead of carbon? — **Gilles Deleuze, *Foucault***

[Women] are confronted virtually with the problem of *reinventing* the world of knowledge, of thought, of symbols and images. Not of course by repudiating everything that has been done, but by subjecting it to exacting scrutiny and criticism from the position of women as subject . . . or knower. — **Dorothy E. Smith, "Ideological Structure and How Women Are Excluded"**

Freedom is a *mystery*. Freedom depends on the very thing that limits or denies it — fate, God, biological or social determinism, whatever. To carry out its mission, fate counts on the complicity of our freedom, and to be free we must overcome fate. The dialectics of freedom and fate is the theme of Greek tragedy and Shakespeare, although in Shakespeare fate appears as passion (love, jealousy, ambition, envy) and as chance. The idea of conditional freedom implies the notion of personal responsibility. Each of us, literally, either creates or destroys his own freedom — a freedom that is always precarious. — **Octavio Paz, intv in *Paris Review* #119**

Learning to speak is like learning to shoot. — **Avital Ronell, *The Telephone Book***

The degree of emancipation of women is an index of the degree of a society's emancipation. — **Charles Fourier**

In the Buddhist tradition, people used to speak of "enlightenment" as a kind of returning home. The 3 worlds — the worlds of form, of non-form, of desire — are not your homes. These are places where you wander around for many existences, alienated from your own nature. So enlightenment is the way to get back. And they speak about efforts to go back — described in terms of the *recovery of oneself, of one's integrity*. — **Thich Nhat Hanh, *The Raft Is Not The Shore***

It is common knowledge that women have historically taken care of the dead in the home before there was an established occupation of undertaking.
— *American Funeral Director*

"Identity politics" regards the discovery of identity as its supreme goal. Feminists even assert that discovering an identity is an act of resistance. The mistake is to view identity as an end rather than a means. Identity is not merely a precursor to action, it is also created *through* action. — **Jenny Bourne, "Homelands of the Mind: Jewish Feminism and Identity Politics"**

I've come up with a new theory about sex. There is a scale, and at one end is absolutely total ecstasy and sheer enlightenment. On the other end is abuse, pain, suffering, rape, power-tripping—everything negative about sex. I guess married life or boring, routine sex would be in the middle. I've traveled virtually the entire line, made a stop at every single point.—**Annie Sprinkle interviewed by Linda Montano, *TDR***

◆

There was one point, for about a year in my sexual evolution, where I went to a kinky sex club. I would be in the center of the room, surrounded by 12 guys on their knees, jerking off, then I'd go get fist-fucked by an amputee without a fist, then have a dog eat crisco off my pussy, then I'd fist-fuck a guy up the ass, piss on someone—all in one night. It was the most liberating, mind-boggling, fabulous, fantastic time in my life. But today, you couldn't get me to do that if you paid me!—**Annie Sprinkle interviewed by Linda Montano, *TDR***

◆

To whip someone now doesn't appeal to me, because I somehow feel that it *hurts* them deep down, even though I whipped people with love. I'd like to take somebody who wanted to be whipped and show them what more pure, direct love is like. And Tantra is the image that I have for that—Tantra and loving myself.—**Annie Sprinkle interviewed by Linda Montano, *TDR***

◆

We now know that our civilization too is mortal.
—**Paul Valery**

◆

There are many women who want to have children. Our planet is overcrowded already, so if a woman doesn't feel like it, it is infinitely preferable that she abstain. A lynx needs 400 kilometers of territory, otherwise it dies. People need space and they haven't got enough.
—**Nelly Kaplan**

◆

People who are evil attack others instead of facing their own failures.—**M. Scott Peck, *People of the Lie***

◆

For Madame Pelletier [see interview with Kerr & Malley], feminine clothes were signs of *servitude*, of being a *sex* and not an individual. Her masculine attire, her short hair, were exterior signs of liberty in a world which was essentially male and in which women don't believe in themselves—for they were taught from childhood that only men have personalities that count. Her male attire was thus not only a sign of *liberty*, but also a passport into the male universe, which from her earliest childhood had seemed the only meaningful one.
—**Charles Sowerwine, *Sisters or Citizens?***

◆

The artist's imagination wards off the despair of the world; creation affords man the possibility of inventing his own future, of imagining his own world and celebrating a ritual which brings him close to the collective unconscious.—**Michel Ciment, *John Boorman***

"Language is not merely a more or less systematic inventory of the various items of experience . . . but actually *defines* experience for us because of our unconscious projection of its explicit expectations into the field of experience . . . the 'real world' is to a large extent built up on the language habits of the group."—**Edward A. Sapir, "Selected Writing in Language, Culture and Personality."**

◆

Aware that the public questioned her own sexual identity, Madame Pelletier suggested that she was essentially a woman like any other, extraordinary only in refusing to be exploited. Her fictional self, Marie, looking back over a celibate life, reflects that "certainly she wasn't without sexuality; she also felt these desires, but she had to repress them in order to remain *free*. She didn't regret it."
—***European Women on the Left*, ed. Jane Slaughter & Robert Kern**

◆

Most of all beware, even in thought, of assuming the sterile attitude of the spectator, for life is not a spectacle, a sea of griefs is not a proscenium, and a man who wails is not a dancing bear.
—**Aime Cesaire, *Return to My Native Land***

◆

All experts serve the state and the media and only in that way do they achieve their status. The most useful expert, of course, is the one who can lie. Whenever individuals lose the capacity to see things for *themselves*, the expert is there to offer an absolute reassurance.
—**Guy Debord, *Comments on the Society of the Spectacle***

◆

Never before has censorship been so perfect. Never before has it been possible to lie to citizens so brazenly. Many things may be unauthorized; everything is permitted. Talk of scandal is thus archaic. "Once there were scandals, but not any more."
—**Guy Debord, *Comments on the Society of the Spectacle***

◆

In a 17th century execution fourteen cats were shut in a cage with a woman who was roasted over a slow fire while the cats in misery and terror clawed her in their own death agonies.
—**Carl Van Vechten, *The Tiger in the House***

◆

To protect yourself from sorcery by cats there was one, classic remedy: maim it. Cut its tail, clip its ears, smash one of its legs, tear or burn its fur, and you would break its malevolent power.—**Robert Darton, *The Great Cat Massacre and Other Episodes in French Cultural History***

◆

The power of cats was concentrated on the most intimate aspects of domestic life: sex. Le chat, la chatte, le minet mean the same thing in French slang as "pussy" does in English, and they have served as obscenities for centuries.—***Ibid***

◆

The worst egoist is the person to whom the thought has never occurred that he might be one.—**Sigmund Freud**

Don't ever be completely masculine because a superior woman is superior to her masculine colleague. In you as a woman there are some exceptional qualities, but they would cease to be so attractive and so remarkable if you got too close to that other part of the human species that is *egoism personified.*—letter to Isabelle Eberhardt quoted in Annette Kobak's *The Life of Isabelle Eberhardt.*

◆

Television has glamorized war for us, whether the movie-drenched jungle palette of the Vietnam War news or the sinister black-and-white film relayed to our living rooms from the nose-cone cameras of Desert Storm's smart bombs, which almost incite the television viewer to become a cruise missile.—J.G. Ballard

◆

Life is a comedy for those who think and a tragedy for those who feel.—Horace Walpole

◆

All forms of eroticism are basically the search for *emotional shock.*—Isha Schwaller de Lubicz, *The Opening of the Way*

◆

The imaginary is that which tends to become real.
—Andre Breton

◆

Mastery of the physical body gives health and strength; mastery of the emotions prevents one from being controlled by others, and opens the inward ear; mastery of the mind, by which the arising thoughts can be either formulated or abolished at will, makes possible intuitive vision.—Isha Schwaller de Lubicz, *The Opening of the Way*

◆

It's not the poet's responsibility to give other people illusions of earthly or heavenly hope, or to weaken people's minds. . . On the contrary, the poet is supposed to keep on saying sacrilegious words and permanent blasphemies.—Benjamin Peret, *The Dishonor of Poets*

◆

The time has come to valorize woman's ideas at the expense of those of man. . . In particular, it is the artist's task to give the greatest priority to everything that comes from the feminine system of the world.
—Andre Breton, *Arcane 17*

◆

Of course, I understand that this is just a dream. . . But if this artificial mind can sustain itself and grow of its own accord, then for the first time human thought will live free of bones and flesh, giving this child of mind an earthly immortality denied to us.—[talking about Artificial Intelligence] computer designer Daniel Hillis, *Daedalus,* Winter 1988

◆

Breakdowns play a central role in human understanding. A breakdown is not a negative situation to be avoided, but a situation of non-obviousness, in which some aspect . . . is brought forth to visibility. A breakdown reveals the nexus of relations necessary for us to accomplish our task.

—Winograd, in Edwards and Gordon, forthcoming

Dig it, this is a planet of women . . . the men are just guests here. They're the mothers, the ones who bear the life of new generations. It's like they have the greatest creative energy going for them. Women today are not satisfied . . . they want men, but all they find are little boys.—Charles Manson

◆

Americans love and hate sex. Sex sells products, fuels popular novels and Hollywood's star system. And yet, when this commodification becomes *literal,* when sexual pleasure is bought and sold, Americans are terrified. Sex professionals bear the burden of this fear. Prostitutes have historically been publicly vilified, leaving them vulnerable to attack, abuse, and harassment from all sides. Yet they never seem to run out of clients. The criminalization of prostitution denies them safe working conditions, and targets them for abuse and violence by johns, cops and criminals..—Excerpt from MANIFESTO by GRAN FURY (NY sex/activist group) WITH P.O.N.Y. (Prostitutes of New York)

◆

[From a letter written to John Adams, who was attending the Continental Congress, by his wife Abigail, 1776]: In the new Code of Laws [our Constitution] Remember the Ladies, and be more generous and favourable to them than your ancestors. Do *not* put such unlimited powers into the hands of the Husbands. Remember: *all men would be tyrants if they could.* If particular care and attention is not paid to the Ladies, we are determined to foment a *Rebellion,* and will not hold ourselves bound by any laws in which we have no voice, or representation.

◆

Eroticism is the magic of vitality, expressed mainly through the awakening of sexual power.
—R.A. Schwaller de Lubicz

◆

When Tarzan first meets La—if one can call it a meeting—she is the priestess assigned to make him into a human sacrifice by piercing his heart. She seems friendly, even *enchanting*—she rescues him from unfriendly gorillas, dances around him, sings in a soft and musical voice. Then she places a rope around his neck and leads him to a bloodstained altar transformed by the fanatical zeal of religious ecstasy into a wild-eyed and bloodthirsty executioner, who, with dripping knife, would be the first to drink her victim's red, warm blood from the little golden cup that stood upon the altar.
—Marianna Torgovnick, *Gone Primitive* (on Edgar Rice Burroughs' *Return of Tarzan*)

◆

Anti and *pro* are two facets of the same thing. . . I force myself into self-contradiction to avoid following my own taste. . . For me there is something else in addition to *yes, no,* and *indifferent*—that is, for instance, the absence of investigations of that type. I am against the word *anti* because it's a bit like atheist, as compared to believer. An atheist is just as much of a religious man as the believer is.
—Marcel Duchamp

[RE]SEARCH Catalog

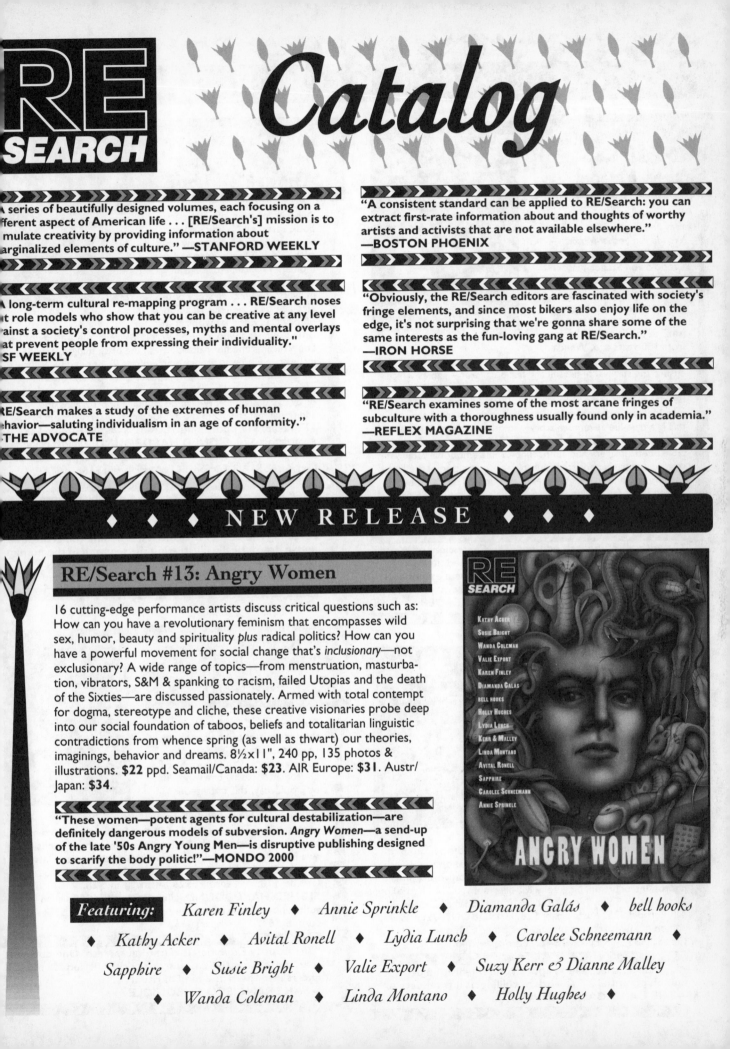

"A series of beautifully designed volumes, each focusing on a different aspect of American life . . . [RE/Search's] mission is to stimulate creativity by providing information about marginalized elements of culture." —STANFORD WEEKLY

"A long-term cultural re-mapping program . . . RE/Search noses out role models who show that you can be creative at any level against a society's control processes, myths and mental overlays that prevent people from expressing their individuality." —SF WEEKLY

"RE/Search makes a study of the extremes of human behavior—saluting individualism in an age of conformity." —THE ADVOCATE

"A consistent standard can be applied to RE/Search: you can extract first-rate information about and thoughts of worthy artists and activists that are not available elsewhere." —BOSTON PHOENIX

"Obviously, the RE/Search editors are fascinated with society's fringe elements, and since most bikers also enjoy life on the edge, it's not surprising that we're gonna share some of the same interests as the fun-loving gang at RE/Search." —IRON HORSE

"RE/Search examines some of the most arcane fringes of subculture with a thoroughness usually found only in academia." —REFLEX MAGAZINE

NEW RELEASE

RE/Search #13: Angry Women

16 cutting-edge performance artists discuss critical questions such as: How can you have a revolutionary feminism that encompasses wild sex, humor, beauty and spirituality *plus* radical politics? How can you have a powerful movement for social change that's *inclusionary*—not exclusionary? A wide range of topics—from menstruation, masturbation, vibrators, S&M & spanking to racism, failed Utopias and the death of the Sixties—are discussed passionately. Armed with total contempt for dogma, stereotype and cliche, these creative visionaries probe deep into our social foundation of taboos, beliefs and totalitarian linguistic contradictions from whence spring (as well as thwart) our theories, imaginings, behavior and dreams. 8½x11", 240 pp, 135 photos & illustrations. **$22** ppd. Seamail/Canada: **$23**. AIR Europe: **$31**. Austr/ Japan: **$34**.

"These women—potent agents for cultural destabilization—are definitely dangerous models of subversion. *Angry Women*—a send-up of the late '50s Angry Young Men—is disruptive publishing designed to scarify the body politic!"—MONDO 2000

Featuring: Karen Finley ◆ Annie Sprinkle ◆ Diamanda Galás ◆ bell hooks ◆ Kathy Acker ◆ Avital Ronell ◆ Lydia Lunch ◆ Carolee Schneemann ◆ Sapphire ◆ Susie Bright ◆ Valie Export ◆ Suzy Kerr & Dianne Malley ◆ Wanda Coleman ◆ Linda Montano ◆ Holly Hughes ◆

The Confessions of Wanda von Sacher-Masoch

Finally available in English: the racy and riveting *Confessions of Wanda von Sacher-Masoch*—married for ten years to Leopold von Sacher-Masoch (author of *Venus in Furs* and many other novels) whose whip-and-fur bedroom games spawned the term "masoch-ism." In this feminist classic from 100 years ago, Wanda was forced to play "sadistic" roles in Leopold's fantasies to ensure the survival of herself and her 3 children—games which called into question who was the Master and who the Slave. Besides being a compelling study of a woman's search for her own identity, strength and ultimately—complete independence—this is a true-life adventure story—an odyssey through many lands peopled by amazing characters. Underneath its unforgettable poetic imagery and almost unbearable emotional cataclysms reigns a woman's consistent unblinking investigation of the limits of morality and the deepest meanings of love. Translated by Marian Phillips, Caroline Hébert & V. Vale. 8½ x 11", 136 pages, illustrations. **$17 ppd.** Seamail/Canada: **$18.** AIR Europe: **$25.** Austr/Japan: **$28.**

"As with all RE/Search editions, *The Confessions of Wanda von Sacher-Masoch* is extravagantly designed, in an illustrated, oversized edition that is a pleasure to hold. It is also exquisitely written, engaging and literary and turns our preconceptions upside down."—**LA READER**

Freaks: We Who Are Not As Others by Daniel P. Mannix

Another long out-of-print classic book based on Mannix's personal acquaintance with sideshow stars such as the Alligator Man and the Monkey Woman, etc. Read all about the notorious love affairs of midgets; the amazing story of the elephant boy; the unusual amours of Jolly Daisy, the fat woman; the famous pinhead who inspired Verdi's *Rigoletto*; the tragedy of Betty Lou Williams and her parasitic twin; the black midget, only 34 inches tall, who was happily married to a 264-pound wife; the human torso who could sew, crochet and type; and bizarre accounts of normal humans turned into freaks—either voluntarily or by evil design! Eighty-eight astounding photographs and additional material from the author's personal collection. 8½ x 11", 124pp. **$17 ppd.** Seamail/Canada: **$18.** AIR Europe: **$25.** Austr/Japan: **$28. SIGNED HARDBOUND:** Limited edition of 300 signed by the author on acid-free paper **$54. ppd.** Seamail/Canada: **$55.** AIR Europe: **$61.** Austr/Japan: **$66.**

"RE/Search has provided us with a moving glimpse at the rarified world of physical deformity; a glimpse that ultimately succeeds in its goal of humanizing the inhuman, revealing the beauty that often lies behind the grotesque and in dramatically illustrating the triumph of the human spirit in the face of overwhelming debility."—**SPECTRUM WEEKLY**

The Torture Garden by Octave Mirbeau

This book was once described as the "most sickening work of art of the nineteenth century!" Long out of print, Octave Mirbeau's macabre classic (1899) features a corrupt Frenchman and an insatiably cruel Englishwoman who meet and then frequent a fantastic 19th century Chinese garden where torture is practiced as an art form. The fascinating, horrific narrative slithers deep into the human spirit, uncovering murderous proclivities and demented desires. Lavish, loving detail of description. Illustrated with evocative, dream-like photos. Introduction, biography & bibliography. 8½ x 11", 120 pp, 21 photos by Bobby Neel Adams. **$17 ppd.** Seamail/Canada: **$18.** AIR Europe: **$25.** Austr/Japan: **$28. HARDBOUND:** Limited edition of 200 hardbacks on acid-free paper **$33. ppd.** Seamail/Canada: **$35.** AIR Europe: **$41.** Austr/Japan: **$46.**

". . . sadistic spectacle as apocalyptic celebration of human potential . . . A work as chilling as it is seductive."—**THE DAILY CALIFORNIAN**

The Atrocity Exhibition by J.G. Ballard

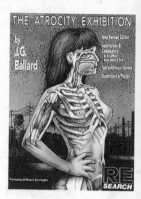

A large-format, illustrated edition of this long out-of-print classic, widely regarded as Ballard's finest, most complex work. Withdrawn by E.P. Dutton after having been shredded by Doubleday, this outrageous work was finally printed in a small edition by Grove before lapsing out of print 15 years ago. With 4 additional fiction pieces, extensive annotations (a book in themselves), disturbing photographs by Ana Barrado and dazzling, anatomically explicit medical illustrations by Phoebe Gloeckner. 8½ x 11", 136pp. **$17 ppd.** Seamail/Canada: **$18.** AIR Europe: **$25.** Austr/Japan: **$28. SIGNED HARDBOUND:** Limited Edition of 300 signed by the author on acid-free paper **$54 ppd.** Seamail/Canada: **$55.** AIR Europe: **$61.** Austr/Japan: **$66.**

"*The Atrocity Exhibition* is remarkably fresh. One does not read these narratives as one does other fiction . . . one enters into them as a kind of ritual . . ."—**SAN FRANCISCO CHRONICLE**

RE/Search #12: Modern Primitives

An eye-opening, startling investigation of the undercover world of body modifications: tattooing, piercing and scarification. Amazing, explicit photos! *Fakir Musafar* (55-yr-old Silicon Valley ad executive who, since age 14, has practiced every body modification known to man); *Genesis & Paula P-Orridge* describing numerous ritual scarifications and personal, symbolic tattoos; *Ed Hardy* (editor of *Tattootime* and creator of over 10,000 tattoos); *Capt. Don Leslie* (sword-swallower); *Jim Ward* (editor, *Piercing Fans International*); *Anton LaVey* (founder of the Church of Satan); *Lyle Tuttle* (talking about getting tattooed in Samoa); *Raelyn Gallina* (women's piercer) & others talk about body practices that develop identity, sexual sensation and philosophic awareness. This issue spans the spectrum from S&M pain to New Age ecstasy. 22 interviews, 2 essays (including a treatise on Mayan body piercing based on recent findings), quotations, sources/bibliography & index. 8½ x 11", 212 pp, 279 photos & illustrations. **$21 ppd.** Seamail/Canada **$22.** AIR Europe: **$30.** Austr/Japan: **$34.**

"**MODERN PRIMITIVES** is not some shock rag parading crazies for your amusement. All of the people interviewed are looking for something very simple: a way of fighting back at a mass production consumer society that prizes standardization above all else. Through 'primitive' modifications, they are taking possession of the only thing that any of us will ever really own: our bodies." —**WHOLE EARTH REVIEW**

"The photographs and illustrations are both explicit and astounding . . . This is the ideal biker coffee table book, a conversation piece that provides fascinating food for thought." —**IRON HORSE**

"**MODERN PRIMITIVES** approaches contemporary body adornment and ritual from the viewpoint that today's society suffers from an almost universal feeling of powerlessness to change the world, leaving the choice for exploration, individuation and primitive rite of passage to be fought out on the only ground readily available to us: our bodies." —**TIME OUT**

"In a world so badly made, as ours is, there is only one road—rebellion."
— Luis Bunuel

"Habit is probably the greatest block to seeing truth." — R.A. Schwaller de Lubicz

RE/Search #11: Pranks!

A prank is a "trick, a mischievous act, a ludicrous act." Although not regarded as poetic or artistic acts, pranks constitute an art form and genre in themselves. Here pranksters such as Timothy Leary, Abbie Hoffman, Paul Krassner, Mark Pauline, Monte Cazazza, Jello Biafra, Earth First!, Joe Coleman, Karen Finley, Frank Discussion, John Waters and Henry Rollins challenge the sovereign authority of words, images & behavioral convention. Some tales are bizarre, as when Boyd Rice presented the First Lady with a skinned sheep's head on a platter. This iconoclastic compendium will dazzle and delight all lovers of humor, satire and irony. 8½ x 11", 240 pp, 164 photos & illustrations. **$21 ppd.** Seamail/Canada: **$22.** AIR Europe: **$31.** Austr/Japan: **$35.**

"The definitive treatment of the subject, offering extensive interviews with 36 contemporary tricksters. . . from the Underground's answer to Studs Terkel." —**WASHINGTON POST**

RE/Search #10: Incredibly Strange Films

A guide to important territory neglected by the film criticism establishment, spotlighting unhailed directors—*Herschell Gordon Lewis, Russ Meyer, Larry Cohen, Ray Dennis Steckler, Ted V. Mikels, Doris Wishman* and others— who have been critically consigned to the ghettos of gore and sexploitation films. In-depth interviews focus on philosophy, while anecdotes entertain as well as illuminate theory. 13 interviews, numerous essays, A-Z of film personalities, "Favorite Films" list, quotations, bibliography, filmography, film synopses, & index. 8½ x 11", 224 pp. 157 photos & illustrations. **$21 ppd.** Seamail/Canada: **$22.** AIR Europe: **$30.** Austr/Japan: **$34.**

"Flicks like these are subversive alternatives to the mind control propagated by the mainstream media." —**IRON HORSE**

"Whether discussing the ethics of sex and violence on the screen, film censorship, their personal motivations, or the nuts and bolts of filmmaking from financing through distribution, the interviews are intelligent, enthusiastic and articulate." —**SMALL PRESS**

RE/Search #8/9: J.G. Ballard

A comprehensive special on this supremely relevant writer, now famous for *Empire of the Sun* and *Day of Creation*. W.S. Burroughs described Ballard's novel *Love & Napalm: Export U.S.A.* (1972) as "profound and disquieting...This book stirs sexual depths untouched by the hardest-core illustrated porn." 3 interviews, biography by David Pringle, fiction and non-fiction excerpts, essays, quotations, bibliography, sources, & index. 8½ x 11", 176 pp. 76 photos & illustrations by Ana Barrado, Bobby Neel Adams, Ken Werner, Ed Ruscha, and others. **$18 ppd.** Seamail/Canada: **$19.** AIR Europe: **$25.** Austr/Japan: **$28.**

"The RE/SEARCH to own if you must have just one . . . the most detailed, probing and comprehensive study of Ballard on the market."—BOSTON PHOENIX

"Highly recommended as both an introduction and a tribute to this remarkable writer."
—WASHINGTON POST

RE/Search #6/7 Industrial Culture Handbook

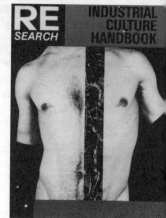

Essential library reference guide to the deviant performance artists and musicians of the *Industrial Culture* movement: *Survival Research Laboratories, Throbbing Gristle, Cabaret Voltaire, SPK, Non, Monte Cazazza, Johanna Went, Sordide Sentimental, R&N,* and *Z'ev.* Some topics discussed: new brain research, forbidden medical texts & films, creative crime & *interesting* criminals, modern warfare & weaponry, neglected gore films & their directors, psychotic lyrics in past pop songs, *art brut,* etc. 10 interviews, essays, quotations, chronologies, bibliographies, discographies, filmographies, sources, & index. 8½ x 11", 140 pp, 179 photos & illustrations. **$17 ppd.** Seamail/Canada: **$18.** AIR Europe: **$24.** Austr/Japan: **$27.**

". . . focuses on post-punk 'industrial' performers whose work comprises a biting critique of contemporary culture . . . the book lists alone are worth the price of admission!"—SMALL PRESS

"A sort of subversive artists directory, profiling an interrelated group of violently imaginative creators/performers whose works blend sex, viscera, machines, crimes and/or noise ... anyone with a strong stomach, twisted imagination and hunger for alternative knowledge, take note: this could be the best $ you'll ever spend."—TROUSER PRESS

RE/Search #4/5: W. S. Burroughs, Brion Gysin, Throbbing Gristle

Interviews, scarce fiction, essays: this is a manual of ideas and insights. Strikingly designed, with rare photos, bibliographies, discographies, chronologies & illustrations. 7 interviews, essays, chronologies, bibliographies, discographies, sources. 8½ x 11", 100 pp. 58 photos & illustrations. **$16 ppd.** Seamail/Canada: **$17.** AIR Europe: **$20.** Austr/Japan: **$22.**

"Interviews with pioneering cut-up artists William S. Burroughs, Brion Gysin and Throbbing Gristle . . . proposes a ground-breaking, radical cultural agenda for the '80s and '90s."—Jon Savage, LONDON OBSERVER

"The unconscious self is the real genius. Your breathing goes wrong the moment your conscious self meddles with it." —G.B. Shaw

"Who wishes to be creative, must first destroy and smash accepted values." —Nietzsche

"Human life is an experience to be carried as far as possible. " —Georges Bataille, *Theory of Religion*

RE/Search #1-2-3

Deep into the heart of the Control Process. Preoccupation: Creativity & Survival, past, present & future. These are the early tabloid issues, 11x17", full of photos & innovative graphics.

◆ **#1** J.G. Ballard, Cabaret Voltaire, Julio Cortazar, Octavio Paz, Sun Ra, *The Slits*, Robert K. Brown (editor, *Soldier of Fortune*), *Non,* Conspiracy Theory Guide, Punk Prostitutes, and more. **$8 ppd.**

◆ **#2** DNA, James Blood Ulmer, *Z'ev,* Aboriginal Music, West African Music Guide, Surveillance Technology, Monte Cazazza on poisons, Diane Di Prima, Seda, German Electronic Music Chart, Isabelle Eberhardt, and more. **$8 ppd.**

◆ **#3** Fela, New Brain Research, The Rattlesnake Man, Sordide Sentimental, New Guinea, Kathy Acker, Sado-Masochism (interview with Pat Califia); Joe Dante, Johanna Went, *SPK, Flipper,* Physical Modification of Women, and more. **$8 ppd.**
Add $1 ea. for Overseas/Canada; **$3** each for AIR Europe; **$5** each for AIR Austr/Japan.

SET OF RE/SEARCH 1-2-3: $18 ppd. Seamail/Canada: **$19.** AIR Europe: **$30.** Austr/Japan: **$34.**

Trilogy: High Priest of California (novel & play); Wild Wives (novel) by Charles Willeford

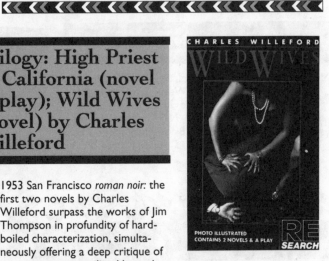

CHARLES WILLEFORD — WILD WIVES

PHOTO ILLUSTRATED
CONTAINS 2 NOVELS & A PLAY

RE/SEARCH

1953 San Francisco *roman noir:* the first two novels by Charles Willeford surpass the works of Jim Thompson in profundity of hard-boiled characterization, simultaneously offering a deep critique of contemporary morality. Unusual plots, tough dialogue starring anti-heroes both brutal and complex, and women living outside the lie of chivalry: *"She wasn't wearing much beneath her skirt. In an instant it was over. Fiercely and abruptly."* Plus the first publication of a play. 304 pp. 5x8". 2 introductions; bibliography; 15 photos by Bobby Neel Adams. **$14 ppd.** Seamail/Canada: **$15.** AIR Europe: **$19.** Austr/Japan: **$25.**
SIGNED HARDBOUND: Limited Edition of 250 signed hardbacks on acid-free paper **$54 ppd.** Seamail/Canada: **$55.** AIR Europe: **$61.** Austr/Japan: **$67.**

"HIGH PRIEST OF CALIFORNIA—The hairiest, ballsiest hard-boiled ever penned. One continuous orgy of prolonged foreplay! WILD WIVES—sex, schizophrenia and sadism blend into a recipe for sudden doom!"
—Dennis McMillan

"Willeford never puts a foot wrong.' —NEW YORKER

Search & Destroy:

SEARCH & DESTROY

Incendiary interviews, passionate photographs, art brutal. Corrosive minimalist documentation of the only youth rebellion of the seventies: punk rock (1977-78). The philosophy and culture, BEFORE the mass media takeover and inevitable cloning.

◆ **#1** Premiere issue. Crime, Nuns, Global Punk Survey.

◆ **#2** Devo, Clash, Ramones, Iggy, Weirdos, Patti Smith, Vivienne Westwood, Avengers, Dils, etc.

◆ **#3** Devo, Damned, Patti Smith, Avengers, Tom Verlaine, Capt. Beefheart, Blondie, Residents, Alternative TV, Throbbing Gristle.

◆ **#4** Iggy, Dead Boys, Bobby Death, Jordan & the Ants, Mumps, Metal Urbain, Helen Wheels, Sham 69, Patti Smith.

◆ **#5** Sex Pistols, Nico, Crisis, Screamers, Suicide, Crime, Talking Heads, Anarchy, Surrealism & New Wave essay.

◆ **#6** Throbbing Gristle, Clash, Nico, Talking Heads, Pere Ubu, Nuns, UXA, Negative Trend, Mutants, Sleepers, Buzzcocks.

◆ **#7** John Waters, Devo, DNA, Cabaret Voltaire, Roky Erickson, Clash, Amos Poe, Mick Farren, Offs, Vermilion & more.

◆ **#8** Mutants, Dils, Cramps, Devo, Siouxsie, Chrome, Pere Ubu, Judy Nylon & Patti Palladin, Flesheaters, Offs, Weirdos, etc.

◆ **#9** Dead Kennedys, Rockabilly Rebels, X, Winston Tong, David Lynch, Television, Pere Ubu, DOA, etc.

◆ **#10** J.G. Ballard, William S. Burroughs, Feederz, Plugz, X, Russ Meyer, Steve Jones, etc. Reprinted by Demand!

◆ **#11** The all photo supplement. Black and White.

$5 ppd. each. Add **$1** each for Seamail/Canada; **$3** ea AIR Europe; **$5** ea Austr/Japan.

SEARCH & DESTROY: COMPLETE SET.
For **$41** we offer #1-11. Seamail/Canada: **$43.** AIR Europe: **$61.** Austr/Japan: **$67.**

Me & Big Joe by Michael Bloomfield

Poignant encounters with some of the last living American blues artists, esp. Big Joe Williams. Entertaining. 5x8", 40pp, photos. **$5 ppd.** Seamail/Canada: **$6.** AIR Europe: **$9.** Austr/Japan: **$10.**

"It was love at first sight when I saw the book . . . A surreal, comic journey . . . It is a beautifully realized American miniature—fully as grotesque and funny as a Fellini dreamscape."—CITY ARTS

BOOKS DISTRIBUTED BY RE/SEARCH

Body Art

From England, a glossy 8½ x 11" magazine devoted to tattoo, piercing, body painting, tribal influences, pubic hairdressing, *et al.* Outstanding explicit Color/B&W photographs, instructive text—a beautiful production. Approx. 48 pgs. Issues #2,3,4 **$17 ppd. per issue.** Seamail/Canada **$18.** AIR Europe **$22.** Austr/Japan **$25.** Issues #5-#15 **$20 ppd. per issue.** Seamail/Canada **$21.** AIR Europe **$25.** Austr/Japan **$28.**

ISSUE #2:	Pubic Hairdressing, Out of the Closet, Shotsie.
ISSUE #3:	Africa Adorned, Tanta, Nipple Jewelry.
ISSUE #4:	Tattoo Expo '88, Tribal Influence, Male Piercings.
ISSUE #5:	Female Piercings, The Year of the Snake.
ISSUE #6:	Body Painting, Celtic Tattoos.
ISSUE #7:	Female Nipple Development, Plastic Bodies.
ISSUE #8:	Tattoo Symbolism, Piercing Enlargement.
ISSUE #9:	Tattoos, Nipple Piercing, The Perfect Body.
ISSUE #10:	Amsterdam Tattoo Convention, Cliff Raven.
ISSUE #11:	Ed Hardy, Fred Corbin, Beyond The Pain Barrier.
ISSUE #12:	Tattoo Expo '90, Genital Modifications.
ISSUE #13:	New Orleans Tattoo Convention 1990.
ISSUE #14:	Krystyne Kolorful, Paris Tattoo Convention.
ISSUE #15:	The Stainless Steel Ball, Bodyshots: Richard Todd

Please list an alternate title for all Body Art selections.

TattooTime edited by Don Ed Hardy

♦ **#1: NEW TRIBALISM.**
This classic issue features the new "tribal" tattooing renaissance started by Cliff Raven, Ed Hardy, Leo Zulueta & others. **$13 ppd.** Seamail/Canada: **$14.** AIR Europe: **$21.** Austr/Japan: **$23.**

♦ **#2: TATTOO MAGIC.**
This issue examines all facets of Magic & the Occult. **$13 ppd.** Seamail/Canada: **$14.** AIR Europe: **$21.** Austr/Japan: **$23.**

♦ **#3: MUSIC & SEA TATTOOS.**
Deluxe double book issue with over 300 photos. **$18 ppd.** Seamail/Canada: **$19.** AIR Europe: **$26.** Austr/Japan: **$29.**

♦ **#4: LIFE & DEATH.**
Deluxe double book issue with fantastic photos, examining trademarks, architectural and mechanical tattoos, the Eternal Spiral, a Tattoo Museum, plus the gamut of Death imagery. **$18 ppd.** Seamail/Canada: **$19.** AIR Europe: **$26.** Austr/Japan: **$29.**

♦ **#5: ART FROM THE HEART.**
All *NEW* issue that's bigger than ever before (128 pgs) with hundreds of color photographs. Featuring in-depth articles on tattooers, contemporary tattooing in Samoa, a survey of the new weirdo monster tattoos and much more! **$23 ppd.** Seamail/Canada: **$24.** AIR Europe: **$31.** Austr/Japan: **$34.**

PopVoid #1: '60s Culture. edited by Jim Morton

Edited by Jim Morton (who guest-edited *Incredibly Strange Films*). Fantastic anthology of neglected pop culture: Lawrence Welk, Rod McKuen, Paper Dresses, Nudist Colonies, Goofy Grape, etc. 8½ x 11", 100 pp. **$13 ppd.** Seamail/Canada: **$14.** AIR Europe: **$22.** Austr/Japan: **$25.**

Halloween by Ken Werner

A classic photo book. Startling photographs from the "Mardi Gras of the West," San Francisco's *adult* Halloween festivities in the Castro district. Limited supply. Beautiful 9x12" hardback bound in black boards. 72 pgs. Black glossy paper. **$14 ppd.** Seamail/Canada: **$15.** AIR Europe: **$27.** Austr/Japan: **$32.**

VIDEOS

Menacing Machine Mayhem — Mark Pauline

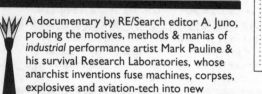

A documentary by RE/Search editor A. Juno, probing the motives, methods & manias of *industrial* performance artist Mark Pauline & his survival Research Laboratories, whose anarchist inventions fuse machines, corpses, explosives and aviation-tech into new prototypes and archetypes appropriate for a war universe. Entertaining! 30 mins. **$30 ppd.** Seamail/Canada **$31.** AIR Europe: **$36.** Austr/Japan: **$40.**

Louder Faster Shorter — *Punk Video*

One of the only surviving 16mm color documents of the original punk rock scene at the Mabuhay Gardens. 20 minute video featuring the AVENGERS, DILS, MUTANTS, SLEEPERS, and UXA. **$23 ppd.** Seamail/Canada: **$24.** AIR Europe: **$29.** Austr/Japan: **$33.**

Baited Trap

Powerful film noir by Jon Reiss, including a nightmare machine sequence by SRL. 13 min. **$20 ppd.** Seamail/Canada: **$21.** AIR Europe: **$28.** Austr/Japan: **$30.**

ALL VIDEOS ARE IN US NTSC VHS FORMAT

RE/SHIRTS

Hand-Screened on 100% Heavyweight Cotton T-Shirts

STYLE A

STYLE C

STYLE D

"WE INTEND TO DESTROY ALL DOGMATIC VERBAL SYSTEMS..."
—W.S. Burroughs

INDUSTRIAL CULTURE HANDBOOK

STYLE E

STYLE F

STYLE I

MODERN PRIMITIVES
Body Piercing

STYLE G

God is my Foundation

STYLE H

MR DEATH
CATCH YOU LATER!

THE GREAT OMI

STYLE J

STYLE L

Deliberately False Statements

STYLE M

STYLE K

Index

A

Abbott, Jack 8
Acconci, Vito 48
ACT UP 18, 157
Against Nature. See Huysmans, J.K.
AIDS 12-14, 18, 31, 45, 49, 63, 127, 158, 192, 193
Aktionists, Viennese 189
Amacher, Maryanne 60
"American Dreams" (poem) 163, 165, 168
Amish 93
Anti-Art 186
Antin, Eleanor 9
Aries, Philip 86
Artaud, Antonin 15, 68
Artificial Intelligence 153
Astrology 173
Atwater, Lee 84

B

Baby Is Born, A 195
Bachhoven 74
Baker, Jim 135
Baldwin, James 88
Bashkirtseff, Maria 68
Bass, Ellen 166
Baudelaire, C. P. 15
Baudrillard, Jean 88
Benjamin, Walter 129, 130, 137
"Black Leather Beavers," 7
Black Looks: Race and Representation 91
Black Panthers 120, 159
"Black Sheep, The" (poem) 43, 47
Blank, Joani 212, 213
Bluest Eye, The. See Morrison, Toni
Briggs Initiative 200
"Bull Dyke of the Month" 218
Burden, Chris 48
Burroughs, William S. 17, 133
Bush, George 142

C

Capra, Fritjof 87
Catholicism 50–52

CBGB's 108
Central Park Jogger 8
Centuries of Childhood. See Aries, Philip
Chance, James 185
Charpentier, Marie Joseph 68
Child Pornography 203
Childbirth 214
Christianity 135, 136
Cixous, Hélène 128, 131, 152
Comfort, Alex 213
Coming to Power. See Samois
Commissioner's Report on Pornography 131–132, 209
Comstock, Anthony 160
Contingency, Irony, & Solidarity. See Rorty, Richard
Courage to Heal, The. See Bass, Ellen
Crack Wars: Literature, Addiction, and Mania 135
"Critique of Violence, The". *See* Benjamin, Walter
Cross-dressing 79–80
Cubeiro, Emilio 32, 105, 108
Curie, Madame 87

D

Dalai Lama 92
Dance 14, 17, 122
Dances With Wolves (film) 91
de Beauvoir, Simone 68, 123
de Nerval, Gerard 15
de Ridder, Willem 28
Deleuze, Gilles 153
Derrida, Jacques 74, 131–132
Dharma Bums. See Kerouac, Jack
Dijkstra, Bram 74
Dildoes 216
Discipline and Punish: The Birth of the Prison. See Foucault, Michel
Dornan, Bob 198
DuBois, W.E.B. 125
Duchamp, Marcel 53, 55–56
Durable Fig Leaf, The. See Strage, Mark
Dworkin, Andrea 128, 201–202

E

Education of Girls, The. See Pelletier, Madame

◆ **Durango Root** *Datisca glomerata*   *Galás*

Toxic Part: Entire plant in flower or fruit.
Symptoms: Depression, diarrhea, increased respiration rate, and death.

◆ **Gloriosa Lily** *Gloriosa rothschildiana*   *Sprinkle*

Toxic Part: The whole plant is poisonous, particularly the tubers. Poisonings have occurred when the tubers were mistaken for sweet potatoes.
Symptoms: Burning pain in the mouth and throat, intense thirst, and difficulty swallowing occurs immediately, followed by nausea and emesis. Abdominal pain and severe diarrhea develop after a two or more hour delay. Extensive fluid and electrolyte loss may lead to hypovolemic shock. Renal involvement is evidenced by hematuria and oliguria. Can be fatal.

◆ **Daffodil** *Narcissus pseudonarcissus*   *Finley*

Toxic Part: Bulbs (often mistaken for onions).
Symptoms: Following ingestion of large amounts, symptoms include nausea, gastroenteritis, vomiting, persistent emesis, diarrhea, and convulsive trembling which can lead to fatality.

◆ **Pawpaw** *Asimina triloba*   *Montano*

Toxic Part: Entire plant.
Symptoms: Causes contact dermatitis.

◆ **Oleander** *Nerium oleander*   *Schneemann*

Toxic Part: Entire plant, green or dried. Smoke from burning wood can also be toxic.
Symptoms: Sometimes, when a branch has been cut from an oleander bush to skewer meat at outdoor barbecues, the poison is transferred to the meat, causing nausea, depression, lowered and irregular pulse, bloody diarrhea, paralysis, and possibly, death.

◆ **Carolina Jessamine** *Gelsemium sempervirens*   *hooks*

Toxic Part: Entire Plant, especially nectar.
Symptoms: Induces muscular weakness, dizziness, falling of the jaw, visual disturbances, dryness of the mouth, slowed pulse, great anxiety, and convulsions. Its strychnine-like action paralyzes motor nerve endings, resulting in respiratory arrest and death. Honeybees are poisoned by the plant causing their honey to become toxic.

◆ **Carolina Rhododendron** *Rhododendron carolinianum*

     Hughes

Toxic Part: The leaves are toxic as is honey made from flower nectar.
Symptoms: Rhododendrons have caused serious intoxications in children who chewed on the leaves. Poisoning also may result from eating honey made from rhododendron nectar. There is a transitory burning in the mouth on ingestion. Several hours later, salivation, emesis, and diarrhea occur, and there is a prickling sensation in the skin. The patient may complain of headache, muscular weakness, and dimness of vision. Bradycardia is followed by severe hypotension. Coma and convulsions are terminal events.

◆ **Poison Hemlock** *Conium maculatum*   *Lunch*

Toxic Part: Entire plant, especially root, seeds, and fruit.
Symptoms: The primary action is on the central nervous system and is similar to nicotine poisoning. Onset of symptoms is usually rapid with irritation of the mucous membranes of the mouth and throat, increased salivation, nausea and vomiting, abdominal pain or diarrhea, thirst, nervousness, headache, dilation of the pupils, sweating, and dizziness. Convulsions occur in severe cases and may be followed by coma or death, the result of respiratory failure.

◆ **Calla Lily** *Zantedeschia aethiopica*   *Coleman*

Toxic Part: Juice of leaves and stems.

Symptoms: Painful irritation of the lips and the mucous membranes of the mouth and throat. In extreme cases swelling of the throat is sufficient to cause choking and inability to swallow. Usually after four days the swelling begins to lessen, eventually disappearing after twelve days. The pain may continue for about eight days. In addition, contact dermatitis commonly occurs.

◆ **Morning Glory** *Convulvulus sepium*   *Ronell*

Toxic Part: Seeds.
Symptoms: Used by thrill seekers because of its LSD-like effect, 50 to 200 powdered seeds from this climbing vine can produce mental effects which have led to suicides. Other side reactions have been nausea, uterine stimulation, visual distortion, restlessness, relaxation, heightened awareness, increased rapport with other persons, and euphoria. Excessive use can result in complete dissociation from reality.

◆ **Baneberry** *Actaea rubra*   *Kerr & Malley*

Toxic Part: Only the berries and roots are toxic.
Symptoms: Upon ingestion there is intense pain and inflammation of the mouth, tongue, and throat, often with blistering and ulceration. Salivation is profuse. Bloody emesis and diarrhea occur in association with severe abdominal cramping. About 30 minutes after ingestion, central nervous system involvement is manifested by dizziness, confusion, syncope, and, in severe cases, convulsions.

◆ **Chaparral Deathcamas** *Zigadenus fremontii* *Sapphire*

Toxic Part: Entire plant, particularly the bulbs.
Symptoms: In humans, burning in the mouth, thirst, dizziness and headache, persistent vomiting, slow heart action, low blood pressure, and convulsions. Drowsiness and staggering progress to a coma with slow and irregular respiration. These symptoms are generally the same in livestock, although some animals may die within a few hours.

◆ **Iris (Blue Flag)** *Iris versicolor*   *Acker*

Toxic Part: Underground rhizome, leaves, and other fleshy portions.
Symptoms: Causes severe, but not usually serious, gastroentic pain, nausea, and pronounced diarrhea; also contact dermatitis.

◆ **Balsam Apple** *Guttiferae clusia rosea*   *Export*

Toxic Part: The golden viscous sap and the fruit are toxic.
Symptoms: Profuse diarrhea occurs after indigestion.

◆ **Naked Lady** *Amaryllis belladonna*   *Bright*

Toxic Part: Bulb.
Symptoms: Ingesting fairly large amounts may induce nausea, persistent vomiting, and minimal diarrhea. This plant also causes both allergic and irritant dermatitis, particularly in florists who are repeatedly exposed to these plants.

◆ **Lily-of-the-Valley** *Convallaria majalis*   *Quotes*

Toxic Part: Any part of the plant may be toxic, including the water in which the cut flowers have been kept, but this species seems to be less of a hazard because of its foul taste.
Symptoms: In humans, irritation to the mucous membranes of the mouth followed by vomiting, dizziness, and abdominal pain caused by the saponins. The digitalis-like glycosides, which have a variable latent period, have toxic effects on the heart.

◆ **Deadly Nightshade** *Atropa belladonna*   *Index*

Toxic Part: Entire plant; the shiny black berries are a potential hazard particularly to children.
Symptoms: On ingestion, dry mouth and difficulty in swallowing and speaking, flushed dry skin, rapid heartbeat, dilated pupils and blurred vision, and neurological disturbances, including excitement, giddiness, delerium, headache, confusion, and hallucinations. Repeated ingestion can lead to dependency and glaucoma.